The Communists
and Chinese
Peasant Rebellions

STUDIES OF THE
EAST ASIAN INSTITUTE
COLUMBIA UNIVERSITY

JAMES P. HARRISON

The Communists
and Chinese
Peasant Rebellions

A STUDY IN
THE REWRITING OF
CHINESE HISTORY

NEW YORK ATHENEUM 1969

To My Parents with Joy

[The Chinese peasant revolts form] a glorious revolutionary tradition. . . . The gigantic scale of . . . peasant uprisings and wars in Chinese history is without parallel in the world. These class struggles of the peasants—the peasant uprisings and peasant wars—alone formed the real motive force of development in China's feudal society.

Mao Tse-tung

"The Chinese Revolution and the CCP" (1939), SWMTT, *vol. 3, pp. 74–76*

We must know from looking at five thousand years of Chinese history that bandit disturbances were frequent, but regardless of the dynasty, no murderous, marauding local bandits were able to succeed. Especially [must this be true of] the present bandits in Kiangsi, the so-called CCP, who like previous bandits such as the Red Eyebrows, Yellow Turbans, Huang Ch'ao, and Li Ch'uang are extraordinarily cruel, footloose, and bestial.

Chiang Kai-shek

Speech at Lu-shan, 1933–34,
in Chiang Chieh-shih, LU-SHAN HSUN-LIEN
CHI, *vol. 1, p. 200*

Preface

THIS STUDY seeks to bring to life an important aspect of one of the most remarkable intellectual revolutions in history, the communist attempt to recast the thought patterns of over 700 million Chinese. The method employed is a case study of communist analysis of the rich legacy of Chinese peasant rebellions, the closest equivalents to the communist movement in Chinese history. The communist handling of the theory of class struggle forms the conceptual basis for this analysis and is also at the core of Chinese communist thought.

Most of the research was completed before the outbreak of the "Great Proletarian Cultural Revolution," but I have tried to include relevant information through 1967. More important, the study well documents the differing approaches to the Chinese past and society which the "cultural revolution" dramatized. Certainly, the fundamentalist emphasis on the class struggle, so much stressed by the Maoists, also dominated the interpretations of the peasant rebellions in the 1960s. Significantly, critics of this approach were the first targets of the "cultural revolution," and one wonders to what extent the attitudes favoring the activities of the Red Guards were fostered by the extreme educational emphasis on "struggle." Beyond the events of the 1960s, the book aims to shed light on Chinese communist idealogy in general and on its relationship with traditional China and with Marxism-Leninism.

Any research depends on the labors of many others, and one covering as many aspects of several different traditions as this is especially indebted. The footnotes and bibliography give some indication of my borrowings but do not express the personal help which I have generously received from many sources.

I would like to thank particularly my adviser, Professor C. Martin Wilbur, and his institution, Columbia University, without whose teaching, advice and facilities the study could not have been completed. Professors Hellmut Wilhelm, Hu Chang-tu, Karl A. Wittfogel, Tong Te-kong, Lu Kuang-huan, Howard Boorman, Albert Feuerwerker, William T. de Bary, Hans Bielenstein, Ainslee Embree, John Meskill, Herschel Webb, James Morley, James Nakamura, Frederick Mote, Arthur Wright, Mary Wright, Fang Chao-ying, James T. C. Lin, Vincent Y. C. Shih, Teng Ssu-yü, Harvey Dyck, John K. Fairbank, Benjamin Schwartz, Lucien Bianco, Richard Sorich, Harold Khan, John Watt, René Goldman, Donald Klein, and Ling Nai-an among others have given me especially valuable reading, discussion and advice. Miss Mervyn Adams, Dale Anderson, Mrs. Charles Granade, and others helped with editing, typing, and innumerable problems.

My father and mother, who have had a lifetime interest in China, gave me the benefit of their broader perspective. Above all, I have been sustained by the encouragement, good humor, and patience of my wife and two young daughters.

Most of the research was done in Hong Kong at the Union Research Center as a Ford Foundation foreign-area fellow, and at Columbia University, New York. I am greatly indebted to all three institutions. I also received generous assistance from the staff of Harvard Yenching Library, the Library of Congress, and the Hoover Institution. Roderick

MacFarquhar and *The China Quarterly*, which hosted the 1964 Ditchley Conference on Chinese Communist Historiography and published an article based on Chapter 5, stimulated much cross-fertilization of ideas and information. Hunter College of the City University of New York has been good to me in providing teaching experience to sharpen my thoughts and time in which to complete my work. It goes without saying that mistakes and weaknesses are mine.

New York City, September 1968

Contents

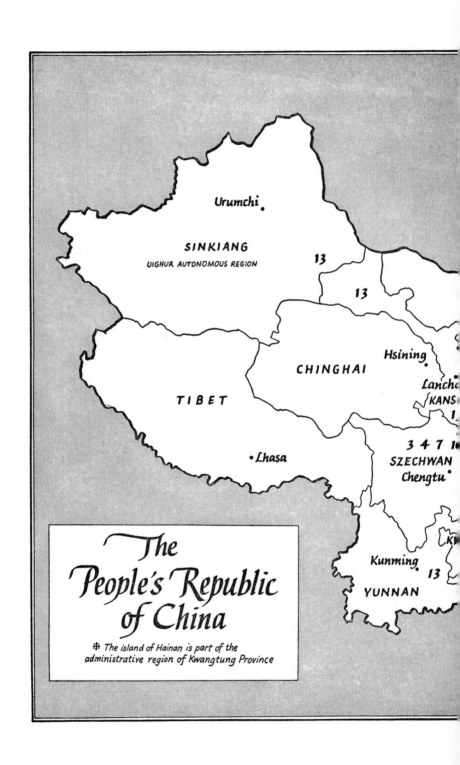

Urumchi.

SINKIANG
UIGHUR AUTONOMOUS REGION

13

13

CHINGHAI

Hsining.

Lancha

KANS

1

TIBET

3 4 7 1

SZECHWAN

Chengtu.

•Lhasa

Kunming.

13

YUNNAN

The
People's Republic
of China

✠ *The island of Hainan is part of the*
administrative region of Kwangtung Province

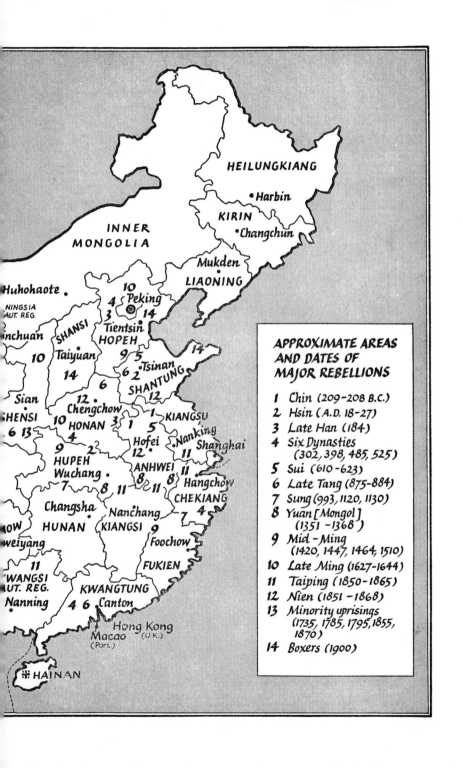

APPROXIMATE AREAS
AND DATES OF
MAJOR REBELLIONS

1 Chin (209–208 B.C.)
2 Hsin (A.D. 18–27)
3 Late Han (184)
4 Six Dynasties
    (302, 398, 485, 525)
5 Sui (610–623)
6 Late Tang (875–884)
7 Sung (993, 1120, 1130)
8 Yuan [Mongol]
    (1351–1368)
9 Mid–Ming
    (1420, 1447, 1464, 1510)
10 Late Ming (1627–1644)
11 Taiping (1850–1865)
12 Nien (1851–1868)
13 Minority uprisings
    (1735, 1785, 1795, 1855,
    1870)
14 Boxers (1900)

PART ONE

Theoretical and Historical Background

CHAPTER ONE

Introduction

IT IS difficult to imagine two philosophies of history more diametrically opposed than Confucianism and Marxism. Where Confucianism describes history as a cyclical process of moral decline and regeneration, Marxism holds that history is a lineal progression determined by material change. Where Confucianism stresses the importance of human example over abstract law and material conditions, Marxism stresses the importance of matter over mind. Above all, where Confucianism emphasizes social harmony, Marxism emphasizes social conflict, the most striking of all changes in modern Chinese historiography.[1]

The Confucian believes that human happiness can be reached only through the patient application of ancient ideals of benevolent moderation. As explained in the *Doctrine of the Mean:*

[1] Arthur F. Wright was among the first to comment on this contrast. See his "Harmony Versus Struggle" in L. Bryson (ed.), *Thirteenth Symposium of Conference on Science, Philosophy and Religion* (New York: Harper and Brothers, 1954), pp. 589–602. Offsetting this contrast of content was an emphasis on the study of history, common to both Confucianism and communism. An analogous contrast of content with similarity of form is evident in the political structure of traditional and Communist China, with Party members replacing the old Mandarin class.

> Let the states of equilibrium and harmony exist in per-
> fection and a happy order will prevail throughout heaven
> and earth and all things will be nourished and flourish.[2]

Disruption of order was the greatest crime, and revolt was
anathema.

To the communist, on the contrary, the ideal of a classless,
stateless society can be achieved only through struggle. Rebellion was and is necessary and just. According to Mao's echo
of Marx:

> Fight, fail, fight again . . . till their victory; that is their
> logic of the people. . . . Classes struggle, some classes
> triumph, others are eliminated. Such is history, such is
> the history of civilization for thousands of years.[3]

The stress on the theory of class struggle also forms the
most characteristic part of the communist revolution in traditional historiography, since most other major changes that
have taken place in Chinese historiography over the past century were already under way as part of the inevitable modernization of Chinese thought. These included emphasis on economic and institutional considerations in place of Confucian
moral determinism, and the adoption of a lineal concept of
historical evolution in place of the Confucian concept of
cyclical aberrations from a permanent ideal. The general
focus for this study of communist interpretations of Chinese
social history will be this contrast between the Confucian
concern with harmony and the communist doctrine of struggle, the single most revolutionary aspect of contemporary
Chinese thought.

How is one to account for Chinese acceptance of Marxism-
Leninism, when its ideals are so directly opposed to Chinese
tradition? [4] First of all, Chinese patriots of the twentieth cen-

[2] James Legge (trans.), *The Four Books* (Shanghai: The Chinese
Book Company, n.d.), pp. 350–51.

[3] Mao Tse-tung, "Cast Away Illusions, Prepare for Struggle" (1949),
Selected Works of Mao Tse-tung (hereafter *SWMTT* Peking edition)
(Peking: Foreign Languages Press, 1961), vol. 4, p. 428.

[4] Of course, as we shall see, "Maoism" has made many adaptations to
Chinese conditions. Moreover, in contrast to much of its content, the

tury became interested, above all else, in results. They looked
to even more radical solutions in the face of decades of national humiliations and frustrations. Thus, one of the founders of Chinese communism defended the Nietzschean statement, "war is to society what movement is to the body," by
posing a question which seemed to have no answer. "The
oriental peoples may regard all this as madness," wrote Ch'en
Tu-hsiu, "but in what condition do all these oriental people
with their love of peace, quiet and harmony now find themselves?" [5] Increasingly since its founding in 1921, the Chinese
Communist Party has valued this concept of "struggle," first
as a means to power and then as a key to the modernization
of China. Following communist victory in 1949, the ideal of
struggle has pervaded the social, political, and economic life
of the mainland, and its intensity of expression has been due
in large part to the conviction that many of China's frustrations were a product of the very different traditional mentality.

Since peasant revolts are the only dramatic evidence of
class struggle in Chinese history, it was natural that the Chinese communists should look to the voluminous record of
peasant unrest in traditional times. In the absence of a significant bourgeois revolution or modern labor movement, the
peasant revolts perforce assume a position of importance
comparable to the modern labor movement in Western
Marxist historiography as the direct forerunners of the communist revolution.[6] Moreover, emphasis on the historical role

---

form of Chinese communism resembles such traditional traits as élitism
and preoccupation with an accepted orthodoxy. Nonetheless, on balance
the contrast between Chinese communist ideology and traditional Chinese thought is very profound.

[5] Ch'en Tu-hsiu, "Basic Differences in the Ideas of Oriental and Occidental Peoples," *Hsing Ch'ing Nien*, vol. 1, no. 4, 1915, cited in Benjamin Schwartz, "Ch'en Tu-hsiu and the Acceptance of the Modern
West," *Journal of the History of Ideas*, January 1951, p. 66.

[6] Hou Wai-lu, one of the ablest mainland historians, spoke of the
Taipings who "replaced the bourgeoisie and heroically shouldered the
responsibility of a modern Chinese revolution." See "Hung Hsiu-ch'uan
and Hung Jen-kan, Ideologists of the T'ai-p'ing Rebellion," Hu Chang-tu
(trans.), *Soviet Press Translations*, vol. 7, no. 15, p. 323 (University of
Washington), citing *Hsien Chien She* (hereafter *HCS*), April 1952.

of the Chinese peasant revolts would assist the process defined by Mao as "throwing away [China's] feudal dross and absorbing its democratic essence." [7] Where the traditional official view either ignored or villified rebels as disturbers of the order and as "bandits," the "new historiography" should "reveal the great revolutionary tradition of the oppressed peoples of China." [8]

Yet, despite the obvious appeals of the study of the Chinese peasant revolts for the communist historian, the theme has been one of the last to be developed during four decades of Chinese communist historiography. The earlier neglect was due not only to more immediate political requirements facing communist historians but apparently also, in the case of the older generation of academic Marxists, to personal preference and to an apparent awareness of the theoretical difficulties inherent in the treatment of the subject.

In the past decade, however, the younger generation of Chinese historians has written hundreds of articles, pamphlets, and books on the subject of the "class struggles of the peasants" in Chinese history,[9] all seeking to demonstrate the "truth that only through struggle is there a way out." [10] One of the polemicists of the Great Proletarian Cultural Revolution of the mid-1960s described the purpose of these writings:

[7] Mao Tse-tung, "On the New Democracy," *Selected Works of Mao Tse-tung* (hereafter *SWMTT*) (New York: International Publishers, Inc., 1954), vol. 3, p. 155.

[8] Chien Po-tsan, "Discussions of China's Ancient Peasant Wars," in *Li-shih Wen-t'i Lun-ts'ung* (Collected Discussions of Problems in History) (Peking: Jen-min Ch'u-pan She, 1962), p. 114.

[9] Between 1949 and mid-1961 over four hundred articles were devoted to the pre-nineteenth-century rebellions alone. Over half of these were written after 1958, and a comparable number of articles have been devoted to the great nineteenth-century rebellions. See the bibliography appended to Shih Shao-pin (ed.), *Chung-kuo Feng-chien She-hui Nung-min Chan-cheng Wen-t'i Tao-lun Chi* (Collected Articles on the Problem of Peasant Wars in Chinese Feudal Society) (hereafter *SSP*) (Peking: San-lien Shu-tien, 1962). Some books and source materials and many pamphlets on the subject have also appeared.

[10] Su Hsing, "Ch'en Sheng, the First Leader of a Chinese Peasant Revolt," *Chung-kuo Ch'ing-nien* (China Youth) (hereafter *CKCN*), no. 72, August 1951, p. 30.

The study of these peasant revolts and wars not only deeply reveals the laws of development of China's feudal society but also the basic Marxist theories of class struggle and feudal society. At the same time the study of the history of peasant wars has very great significance in the elevation of our country's glorious revolutionary tradition, and in the education of the people's progressive class struggle.[11]

In short, the "mass nature and revolutionary nature of the peasant movements . . . is the historical textbook of the Chinese laboring people." [12] Long before the "cultural revolution" of the mid-1960s there were recommendations that materials on peasant rebellions supply up to one quarter or one third of the curriculum on Chinese history, even in the upper levels of grade school.[13]

The place of the interpretations of the peasant revolts in ideological education will be covered later, but it is essential for the reader to bear in mind from the outset the extraordinary tensions under which mainland historians have had to work. Ideological indoctrination of the tenets of "Marxism-Leninism and the thought of Mao Tse-tung" has been continuous in China since 1949, building to great intensity in such campaigns as those of the early and late 1950s and of the mid-1960s. The control of the lives and, so far as possible, of the thoughts of the people has been achieved through inten-

11 Shih Shao-pin, "On the Discussion of Problems in the Peasant Revolutionary Wars in Chinese Feudal Society," SSP, p. 499. Ch'i Pen-yü, another prominent leader of the "cultural revolution," made a similar statement in late 1965, "Study History for the Sake of Revolution," SCMM 506, p. 19, citing *Hung ch'i*, no. 13, 1965 (December). Shih reportedly changed his given name from Shao-pin to Hung Ping (Red Guard) in honor of the "cultural revolution."

12 Hou Wai-lu, "The Development of the Peasant Wars and Their Programs and Slogans in Early and Late Periods of China's Feudal Society," SSP, p. 47.

13 *Hsiao-hsueh Kao-nien-chi, Li-shih Chiao-hsueh Shou-ts'e* (Shanghai: Shang-wu Yin-shu Kuan, 1951), pp. 22–23. Chinese history in general was emphasized as seen in the fact that 37 of the 127 courses at Peking University in the early 1960s were devoted to Chinese history and 40 to the history of Chinese philosophy. *China News Analysis* (hereafter CNA) 690, January 5, 1968, p. 6.

sive organizational work, through a steady procession of mass movements, and, above all, through the manipulation of enormous pressures to conform in the name of socialism and Chinese nationalism. Ideological pressures, of course, have been directed primarily at the five million "intellectuals" of communist China.[14] Nowhere have these pressures been more intense than in historical studies, whose "primary aspect," we are told, "is in the advancement of thought as a weapon in the class struggle . . . and whose development cannot be separated from the class struggle [in contemporary life]." [15] Historians figured especially prominently in the anti-rightist movement of 1958 and in the "great cultural revolution" of 1966.[16]

Historical studies played an expected role in the inculcation of Chinese nationalism and self-respect under the Nationalists, and continue to do so under the communists.[17] One of the first goals of history teaching is to "nurture patriotism and the love of the people" by revealing the greatness

[14] According to Mao in 1957, 1 to 3 percent of the five million "intellectuals" were "hostile" to the Chinese revolution, 10 percent were "firmly proletarian," and the remainder were either neutral or unfamiliar with Marxism-Leninism. Mao Tse-tung, "Talk at the National Conference on Propaganda Work of the CPC" (March 12, 1957), trans. in *Current Background* (hereafter *CB*) 740, August 31, 1964, pp. 9–10. Other sources give variant but similar statistics and proportions for the Chinese intellectuals. In the early 1950s there were several hundred thousand "higher intellectuals" (with higher degrees) in China.

[15] Liu Yao-t'ing *et al.*, "The Development of Historical Science in the Light of Ten Years of Struggle on the Intellectual Front," *Shih-hsueh Yueh-k'an* (hereafter *SHYK*), no. 10, 1959, p. 5.

[16] Thus, the criticisms of the well-known historian Wu Han in 1965 and 1966 served as a "warm-up" for the widespread purges which followed. The best general accounts of ideological reform in the 1950s are Theodore H. E. Ch'en, *Thought Reform of the Chinese Intellectual* (Hong Kong: Hong Kong University Press, 1960), and Merle Goldman, *Literary Dissent in Communist China* (Cambridge: Harvard University Press, 1967). For its effects on historians, see James P. Harrison, "The Ideological Training of Intellectuals in Communist China," *Asian Survey*, October 1965, and Chapter 10 below.

[17] See Cyrus H. Peake, *Nationalism and Education in Modern China* (New York: Columbia University Press, 1932), and Hsu T'e-li *et al.*, eds. *Lun Ai-kuo Chu-yi te Chiao-yü* (On the Education of Patriotism) (Peking: Ch'un-ch'ung Shu-tien, 1951).

of China and the evils of Imperialism.[18] Along with the ubiquitous calls for patriotism there has also been stress on the duties of internationalism,[19] but developments in historical studies as well as in foreign affairs suggest that the primary Chinese wish is to see their country placed at the head of international developments in the future as in the past. In historical studies there have been calls for the destruction of the old "Europe as the center theory of world history" and the parallel construction of a new system of world history based on the development of the class struggle. "World history should be a history of the struggle of all the laboring people of the world, and it is known that geographically the center of world history varies according to . . . the class struggle." [20] This interpretation places China in the vanguard of the world class struggle in many periods of ancient history as well as in contemporary times.

> . . . the Chinese revolution like the October Revolution was of world significance and the summation of the experience of our revolutionary struggles will not only be a great help for our people's task of construction but

---

[18] *Chung-hsueh Chiao-hsueh Tsan-k'ao Tzu-liao* (Reference Materials for High School Education) (Tientsin: Tienchin Chiao-yü She, 1950), p. 86. See also Chiao-yü Tzu-liao She, ed., *Hsueh-hsiao Chung te Ai-kuo Chu-yi Chiao-yü* (The Education of Patriotism in the Schools) (Peking: Jen-min Ch'u-pan She, 1951), p. 13.

[19] E.g., the warnings of Liu Shao-ch'i in 1949 that "proletarian internationalism [is] closely connected with patriotism" (*Internationalism and Nationalism* [Peking: Foreign Languages Press, 1951], p. 49), and of Mao Tse-tung in 1956 that "we should resolutely and thoroughly get rid of great power chauvinism, lock, stock and barrel" ("In Commemoration of Dr. Sun Yat-sen," in *Dr. Sun Yat-sen, Commemorative Articles and Speeches* [Peking: Foreign Languages Press, 1957]).

[20] "Departments of Szechwan Normal Institute and Chungshan University Eagerly Discuss the Question of the Center of World History," *Survey China Mainland Press* (hereafter *SCMP*) 2531, p. 27, citing *Kuang-ming Jih-pao* (hereafter *KMJP*), May 7, 1961. See also Wu T'ing-ch'iu, "Establish a New System of World History," *SCMP* 2503, p. 16, citing *KMJP*, April 9–10, 1961. Soviet historians have criticized this "sinocentric" view of the world. See R. V. Viatkin and S. L. Tikhvinsky, "On Questions in Chinese Historical Sciences," *Voprosy Istorii* (hereafter *VI*), no. 10, 1963, pp. 6–11. This article has been translated in *Current Digest of the Soviet Press*, February 19, 1964.

moreover will have real significance for the various oppressed peoples in their struggle for independence
against the slavery of American imperialism. We must
continually increase the research of Asian history, because our country and the various countries of Asia will
have increasingly close connections.[21]

The most significant aspect of Chinese communist nationalism is this stress on a revolutionary ideology as the best
means of serving national interests.

The following study will seek to analyze the most obvious
manifestation of this revolutionary nationalism in historical
studies, the historiography of the Chinese peasant movements. The most frequently studied rebellions are those
against the Ch-in (209 B.C.), Wang Mang (A.D. 18–27), the
later Han (A.D. 184), the Sui (611–24), the T'ang (874–84),
the Yuan (1351–68), the Ming (1627–45), and the Taiping movement (1851–64), as well as other smaller revolts of
the Six Dynasties (222–589), Sung, Ming, and Ch'ing periods.[22]

Among the many large-scale internal disruptions in Chinese history, only the rebellion of An Lu-shan in the T'ang
dynasty[23] and certain smaller, particularly aimless "bandit"

---

[21] Chung-hua Jen-min Kung-ho-Kuo Kao-teng Chiao-yü Pu, eds.,
K'ai-hsueh Chih-tao (Guide for Beginning School) (Peking, 1957), pp.
160 ff.

[22] Mao Tse-tung speaks of "several hundred big and small uprisings"
("The Chinese Revolution and the CCP," *SWMTT*, vol. 3, p. 78), and
Chien Po-tsan mentioned over one thousand peasant revolts in the last
fifteen hundred years of Chinese history and "uninterrupted, scattered,
small-scale revolts" ("Discussing the Peasant Wars of Ancient China,"
in Chien Po-tsan, *Li-shih Wen-t'i Lun-ts'ung* [Collected Discussions of
Problems in History] [Peking: Jen-min Ch'u-pan She, 1962]).

[23] The rebellion of An Lu-shan is described as a "war between different races" and as the result of a "contradiction within the governing
class." See Wang Tan-ling, *Chung-kuo Nung-min Ke-ming Shih-hua*
(Talks on the History of Chinese Peasant Revolution) (Shanghai: Kuo-
chi Wen-hua Fu-wu She, 1953), p. 185. For an example of communist
writers' refusal to "slander the peasant class" by including certain un-
savory movements as "peasant uprisings," see Wang P'ing-sheng, "Regarding the Article 'A Tentative Discussion of Peasant Uprisings of the
Mid-Northern Sung,'" *SHYK*, no. 9, 1959.

movements are omitted from the list of what are called "righteous uprisings of the peasantry" (*nung-min ch'i-yi*, hereafter referred to as peasant uprising or revolt) or "peasant wars" (*nung-min chan-cheng*). The latter were larger than the former and are said to have affected the whole country (*ch'uan-kuo te*).[24] Still smaller disturbances are referred to as "riots" (*pao-tung*), but the early stage of development from riot to rebellion and other key problems in the history of the peasant wars are generally ignored in communist historiography of the subject.[25] Other phenomena in Chinese history, including tax evasion and flight from the land, are also cited but generally only in passing as evidence of the continuing struggle of the peasantry against the ruling landlord class.

The large-scale mass movements mentioned above—there were a dozen or more as large as or larger than the greatest comparable movements of medieval Europe[26]—have indeed been a feature of Chinese history and an important but little-known strand in world social history. Although the size of the Chinese rebel armies, sometimes estimated to have been a million or more strong, has often been greatly exaggerated in

[24] "The Differences and Connections Between Peasant Revolts and Wars," *Wen Hui Pao* (Shanghai), July 9, 1961. Their term *ch'i-yi* was occasionally used in traditional times at least from the fifth century on, but only to refer to successful rebels such as the founder of the Han and of the later T'ang (923). Although communist writers sometimes use the word "revolution" (*ke-ming*) to refer to the peasant revolts, they have followed Marx in stressing the difference between revolt and revolution.

[25] Wolfram Eberhard has given a brief presentation of the stages of development of the Chinese peasant movements from "banditry" to "robber gang" to rebel army. See his *Conquerors and Rulers: Social Forces in Medieval China* (Leiden: E. J. Brill, 1952), pp. 62–63. See also Hsiao Kung-ch'uan, *Rural China: Imperial Control in the Nineteenth Century* (Seattle: University of Washington Press, 1960), pp. 418–500.

[26] This comparison refers to such European movements as those of the *Jacquerie* and the Lollards in the fourteenth century, the Hussites in the early fifteenth century, the German peasant revolt of 1524–25, and the Russian peasant revolts of the seventeenth and eighteenth centuries. The statement does not imply that the impact of the Chinese revolts was any greater than that of the European peasant movements but only that their scale was vast.

both traditional and communist accounts, there is no doubt that the Chinese peasant movements were major social upheavals involving armies of tens and occasionally hundreds of thousands, roaming over wide areas of the subcontinent of China.

Any generalizations about this extraordinary pattern of unrest must reckon with the vastness of the time span and area and with the complexity of the social problems involved. Nevertheless, many besides the communists have been impressed by the cyclical nature of the political crises and mass rebellions in Chinese history. In a society such as traditional China, marked not only by economic insecurity but also by a partially developed money economy and a high degree of social and political organization with their concomitant tensions, the possibility of social unrest was always latent.[27] Such crises did erupt with disconcerting regularity, and similarities among them stimulated an enormous literature on one or another aspect of the subject. While no definitive picture of the Chinese rebellions is possible at this stage, an analysis of the differing views of them is an essential preliminary step and provides a striking testament to the diversity of human understanding of the same phenomenon.

Where traditional writers saw these movements as "disruptions" (*luan*) of the existing and—by implication—just order, the communists portray them as "armed struggles of the peasantry against the landlord class" and as the "highest form of class struggle" in the history of Imperial China. For our purposes the most militant and organized of the peasant rebellions might be described as movements of large groups of rural inhabitants, predominantly of lower-class origin,

---

[27] Barrington Moore found evidence of class struggle where similar conditions existed in nine of twenty societies (including ancient China); see "A Comparative Analysis of the Class Struggle," *American Sociological Review*, no. 10, 1945, pp. 31–37. However, most social scientists deny the existence of the class struggle either in traditional agrarian societies or in highly industrialized societies; see John H. Kautsky, *Political Change in Underdeveloped Countries* (New York: John Wiley & Sons, 1962), p. 7. The answer may be that for several thousand years China has been a peculiar form of "transitional society," neither totally agrarian nor modern.

though often with middle- or upper-class leaders, who are
mobilized in the belief that they are acting in their own interests and in the interests of the majority of their kind and
who take action that brings them into conflict with the existing government and with the social and economic status quo.

Many of the problems raised in such a definition are considered later. Here we may note that the use of the word
"peasant" is not entirely unjustified.[28] While it is true that
in a rural society such as traditional China the great majority
of the populace and of the government army were peasants,
most government recruits were mercenaries or conscripts, and
the scholar-gentry almost universally supported the legitimate
dynasty in the early stages of any popular rebellion. While
economic grievances of smugglers, merchants, and other
"middle"-class groups were important motives at times, most
participants in the rebel armies, on the other hand, joined
with a sense of grievance over some problem connected with
land or taxation. In that sense these mass movements could
have been, and often were, "peasant revolts," and the communists are at least partially justified in saying a nonpeasant
could lead a peasant uprising if he genuinely sought "peasant
goals." The problem lies in the sincerity and tenacity of the
leaders' convictions.[29]

Another issue of great controversy raised in any definition
of the subject concerns the distinction between rebellion and
revolution. The Chinese peasant movements were revolts
against the existing government but were not revolutions in
the sense of calling for a fundamental change in the existing
order.[30] Yet some of the Chinese rebellions at least hinted at

[28] As charged by the eminent Taiping scholar Chien Yu-wen ("The
Marxian Interpretation of the T'ai-p'ing T'ien-kuo [hereafter *TPTK*],"
*Proceedings of the Second Biennial Conference of the International
Association of Asian Historians*, Taipei, 1962, p. 760), who stated that
the Taipings "might just as well be called a 'human revolution'" as a
peasant revolution, since "every single person under its banner was also
a human being."
[29] See Chapters 6 and 7.
[30] E.g., Thomas Taylor Meadows wrote in 1856, ". . . revolutionary
movements are against principles; rebellions against men. . . . Bearing
the above distinction clearly in mind . . . Of all nations that have at-

the latter in various utopian slogans which contrasted sharply with contemporary traditional teachings.[31] Therefore, they might be thought of as "potential revolutions," although there was no real possibility of their fulfillment prior to modern times, when better organization and communications might enable the popularization and execution of their ideas. These movements were revolts, but in theory some mentioned what would have been revolutionary programs if carried out. The Chinese peasant revolts can be further categorized either according to their ideology—as spontaneous, millenarian, or anarchist—or according to their type and size—as banditry, riots, or rebellions.[32]

The communists seek to avoid such considerations, since these might qualify the simple force of their historical analysis. Their goal is, above all, to write didactic, popular history, and their methods follow from this. They select those sources which "reveal the real facts of history" rather than those which "slander the peasant revolts," and they are instructed to use those materials which "show the crimes of the

---

tained a certain degree of civilization, the Chinese are the least revolutionary and the most rebellious." *The Chinese and Their Rebellions* (Stanford: Academic Reprints, n.d.), p. 25. Revolutions of the modern type are thought to have emerged only with the French Revolution of 1789. See Hannah Arendt, *On Revolution* (New York: Viking Press, 1963), pp. 34 ff.; and J. Talmon, *Political Messianism* (New York: Praeger, 1960), p. 10. Communists since Marx have also stressed the distinction between rebellion and revolution, although they maintain that some rebellions have "revolutionary effects."

[31] Long before the Taipings, Chinese rebels advanced certain vague utopian and egalitarian notions. These ideas had precedents in classical Chinese philosophy, but their execution would have been "revolutionary" in Imperial China. See Chapter 6.

[32] Chalmers Johnson lists six categories of violent social change, of which three types would apply to the historical Chinese peasant revolts —namely *Jacquerie*, millenarian movements, and anarchistic rebellion. See his *Revolution and the Social System* (Stanford: The Hoover Institution, 1964), especially pp. 27–45. A fourth type, the militarized armed insurrection, is descriptive of the Chinese communist struggle for power. "Conspiratorial coups d'état" and "Jacobin Communist Revolutions" were the other two types. Hsiao Kung-ch'uan defines four types of rural violence in Chinese history—namely, feuds, riots, banditry, and rebellion, the last applying to the peasant revolts mentioned above (*op. cit.*, pp. 418–86).

governing class" rather than those which "glorify the government at the expense of the people." [33] Criticism of traditional sources and praise of "people's history" at times goes to extraordinary lengths. The now disgraced historian and former Vice Mayor of Peking, Wu Han, once wrote that only oral testimony, such as had been gathered from old peasants about the Boxer movement, "reflected historical truth," while the written record was bound to reflect "the class stand of the recorder." [34]

Despite such idiosyncrasies, the millions of words devoted to the subject of the peasant movements provide the historical documentation for the most massive attempt at ideological re-education in human history. The aim is nothing less than the transformation of the world view of the world's largest people. If the communists fall short of this fundamental revolution, the writings on the peasant rebellions reveal the unremitting struggle they have waged to achieve this goal.

[33] Liu Chih-chien, "A Brief Discussion of Selection and Use of Historical Materials," *KMJP*, August 6, 1959; and Fan Wen-lan, *Chung-kuo T'ung-shih Chien-pien* (A Simple General History of China) (Shanghai: Hsin chih-shih Shu-tien, 1947), Preface, p. 2.

[34] Wu Han, "On the True Nature of History, *KMJP*, December 3, 1960.

CHAPTER TWO

The Theory of the Class Struggle

COMMUNIST theorists attempt to fit historical phenomena into a pattern which on the one hand will show the inevitability of communism and which on the other will foster its implementation. The Chinese communists believe the study of the peasant wars in the history of their country to be eminently suited to both these tasks. Yet from both the point of view of Marxist theory and the facts of Chinese history, their efforts encounter immense problems of interpretation.

The twin pillars of the Marxist analysis of history are the primacy of economics and the class struggle. Engels expressed the first:

The materialist conception of history starts from the proposition that the production of the means to support human life and, next to production, the exchange of things produced, is the basis of all social structure. . . .[1]

[1] Karl Marx and Friedrich Engels, "Socialism, Utopian and Scien-

The second is expressed in the famous line of the *Communist Manifesto*, "the history of all hitherto existing society is the history of class struggles." [2] If economics is the basis, "revolution is the driving force of history." [3] Moreover, because the communists believe violence necessary to overthrow impediments to economic progress, the two theories of economic evolution and social revolution are inseparably linked in classical Marxism.

Problems in the coordination of the two theories, however, are immediately apparent. In fact many, including one of the founders of the Chinese Communist Party (CCP), Li Ta-chao, have held that the theory of social revolution and class struggle was in basic conflict with the theory of economic evolution.[4] If history really were determined by inevitable economic evolution, the class struggle would seem to be unnecessary. In fact, it often seemed the other way round—that politics, not economics, was determinant, as the course of twentieth-century communism seems to prove. There is also difficulty in applying Marxist views to earlier and to non-European history. Marx and Engels themselves appear to have had doubts about the nature of ancient class struggles, and even more about the class structure of pre-modern society.[5]

---

tific," in *Selected Works in Two Volumes* (hereafter *MESW*) (Moscow: Foreign Languages Publishing House, 1958), vol. 2, p. 136.

[2] Engels later added "since primitive communal society" to this phrase, because there obviously could have been no class struggle before the formation of classes in the epoch of slavery.

[3] Marx and Engels, *The German Ideology* (New York: New World paperback edition), p. 29.

[4] See Chou Tse-tsung, *The May Fourth Movement* (Cambridge: Harvard University Press, 1960), p. 298; and Maurice Meisner, *Li Ta-chao and the Origins of Chinese Marxism* (Cambridge: Harvard University Press, 1967), pp. 19–20.

[5] E.g., the opening paragraphs of the Communist Manifesto, *MESW*, vol. 1, p. 34. The ambiguity of class definition, of course, is one of the major weaknesses of the Marxist theory of class struggle, criticized by some socialists (e.g., Georges Sorel) and most non-Marxists. See R. N. Carew Hunt, *Marxism, Past and Present* (London: Geoffrey Bles, 1954), pp. 87–88; Crane Brinton, *Anatomy of Revolution* (Englewood Cliffs, N.J.: Prentice-Hall, 1952), p. 54; Ralf Dahrendorf, *Class and Class Conflict in Industrial Society* (Stanford: Stanford University Press,

Another serious problem arises from the fact that prior to the socialist revolution all transitions from lower to higher stages of production were led by representatives of a minority and not of the majority, by emergent economic leaders and not by the masses of the workers. Only with the proletarian revolution would the leading economic class also happen to represent the mass of the workers. Hence, "all previous historical movements were movements of minorities or in the interests of minorities. [Only] the proletarian movement is the self-conscious, independent movement of the immense majority." [6] In other words, the strife between "ruling class" proponents of the new and old orders is the dominant consideration for Marx and Engels, and not the class struggle between rich and poor.[7] For this reason they insist that every meaningful class struggle is essentially a struggle for political power.[8]

Equally great problems occur for Marxist analysis of class struggles in the early period of each stage of production, whether in the period of slavery, feudalism, or capitalism. In his most concise statement of the economic role of the class struggle, Marx wrote:

> At a certain stage of their development, the material productive forces of society come in conflict with the existing relations of production . . . from forms of development of the productive forces these relations turn into their fetters. Then begins an epoch of social revolution. . . .[9]

1959), pp. 117 ff.; R. Bendix and S. M. Lipset (eds.), *Class, Status and Power* (Glencoe: Free Press, 1953), pp. 75 ff., 81 ff., 598, and 607; and Karl Deutsch, *Nationalism and Social Communication* (Cambridge: M.I.T. Press, paperback, 1966), pp. 31 ff.

[6] Manifesto of the Communist Party, *MESW*, vol. 1, pp. 42–43.

[7] See F. Engels, "Feuerbach and the End of Classical German Philosophy," *MESW*, vol. 2, p. 393. Elsewhere Engels even spoke of the "great antithesis between the burgher and peasant—plebeian oppositions which caused the defeat of the peasant war [of 1525 in Germany]. This antithesis is evident all down the later Middle Ages." *The Peasant War in Germany* (Moscow: The Foreign Languages Publishing House, 1956), p. 56.

[8] Manifesto of the Communist Party, *MESW*, vol 1, pp. 42–43.

[9] Preface to the "Critique of Political Economy," *MESW*, vol. 1, p. 363.

If revolution "begins" when the productive forces come into conflict with the existing productive relations or conditions of work, what is the role of class struggle at the beginning of a stage of production? On the one hand, class struggle is held to be omnipresent, but on the other, in the early period of a given mode of production, when productive forces and relations are in accord, production is developing satisfactorily and there should be no need of class struggle. Only later, when productive relations "turn into the fetters" of productive forces, is there a clear role for the class struggle.

For Soviet and Chinese historians a still more fundamental loophole in the classical theory of the class struggle was the omission of non-Western civilizations in general and of "Oriental society" in particular from Marxist theories. The implication that Marxism might not apply to non-European areas was, of course, anathema to Soviet and Asian communists, and after intense debates in the 1920s and 1930s the very existence of classical Marxist statements about the "peculiarities of Oriental society" was denied. Yet such statements were made in the writings of Marx and Engels.[10] Thus, Marx began his critical comments about the Taiping Rebellion with the statement, "the Oriental empires present us with permanent changelessness in the social substructure . . . [although there is] restless change among the persons and tribes that seize the political superstructure." [11] Elsewhere Marx elaborated on the passivity of the Indian village, "the social foundation of Oriental despotism." [12] Marx saw no evidence of social revolutions in the history of the changeless East. Similarly, Engels, who described village-based Oriental society as the "most barbarous form of state," [13] warned that the religious revolts of the Moslem world did not have the

[10] This is now admitted again in the Soviet Union; see articles in *Narody Azii i Afriki* (Peoples of Asia and Africa, hereafter *NAA*), 1965, no. 1 *et seq.* For a discussion of such references see D. M. Lowe, *The Function of China in Marx, Lenin, and Mao* (Berkeley: University of California Press, 1966), pp. 6 ff.

[11] Cited in Karl A. Wittfogel, "The Marxist View of China," *The China Quarterly*, no. 11, July–September 1962, p. 6.

[12] Marx, "The British Rule in India," *MESW*, vol. 1, p. 350.

[13] Engels, *Anti-Duhring* (New York: International Publishers, Co., 1939), p. 206.

same immediate effect on the old economic order that such movements had in the West:

> Even when they are victorious, they allow the old economic conditions to persist untouched. So the old situation remains unchanged and the collision recurs periodically [between the townspeople and the more fundamentalist bedouins]. . . .[14]

The similarity between the results of such recurring but ineffectual Moslem revolts and the results of Chinese peasant revolts is evident. Yet, it could be argued, as the Chinese communists do, that while the turmoil in their history did not have readily discernible effects, the class struggle nonetheless affected the deeper undercurrents of history.

It may be said that while Marx and Engels led a revolution in the interpretation of social history,[15] they themselves were confused and cautious in the evaluation of the role of the class struggle in pre-modern and non-Western society. Even for the modern West there is very little concrete explanation of the theory of class analysis and class struggle.[16] The burden of the work of Marx and Engels was economic, and the truth of what Engels called "the great law of motion of history" [17] was left to later writers to document.

----

[14] Engels, "On the History of Early Christianity," in *K. Marx and F. Engels on Religion* (Moscow: Foreign Languages Publishing House, 1957), p. 317.

[15] Hence, even those who reject the theory of the class struggle no longer see the conflicts between economic groups as aberrations but as normal and perhaps even as desirable activities in the course of human development. Actually Marx did not claim to have discovered the theory of class struggle (see Marx, "Letter to J. Weydemeyer," *MESW*, vol. 2, p. 452). Rather he took an old idea (e.g., Plato's references to war between rich and poor), which was immeasurably developed as a result of the French revolution (see the statement of Augustin Thierry cited in Fritz Stern [ed.], *The Varieties of History* [New York: Meridian Books, 1957], p. 70) and made it one of the most familiar concepts of modern thought. He also developed its political implications, of course, insisting that meaningful class struggles were those fought for political power.

[16] See R. Bendix and S. M. Lipset, "Karl Marx' Theory of Social Classes," in Bendix and Lipset, *op. cit.*, p. 26; and G. Lichtheim, *Marxism: An Historical and Critical Study* (New York: Praeger, 1961), p. 86.

[17] F. Engels, Preface to "The Eighteenth Brumaire of Louis Bonaparte," *MESW*, vol. 1, p. 246. Engels compared Marx's theory of the

Nonetheless, the impact of this aspect of Marxist theory has been immeasurable, largely because of the emphasis given to it by twentieth-century communist theorists. With the development of Bolshevism, cautious earlier appraisals of the class struggle in history have given way to far more assertive Soviet and Chinese views. Lenin, of course, had most to do with this, because it was he who first successfully wed the theory with the practice of class struggle. The latter he defined as

> the struggle of one part of the people against the other; the struggle waged by the masses of the rightless, the oppressed, the toilers; against the privileged, the oppressors, the parasites, the struggle of the wage laborers, or proletarians against the property-owners or bourgeoisie. This great struggle has always gone on and is now going on. . . .[18]

More important than Lenin's understanding of the theory of class struggle was his development of a theme already hinted in Marx, "that the class struggle necessarily leads to the dictatorship of the proletariat." [19] Lenin wrote:

> He who recognizes only the class struggle, is not a Marxist. . . . A Marxist is one who extends the acceptance of class struggle to the acceptance of the dictatorship of the proletariat. Herein lies the deepest difference between a Marxist and an ordinary (or even big) bourgeois.[20]

---

class struggle for social development with Darwin's concept of the survival of the fittest for natural evolution ("Speech at the Graveside of Karl Marx," *MESW*, vol. 2, p. 167).

[18] V. I. Lenin, "To the Rural Poor" (1903), in *Alliance of the Working Class and the Peasantry* (Moscow: Foreign Languages Publishing House, 1959), p. 81.

[19] K. Marx, "Letter to J. Weydemeyer," *MESW*, vol. 2, p. 452.

[20] V. I. Lenin, "Marx on the Class Struggle and the Dictatorship of the Proletariat," in *Marx, Engels, Marxism* (Moscow: Cooperative Publishing Society, 1934), p. 160. Lenin was fully aware of the possibilities of distorting history and once wrote, "In view of the extreme complexity of the phenomenon of social life, it is always possible to select any number of examples or separate data to prove any proposition." "Imperialism, the Highest Stage of Capitalism," *Collected Works of V. I. Lenin* (New York: International Publishers Co., 1942), vol. 19, p. 86.

The corollary to this dictum is the proposition that without the leadership of the vanguard of the modern working class, the Communist Party, there can be no successful conclusion to the class struggle. In fact, party had replaced class as the maker of communist revolution.[21]

The concept of the class struggle entered China on the heels of social Darwinism. The translation of Huxley's *Evolution and Ethics* in 1898 was the first systematic introduction of what became accepted beliefs among some Chinese—the concepts of "the struggle for existence" and "survival of the fittest." [22] Already in the first decade of the twentieth century a small group of men was arguing in socialist terms about the meaning and manner of historical progress. In Paris and Tokyo, Chinese converts to anarchism contended that "the world progressed through competition, and thus the struggle between rich and poor, between ruler and people, constituted a part of the inevitable historical process." [23]

Chinese intellectuals, however, were far more willing to accept the idea of struggle in the world of nature than in the history of mankind. Many, including revolutionaries such as Sun Yat-sen, criticized the theory of progress through competition between classes, favoring instead belief in social progress through cooperation and mutual aid.[24] As young revolutionaries, they realized that only in an acceptance of the idea that life constantly progressed was there hope for China. Yet few embraced the idea that class competition was necessary or desirable for that progress.

[21] See George Lichtheim, "The Transmutations of a Doctrine," *Problems of Communism*, July/August 1966, pp. 14–25.

[22] See Benjamin I. Schwartz, *In Search of Wealth and Power: Yen Fu and the West* (Cambridge: Harvard University Press, 1964), pp. 45–46, 55 ff., and 99. See also O. Brière, *Fifty Years of Chinese Philosophy* (London: George Allen & Unwin, 1956), p. 19; and Chou Tse-tsung, "Yen Fu," in Howard Boorman (ed.), *Men and Politics in Modern China: Preliminary Fifty Biographies* (New York: Columbia University Press, 1960), p. 166.

[23] See Robert A. Scalapino and George T. Yu, *The Chinese Anarchist Movement* (Berkeley: University of California Center for Chinese Studies, 1961), p. 19.

[24] For this, many looked to the writings of the Russian anarchist Kropotkin.

According to Sun Yat-sen, "The main force of human progress is in mutual help. It is not in competition as it is for other animals." [25] He specifically rejected an interpretation of history as a struggle between classes, at least in the pre-capitalist period in which China found itself. Other Chinese reformers, including Liang Ch'i-ch'ao and Yen Fu, like Sun Yat-sen acknowledged the existence of the class struggle in the history of the West but felt that in China this would be subordinated to the national struggle for survival.[26] As Nationalists they looked for war between oppressed and oppressor nations rather than for a class war within China.[27] This orthodox interpretation of social history, picturing life as a struggle for subsistence and survival, requiring cooperation rather than class struggle, continued under the Republic. One of the principal aims of the teaching of history in Nationalist China was to cultivate "the spirit of cooperation . . . through the development of human sympathy." [28] After the break with the communists in 1927, the Kuomintang, (hereafter KMT) specifically sought to contrast favorably their theory of mutual cooperation with communist conceptions of the class struggle.

Nationalist leaders correctly single out the concept of class struggle as the most characteristic and most un-Chinese aspect of communist ideology. Yeh Ch'ing, a leading Marxist of the 'thirties who became one of the major nationalist ideologists on Taiwan, wrote that as of 1951 few Chinese had written criticisms of the theory of class struggle, although it

[25] *Tsung-li Ch'uan-chi* (Collected Works of the President [Sun Yat-sen]), vol. 1, p. 694, cited in Yeh Ch'ing, *Chieh-chi Tou-cheng Lun P'i-p'an* (Critique of the Theory of Class Struggle) (Taipei: Po-mi-erh Shu-tien, 1952), p. 27.

[26] See Joseph R. Levenson, *Liang Ch'i-ch'ao and the Mind of Modern China* (Cambridge: Harvard University Press, 1953), p. 116.

[27] E.g., see Sun Yat-sen, *San-min Chu-yi*, trans. by Frank W. Price (Chungking: Ministry of Information of the Republic of China, 1943), p. 18. This reorientation of the concept of class struggle in terms of international struggle between nations was accepted by some leading Chinese communists. See Meisner, *op. cit.*, pp. 176 ff.

[28] Cyrus H. Peake, *Nationalism and Education in Modern China*, p. 113.

alone separated real communists from mere Marxists. Yeh argued that "revolution is not class struggle, but is mutual aid, because revolution is the majority of all men rising to smash the old system and build a new, a movement for the improvement of life." [29]

The first Chinese to accept communism did so as a result of ever greater frustrations at China's humiliations. They had accepted Darwinian ideas of struggle and evolution in common with other intellectuals of the time, but, unlike most, they eventually moved from these beliefs to an acceptance of the theory of the class struggle. Ch'en Tu-hsiu, with Li Ta-chao one of the co-founders of the Chinese Communist Party, became a communist only in 1920, but by 1915 he had clearly stated his belief that Western superiority was rooted in competitive ideals, writing, "The West is dynamic, warlike and enterprising while the East is passive, inert and pacifist." By 1917 he went so far as to state, "War is to society what movement is to the body." [30]

After the May Fourth Movement of 1919, Ch'en moved from advocacy of individualism, democracy, and science toward the communist idea of class struggle.[31] In one respect central to our analysis, however, Ch'en differed from Li Ta-chao and the later dominant strain of the Chinese Communist Party. That was his distrust of the peasant masses, both in history, as seen in some of his earlier statements on the

[29] Yeh Ch'ing, *op. cit.*, p. 27. Even a progressive warlord like Yen Hsi-shan agreed that the doctrine of class struggle was the only really unacceptable feature of Marxism. See Donald G. Gillin, "China's First Five-Year Plan: Industrialization Under the Warlords as Reflected in the Policies of Yen Hsi-shan in Shansi Province," *Journal of Asian Studies* (hereafter *JAS*), February 1965, p. 253.

[30] See Ch'en's writings in *Hsin Ch'ing Nien*, which he founded in September 1915. See also Benjamin I. Schwartz, "Ch'en Tu-hsiu and the Acceptance of the Modern West," *Journal of the History of Ideas*, January 1951, pp. 65–66; Julie How, "The Development of Ch'en Tu-hsiu's Thought, 1915–1938," unpublished Columbia University Master's Essay, 1949; and D.W.Y. Kwok, *Scientism in Chinese Thought, 1900–1950* (New Haven: Yale University Press, 1965), pp. 59 ff.

[31] Benjamin I. Schwartz, *Chinese Communism and the Rise of Mao* (Cambridge: Harvard University Press, 3d ed., 1958), pp. 17 ff. See also Chou Tse-tsung, *op. cit.*, p. 176, and Y. C. Wang, *Chinese Intellectuals and the West* (Chapel Hill: University of North Carolina Press, 1966), p. 316.

Boxers,[32] and in his rather paternal ideas of leadership.

Li Ta-chao, who in 1918 was the first to hail the October Revolution, did so from an "idealist" position. He regarded it as a triumph of man's spirit rather than of economic processes, and he criticized historical materialism as too fatalistic. Later he apparently overcame this objection to communist theory by stressing spiritual rejuvenation as a result of class struggles.[33] He resolved the conflict between traditional concern for harmony and the requirements of class struggle by arguing that there was no ultimate contradiction between the Chinese ideal of *great unity* (*ta-t'ung*) and social revolution, because the communist revolution would usher in a new classless society in the future. He wrote:

> In the present world, tyranny has reached an extreme point . . . we must make a fundamental change . . . wash clean the previous world of class struggle and . . . bring forth a glorious new world of cooperation.[34]

Li continued to stress that the essence of historical materialism lay in seeing history as constant movement and in seeing the interconnections in this movement. This state of flux was due to the struggle of opposites, "have and have not, relative and absolute; in today's terminology, contradictions." [35]

It cannot be said that in these years Ch'en, Li, or any other Chinese intellectual had profound understanding of Marxism, nor could they have had. Books on socialism were published in 1903, part of the *Communist Manifesto* was translated in 1906, and excerpts from the writings of Engels in 1907 and 1912, but there were no further translations of this alien

[32] See Chapter 3 and Meisner, *op. cit.*, pp. 80 ff. and 237 ff.

[33] See Maurice Meisner, *op. cit.*, pp. 13–14, 91–92, 112, 140–146, and Meisner, "Li Ta-chao and the Chinese Communist Treatment of the Materialist Conception of History," *China Quarterly*, no. 24, October–December 1965; Schwartz, *Chinese Communism and the Rise of Mao*, chap. 1; Chou, *The May Fourth Movement*, pp. 298–99; and Huang Sung-k'ang, *Li Ta-chao and the Impact of Marxism on Modern Chinese Thinking* (Paris: Mouton and Co., 1966).

[34] *Li Ta-chao Hsuan-chi* (Peking: Jen-min Ch'u-pan She, 1962), p. 224.

[35] Kuo Chan-po, *Chin Wu-shih-nien Chung-kuo Ssu-hsiang Shih* (History of the Last Fifty Years of Chinese Thought) (Peiping: Jen-wen Shu-tien, 1936), pp. 152 and 144.

philosophy until 1919.[36] The first relatively thorough exposition of Marxism in *Hsin Ch-ing Nien,* May 1919, had several articles on historical materialism, but these neither expounded nor accepted Marxism fully. The first efforts to interpret Chinese history in the light of historical materialism were made in the same year,[37] and ideas common to the Marxist view of history continued to spread. Karl Kautsky's *The Class Struggle* is said to have been the first full book on Marxism translated into Chinese.[38]

The vigorous attack on the old Confucian order, led by some radical Chinese thinkers after 1915, was instrumental in preparing the way for Marxism in China. The past seemed to offer no answers for China's problems. As Li Ta-chao put it,

> Our nation has gone through an extremely long history, and the accumulated dust of the past is heavily weighing it down. By fettering its life it has brought our nation to a state of extreme decay . . . what we must prove to the world is not that the old China is not dead, but that a new youthful China is in the process of being born.[39]

As for the future, the only certainty seemed the necessity for action. For this Marxism had enormous appeal, since it offered an antidote to the West and, above all, a successful

[36] Chou, *The May Fourth Movement,* p. 298; and Wei Li, "Introduction of the Classical Works of Marxism-Leninism to China . . . ," *SCMP* 2021, pp. 7 ff., citing *JMJP,* May 5, 1959. For a more complete listing of translations of Marxist works into Chinese see Chang Ching-lu, *Chung-kuo Ch'u-pan Shih-liao Pu-pien* (Expanded Edition of Historical Materials on Chinese Publishing) (Peking: Chung-hua Shu-chü, 1957), pp. 442 ff.

[37] Chou Tse-tsung, *The May Fourth Movement,* pp. 298–99.

[38] K'o Tzu-chi (Kautsky), *Chieh-chi Cheng-tou* (Class Struggle), Yun Tai-ying (trans.) (Shanghai, Hsin Ch'ing Nien She, 1921). This was presumably a translation of the American version, published in Chicago in 1910, of Kautsky's *Das Erfurt Programm* (1891). Despite its title, this book does not give a systematic account of the class struggle but rather a description of the contemporary labor movement in Europe. Along with Kirkup's *History of Socialism,* which criticized Marxism as too stereotyped, and the Communist Manifesto, it was particularly influential on the growing convictions of Mao Tse-tung. Edgar Snow, *Red Star over China* (New York: Random House, 1938), p. 139.

[39] Cited in Benjamin I. Schwartz, *Chinese Communism and the Rise of Mao,* p. 12.

system of organization based on a variant of the needed Western mentality.[40] It seemed both "scientific" and anti-Western. To these attractions was added a cogent explanation of imperialism and a style of work and ideological framework superficially in accord with the élitist ideas of most young Chinese revolutionaries.

Nevertheless, offsetting these appeals were traditional values antithetical to much of Marxist theory. This was especially true of the doctrine of class struggle. Other aspects of Marxist theory were accepted to a great extent in the 1920s and 1930s, their way having been prepared by more moderate Western theories, but a belief in the desirability of class struggle had to overcome many deeply rooted habits of mind. The doctrine of class struggle also appeared to many to conflict with nationalism, the dominant belief of the age.

Another factor discouraging a ready acceptance of Marxist theory was the widespread criticism of it in the West. This is well and surprisingly illustrated by Li Ta-chao in a book published in 1924. Now hailed as the real founder of Chinese Marxism, Li timidly stated that Marxism was one possible interpretation of history but noted that it had been criticized by later historians, since the "laws of historiography [also] evolve." He concluded by observing that the current validity of Marxism as an historical science was still under debate.[41]

Another Li, Li Ta, was acknowledged as the first to give Chinese readers a complete and systematic explanation of Marxism. After participating in the founding of the Chinese Communist Party in 1921, he wrote *Wei-wu Shih-kuan Chieh-shuo* (An Explanation of Historical Materialism) and *Hsien-tai She-hui Hsueh* (Modern Sociology).[42] The latter work, first published in 1926, has been described as the "most learned work published in China on this school." [43] It in-

[40] See Y. C. Wang, *op. cit.*, p. 315.

[41] Li-Shou-ch'ang (Li Ta-chao), *Shih-hsueh Yao-lun* (Discussion of the Essentials of Historiography) (Shanghai: Shang-wu Yin-shu Kuan, 1924), pp. 60–62. This book may have been written several years earlier. See also Chou Tse-tsung, *The May Fourth Movement*, pp. 220 and 298.

[42] Kuo Chan-po, *op. cit.*, p. 238.

[43] Brière, *op. cit.*, pp. 76–77.

cluded a thorough discussion of Marxist principles of class struggle, beginning with the statement, "Revolution is the mother of progress. Society without revolution is a society without progress. This is a law of history." [44]

The cause of class opposition, Li continued, is "private ownership of property," while the cause of the final stage of social revolution is "the obstruction of productive forces by social organization [productive relations]." He attempts to resolve the contradiction between Marxist economic determinism and the Marxist theory of class struggle; "the productive forces develop the basic conditions for the transformation of the productive relations [while] at the same time, the class struggle is the motive force of social revolution." Finally he notes a division of the class struggle into two periods. At first, when productive forces and relations are in accord, "class struggle is only an economic struggle . . . for economic advantages." Later, when productive relations no longer suit the development of the productive forces, "the class struggle . . . is political struggle, namely a struggle for political power." [45]

Interestingly enough, however, Li Ta heeded Marx's warning[46] not to try to apply these theories derived from Western experience to all societies regardless of their peculiarities. Thus, Li introduced his book with the following statement: "The theories in this book are mostly directed at European, American and Japanese capitalist society and cannot explain clearly much in semi-feudal Chinese society." [47]

Marxist ideas are said to have become dominant among Chinese youth as early as 1927 or 1928.[48] Certainly by the mid-1920s Marxism was one of the leading schools of thought

[44] Li Ta, *Hsien-tai She-hui Hsueh* (Modern Sociology) (Shanghai: K'un-lun Shu-tien, 2d ed., 1929), p. 127.

[45] *Ibid.*, pp. 130–34, 140–43.

[46] See Karl A. Wittfogel, "Marxist Views of Russian Society and Revolution," *World Politics*, vol. 12, July 1960, pp. 493–94.

[47] Li Ta, *op. cit.*, p. 2. Perhaps not surprisingly, considering his unorthodox career, Li was denounced as "anti-party" in the 1966 purges. *New York Times*, Aug. 5, 1966, p. 4.

[48] Brière, *op. cit.*, p. 19; Kuo Chan-po, *op. cit.*, p. 196; and Chou Tse-tsung, *op. cit.*, p. 297.

among modern educated intellectuals, but the distinction between appeals of the theory and organizational commitment must be kept in mind. Furthermore, by the early 1930s the ascendancy of Marxist historians was measured more in vociferousness than in numbers[49] or quality of work. It is therefore misleading to say that the intellectual battle for China was already won by the communists in the early 1930s.[50] There were still influential supporters of Western liberal ideals in the 1930s and '40s, such as members of the *Tu-li P'ing-lun* group. Their lack of influence was due more to political isolation than to a lack of talent; and had there been a strong party behind the liberal intellectuals, the academic climate of China might have been far different. As it was, the prewar period was one of great intellectual diversity, with many schools contending for theoretical solutions to China's problems. Moreover, Marxist-oriented literature of the years before 1949 was itself far freer of dogmatism than was the case once the CCP was in a position to dictate desired interpretations. Prewar Marxism was an increasingly popular intellectual position, but it is by no means to be equated with the Party-dictated orthodoxy which emerged later.[51]

Proof of this is offered by the examples of T'ao Hsi-sheng and Yeh Ch'ing. They were among the most active participants in the Marxist debates of the time, but neither became a communist. On the contrary, both are now leading nationalist ideologists in Taiwan. Yet T'ao, along with Kuo Mo-jo, was the first Chinese to use historical materialism in depth for the study of Chinese history, and Yeh Ch'ing was "hailed

[49] Israel agrees with Olga Lang and others that perhaps one third of college students in the mid-1930s were "radical" and hence "ideologically pro-communist." John Israel, *Student Nationalism in China, 1927–1937* (Stanford: Stanford University Press, 1966), p. 181.

[50] E. S. Kirby, *Introduction to Economic History of China* (London: George Allen & Unwin, 1954), p. 23. See also Kwok, *op. cit.* Sun Yat-sen claimed in the early 1920s that already a majority of Chinese youths favored communism.

[51] Even within the Party absolute orthodoxy was difficult to maintain. Ch'en Tu-hsiu was expelled in 1929 and formed an opposition "Trotskyist" party. After release from a Kuomintang prison in 1937, Ch'en appeared to renounce at least basic aspects of "Stalinism." See Y. C. Wang, *op cit.*, p. 319.

as one of the new leaders of Marxist thought." [52] Even Ku Chieh-kang, one of the best-known modern Chinese histor-ians, who certainly would not be considered an orthodox communist historian, declared in 1933 that "the materialistic interpretation of history was the most fruitful guide for the study of ancient thoughts and institutions." [53]

It is not argued that the widespread acceptance of the evo-lutionary and economic aspects of Marxist theory did not help the communist military and political triumph on the mainland, but only that there was a distinction between Party theorists and Marxist intellectuals in pre-1949 China. In fact, there was a marked contrast between the academic situation in China and in pre-revolutionary Russia, where few intellectuals accepted Marxism before 1917.[54] In China not only did most well-known historians remain on the mainland in 1949, but a significant proportion of these historians were al-ready accustomed to using the Marxist approach to history.[55]

The reasons for the wide intellectual acceptance of Marx-ism in China before 1949 were a craving for a sense of na-

[52] Brière, *op. cit.*, p. 82; and Kwok, *op. cit.*, pp. 170 ff. Among other prominent "unorthodox Marxist historians" were Li Chi, Yen Ling-feng, Hu Ch'iu-yuan, Wang Li-hsi, Ch'en Pang-kuo, and Wang Yi-ch'ing. Li Ta, Liu Meng-yuan, and Liu Su-hua were the earliest important aca-demic proponents of "orthodox" Marxism, followed by Kuo Mo-jo, Lü Chen-yü, and others among the historians in the 1930s. See Lü Chen-yü, *Shih Lun-chi* (Discussions of History) (Peking: San-lien Shu-tien, 1960), pp. 25 ff.; and Ho Kan-chih, *Chung Kuo Ch'i-meng Yun-tung Shih* (History of China's Movement for Enlightenment) (Shanghai: Sheng-huo Shu-tien, 1947).
[53] Cited in Robert H. G. Lee, "The Study of History, Some Con-temporary Views," in John E. Lane (ed.), *Researches in the Social Sciences on China* (New York: East Asian Institute of Columbia Uni-versity, private distribution, 1957), p. 19.
[54] K. F. Shteppa, *Russian Historians and the Soviet State* (New Brunswick: Rutgers University Press, 1962), p. 12.
[55] See Kwok, *op. cit.*, pp. 162 ff. According to the Chairman of the Department of History at Nankai University in 1957, Cheng T'ien-t'ing, "the former study methods of [all old historians over sixty or seventy] . . . were close to Marxist-Leninist methods [before 1949]. So it was comparatively easy for them to accept Marxism-Leninism." "Professors' Views in Respect of 'Contention of Diverse Schools of Thought,' " *Un-ion Research Service* (hereafter URS), vol. 7, no. 20, p. 47, citing *JMJP*, April 21 and 22, 1957.

tional identity, spiritual insecurity, a long tradition of authoritarianism, orientation toward state service, and a rejection of capitalist values.[56] The widespread early acceptance of academic Marxism in China is not, however, to be equated with a political commitment to the Communist Party.[57]

The relative freedom from dogmatism prior to the communist conquest is illustrated in the early debates over the nature of Chinese society which dominated Marxist historiography of the late 1920s and 1930s in China. Many different approaches and viewpoints were presented in these arguments, and their outcome had important implications for the historiography of the Chinese peasant revolts, since the causes and forms of the class struggle are held to differ greatly according to the existing mode of production.

Following years of wide-ranging and intensive discussion about the nature of Chinese society and economics by Soviet and Japanese as well as by Chinese scholars, Stalin's theorists "decided" that Marx's references to an "Asiatic mode of production"—characterized by isolated village communities, large-scale government public works projects for irrigation and defense, absence of private ownership in land, and absence of a meaningful class struggle[58]—applied only to ancient history and specifically to a variant period of development during the transition from primitive communal society to slavery. By thus isolating and minimizing the "Asiatic mode," China, like every other great civilization, could be shown to have advanced through the four stages of communal, slave, feudal, and bourgeois society on the inevitable

---

[56] Benjamin I. Schwartz, "The Intelligentsia in Communist China, a Tentative Comparison," *Daedalus*, Summer 1960, p. 616.

[57] The situation in Japan is comparable in this respect.

[58] After several decades of embarrassed silence, Soviet theorists have revived discussion of the Asiatic mode of production (see *NAA*, 1965, no. 1 *et seq.*). Of special interest here is their emphasis on the lack of a role for the class struggle in Oriental societies and consequent communist rejection of this theory for China after ancient times. They maintain that ancient China did have some of the characteristics of "Oriental society," but those were destroyed by the coming of the West and subsequent developments. See *NAA*, 1965, no. 5, pp. 85–86; and Wittfogel, *Oriental Despotism* (New Haven: Yale University Press, 1963), pp. 327 ff.

path to communism. Therefore, China did not stagnate in an "Oriental mode of production," as suggested by statements in the Marxist classics and by many later writers, but progressed in the past as in the present. Most important, according to this orthodox dictation of history, the two millennia of Chinese history preceding the coming of the West were characterized by a "feudal" society and economy and not by a "pre-capitalist" or "Asiatic mode of production," as argued by the "Trotskyists." It was argued that the immediate task of the Chinese revolution was to overthrow feudalism, not capitalism. Similarly, in pre-modern times the Chinese peasant revolts were "anti-feudal" rather than "anti-commercial capital," and their struggles were better characterized as opposition to the landlord class as a whole than as opposition to an "unholy alliance" of usurers, merchants, officials, and landlords.[59]

Therefore communist periodization schemes included both a slave and a feudal period. According to most, a slave system had replaced the original communal form of production by the time of China's first documented civilization during the Shang (traditionally dated 1766–1122 B.C.).[60] The start of the

[59] For further discussion of the debates over the structure of ancient Chinese society see *Ibid.*, pp. 369–412; Wittfogel, "The Marxist View of China," *China Quarterly*, nos. 11 and 12, 1962; Benjamin I. Schwartz, "A Marxist Controversy on China," *Far Eastern Quarterly* [hereafter *FEQ*], February 1954, pp. 143–54; Wolfram Eberhard, *Conquerors and Rulers, Social Forces in Medieval China* (Leiden: E. J. Brill, 1952), pp. 44 ff.; Shteppa, *op. cit.*, pp. 6–11 and 152 ff.; Kwok, *op. cit.*, pp. 166 ff.; Ho Kan-chih, *op. cit.*, pp. 183–84; Hou Wai-lu, *Su-lien Li-shih-hsueh Chieh Chu Lun-cheng Chieh-ta* (Exposition of the Debates in Soviet Historical Circles) (Shanghai: Chien-kuo Shu-tien, 1946), pp. 26 ff.; Huang Yuan-ch'i, "The Spread and Development of Chinese Historical Science Under the Glorious Reflection of the October Socialist Revolution," *SHYK*, 1957, no. 11, p. 4; Lü Chen-yü, *Chung-kuo She-hui Shih Chu Wen-t'i* (Problems of Chinese Society) (Peking: San-lien Shu-tien, 1961; first published 1940), p. 37; and Lü Chen-yü, *Shih Lun-chi*, pp. 32–37.

[60] It is also admitted, however, that the communal forms persisted until well into the Chou, a concession to the arguments about an "Asiatic mode of production." Some even argue that the slave system began only in the Chou, and during the One Hundred Flowers period it was revealed that some mainland historians (e.g., Lei Hai-tsung) still, as in the 1930s, favored dispensing altogether with the artificial insistence on a slave period.

next mode of production, feudalism, is still a matter of heated debate, with dates from roughly 1100 B.C. to A.D. 200 advanced for its inception, although most now agree the transition occurred in the Chankuo period (403–221 B.C.).[61] The end of the feudal period is generally agreed to date from the beginning of imperialist domination of China in 1840.

The Chinese communists have even greater difficulty in accounting for the fact that their "feudalism" began about the time of the unification of the country. This obvious discrepancy from the noncommunist use of "feudal" to denote divided and localized political power, is sometimes covered by calling China from the Ch'in to the nineteenth century a "feudal absolutist state," an "Eastern feudal despotism," or a "centralized despotic feudal society." [62] In his 1930 book on ancient Chinese society, Kuo Mo-jo noted the unfortunate discrepancy in the communist and traditional uses of the

[61] For an account of those who argue that feudalism began in early Chou and those who argue that it began in later Chou, see A. Feuerwerker, "China's History in Marxian Dress," *American Historical Review*, 1961, no. 1, pp. 338–39. At least until recently there has also been a vigorous third school, including most Soviet sinologists, which holds that slavery persisted through the Han as the leading mode of production. For instance, the leading Soviet textbook of world history, compiled by the Soviet Academy of Sciences in the early 1950s and translated into Chinese in 1960, takes this position. See *Shih-chieh T'ung-shih* (General History of the World), E. M. Ju-Ka-fu (ed.) (Peking: San-lien Shu-tien, 1960), vol. 2, p. 754. Among Chinese proponents of this periodization, see Wang Chung-ying, *Kuan-yü Chung-kuo Nu-li Shehui te Wa-chieh chi Feng-chien Kuan-hsi te Hsing-ch'eng Wen-t'i* (On the Problem of the Breakup of Chinese Slave Society and the Formation of Feudal Relations) (Wuhan: Hupei Jen-min Ch'u-pan She, 1957), p. 86.

[62] E.g., see Hou Wai-lu, "The Development of the Peasant Wars and Their Programs and Slogans in Early and Late Periods of Chinese Feudal Society," SSP, p. 41; and Chien Po-tsan, "Regarding the Problem of Public and Private Slaves During the Two Han," LSYC, 1954, no. 4, p. 1. Part of the explanation for this confusion arises from the fact that the terms for slavery and feudalism arose in a European context. Hence, the so-called "slave" period coincides with what all noncommunist sinologists and the classical texts call the "feudal" period of China, while what most communist historians term the early "feudal" period includes the Han, possibly the period of maximum utilization of slaves in China. Even then, however, slaves probably did not exceed 1 percent of the population. See C. Martin Wilbur, *Slavery in China During the Former Han Dynasty* (Chicago: Field Museum of Natural History, 1943), p. 237.

term "feudal," but he made it plain that he applied this term in its economic sense.[63] This economic interpretation, hinging on what are called "feudal land relations," is still followed and defended against all denials.

The Chinese, in part, have changed the content of the original Marxist concept of a "feudal mode of production" until its only meaning is to convey the image of an oppressive society. Moreover, in recent years, under the assertive nationalism of the Chinese communist government, the whole argument of the 1930s has been turned on its head, and it is asked why the admittedly "Asiatic" forms of Chinese history should not be the model for world history instead of the historical development of the Western world. Whereas in the 1930s historians did not wish to class China as a distinctive "Asian" society, since this would imply inferiority, now mainland historians, under a movement known as "oppose the Europe-as-the-center theory of world history," endeavor to make a virtue of their differences, claiming that their experience has been more typical of world history than Europe's.[64] Furthermore, there is clear evidence of continued Chinese concern with the problem of the nature of "Oriental society," [65] and on occasion China is still referred to as "an an-

[63] Kuo Mo-jo, *Chung-kuo Ku-tai She-hui Yen-chiu* (Research in Ancient Chinese Society) (Peking: K'o-hsueh Ch'u-pan She, 1960, reprint), p. 167. See also Ho Kan-chih, "Problems of the Laws of Development of Feudal Society," *Shih-ti She-hui Lun-wen Chai-yao Yueh K'an* (Abstract Monthly), October 1936. For a general discussion of the Marxist description of Chinese "feudalism," see Benjamin I. Schwartz, "A Marxist Controversy on China," *FEQ*, February 1954, pp. 148–50. For a recent explanation of the development of "feudalism" primarily in terms of the increasing concentration of land ownership, see Ch'i Hsia et al., *Ch'in-han Nung-min Chan-cheng Shih* (History of the Peasant Wars of the Ch'in and Han) (Peking: San-lien Shu-tien, 1962, pp. 3–7.

[64] E.g., see Wu T'ing-chiu, "Establish a New System of World History," *SCMP* 2503, p. 16, citing *KMJP*, April 9–10, 1961. The rationale of this campaign has been described as "to establish national self-respect. . . . As everybody knows the 'Europe as the center theory' was a reflection in the realm of the study of history of the imperialist aggressive policies of the western bourgeoisie who sought to conquer the world." See Teng T'o, "The Thought of Mao Tse-tung Opens the Way for the Development of China's Science of History," *ECMM* 264, p. 9, citing *LSYC*, 1961, no. 1.

[65] E.g., see "The Form of Land Ownership Under Feudal Society

cient Oriental type of state with large scale water works and public works projects." [66]

Since early Chinese Marxist writings on history were part of the effort to construct a theoretical basis for the "new China" all wished to see fulfilled, many must have consciously or unconsciously argued positions they knew to be not entirely logical in the interests of establishing this theoretical framework. They used the terms "slave" and "feudal" as a code or shorthand for previously established meanings.[67] In the 1930s and 1940s, as the Communist Party played skillfully on the growing frustrations and nationalism of the Chinese intelligentsia, these basic Marxist interpretations and approaches to history gained ever increasing currency.[68] Yet this did not appear to be true of "pre-liberation" attitudes toward the class struggle in history.

in China," *SCMP* 2479, pp. 23–24, citing *KMJP*, March 11, 1961; and articles listed in *Chung-kuo Ku-tai chi Chung-shih-chi Shih Pao-k'an Lun-wen Tzu-liao So-yin* (Index to Periodical Literature for Ancient and Medieval Chinese History), Hua-tung Shih-fan Ta-hsueh (eds.) (Shanghai, 1959), p. 46.

[66] *SSP*, p. 503.

[67] For a general discussion of Chinese historiography during this period, see Teng Ssu-yü, "Chinese Historiography in the Last Fifty Years," *FEQ*, February 1949; Chou Yü-t'ung, "China's New Historiography of the Last Fifty Years," *Hsueh lin*, vol. 1, 1941; and Ch'i Ssu-ho, "A Criticism of Modern Chinese Historiography," *Ta Chung*, 1946, vol. 1. See also Arthur Wright, "On the Uses of Generalization in the Study of Chinese History," in Louis Gottschalk (ed.), *Generalization in the Writing of History* (Chicago: University of Chicago Press, 1963), pp. 36–58.

[68] However, this pre-1949 Marxist historiography continued to be marked by considerable diversity. In fact, of the Marxist historical studies written before 1949, a Chinese communist publication recommended only those of Kuo Mo-jo, Ch'en Po-ta, Fan Wen-lan, Lü Chen-yü, Hou Wai-lu, and Chien Po-tsan. See Liu Ta-nien, "Present State of China's Historical Science," *KMJP*, July 22, 1953. Most of these historians were denounced in turn in 1966. Of course, many other historians now on the mainland were active before 1949. Other well-known historians whose "pre-liberation" works used Marxist theories to greater or lesser degree included Wu Han, Hsieh Kuo-chen, Chang Yin-lin, Li Wen-chih, Lo Erh-kang, Chou Ku-ch'eng, and Pai Shou-yi. Today their early works are recommended for specific information but not for point of view. This is true to a still greater extent of such eminent mainland historians as Ch'en Yin-ch'ueh, Ku Chieh-kang, T'ang Yung-t'ung, and others. We will come across many of these names again in our consideration of the historiography of the peasant rebellions.

Before 1949 even the most radical of the "orthodox Marxist" historians generally preferred to speak of economic or broad social forces rather than of the class struggle between the peasants and the landlords in Chinese history. According to a Chinese communist account, the first to analyze China's feudal society according to the development of its internal class contradictions was a one-time chief of the Comintern Far Eastern Bureau, G. Safarov.[69] In a work published in 1928 he allegedly used the class struggle rather than the traditional dynastic approach to periodize Chinese history. In fact, this book stressed economic and sociological data and their effects on the ruling class rather than such evidences of class struggle between exploiters and exploited as the medieval peasant movements.[70] The same socio-economic emphasis is found to a great degree in the works of Kuo Mo-jo, Lü Chen-yü, and the elder generation of Marxist historians in China. They sought to base their arguments about the nature and development of Chinese society upon changes in the economy. Like Marx himself, they used archeological and sociological data, such as increases in landholding, commercial developments, evidences of slaves, and so forth, as well as traditional legal and ethical statements to document their arguments.[71] This approach differs profoundly from traditional Chinese "moral determinism" with its consideration of the ethical qualities of the rulers and the cyclical pattern of history. But these historians did not take the further step of considering the effects of social manifestations on the lower classes. Their *dramatis personae* were still the gentry and

[69] Ho Kan-chih, *op. cit.*, p. 190. Safarov was a member of the Communist Academy and an editor of *Leningrad Pravda* but was apparently a victim of the Stalinist purges of 1937. Accordingly, his work is listed in the 1932 edition of P. E. Skachkov's *Bibliografiya Kitaya* but has been dropped from the revised and enlarged 1959 edition. This is perhaps also because of the evident influence of the theories of Asiatic production and of merchant capitalism in his work.

[70] *Klassy i Klassovaya Borba v. Kitaiskii Istorii* (Classes and Class Struggle in Chinese History) (Moscow: Gos. Izdat., 1928).

[71] See, for instance, Kuo Mo-jo, *op. cit.*, p. 107; and Lü Chen-yü, *Shih Ch'ien-ch'i Chung-kuo She-hui Yen-chiu* (Researches into Chinese Society before the Historical Period) (Peiping: Jen-wen Shu-tien, 1934), pp. 16 ff.

rulers, although now the focus was on the material and social conditions which shaped these leaders. Socially, if not economically speaking, the Chinese Marxist historians still looked on history from the top down.[72]

For Party leaders the situation was somewhat different. As believers in the "unity of theory and practice," they of necessity initiated discussion of the theory of class struggle and of the historic role of the masses as an integral part of their revolutionary tactics. Yet because of the lag of Marxist historians in developing these theories and because of other preoccupations of both the revolutionaries and the theorists, the historical aspects of the theory of the class struggle were not widely discussed before 1949. This is evident even in the writings of Mao Tse-tung. Nevertheless, the emphasis of the Party leaders on "struggle" and on the "mass line" set the stage for what was to come, the key role of the concept of class struggle in the ideological education of the Chinese people after 1949.

[72] Fan Wen-lan's work in compiling a general history of China (*Chung-kuo T'ung-shih Chien-pien*) in Yenan (first published in 1941) is perhaps an exception. In fact, he later criticized his failure to stress the leading rulers of Chinese history in his concern for the role of the masses. But this work was compiled under Party direction and in fact did not stress the role of the masses as much as have most publications since 1949.

CHAPTER THREE

Peasant Rebellions
and Communist Theory

THE growing concern with the theory of the class struggle parallels a growing emphasis on the role of the peasant class in that struggle. Both of these progressions were natural developments, determined by an increasing need for struggle to change the apparent evolution of history in non-Western areas, and by the increasingly agrarian nature of society as communism moved eastward. For European Marxists the primary concern in class theory was the attitude and behavior of the urban bourgeois and proletarian classes. In Russia, and far more in China, the question of the political nature of the peasantry became the dominant concern.

Marx and Engels generally considered the peasantry conservative, if not reactionary, for they "try to roll back the wheel of history."[1] But they also were impressed by the past

[1] E.g., see the famous statements in the "Manifesto of the Communist Party," MESW, vol. 1, p. 44, and in Engels, The Peasant War in Germany, p. 52, and other references such as Engels, "the peasant has so far largely manifested himself as a factor of political power, only by his apathy . . ." ("The Peasant Question in France and Germany," MESW, vol. 2, p. 420). See also K. A. Wittfogel, "The Peasants," in Handbook on Communism, F. M. Bochensky and G. Niemeyer (eds.)

outbursts and future revolutionary potential of the peasantry. They recognized that the peasantry had a radical as well as a conservative side, since they were not only a property-owning but also a laboring class. Several times they called for an alliance between the proletariat and the peasantry,[2] "the class nearest the industrial workers in the towns." [3]

Engels contrasted peasant "revolutionary energy and resolution" with the vacillation of bourgeois leaders, and he sought to reveal to the "German people . . . their revolutionary tradition" in his work on the German peasant war of 1525,[4] the first model for Soviet and Chinese historians on the subject. However, both men also condemned peasant narrow-mindedness and generally showed contempt for any such predominantly peasant movement as envisaged by the Russian populists[5] or as actually took place in mid-nineteenth-century China. In an 1862 commentary on the Taiping Rebellion, Marx linked the stagnation of Oriental society to the weaknesses of the Eastern peasantry:

> From the start the [Taiping] movement had a religious coloration, but it shared this with all Oriental movements. . . . Original in this Chinese Revolution are only its protagonists. They are aware of no tasks except the change of the dynasty. They have no slogans. Their goal seems to be only to assert . . . destruction in grotesque, repulsive forms, destruction without any germ of a new formation. After ten years of noisy pseudo-activity, they have destroyed everything and produced nothing.[6]

(New York: Praeger, 1962), pp. 357–61; and David Mitrany, *Marx Against the Peasant* (Chapel Hill: University of North Carolina Press, 1951).

[2] E.g., see Letter, Marx to Engels (1856), *MESW*, vol. 2, p. 454; and Mitrany, *op. cit.*, p. 43.

[3] Engels, *The Peasant War in Germany*, p. 25.

[4] *Ibid.*, pp. 35 ff.

[5] See Engels, "On Social Relations in Russia," *MESW*, vol. 2, pp. 49–61.

[6] Cited in Karl A. Wittfogel, "The Marxist View of China," *The China Quarterly*, nos. 11 and 12, July 1962, pp. 6–7. Ironically, this passage is also cited in *Ma-k'o-ssu En-ko-ssu Lun Chung-kuo* (Marx and Engels on China) (Peking: Jen-min Ch'u-pan She, 1957), p. 137.

In short, ambivalent interpretations, first emphasizing the conservative and then the violent aspects of peasant character, alternate in the works of Marx and Engels, as of later Marxist writers. Yet, on the whole, early European Marxists tended to stress the conservative or property-owning aspects of the peasantry, rather than their revolutionary or working-class aspects. This was even more true of such prominent disciples as Ferdinand Lasalle and Karl Kautsky than it was of Marx and Engels.[7] Soviet and, to a much greater degree, Chinese theorists have reversed this emphasis, assigning ever more emphasis to the revolutionary side of the "dual nature" of the peasant class. This was not always the case, however, either in Russia or in China.

Indeed, in late nineteenth-century Russia the introduction of Marxism was in large part due to a reaction against and a disillusionment with the indigenous populist faith in the peasant. Therefore, a large part of the late nineteenth-century polemics between the social democrats (Marxists) and the Narodniki (populists) concerned a fundamentally different concept of the political nature of the peasantry.[8] In general, the populists hoped to rely on the innate qualities and communal social organization of the Russian peasant to achieve an immediate transition to socialism, while the Marxists argued that this could be brought about only by the proletariat as a result of the processes of capitalism. The 1887 program of the Marxist group founded by Plekhanov and others stated, "the main bulwark of absolutism lies in the political indifference and the intellectual backwardness of the peasantry,"[9] an argument which was upheld by the social democrats in the 1890s and by the Mensheviks later.

Lenin at first also condemned excessive reliance on the peasantry, whose "reactionary features [as a] small producer

[7] E.g., see Karl Kautsky, *The Class Struggle* (Chicago: Charles H. Kerr and Co., 1910), p. 165; and Leo Yaresh, "The 'Peasant Wars' in Soviet Historiography," *American Slavic and East European Review*, October 1957, p. 242.

[8] Yet, in many respects Chinese communist views of the peasantry are closer to the populist than to classical Marxist views.

[9] Cited in Merle Fainsod, *How Russia is Ruled* (Cambridge: Harvard University Press, 1959), p. 3.

. . . compel him to be an enemy of all agitation . . . ," [10] and he was in the forefront of the late nineteenth-century arguments with the populists. Yet in the early years of the century Lenin led what has been called a fusion of Russian Marxism and populism. [11] Believing, above all, in successful revolution, he increasingly stressed the necessity for an alliance with the exploited peasantry, [12] especially the "rural proletariat"—in short, for a "union consisting only of laborers and poor peasants to fight all those who live on the labor of others." [13]

After the revolution of 1905 Lenin made a more explicit call for a worker-peasant alliance against the government. He sought to answer more orthodox critics of such an alliance by pointing out that eventually the workers alone would lead the struggle against all private property, including that of the peasants. [14] Until that time, however, Lenin argued that the two classes would have to work together under "the slogan of the 'revolutionary democratic dictatorship' of the proletariat and the peasantry." [15]

In short, Lenin subscribed to Marx's and Engels' reservations about the political outlook of the peasantry, the complexity of pre-modern society, and the role of the class struggle in ancient times. [16] But more than they, he saw the revolutionary potential of a peasant-worker alliance:

[10] Lenin, "The Economic Content of Narodnism" (1895), *Collected Works* (Moscow: Foreign Languages Publishing House, 1960), vol. 1, pp. 403–4.

[11] George Lichtheim, "The Transmutations of a Doctrine," *Problems of Communism*, July/August 1966, pp. 20–21.

[12] E.g., Lenin, "To the Rural Poor" (1903), in *Alliance of the Working Class and the Peasantry* (Moscow: Foreign Languages Publishing House, 1959).

[13] Lenin, "From Narodnism to Marxism (1905), *Collected Works* (Moscow: Foreign Languages Publishing House, 1962), vol. 8, pp. 86–87. See also his "What the Friends of the People Are and How They Fight Against the Social Democrats," *Selected Works in Twelve Volumes*, vol. 1, p. 445.

[14] See Lenin, "From Narodnism to Marxism," *loc. cit.*

[15] Lenin, "Two Tactics of Social Democracy in the Democratic Revolution," *Alliance of the Working Class and the Peasantry*, pp. 104–107.

[16] E.g., see Lenin, "The Agricultural Program of the Social Democ-

In the period of serfdom, the entire mass of the peasants
fought against their oppressors, the landlord class . . .
[but] the peasants then were unable to unite, they
were utterly crushed by ignorance, they had no helpers
. . . nevertheless they fought as best they could. . . .
Meanwhile after the abolition of serfdom, a new class
struggle arose, the struggle of the proletariat against the
bourgeoisie. . . . The urban workers started a new great
struggle of all the poor against all the rich. . . . The
peasants were defeated [in the past], but they will rise
again and again . . . [and] the class conscious workers
will do all in their power to help. . . .[17]

Stalin also stressed the class struggle and the necessity of a
peasant alliance. He called the former "the principal feature
of the feudal system" [18] and stated "the history [of Russia,
circa 1910–17] is the history of the struggle of the Kaydets
and Bolsheviks for the peasantry." [19] But above all, Stalin
stressed questions of leadership and power. Hence, he denied
that "the fundamental thing in Leninism is the peasant question," arguing rather that it was the dictatorship of the proletariat.[20] He also drew a sharp distinction between pre-
modern peasant revolts and the socialist revolution.[21]

In China the peasant problem was particularly acute, because by 1930 it was apparent that the communists, if they
were to win at all, must do so first in the countryside, contrary to the classical theory of revolution. The formula of a
peasant war led by communist representatives of the urban
workers, only hinted at in Marx and developed by Lenin, was

racy in the First Russian Revolution" (1905–7), *Collected Works*
(1962 ed.), vol. 13, p. 279.
   [17] Lenin, "To the Rural Poor," pp. 81–82.
   [18] Stalin, "Dialectical and Historical Materialism," *Selected Writings*
(New York: International Publishers, 1942), p. 426.
   [19] See D. Treadgold, *Lenin and His Rivals: The Struggle for Russia's
Future* (New York: Praeger, 1955), p. 266; and K. A. Wittfogel, "The
Peasants," pp. 357 ff.
   [20] Stalin, *Foundations of Leninism* (Moscow, 1934), p. 52. He
went on to stress the revolutionary nature of the Russian peasantry, however. See *ibid.*, p. 59.
   [21] See Chapter 4.

fully applied for the first time in China. However, the theoretical justification for carrying this policy to the Chinese extreme of temporarily abandoning the cities altogether was developed only with difficulty, and the struggles over the issue are a key aspect of the early history of Chinese communism.

The Comintern and most Chinese communist leaders assumed an important revolutionary role for the peasantry from the beginning of communist efforts in China,[22] but they stressed the necessity of "actual" proletarian leadership until they were forced by events to settle for "nominal" proletarian leadership of the Chinese revolution. The theoretical question involved here centered on the problem of the ability of communist leaders, without direct involvement in the urban worker movement, to maintain "proletarian ideology" or commitment to the creation of a communist, industrialized society. Throughout the 1920s it was assumed both by Soviet and by Chinese leaders that effective "proletarian leadership" could be realized only if a proper balance was maintained between urban and rural work. Not until after 1930 did events force acceptance of the Maoist rationalization that "proletarian leadership" could be maintained by leaders of a peasant movement quite cut off from the cities.[23] Even then many attacked the Comintern and Chinese leaders for what they considered the abandonment of traditional Marxist tenets in China. As Trotsky put it:

> It is one thing when the Communist Party firmly resting upon the flower of the urban proletariat strives through the workers to lead the peasant war. It is an altogether different thing when a few thousand or even tens of thousands of revolutionists assume the leadership of the peasant war . . . without having serious support from the proletariat. This is precisely the situation in China. . . .[24]

[22] E.g., see Jerome Ch'en, *Mao and the Chinese Revolution* (London: Oxford University Press, 1965), pp. 106 ff.

[23] See James P. Harrison, "The Li Li-san Line and the CCP in 1930," *China Quarterly*, nos. 14 and 15 (1963).

[24] Leon Trotsky, "Peasant War in China" (1932 letter), in *The Chinese Revolution*, (Bulletin of Marxist Studies, no. 1) (New York:

Leaving aside the debate about whether the rise to power of Chinese communism involved a new departure in communist theory,[25] it is clear that the Chinese communists manipulated the peasantry rather than the other way around. The point was to come to power, and then to shape the revolution from above. Furthermore, there were constant efforts to restate the theory of proletarian leadership despite the reality of enforced seclusion in the villages. The goal of the peasant was still the city. As a Party resolution put it, "The rural bases will have accomplished their historical task when the enemy-occupied cities are liberated. . . ." [26]

The protracted discussions over the issue of the proportion of proletarian leadership essential to victory were more important for revealing another primary trait of Chinese communist theory—namely, the belief that a man can shape his ideology through commitment and need not depend on material environment and historical evolution. Contrary to classical Marxist theory but logically extending Leninist voluntarism, they have held that a communist peasant leader could maintain "proletarian" ideology even when isolated from the urban workers for an extended period.

During the late 1920s and 1930s, the Chinese communists worked out a formula for the organization of the peasants which by its success made much of the argument academic. Stressing both the revolutionary potential of the masses and, simultaneously, the peasant's need for "advanced class" leadership, they were able to create a disciplined, tightly or-

Pioneer Publishers), pp. 15–16. See also Steven Levine, "Trotsky on China," *Harvard Papers on China*, no. 18, December 1964.

[25] As we have seen, it was only natural that there should have been a progression from Marx to Lenin to Mao on the use of the peasantry, since the basic problem was that of the "successful revolution." For discussion of this question, see articles by K. A. Wittfogel and Benjamin Schwartz in *The China Quarterly*, nos. 1 and 2, January and April 1960; Stuart Schram, *The Political Thought of Mao Tse-tung* (New York: Praeger, 1963), pp. 34 ff.; R. North, "M. N. Roy and the Fifth Congress of the CCP," *The China Quarterly*, Fall 1961; and Shanti Swarup, *A Study of the Chinese Communist Movement, 1927–1934* (London: Oxford University Press, 1966), pp. 108 ff.

[26] Resolution on Questions in the History of the Party, SWMTT, vol. 4, p. 197.

ganized peasant army with which to achieve their goals, defined as "proletarian revolution." The development of this technique of mobilizing revolutionary energy through the arousing and channeling of social ferment must be traced because it also determines later interpretations of mass movements in history.

We have already noted the contrast between Li Ta-chao's emphasis on the potentiality of the masses and the more paternal attitudes of Ch'en Tu-hsiu. Ch'en's views were, in fact, closer to the original élitist Marxist mistrust of the peasantry, while Li's views followed Leninist emphasis on mass organization.

In 1919 Li called on Chinese youth to emulate Soviet youths in "going to the countryside." [27] He maintained that "our China is a rural nation and a majority of the laboring class is composed of these peasants. If they are not liberated, then our whole nation will not be liberated." In 1920 he spoke of the Chinese people as a "proletarian nation," making no distinction between peasant and urban worker. He continued to stress the role of the peasantry and in 1926, without mentioning the lead of the proletariat, called on the peasants to "rely on their own strength." [28] In 1924 Li wrote that "the new history, unlike the old, does not concentrate on the activities of sages and kings but teaches that the people are the real makers of history." [29]

Ch'en Tu-hsiu, on the other hand, although instrumental in inculcating the principles of historical progress through struggle, hesitated to credit the masses with being the force of this change. In 1923, he stated, ". . . the main force of the communist movement must be the industrial proletariat. In

[27] Li Ta-chao, "Youth and the Village," *Li Ta-chao Hsuan-chi* (Selected Works of Li Ta-chao) (Peking: Jen-min Ch'u-pan She, 1962), p. 146.

[28] Cited in Schram, *op. cit.*, pp. 18, 25, 33; see also Maurice Meisner, *Li Ta-chao and the Origins of Chinese Marxism*, pp. 80 ff., 237 ff.

[29] Robert H. G. Lee, "The Study of History: Some Contemporary Views," p. 19. Of course, Li was not the first to argue for popular history in China. Liang Ch'i-ch'ao had stressed this (J. R. Levenson, *Liang Ch'i-ch'ao and the Mind of Modern China*, p. 82), but Li was the first influential Marxist to do so.

a small-peasant country such as China, over half the farmers
are petit bourgeois landowners with firmly rooted concepts of
private ownership. How can they accept communism?" [30]
Earlier he spoke of the Boxers as representing "the obscurant-
ist path of despotism, superstition and theocracy," and although he later criticized such negations of the Boxer movement,[31] he continued to think of the educated as being the
vanguard of the revolution. Ch'en reportedly felt that the
"peasantry had no historic creativity of its own . . . was a
repository of the past and the traditional, a huge force of in-
ertia standing in the way of Westernization and enlightenment," [32] and remarked, "the peasantry's cultural level is
low, their forces are scattered, and they are inclined toward
conservatism." [33]

Similarly, Chang Kuo-t'ao, after Ch'en the most conspicuous dissident in the history of the Chinese communist
movement, wrote in 1922:

> The peasants take no interest in politics. This is com-
> mon throughout the whole world but is particularly true
> in China, for most of the Chinese peasants are small-
> holders. They are not interested in politics. All they care
> about is having a true son of heaven to rule them and a
> peaceful, bumper year.[34]

In the early years of the history of the CCP, such assumptions of the dependence of the peasant movement on the
proletarian revolution were in line with Comintern policies.

[30] Ch'en Tu-hsiu, answer to letter in "Voice of the Readers," *Hsiang-
tao Chou-pao*, no. 34 (August 1, 1923).
[31] Ch'en Tu-hsiu, "Our Two Mistaken Views of the Yi Ho T'uan,"
Hsiang-tao Chou-pao, no. 81, September 3, 1924. The earlier view was
expressed in *Hsin Ch'ing-nien*, November 15, 1918, cited in B. Schwartz,
Chinese Communism and the Rise of Mao, p. 15. See also D. W. Y.
Kwok, *Scientism in Chinese Thought, 1900–1950*, pp. 70–71; and R.
A. Scalapino and G. T. Yü, *The Chinese Anarchist Movement*, p. 56.
[32] B. Schwartz, "Ch'en Tu-hsiu and the Acceptance of the Modern
West," *Journal of the History of Ideas*, January 1951, pp. 70–71. See
also his *Chinese Communism and the Rise of Mao*, p. 65.
[33] *Ibid.*, p. 65.
[34] Chang Kuo-t'ao in *Hsiang-tao Chou-pao*, no. 12, December 1922,
cited in Jerome Ch'en, *op. cit.*, p. 193.

The latter consistently stressed the importance of the peasantry in the Chinese revolution but stressed even more the necessity for proletarian leadership and the maintenance of the alliance with the Kuomintang. Accordingly, the early efforts of P'eng Pai in Kuangtung and of other early peasant leaders were largely ignored by communist leaders until the breakdown of the KMT alliance in 1927. Even then the successors of Ch-en Tu-hsiu continued to press for a supposedly essential proletarian base until persistent failure in the cities left the Party no alternative but to retreat to the countryside, a development which eventually enabled Mao Tse-tung to acquire leadership of the Party.

The views of Mao on the political role of the peasantry are, of course, the most determinant of all for Chinese communist attitudes toward the peasant class. In his autobiography Mao spoke of an early sympathy for the struggles of the peasants. He claimed he had early recognized the ruling-class bias against the peasantry which prevailed in Chinese literature and had understood the causes of the local disturbances which broke out in his native area.[35] According to a sympathetic biographer of Mao, the communist leader "set his face away from the townspeople" and placed his hopes in the peasantry from his earliest years. "He approved of peasants. He approved of no one else. What he particularly approved of in the peasants was their courtesy and their loyalty to one another."[36]

If this childhood approval of the peasantry was true—and this would be natural for a country youth—Mao nonetheless placed his hopes for change elsewhere. He stated that his real hopes lay in such upper-class reformers as K'ang Yu-wei and Liang Ch'i-ch'ao at the time of the 1911 revolution.[37] He was acquainted with the evolutionary ideas of the Chinese reformers but opposed to more radical proposals. After 1915 Mao came under the influence of Ch'en Tu-hsiu and Li Ta-

[35] Snow, *op. cit.*, pp. 116–18.
[36] Robert Payne, *Portrait of a Revolutionary* (New York: Abelard-Schuman, 1961), p. 44, citing Hsiao San.
[37] Snow, *op. cit.*, pp. 120–21.

chao, but it was not until 1920 that he became convinced of the need for mass organization and turned to Marxist theory and the history of the European socialist movements for guidance.[38]

In 1919, under the influence of Li Ta-chao, Mao emphasized "the great union of the popular masses" of all classes against their oppressors. In the following years, however, his writings are concerned almost exclusively with the urban workers, with whom he was assigned to work.[39]

Later, in at least two places, Mao confessed to a youthful intellectual's contempt for manual laborers and to feeling that "the peasants were somehow wrong." [40] "At that time," Mao wrote, "it seemed to me that the intellectuals were the only clean persons in the world, and the workers and peasants seemed rather dirty beside them." [41] Then, as a result of organizational work in rural areas in 1925, Mao claimed "a fundamental change . . . in the bourgeois and petty-bourgeois feelings implanted in me by the bourgeois schools," and he might have added, by traditional Marxism.[42] He said he realized that he had been "mistaken and that the peasants' views were right" [43] and promptly went to the other extreme, from the point of view of Marxist theory, overemphasizing the revolutionary role of the peasantry in his writings of the immediately succeeding years. Although Mao declares in his 1926 "Analysis of the Classes in Chinese Society" that the "industrial proletariat, though small in number, has become the major force of the national revolutionary movement," he devotes by far the greatest space to an analysis of the six of the thirteen strata which derived from the mid- and poor peasantry.[44]

[38] *Ibid.*, p. 139. See also Schram, *The Political Thought of Mao Tse-tung*, pp. 9 ff.

[39] Schram, *op. cit.*, pp. 18 ff.

[40] "Report of an Investigation into the Peasant Movement in Hunan," *SWMTT*, vol. 1, p. 56.

[41] "Yenan Forum on Art and Literature," *SWMTT*, vol. 4, p. 67.

[42] *Ibid.*

[43] "Report of an Investigation into the Peasant Movement in Hunan," *SWMTT*, vol. 1, p. 56.

[44] Cited in Schram, *op. cit.*, p. 177; see also *SWMTT*, vol. 1, p. 20.

In another article published in October 1926 but not included in the *Selected Works*, Mao openly acknowledges the autonomous leadership of a peasant movement. Reporting on the investigation of some peasant communities in Kiangsu and Chekiang provinces, he noted that in 1922 a peasant riot broke out in Ch'ungming, Kiangsu, quite independent of any outside agitation. He wrote, "Without any Red party or radical party to stir them [the peasants] up, they themselves grouped and rose to smash the police station, 'cut off the landlords' ears,' stir up the *hsien* and demand tax reductions." [45] However, he does blame the failure of this movement in part on its inadequate organization.

Mao's greatest statement of faith in the peasants is found in his famous "Report of an Investigation into the Peasant Movement in Hunan." In it he wrote:

All kinds of arguments against the peasant movement must be speedily set right. . . . For the rise of the peasant movement is a colossal event. In a very short time, in China's central, southern and northern provinces, several hundred million peasants will rise like a tornado or tempest, a force so extraordinarily swift and violent that no power, however great, will be able to suppress it. They will break all trammels that now bind them and rush forward along the road to liberation. . . . All revolutionary parties and all revolutionary comrades will

[45] Jun chih (Mao Tse-tung), "The Bitter Sufferings of the Peasants in Kiangsu and Chekiang," *Hsiang Tao Chou-pao*, no. 179, October 25, 1926, p. 1869. There are other reports of the spontaneous nature of many peasant movements of this time. One wrote that "in this suddenly developed peasant movement, the Party in fact lagged behind [*lo le hou*]." The report added that often there was not a single cadre even among several hundred peasants and blames the subsequent defeat of the movement on this lack of communist leadership. See "Report of Hunan Mass Work Group," June 1927, in *Ti-yi-tzu Kuo-nei Ke-ming Chan-cheng Shih-ch'i te Nung-min Yun-tung* (The Peasant Movement During the Period of the First Revolutionary Civil War) (Peking: Jenmin Ch'u-pan She, 1953), p. 320. Chu Te makes the same point, relating that peasant uprisings often occurred well before the Red Army arrived on the scene. See Agnes Smedley, *The Great Road* (New York: Monthly Review Press, 1956), p. 215.

stand before them to be tested and to be accepted or rejected as they decide. . . .[46]

The most striking thing about this 1927 essay from the Marxist point of view is the latitude allowed to peasant leadership. The contrast with later Party efforts to hinge all peasant success on proletarian leadership is virtually complete. Over and over, Mao speaks of the peasant movement as an autonomous force acting on its own initiative.[47]

The early enthusiasm of Mao for the revolutionary qualities of the peasantry did not continue unchanged. Like the classical Marxists, he and other Chinese theorists later recognized that to attribute too high a degree of autonomy to the peasants would compromise the uniqueness of their own leading role in the Chinese revolution. This is made quite clear by the revisions made in many of Mao's original texts dealing with the peasantry. For instance, the two phrases which refer to proletarian leadership of the peasantry in the current version of the "Report of an Investigation into the Peasant Movement in Hunan" were later additions. Where the official version reads, ". . . the poor peasants have fought militantly all along. They accept most willingly the leadership of the Communist Party," [48] the Chinese original, after the statement "the poor peasants have fought militantly all along," added, "The organization was their organization, the revolution was their revolution." [49] Nothing was said about the leadership of the proletariat. In the section on "peasant prohibitions," the authorized version now reads, "When under Communist leadership the peasant association has established its authority in the countryside, the peasants begin to place prohibitions or restrictions on things they dislike." [50] The Chinese original simply states, "When the peasant asso-

[46] *SWMTT*, vol. 1, pp. 21–22.
[47] See *ibid.*, pp. 22, 25, 27, 32, 34 ff.
[48] *SWMTT*, vol. 1, p. 31.
[49] Mao Tse-tung, *Hunan Nung-min Yun-tung K'ao-ch'ao Pao-kao* (Report of an Investigation into the Peasant Movement in Hunan) (Shanghai: Hsin-hua Shu-tien, 1949), p. 10.
[50] *SWMTT*, vol. 1, p. 50.

ciation established its authority in the countryside. . . ." [51]
The term "the leadership of the Communist Party" was a
later addition in both cases. [52] If Mao conceived of the
Party's infiltrating a "going" peasant organization, Party theorists later wished to have it appear that the peasants were
under Party or proletarian leadership from the beginning.
Also impermissible and deleted from the authorized version
of Mao's works was his statement that the peasants were contributing 70 percent of the force of the revolution, the proletariat and military only 30. [53]

In August and September 1927, on the heels of the final
rupture with the Kuomintang, Mao was assigned to organize
his projected peasant movement. However, the subsequent
failure of the "Autumn Harvest Uprising" led to changes in
his estimate of the peasantry, as well as to the temporary
eclipse of Mao and his theories in the eyes of the Central
Committee. [54] At least in the current versions of Mao's writings of the following year, there is definitely more emphasis
on peasant weaknesses and the need for Party leadership. In
November 1928 he complained, "The Party organizations in
the border area are composed almost entirely of peasants, who
will go astray without proletarian ideological leadership." [55]

[51] Mao Tse-tung, *op. cit.*, p. 30.

[52] Of course, in part the failure to mention Party leadership may have
been due, as Wittfogel pointed out ("The Legend of 'Maoism' [con-
cluded]," *China Quarterly*, no. 2, April–June 1960, pp. 18–19), to the
fact that the Comintern was then still recommending the alliance with
the KMT. But this would not influence the degree of initiative allowed
to the peasantry.

[53] See Schwartz, *Chinese Communism and the Rise of Mao*, p. 75.
Ch'en Po-ta and other later commentators also add stress on the "leadership of the Communist Party" where none existed in the original and
where documents confirm that, in fact, the Party lagged behind. See
Ch'en Po-ta, *Notes on Mao Tse-tung's "Report of an Investigation
into the Peasant Movement in Hunan"* (Peking: Foreign Languages
Press, 1954), p. 53. See also Yu Yen-kuang, "The Kwangtung Peasant
Movement in the First Internal Revolutionary War Period," *LSYC*,
1958, no. 9, p. 24; and *Kao-chi Chung-hsueh K'o-pen Chung-Kuo Li-
shih* (Upper-Level High School Text of Chinese History) (Peking:
Jen-min Ch'u-pan She, 1958), vol. 4, p. 29.

[54] See Schwartz, *Chinese Communism and the Rise of Mao*, pp.
100–1.

[55] *SWMTT*, vol. 1, p. 98.

The following year he dedicated an entire article to manifestations of peasant weaknesses in the Party.

> The source of various incorrect ideas in the Party organization in the Fourth Army lies of course in the fact that the Party's organizational basis is largely made up of peasants and other elements of petty-bourgeois origin. . . .[56]

Mao apparently shifted from a more orthodox mistrust of the peasants in the early 1920s to an excessively enthusiastic appraisal of their revolutionary potential in 1926–27. Then, after the failure of the Autumn Harvest Uprising and difficulties in organizing the newly formed Red Army,[57] and perhaps also because of a growing acquaintance with the Marxist theory of the peasantry, Mao and later Party editors paid more attention to the difficulties of correct leadership of the peasants. Nevertheless, by the early 1930s Mao had developed key aspects of his theory of the "revolutionary character of the Chinese peasantry" and this became an important issue in his disputes with more orthodox comrades, then in control of the Party.

After winning control of the CCP in early 1935, Mao con-

---

[56] "On the Rectification of Incorrect Ideas in the Party," *SWMTT*, vol. 1, p. 105. The emphasis on the weaknesses of the peasantry has been increased in the authorized version and, according to Stuart Schram, there were extensive changes in the text of the latter work, removing some of the descriptions of the "roving insurgents" ("rural lumpen-proletariat" or vagrants [*yu min*]), emphasizing their weaknesses and minimizing their part in the Red Army. Stuart Schram, "Chinese and Leninist Components in the Thought of Mao Tse-tung," *Asian Survey*, June 1963, p. 168.

Similarly, in the 1930–31 investigation of Hsing-kuo Hsien in Kiangsi, which was not included in the authorized version of Mao's *Selected Works*, Mao states that the poor peasants are the "leading class in the village." *Mao Tse-tung Hsuan-chi* (1948 ed.), p. 83. He emphasized the revolutionary potential of the "vagrant" class who "all welcomed the revolution" and often served well in leading positions of the village government (*ibid.*, p. 92), whereas in the authorized versions the destructive nature of this group is stressed.

[57] In late 1928 Mao admitted, "wherever the Red Army goes, it finds the masses cold and reserved; only after propaganda and agitation do they slowly rouse themselves. . . ." *SWMTT*, vol. 1, p. 99.

tinued this double theme of great stress on the organizational needs as well as revolutionary potential of the peasantry. In 1939 Mao defined "the armed struggle of the CCP [as] a peasant war under the leadership of the proletariat," [58] and in 1940 he stated that the "first stage [of the Chinese revolution] is to end with the establishment of a new-democratic society under the joint dictatorship of all Chinese revolutionary classes headed by the Chinese proletariat." [59] Here Mao gives formal expression to the concept of "the people" as all who accept the leadership of the CCP, a definition which ensured the majority, if not leading, role for the peasant masses. He also noted that "because the Chinese proletariat is largely made up of bankrupt peasants, it has natural ties with the vast peasantry which facilitate their close alliance," but he immediately added, "the Chinese revolution certainly will not succeed without the leadership of the proletariat." [60] In 1949 he asserted that the "people's democratic dictatorship needs the leadership of the working class. For it is only the working class that is most far-sighted, most selfless and most thoroughly revolutionary." [61]

In that year Mao also told a session of the Seventh Central Committee:

Some muddle-headed comrades think we should rely not on the working class but on the masses of the poor. Some comrades who are even more muddle-headed think we should rely on the bourgeoisie. . . . We must criticize these muddled views. We must whole-heartedly rely on the working class, unite with the rest of the laboring classes, win over the intellectuals and win over to our side as many as possible of the national bourgeois elements. . . .[62]

[58] "Introductory Remarks to 'The Communist,'" *SWMTT*, vol. 3, p. 60.
[59] "On the New Democracy," *ibid.*, p. 115.
[60] "The Chinese Revolution and the CCP," *ibid.*, p. 94.
[61] "On the Dictatorship of the People's Democracy," *SWMTT* (Peking edition), vol. 4, p. 421.
[62] *Ibid.*, p. 364.

With respect to Chinese history, Mao wrote that Chinese "peasant revolutions invariably failed" since they lacked "such correct leadership as is given by the proletariat and the Communist Party today." [63] This statement has established the limits to which emphasis on the revolutionary potential of the peasant wars can go in Chinese communist historiography.

In terms of tactics, however, greater attention to the necessity of correct leadership for the peasantry meant more rather than less Party concern for the mobilization of the peasants. Party documents after 1927 confirm the policy of using peasant movements where they already existed and of organizing them elsewhere. Communist agitators instructed the peasantry to avoid taxes, open granaries, and distribute the property of the rich to the poor. Where there was no indigenous "spontaneous struggle," cadres were instructed to organize guerrilla warfare, kill the landlords, and burn houses. Above all, there must be "mass activities and not just military activities." [64] Cadres are warned not to make the mistake of underestimating the power of the peasantry, who, despite their ignorance, can be organized to understand their interests.[65] An enormous amount of analysis of rural conditions went into this effort to organize the peasantry.

While the theory of proletarian leadership was maintained, the great majority of the Chinese communists were in fact ever more deeply immersed in rural life.[66] The enthusiasm of

[63] "The Chinese Revolution and the CCP," p. 76.

[64] E.g., see *Nung-min Yun-tung Fang-fa Ta-yao* (Outline of Methods of Peasant Movement) (Taipei: Nei-cheng pu, Tiao-ch'a chu [Investigation Bureau of Internal Government Section], document number 554–4971–804).

[65] Wang Chung-ming (ed.), *Chung-kuo Nung-min Wen-t'i yü Nung-min Yun-tung* (The Chinese Peasant Question and the Peasant Movement) (Shanghai: P'ing-fan Shu-chu, 1929).

[66] Two thirds of the Eighth Central Committee of the CCP elected in 1956 have rural backgrounds, and of necessity almost all worked in the rural areas prior to 1949. However, over half of these came from landlord backgrounds and most of the rest, including Mao, were of rich peasant background. Only 4 of the 97 members of the Eighth Central Committee were of poor peasant background. See F. W. Houn, "The Eighth Central Committee of the CCP," *American Political*

Mao himself for work among the masses, evident in passages already cited, gradually became formalized in the Party "style of work." In 1936 Mao addressed the Elder Brother Secret Society, showing a "genuine feeling of fellowship" for a fellow mass-conspiratorial society.[67] In 1939 he put the question of mass organization in an unmistakably central position. Asking, "What is the lesson of the revolution in the last fifty or more years?" Mao replied, "fundamentally it is a lesson of 'arousing the masses of the people.' "[68] He warned the intellectuals:

> In the movement of the Chinese Democratic Revolution, the intellectuals were the first section of people to be awakened . . . but if the intellectuals do not become one with the masses of the workers and peasants then they will accomplish nothing.[69]

Elsewhere he wrote, "it must be understood that the masses are the real heroes, while we ourselves are often ridiculously childish, and unless we grasp this point we shall never be able to acquire even elementary knowledge."[70] The "masses of the people" in China, of course, were the peasants, and in 1940 Mao went so far as to state, "the Chinese Revolution is virtually the peasants' revolution. . . ."[71] Similarly, Liu Shao-ch'i wrote, "the present revolution in China is essentially a peasant revolution."[72]

For all the emphasis on working with the peasants, it must not be thought that the Chinese communists ever intended

---

Science Review, June 1957, p. 395. Only Khrushchev among recent leaders of the CPSU came from a peasant background.

[67] Stuart R. Schram, "Chinese and Leninist Components in the Thought of Mao Tse-tung," *Asian Survey,* June 1963, p. 268. For a partial translation of this address, see Schram, *The Political Thought of Mao Tse-tung,* p. 189.

[68] "The Orientation of the Youth Movement," *SWMTT,* vol. 3, p. 16.

[69] "The May Fourth Movement," *SWMTT,* vol. 3, p. 10.

[70] "Preface to Rural Survey," *SWMTT,* vol. 4, pp. 8–9.

[71] Mao Tse-tung, "On the New Democracy," *SWMTT,* vol. 3, p. 137.

[72] Liu Shao-ch'i, *On the Party* (Peking: Foreign Languages Press, 1951), p. 26.

simply to follow the masses. The question was rather one of manipulation according to the principle of mass organization summarized in the slogan "from the masses to the masses." In 1943 a resolution of the Central Committee elaborated:

> In all practical work of our Party, correct leadership can only be developed on the principle of "from the masses to the masses." This means summing up (i.e., coordinating and systematizing after careful study) the views of the masses (i.e., views scattered and unsystematic) then taking the resulting ideas back to the masses, explaining them and popularizing them until the masses embrace the ideas as their own, stand up for them and translate them into action by way of testing their correctness. Then it is necessary once more to sum up the views of the masses and once again take the resulting ideas back to the masses so that the masses give them their whole-hearted support . . . and so on over and over again.[73]

The idea is to see what issues can mobilize the peasants and then to manage these issues so as to suit Party purposes and have the "masses embrace the ideas as their own." After 1949 this exploitation of the "wishes of the masses" became much more obvious. For instance, the acceleration of the cooperativization movement of 1956 was attributed to the Party's lagging behind the wishes of the masses.[74]

These principles of contemporary mass organization obviously affect the official interpretation of mass movements in history. The need to respect "the spontaneous revolutionary actions and creative energy of the masses" applies to the historical treatment of peasant movements, as does the belief that the masses were helpless to carry through any thorough revolution without the leadership of the "vanguard of the proletariat." The interplay between these two somewhat con-

[73] *SWMTT* 4, p. 113. See also Ch'en Po-ta, *op. cit.*, p. 2. Of Mao's principles of working with the masses in guerrilla warfare, see Mao Tse-tung, *On Guerrilla Warfare*, S. D. Griffith (trans.) (New York: Praeger, 1961).

[74] See Mao Tse-tung, "Introducing a Cooperative," *SCMP* 1784, citing *Hung Ch'i*, no. 1, 1958.

tradictory dogmas provides the framework for the millions of words written about the nature of the peasant wars in Chinese history. It also helps explain the many ambiguities and inconsistencies which show up in communist historiography of the peasant revolts.

Following their successful drive to power, Chinese theorists have continued to acknowledge both sides of the dual—working class, property owning—nature of the peasantry, but they increasingly stress the theory as well as the practice of a revolutionary peasantry. Liu Shao-ch'i repeated the negative, more orthodox view of the peasant in several passages. He wrote that since classes have

> a given position in social production and have for a long time produced, lived, and struggled in a given manner, they will create their particular mode of life and their particular interests and demands. . . . It follows that the peasantry, who have long been tied to the land in scattered small production, are marked by "lax ways, conservatism, narrow-mindedness, backwardness, and the outlook of private owners." . . .[75]

Elsewhere, Liu stated that "the chief intrinsic contradictions inside our party are those between proletarian and non-proletarian ideologies, of which the most important is the contradiction between the ideology of the proletariat on the one hand and the ideology of the peasantry and the petty-bourgeoisie on the other." [76]

If an economically underdeveloped country as well as Marxist theory constantly brought peasant backwardness to the attention of Party leaders, they also reminded Chinese

[75] Liu Shao-ch'i, "The Class Nature of Man," Appendix to *How to Be a Good Communist* (Peking: Foreign Languages Press, 1951), p. 116. Gradually, according to mainland theorists, this peasant backwardness will disappear; they maintain that the "weak points and a certain backwardness" of the peasants are being overcome and changed under the guidance of the Communist Party and the worker class" (see URS 2, 21, p. 309, citing CKCN, October 16, 1955), and with the establishment of communism not only peasant backwardness but all distinction between peasant and townsman will disappear.

[76] Liu Shao-ch'i, *On the Party*, p. 20.

leaders of their dependence on the peasantry. Therefore, parallel with standard criticism of peasant backwardness, there has been continuous praise for the role of the peasantry in the Chinese revolution and reconstruction. This discrepancy has been resolved by a matter of semantics. The Chinese communists have substituted "all those who were oppressed" for the proletariat of the classical formulas. Mao had already said that "certain sections of the peasants and handicraftsmen were predecessors of the Chinese proletariat" and called for a united front of "all revolutionary classes headed by the Chinese proletariat." [77] The oppressed of whatever class replace the proletariat of orthodox Marxist theory,[78] and ideology replaces class origin as the arbiter of revolutionary character. As Mao put it:

> The term "the people" has different meanings in different countries and in different historical periods in each country. . . . [In China all those who supported the Party before 1949 and] at this stage . . . all classes, strata and social groups which approve, support and work for the cause of socialist construction belong to the category of the people.[79]

Similarly, Liu Shao-ch'i wrote of the Party member:

> The social origin of the Party membership alone cannot determine everything. The determining factors are our Party's political struggles and political life, its ideological education and its ideological and political leadership.[80]

[77] Mao Tse-tung, "The Chinese Revolution and the CCP," *SWMTT*, vol. 3, p. 77; and "On the New Democracy," *SWMTT*, vol. 3, p. 115.

[78] According to one writer, Marx and Lenin "placed the historical mission of transforming the bourgeois world on the shoulders of the proletarian class . . . [but] Comrade Mao Tse-tung has often told us that the people [*jen-min*] . . . are the true creators of the history of the world." Sun Ting-kuo, "We must Treat the Revolutionary Mass Movement Correctly," *SCMP* 2099, p. 2, citing *JMJP*, September 1, 1959.

[79] Mao Tse-tung, *On the Correct Handling of Contradictions Among the People* (Peking: Foreign Languages Press, 1960), p. 8.

[80] Liu Shao-ch'i, *On the Party*, p. 20.

Given the majority role of the peasantry within the united front of "all revolutionary classes," Chinese revolutionary theory has naturally emphasized the radical rather than the conservative side of the "dual nature" of the peasantry. We are told that those deviationists who sought to uphold the traditional emphasis on the urban workers at all costs were "erroneously opposing the so-called 'peculiar revolutionary character of the peasants.' " [81] According to a leading Party member, "those who ignore the great powers of our peasants do not understand the revolution and the construction in our country." [82]

In recent years the emphasis on the role of the peasantry in the Chinese revolution has been involved with the competition with the Soviet Union for the leadership of the revolution in agrarian countries of Asia and elsewhere. Already in 1949 Liu Shao-ch'i termed the peasant-based Chinese revolution the model for revolution in all underdeveloped countries.[83] A decade later Liu openly attributed communist victory to this strategy and acknowledged the equation of the Chinese peasantry with the proletariat:

> The peasant question was the central question in our democratic revolution . . . the CCP therefore went deep into the villages for twenty-two years to lead the armed revolutionary struggle which used the village to encircle the cities. . . . This enabled the Party to build powerful and reliable revolutionary bastions in the rural areas, to build up the revolutionary army and revolutionary base and gradually raise the revolutionary enthusiasm

[81] "Resolution on Some Questions in the History of Our Party," *SWMTT*, vol. 4, p. 192. As early as 1932 Ch'en Shao-yu criticized those in the Party who sought to create a "theory of the universal revolutionary character of the peasantry in colonial and semi-colonial countries." See Hsiao Tso-liang, *Power Relations Within the Chinese Communist Movement, 1930–1934* (Seattle: University of Washington Press, 1962), p. 205.

[82] Po Yi-po, cited in Wu Yuan-li, "The Economic Challenge of Communist China," in E. S. Kirby (ed.), *Contemporary China, 1958–1959* (Hong Kong: Hong Kong University Press), p. 49.

[83] See O. Edmund Clubb, *Twentieth Century China* (New York: Columbia University Press, 1964), pp. 335–36.

and revolutionary discipline of the broad masses of impoverished peasants close to the level of the revolutionary proletariat and receive from them the continuous supply of manpower and material reserves needed by the Party and the People's Army led by the Party.[84]

In the polemics between the Soviet Union and China, the Russians alleged that they had been correct in denouncing peasant domination of the CCP in the 1930s. They charged that Liu Shao-ch'i had stated that the Chinese peasantry were superior to the Western proletariat, and said: "Marx never knew such people . . . they are even more disciplined than the industrial proletariat." [85] At least one high-ranking Chinese communist has said that "the peasants of China are the most revolutionary people on earth." [86]

Numerous articles from the late 'fifties on stressed the tactics of the united front with the peasants, terming it "the fundamental question in the national and democratic revolution in all colonial and semi-colonial countries. . . ." [87] China had led the way in the development of this tactic, since, as one historian put it, there had been only a partial union of the peasants' and workers' struggles in Russia, but in China the "combination of a workers' movement with a peasant war . . . was completely realized." [88]

An important article on the role of the peasantry in the modern revolution elaborated on these themes and specifically distinguished the "revolutionary Chinese peasantry" from the conservative peasantry of "certain capitalist countries," obviously referring to the originally critical Marxist view of the peasantry.

[84] Liu Shao-ch'i, "The Victory of Marxism-Leninism in China," *Peking Review*, October 1, 1959.

[85] See *Current Digest of the Soviet Press*, vol. 16, no. 21, p. 5, citing *Izvestia*, May 17, 1964. No Chinese statements on the peasant question were carried in the Soviet press after 1960.

[86] Chu Te, as cited by Smedley, *op. cit.*, p. 217.

[87] Li Wei-han, "The Struggle for Proletarian Leadership in the New Democratic Revolution in China," *Peking Review*, February 23, 1962.

[88] Li Shu, "Comrade Mao Tse-tung's 'Reform Our Studies' and China's Science of History," *SCMP* 2546, p. 8, citing *JMJP*, July 8, 1961.

The poor peasants were the semi-proletariat of the countryside. Although China's proletariat was smaller in
number, she possessed an extremely large semi-proletariat [i.e., the peasantry] which was tempered in pro-
longed struggles against imperialism and feudalism and
was highly revolutionary.

Both right and left opportunists ignored this reality.
They were blind to the revolutionary character and revolutionary tenacity of the Chinese peasantry, hence their
failure to understand that *one could not speak of the
Chinese peasantry and the relatively conservative peasantry of certain capitalist countries in the same breath.*

Through the land and all other struggles, the revolutionary initiative and discipline of the broad masses of
poor peasants were gradually raised to a level approaching that of the revolutionary proletariat, making them an
inexhaustible source of the Party's strength and the people's armed force.[89]

These statements on the role of the peasantry in the Chinese revolution were clearly intended for an international audience, and it is significant that one of the points at issue
between Moscow and Peking is the theoretical and tactical
evaluation of the political nature of the peasantry. Indeed,
Russian commentators often attribute the origins of the
Maoist heresy to a "petty-bourgeois peasant mentality." [90]

[89] Lin Yi-chou, "The Peasant Question in the Democratic Revolution," *Peking Review*, March 31, 1961, no. 13, p. 9 (italics added).
This article was followed by a companion piece on the role of the peasantry in the socialist revolution after 1949. See Hsiao Shu, "The Peasant Question in the Socialist Revolution," *Peking Review*, no. 21, May
26, 1961, p. 12.
[90] E.g., see T. Timofeyev, "Scientific Socialism and Petty Bourgeois
Ideology," *Current Digest of the Soviet Press*, November 16, 1966, citing *Pravda*, October 24, 1966.

CHAPTER FOUR

Pre-1949 Interpretations

THE most significant Chinese revolution prior to contemporary times was the transition from classical Chou society to the Imperial Chinese system in the last half of the first millennium B.C. Paradoxically for the communists, no mass rebellions occurred before this or were associated with the far-reaching changes of these centuries. On the contrary, mass disturbances arose only after the transformation from the Bronze to the Iron Age, the rise of private property in land, the development of a centralized, bureaucratic state, and many other changes of the late Chou period. In other words, "social revolution" followed rather than triggered, as it should have according to Marxist theory, the greatest socio-economic revolution of ancient China. Communist historians must look to disputes in classical philosophy and literature, not to mass rebellions, to document the existence of the class struggle in earliest times.

From the time of the founding of the Imperial Chinese state in the third century B.C., however, a series of massive uprisings, perhaps unique in world history in size and intensity, burst forth in the next two thousand years of Chinese history. The nature of these enormous disturbances remains unclear and in need of much further research both individually and collectively. Yet, without too much injustice to individual differences, over a dozen of these can be described as great "peasant rebellions."[1]

These included:[2]

1. The rebellion led by Ch'en Sheng and Wu Kuang against the Ch'in in north China in 209 B.C.

2. The revolts of the Red Eyebrows, Green Forest, and other "peasant armies" which overthrew Wang Mang's short-lived Hsin dynasty, A.D. 18–27.

3. The Taoist Yellow Turban Rebellion of A.D. 184 in east China and in Szechwan.

4. Revolts in the Six Dynasties Period, including those of the "vagrants" in the early fourth century and those led by Sun En and Lu Hsun in the lower Yangtze area, 398–417, by T'ang Yü-chih in Chekiang in 485, and by Ko Jung and others in Hopeh 525–28.

5. The revolts against the Sui dynasty, especially those led by Wang Po, Li Mi, Tu Fu-wei, Tou Chien-te, and Liu Hei-ta, from 610 to 624.

6. Late T'ang rebellions led by Ch'iu Fu, 859–60, and P'ang Hsun, 869, and the great rebellion led by Wang Hsien-chih and Huang Ch'ao, 874–84, which had its own "Long March" as far as Canton and which took the T'ang capital of Ch'ang An.

7. The revolts of the Sung period, led by Wang Hsiao-po and Li Hsun in Szechwan, 993–95, by Fang La in Fukien and Chekiang, 1120–22 and by Chung Hsiang and Yang Yao in northern Hunan and southern Hupeh, 1130–35.

8. The rebellions which overthrew the Mongol Yuan dynasty, associated with the White Lotus Sect from 1351 and later led by Chu Yuan-chang and others.

9. The rebellions of the middle Ming period, led by T'ang

---

[1] See definitions in Introduction. For some modern noncommunist interpretations of these rebellions, see Vincent Shih, "Some Chinese Rebel Ideologies," *T'oung Pao*, no. 44, 1956, carried also in his *The Taiping Ideology* (Seattle: University of Washington Press, 1967); Teng Ssu-yü, "A Political Interpretation of Chinese Rebellions," *Tsing Hua Journal of Chinese Studies*, September 1958; and Yuji Muramatsu, "Some Themes in Chinese Rebel Ideologies," in Arthur F. Wright (ed.), *The Confucian Persuasion* (Stanford: Stanford University Press, 1960).

[2] For brief sketches of these rebellions, see Appendix.

Sai-erh in Shantung, 1420–21; by Yeh Tsung-liu, 1442–49, and Teng Mou-ch'i, 1447–49 in Fukien, Chekiang, and Kiangsi; by Liu T'ung and Li Yuan in Hupeh, in the 1460s and 1470s; and by the Liu brothers in various areas of north China 1510–12.

10. The rebellions led by Li Tzu-ch'eng and Chang Hsien-chung, which overthrew the Ming dynasty, 1627–45.

11. The Taiping rebellion, which probably was the greatest pre-modern mass movement in history, 1851–64.

12. Other Ch'ing rebellions against the Manchu Ch'ing Dynasty, notably of the White Lotus Society in north China in the late eighteenth and early nineteenth century, of the Moslem and other minorities in southwest and northwest China, and of the Nien and Boxer Societies in the nineteenth century.

One Communist historian grouped these and other lesser rebellions into five categories: (1) those which were limited in area and activities and which did not establish a government or have clear slogans and goals; (2) large-scale revolts which established governments but which did not have clear goals and were quickly suppressed or transformed into feudal governments, such as the revolt led by Ko Jung (c. A.D. 525); (3) a small-scale revolt involving one or several *hsien* or *chou* but which lasted for a long time and whose actions accorded with the wishes of the masses, such as that led by Chang Lu (late second century in Szuchwan) and Chung Hsiang and Yang Yao (1130–35 in Hunan and Hupeh); (4) a big peasant war, perhaps with a clear program, but which was soon subverted by representatives of the landlord class into an instrument of dynastic change, such as the peasant wars of the Ch'in and the Han interregnum and of the Sui and Yuan; and, finally, the large-scale peasant war with clear programs which were consistently in the interests of the peasants and struck at the interests of the landlord class, such as the revolts led by Huang Ch'ao in the late T'ang and Li Tzu-ch'eng in the late Ming.[3] Most mainland historians would also include

[3] Ch'i Li-huang, "On the Double Nature of 'Peasant Government' in Chinese Feudal Society and Its Necessary Transformation into a Feudal Government," *LSYC*, no. 3, 1962, p. 135.

the revolts of the Yellow Turbans and Taipings here.

The Rebellion of An Lu-shan and Shih Ssu-ming, 756–63, which divides the history of the T'ang Dynasty, is considered a result of "contradictions within the governing class" rather than a peasant war.[4]

Eight of the twenty or so major rebellions mentioned above (those against the Ch'in, Wang Mang, the late Han, Sui, late T'ang, Yuan, late Ming, and the Taipings) either fatally weakened, overthrew, or accompanied the fall of the ruling dynasty. Their armies ranged from tens to hundreds of thousands. The record of this striking recurrence of rural unrest has impressed many observers of Chinese history besides the Communists.

TRADITIONAL INTERPRETATIONS

For thousands of years before the communists, Chinese philosophy has been deeply concerned with the life of the peasantry. By late Chou times, an understanding of the political importance of the peasantry was clearly stated as essential to successful rule,[5] and in Imperial times concern for the rural order became the basis of Chinese political thought.[6] With the development of an authoritarian state after the third century B.C., this concern turned increasingly on relations between the ruling class and the masses of the governed, of whom the overwhelming majority were peasants. Internecine strife between military aristocrats gave way to struggles between the government and its supporters, on the one hand, and discontented subjects of all classes, on the other. Han Fei's (d. 233 B.C.) statement, "Superior and inferior wage one

[4] See Chapter 1.

[5] As Mencius put it, "Win the people and you win the empire." See W. T. de Bary, *et al.* (eds.), *Sources of the Chinese Tradition*, p. 107.

[6] The communists maintain that the impact of the peasant wars was the greatest single reason for this. See Jen Chi-yü, "The Function of the Peasant Revolutionary Struggles for the History of Chinese Philosophy," *SSP*, pp. 397 ff. See Chapter 8 for further discussion of this point.

hundred battles a day," [7] may have exaggerated this tension, but it doubtless existed in Imperial China. Hence, it is not surprising that the first large-scale peasant unrest recorded in Chinese history dates from the last years of the first empire.

Because of their hatred of the legalists, later historians in the Confucian tradition regarded the anti-Ch'in rebellion in a special light. Chia Yi, an influential early Han poet and statesman (d. 169 B.C.), first expressed a sympathetic view of the rebellion against the Ch'in. He wrote that the reason Ch'en She had been able to start the chain of events leading to the overthrow of the mighty Ch'in was because the Ch'in rulers "failed to rule with humanity and righteousness and to realize that the power to attack and the power to retain what one has thereby won are not the same." [8] Ssu-ma Ch'ien, the first great Chinese historian, followed this interpretation. His introduction to the biography of Ch'en She stated, "When . . . the last rulers of the Hsia and Shang [dynasties] sank into evil, T'ang and Wu rose to replace them. When the way of Chou faltered, the *Spring and Autumn Annals* were made [to reveal the faults of the Chou rulers]. When Ch'in's rule failed, Ch'en She marched forth." [9] Thus, the Confucian idea of "moral determinism" already manifest in the classics was applied specifically to the fall of the first Imperial dynasty.

Mencius had long before declared the necessity of the emperor's sanction by Heaven and by his people, and he had implied the "moral right" of the people to overthrow a ruler who was "a scourge or a scoundrel," since such a ruler did not deserve the title of "sovereign." [10] If, however, "the prince is the boat and the people the water," as Hsun Tzu put it,[11]

[7] *The Han Fei-tzu*, W. K. Liao (trans.) (London: Arthur Probstain, 1959), vol. 1, p. 59.

[8] "Kuo Ch'in Lun," cited in de Bary, *et al.* (eds.), *Sources of the Chinese Tradition*, p. 168.

[9] Cited in Burton Watson, *Records of the Grand Historian of China*, vol. 1, p. 19.

[10] See de Bary, *et al.* (eds.), *Sources of the Chinese Tradition*, p. 111.

[11] See Lin Mou-sheng, *Men and Ideas* (New York: The John Day Co., 1942), p. 58.

the so-called "right of rebellion" was no legal right and certainly no obligation or responsibility. It was a warning to the ruler to follow Confucian ideals of "noblesse oblige" and not an invitation to the people to revolt. Along with this code of ethics for the ruler and the superior man went its equally fundamental complement, that subjects should accept the rule of just superiors. Mencius recognized that material well-being was necessary for social tractability, but he also insisted on a well-defined political hierarchy.

> "Some labor with their minds and some labor with their strength. Those who labor with their minds govern others; those who labor with their strength are governed by others. Those who are governed by others support them; those who govern others are supported by them." This is a principle universally recognized.[12]

As is evident in this passage, there are striking similarities as well as differences in the Confucian and communist views of class. Basically, the former as "idealists" believed that class status determined economic function, while the "materialists" believe it is the other way around.

Hsun Tzu vividly warned of the dire results of not maintaining social distinctions,[13] and legalists such as Han Fei went still further in insisting on the absolute subservence of ruled to ruler. The followers of Mo Tzu and even the Taoists also subscribed to the ideal of political order. Hence, from the beginning of Chinese thought there has been a diversity of opinion regarding peasant unrest, with general sympathy for its causes, but a simultaneous and somewhat contradictory antipathy toward "disruption."

With the founding of the Imperial state, the latter tendency became still stronger. Historians for the first time were appointed by the government to write specific histories re-

---

[12] James Legge (trans.), *The Four Books* (Shanghai: The Chinese Book Company), p. 627.
[13] See Derk Bodde, "Harmony and Conflict in Chinese Philosophy," in A. F. Wright (ed.), *Studies in Chinese Thought* (Chicago: University of Chicago Press, 1953), p. 47.

flecting an increasingly state-oriented Confucianism.[14] This in turn led to an ever more disparaging view of social malcontents and to the orthodox tradition which contrasts so strikingly with communist praise of rebellion.

The tendency to a more socially conservative historiography is strikingly revealed by a comparison between two great Han historians, Ssu-ma Ch'ien (d. 85 B.C.) and Pan Ku (d. A.D. 92). While contradictory statements may be found in both writers, there is a clear change of emphasis from Ssu-ma Ch'ien's praise of dissident groups such as the "wandering knights" (*yu-hsia*) to their condemnation by Pan Ku a century or so later.[15] The change reflects, at least in part, the greater commitment of the state-appointed historian to the status quo.

Pan Ku's favorable treatment of the rebellion of Ch'en She and Wu Kuang is similar to that of Ssu-ma Ch'ien, but this is probably because of the alleged inequities of Ch'in rule. Later Han interpretations make clear that no later rebels, unless they should also be of the Han Imperial line, founded by the successful rebel Liu Pang, could hope for similar profit from revolt. In order to discourage any such ideas, Pan Ku's father had written an impassioned defense of the status quo:

If . . . even poverty and misery are meted out by destiny, how much more so the honor of the throne, the

[14] See A. F. P. Hulsewé, "Notes on the Historiography of the Han Period," in W. G. Beasley and E. G. Pulleyblank (eds.), *Historians of China and Japan* (London: Oxford University Press, 1961), p. 43.

[15] The *yu-hsia* were a social group who "preferred action to moralizing." Burton Watson ("Memoirs of the Yu Hsia," unpublished Columbia University master's essay, 1951, preface), Tatsuo Masubichi ("The Yu Hsia and the Social Order in the Han Period," *Annals of the Hitotsubashi Academy*, October 1952, pp. 54 ff.), and James J. Y. Liu, *Chinese Knight Errant* (Chicago: University of Chicago Press, 1966) follow Ssu-ma Ch'ien's favorable opinion of *yu-hsia* and generally translate the term as "wandering knight." Ho Ping-ti ("Records of China's Grand Historian: Some Problems of Translation," *Pacific Affairs*, Summer 1963, pp. 171–80) follows the lead of Pan Ku and most traditional Chinese historians, however, and favors the term "underworld leaders," since the "yu hsia were in reality the stalwarts of the underworld of the former Han society." See also Robert Crawford, "The Social and Political Philosophy of the *Shih Chi*," *JAS*, August 1963, p. 406.

riches of all within the four seas, and the blessings of the
gods. How could one recklessly try to arrogate to oneself
such a position? True, there are some who, happening
upon an age of trouble and peril . . . manage to seize
authority for a time. Yet all must end cast into the caul-
dron or bowed beneath the stroke of an axe, boiled alive
or struck down and quartered. . . . As a man cannot
ride a thousand mile journey on a crippled jade . . . no
more can any mere dullard shoulder the burden of imperial rule.[16]

Pan Ku's treatment of the uprisings against Wang Mang
also contains a revealing distinction. Where neither commoner
nor noble rebels against the Ch'in are termed "thieves and
robbers," some of the peasant rebel groups which arose in the
late years of Wang Mang's rule are.[17] Pan Ku usually uses
the more favorable term "troops" (*ping*) to refer to the
rebels from P'ing-lin, Hsin-shih, and the lower Yangtze, since
these later allied with Liu Po-sheng members of the Han ruling
house to overthrow the usurper Wang Mang, but he calls the
unsuccessful Red Eyebrows and other groups "bandits." [18]
The pejorative terms "thieves" and "bandits" (*tao-tsei, t'u-fei,*
etc.) are thus reserved for unsuccessful rebel commoners and,
beginning with the Yellow Turban revolt of A.D. 184, are applied to all such rebels with few exceptions.[19]

A leading scholar of Han historiography argues that the
next major Chinese historical compilation, Fan Yeh's *Later
Han History*, is "remarkably objective," but he notes Fan's
bias against rebels "who through their actions had placed
themselves outside orderly relations." [20] He reports that the

[16] Cited in de Bary, *et al.* (eds.), *Sources of the Chinese Tradition,*
pp. 193–94.
[17] H. H. Dubs (trans.), *History of the Former Han Dynasty* (Baltimore: The Waverly Press, 1955), vol. 3, pp. 370–71, 379, 385, 436.
[18] *Ibid.*, pp. 430, 435, 437.
[19] E.g., since the rebellion of Chu Yuan-chang resulted in the founding of the Ming dynasty, the *Ming History* naturally uses the favorable
term for the initiation of this revolt.
[20] See Hans Bielenstein, *The Restoration of the Han Dynasty*, vol. 1,
p. 44.

Later Han history typically gives a stylized picture of rebels as bandits who oppress the people, but he believes that this is not a matter of class bias but of demonstrating the propriety of the Mandate of Heaven. In sum, "the traditional historian exaggerates, distorts and shifts emphasis in order to show why one man was worthy of the Mandate of Heaven and all others unworthy. . . ." [21]

For our purposes, this is the most fundamental feature of traditional historiography. It is well summarized in the common saying, "If you succeed you are king, if you fail you are a bandit" (*ch'eng-che wei wang, pai-che wei k'ou*). When a rebel is victorious, then the Confucian historian can be expected to endeavor to show that he was predestined to succeed by his worthiness and the unworthiness of his opponents. If he fails to accomplish any more than the disruption of a relatively peaceful, even if decadent, rule, he is a disturber of the peace and a "bandit." [22] This view became one of the basic beliefs of the Confucian historian, who praised harmonious social relations, vilified rebellion, and placed great emphasis on showing the worth of the reigning dynasty. The contrast with communist praise of class struggle is complete.

Liu Chih-chi (d. 721), who wrote the world's first book of historical criticism, further strengthened the anti-rebel bias in Chinese historiography. He criticized most Chinese historians for demeaning the principle of legitimate rule by falsely portraying successful rebels as legitimate heirs to the throne when they had in fact opposed the legitimate line. [23] According to the reasoning of Liu Chih-chi, it was wrong for the early dynastic histories to make the transfer of the Imperial Mandate seem predestined or just if the transfer of power

[21] *Ibid.*, vol. 2, p. 253.

[22] See Wolfgang Franke, *Das Jahrhundert der Chinesischen Revolution, 1851–1949* (Munich: R. Oldenbourg, 1958), p. 16.

[23] For instance, Liu called the authors of the *Han Shu, San Kuo Chih, Chin Shu,* and especially the *Wei Shu* "scoundrels" (*chien-tsei*) for this error. See Liu Chih-chi, *Shih-t'ung* (Generalities on History), chüan 7, section 25, pp. 8b–9a. For a commentary on this see E. G. Pulleyblank, "Chinese Historical Criticism: Liu Chih-chi and Ssu-ma Kuang," in Beasley and Pulleyblank, *op. cit.*, pp. 147–48.

was accompanied by violence.[24]

An exception to the practice of regarding a successful "bandit" as the rightful "emperor," which proves the rule of traditional bias against rebels, occurs in the treatment of Chu Wen, a former lieutenant of Huang Ch'ao, who deserted to the T'ang and went on to found the later Liang dynasty in A.D. 907. Sixteen years later Li K'o-yung, an aristocratic general of Turkish extraction, avenged earlier defeats and founded the later T'ang, the second of the ephemeral "five dynasties." According to a modern scholar of the historical records of the period, since it was "easier for a Chinese Mandarin to live under the provisional government of an aristocratic [Turk] than under a low class rebel, such as Chu Wen, contemporary historians had a violent aversion to the later Liang dynasty and favor wherever possible the later T'ang." [25]

An obvious explanation for the historian's low esteem for Chu, besides the anti-rebel bias mentioned here, was the short period of his rule. Had he succeeded in establishing a more durable dynasty, later historians would no doubt have honored him. Analogous situations arose after the peasant rebel Chu Yuan-chang established the Ming dynasty and after the Manchu defeat of the late Ming rebel Li Tzu-ch'eng in 1644. The long rule of the Ming founder and of his dynasty assured him respectful, if not uniformly laudatory, treatment. On the other hand, Li Tzu-ch'eng's defeat doomed him to the condemnation of Ch'ing historians both for rebelling against the Ming and for resisting the victorious Manchus. The paramount consideration is clearly "moral" and not geographical, and for most scholars in the Confucian tradition the sinicized alien who appeared to accept the Confucian order was preferable to the native rebel who did not.

The Confucian revival in the Sung dynasty led to an increased scholarly concern with history and with the moral lessons revealed in history.[26] There was a reinforcement of

---

[24] *Ibid.,* p. 148.
[25] W. Eberhard, *Conquerors and Rulers: Social Forces in Medieval China,* pp. 103 and 106.
[26] Ma Tuan-lin, although stressing the continuity of institutional

Confucian paternalism and principles of legitimacy which in
turn led to a further hardening in the historical treatment of
rebellion. This is well revealed in the writings of Chu Hsi
(d. 1200), the foremost exponent of Sung Confucianism. Chu
instructed his disciples to use a very exact terminology, in the
tradition of the *Spring and Autumn Annals*,[27] in order to
make the moral of the narration clear. For instance, the historian should speak of "raising troops" (*ch'i ping*) [28] if the expedition was altogether worthy, as was the case in the revolts of
the late Ch'in nobles and of Liu Yen and Liu Hsiu against
Wang Mang. If neither the rebels nor their opponents were
considered worthy, as was the case when the Red Eyebrows
revolted against Wang Mang, then one could only say
"troops rose [in rebellion] " (*ping ch'i*).[29] If there was a
rebellion against the legitimate line or government (*t'ung-hsi*
or *cheng-t'ung*), it should be termed "making a disturbance"
(*tso-luan*). If there were only a few insignificant participants,
rebels should be called "robbers" (*tao*) or, if their number
was large, a "host of robbers" (*chun tao*). Those who violate
principles (*fan hsun*) should be termed "thief" (*k'ou*).[30]
Notes to those instructions elaborate on the relatively favorable treatment given the Red Eyebrows by Chu Hsi. The
tolerance of this rebellion is explained as due to the despic-
able nature of their opponent, the usurper (*ts'uan-tsei*)
Wang Mang. It was proper for Chu Hsi to use the term "kill
righteously" (*chu*) in describing the Red Eyebrow defeat of

history, dissented from the usual Confucian view that there was an
underlying principle behind the rise and fall of dynasties. He wrote,
". . . periods of order or disorder, of the rise and fall of different dynasties, are not inter-related. . . . Each period has its own history." See
de Bary, *et al.* (eds.), *Sources of the Chinese Tradition*, pp. 499–501.
Wang Fu-chih (seventeenth century) held similar views, according to
Lin Mou-sheng, *op. cit.*

[27] See P. Van der Loon, "The Ancient Chinese Chronicles and the
Growth of Historical Ideals," in Beasley and Pulleyblank, *op. cit.*, p. 26.

[28] The communists now use the term *ch'i ping* only to refer to landlords or the government raising troops, as distinguished from righteous
uprisings (*ch'i yi*) of the peasants.

[29] Chu Hsi, *T'ung-chien Kang-mu* (Outline and Digest for the General Mirror), Fan li section (guiding principles), p. 10a.

[30] *Ibid.*, p. 14a.

one of Wang Mang's generals, even though this was the case of a rebel opposing the existing government. This was so because "both [the Wang Mang government and the Red Eyebrows] were bandits" (*tsei*).[31]

In addition to the stress on the legitimacy of the reigning dynasty evident in the quibbling over terminology, there is also an element of social distinction in Chu Hsi's historiography. Where the revolts of the nobles against Wang Mang are considered righteous (*yi-che*), those of peasant rebels such as the Red Eyebrow leader Fan Ch'ung are not.[32]

For the most part, the Sung histories and literature continue this unfavorable presentation of rebels against the government. The movement led by Fang La (1120–1122) is described in contemporary histories as the "plunder of bandits," while its religious aspects are called "deluding stupid people with prophecies." [33] Several Sung short stories are concerned with peasant rebellions and also present them in an unfavorable light.[34]

More sympathetic interpretations of Chinese rebellions are also to be found in Chinese literature, however, and this alternate stress of good and bad deeds of the rebels presents problems of interpretation for noncommunist as well as for communist historians.[35] The continuing contradictions in modern interpretations of Chinese rebels, as of the communists themselves, verify the ambiguities in the reports of traditional Chinese historians for two millennia. Naturally,

[31] *Ibid.*, chüan 8, p. 17b. For a partial translation of this document see de Bary, et al. (eds.), *Sources of the Chinese Tradition*, pp. 507–9.

[32] Chu Hsi, *op. cit.*, Fan li section, p. 10a.

[33] See Kao Yü-kung, "A Study of the Fang La Rebellion," unpublished Harvard University doctoral dissertation, 1962.

[34] E.g., H. F. Schurmann, "On Social Themes in Sung Tales," *HJAS*, June 1957, p. 242; and *Wang Hsin chih Yi-ssu Chiu Ch'uan-chia* (The Death of Wang Hsin Saves His Whole Family).

[35] Thus, harsh criticisms of rebels are often followed by favorable and seemingly contradictory remarks. E.g., Teng Ssu-yü, *The Nien Army and Their Guerrilla Warfare, 1851–1868*, pp. 62, 68, 91, 146–47, and then the favorable judgment given on p. 69. Similarly, see Hsiao Kung-ch'uan, *Rural China: Imperial Control in the Nineteenth Century*, p. 405, and then pp. 476, 483, 385; and Franz Michael, *The Taiping Rebellion*, vol. 1, pp. 195 and 199.

those who stress law and order tend to emphasize one interpretation, and those who emphasize struggle tend to emphasize the other, with varying degrees of emotional commitment.

The *Tzu-chih T'ung-chien* (Mirror of History), by the
great Sung historian Ssu-ma Kuang (d. 1086), illustrates this
two-sided approach. His treatment of the peasant revolts in
Chinese history, while somewhat fuller than most, essentially
follows traditional views. He sympathizes with the uprisings
against the hated Ch'in and Wang Mang governments, but
thereafter he disparages all peasant rebels as "bandits." On the
other hand, Ssu-ma Kuang was too great a historian to obscure
information which might be favorable to the rebels, and this
information supplies data which communist writers frequently
cite as examples of "peasant justice." [36] Even as he criticized
the rebellion of Huang Ch'ao (d. 884), Ssu-ma reported that
the rebels gave some of their "ill-gotten wealth" to the poor.[37]
Since traditional historians also reported that Huang Ch'ao's
army especially hated the officials and killed all they captured,
the communists naturally cite these actions as proof of the
rebels' class hatred of the rich and as the explanation for government class slanders of the rebels.[38]

One explanation for this contradiction between oppro-
brium of the rebels and reporting of information favorable to
them is to be found in the importance most traditional historians attached to imparting factual information.[39] While the
emphasis varied according to the historian, the more important Chinese historians saw no conflict between the two and

[36] See Hou Wai-lu, *et al.* (eds.), *Chung-kuo Ssu-hsiang T'ung-shih*
(A General History of Chinese Thought) (Peking: Jen-min Ch'u-pan
She, 1957–59), vol. 2, p. 137. A Western scholar also credits Ssu-ma
Kuang with assisting the development of a political, if not social, autoc-
racy in the Sung period. F. W. Mote, "The Growth of Chinese Despot-
ism," *Oriens Extremus*, August 1961, p. 13.

[37] Ssu-ma Kuang, *Tzu-chih T'ung-chien* (Comprehensive Mirror for
Self-Government) (Peking: Ku-chi Ch'u-pan She, 1956, Reprint), vol.
9, p. 8240.

[38] E.g., Ho Lin-t'ien, "How to Look on the Two Mistaken Traditions
Concerning Huang Ch'ao and the Boxers," *Hsiao-hsueh Chiao-shih*
(Elementary School Teacher), September 1954.

[39] See James B. Parsons, "Attitudes Toward the Late Ming Rebellions," *Oriens Extremus*, December 1959, p. 190.

were confident that the fullest possible record of events would speak for itself. They therefore reported information favorable to the rebels along with much more which was unfavorable.

Another factor responsible for a relatively balanced picture of peasant rebellion in certain traditional writings was the importance attached to responsible rule. In fact, more emphasis was given to conducting proper government than to good citizenship, because the latter was assumed to follow from the former. Confucians paid great attention to political conditions and commonly attributed the cause of disorder and rebellion to misgovernment, as in the saying "the officials compel the people to rebel" (*kuan pi min fan*). Early Han Confucians were quick to adduce the first rebellions against the newly established Imperial order as proof of this assumption, and this interpretation was followed by all later historians.[40]

Traditional records contained occasional evidences of sympathy for rebels with a cause. This underground current in Chinese literature increased in Sung times, probably in reaction to the ever more rigid élitist views of the Confucian bureaucracy. Certainly by the time of the writing of the Shui-hu Chuan (*Water Margin*) in the Ming dynasty, an attitude of sympathy for commoner rebels had become one variant of the literary tradition.[41]

In addition there were varied interpretations of the true popularity of the rebels. Many critics of revolt, both traditionally and in modern times, have argued that the peasant rebels, like their communist successors, coerced an unwilling populace to follow them. But there is conflicting evidence

[40] See Chapter 5.

[41] This story presents the adventures of a band of 108 rebels of the Sung in a manner similar to that of the Robin Hood cycle. Although the novel presents a picture of what one scholar calls "gang morality" and the corruption of the rebels themselves (C. T. Hsia, "Comparative Approaches to Water Margin," *Yearbook of Comparative and General Literature*, no. 11, 1962, pp. 121 ff.), it is most remembered for its sympathetic understanding of the reasons these men became outlaws, namely, because of official corruption and of other frustrations of a complex society. The novel has been translated by Pearl Buck as *All Men Are Brothers*.

about the true popularity of the peasant movements and the degree of their spontaneity or manipulation by unscrupulous leaders. On occasion rebel chieftains utilized a variety of methods, ranging from terror to promises of reward, to recruit new followers,[42] and there were often revolts against rebel leadership by disillusioned or resentful underlings.[43] Yet reports of rebel unpopularity[44] are outnumbered by evidence that the people at least favored the rebels over government troops.[45] Hence, a Han saying stated, "We would rather meet the Red Eyebrows than T'ai-shih" (one of Wang Mang's generals), and a late Ming and nineteenth-century refrain complained, "The rebels comb coarsely, the government armies comb finely."

One of the most consistent themes in the communist historiography of the peasant revolts is the belief that most of the unfavorable reports of the peasant revolts were "slanders" written by the governing class, whose vested interests were at stake.[46] One need not accept this argument, but it must be recognized that rebellions of masses of the poor, who could expect little in the way of safety or immediate riches, probably were spontaneous movements of one sort or another and not simply the result of machinations by wicked leaders.

[42] E.g., see K. C. Hsiao, *op. cit.*, p. 476.

[43] See Hsiao's account of resentment against the Taipings, *ibid.*, pp. 483–85. Some communist writers also discuss such incidents. E.g., Mou An-shih, *T'ai-p'ing T'ien-kuo*, p. 424; and Ch'i Lung-wei, "Discussing Current Prejudices in Research on the History of the T'ai-p'ing T'ien-kuo," *KMJP*, May 23, 1957.

[44] As the populace stoning the departing troops of Huang Ch'ao. See Ssu-ma Kuang, *Tzu-chih T'ung-chien*, cited in Howard Levy, *Biography of Huang Ch'ao* (Berkeley: University of California Press, 1961), pp. 80–81.

[45] E.g., *ibid.*, p. 24 ff. See also sources collected in Pei-ching Ta-hsueh Wen-hsueh Hsi (eds.), *Chung kuo Lit-tai Nung-min Wen-t'i Wen-hsueh Tzu-liao* (Literary Materials on the Peasant Question in Chinese History) (Peking: Chung-hua Shu-chü, 1959); and Rewi Alley (trans.), *Poems of Revolt* (Peking: New World Press, 1962). Evidence of rebel popularity is supported by some non-communist studies. E.g., James Parsons, "The Rebellion of Chang Hsien-chung as an Example of Internal Disturbances in China During the Late Ming Dynasty," unpublished University of California doctoral dissertation, 1954, and Teng Ssu-yü, *The Nien Army*, pp. 62, 68, 91, 146–47.

[46] E.g., see Ho Lin-t'ien, *op. cit.*, *Hsiao-hsueh Chiao-shih*, September 1954.

The existence of a number of statements favorable to the rebels in Chinese history, whether because of the historians' own sympathy or because of the Chinese tradition of presenting the fullest possible historical record, has provided communist historians with a considerable amount of historical documentation for the glorification of the peasant rebels.

Yet, whatever the expression of extenuating circumstances, the underlying assumption behind all traditional Chinese literature was the desirability of harmony and order. The process of consolidation of this orthodox, anti-rebel ideology, furthered in the Sung, was continued in the Ming and Ch'ing dynasties. The founder of the Ming dynasty, who himself rose from the status of impoverished peasant to emperor after more than a decade of strife, had a paranoid suspicion of similar rebellions against his own rule. Accordingly, he instituted a more centralized administration and forbade all activities by potentially subversive societies. Furthermore, he sought to delete passages of the Confucian canon which were ambiguous in their condemnation of rebels. Unable to impose such a wholesale censorship, he settled for the removal of the passages in Mencius implying the "right of rebellion," [47] as did early Manchu rulers.

Despite the efforts of the Ming founder and later conservatives, the record of peasant revolts continued to attract the attention of traditional historians. Fang Hsiao-ju, a scholar of the period (d. 1402), wrote, "The people began to rise and cause disorder with the Ch'in dynasty. In later times all who overthrew dynasties were mostly common people." [48] Seventeenth-century thinkers, influenced by the revolts of Chang Hsien-chung and Li Tzu-ch'eng and by the fall of the country to the Manchus, were naturally concerned with the causes of these catastrophic events. Huang Tsung-hsi, whose thought the communists maintain was influenced deeply by the peasant movements,[49] did indeed bemoan the plight of the

[47] See Franke, *op. cit.*, p. 17.
[48] Cited in K. C. Hsiao, *op. cit.*, p. 372.
[49] E.g., Chao Hsi-yen *et al.*, "Criticisms of Several Mistaken Views of the Historical Function of Chinese Peasant Wars in [Sun Tso-min's] . . . *T'an-su,*" SSP, p. 420.

masses. Lamenting the ever-rising taxes and other burdens of government, Huang went much further than most Chinese scholars in advocating far-reaching reform. Implicitly accepting Mencius' theory of the "right of revolution," he wrote, "Whether there is peace or disorder in the world does not depend on the rise and fall of dynasties but upon the happiness or distress of the people." [50]

The Manchu Ch'ing dynasty, however, dictated a rigid Confucian view of the world and imposed a strict censorship, particularly of unfavorable references to their own status.[51] While some unorthodox philosophical views were tolerated, dissenting political views were not. Among historical subjects the Ch'ing treatment of peasant revolts followed and elaborated traditional interpretations. Historians devised some of the most imaginative of all criticisms of peasant rebels, as illustrated by the various fabrications and violent denunciations of the late Ming rebels. For instance, the *Ming Shih* stated that 600 million persons lost their lives in the terror perpetrated by Chang Hsien-chung, and that Li Tzu-ch'eng was "by nature . . . suspicious and repressive. Every day he killed people, severed their feet and cut out their hearts as a sport. . . ." [52] Yet, for reasons we have mentioned, relatively complete information, including favorable references to the rebels, was also included.

The two greatest historians of the eighteenth century, Chang Hsueh-ch'eng and Chao Yi, both sought to improve the methodology of traditional historiography.[53] While

[50] Cited in W. T. de Bary, "Huang Tsung-hsi, a Plan for the Prince," unpublished Columbia University doctoral dissertation, 1953, pp. 150–151.

[51] See L. C. Goodrich, *Literary Inquisition of Ch'ien Lung* (Baltimore: The Waverly Press, 1935).

[52] James Parsons, "The Culmination of a Chinese Peasant Rebellion: Chang Hsien-chung in Szechwan, 1644–5," *JAS*, May 1957, p. 395, and "Attitudes Toward the Late Ming Rebellions," *Oriens Extremus*, no. 2, December 1959, p. 186. The latter is the most detailed description of traditional views of peasant revolts in a Western language.

[53] See P. Demieville, "Chang Hsueh-ch'eng and His Historiography," in Beasley and Pulleyblank, *op. cit.*, pp. 167–85, and David Nivison, *The Life and Thought of Chang Hsueh-ch'eng* (Stanford: Stanford University Press, 1966).

avoiding extreme theoretical positions and calling for an objective presentation of the facts, they were well within the Confucian tradition in their attitudes toward the social order. Thus, Chao Yi, while noting the neglect of popular revolts by traditional historians and devoting comparatively much attention to them, continued to condemn rebel motives and actions in the time-honored way.[54]

In the nineteenth century, with the social order moving toward collapse for both internal and external reasons, the Ch'ing rulers vainly sought to shepherd their people back to peaceful ways. The Chia-ch'ing emperor pontificated on the suppression of the eight-diagrams secret society in 1813. Beyond Confucian principles, he stated, "no so-called religion exists, and outside the principles of nature and the laws of the ruler, happiness may not be sought after: happiness proceeds from complying with orthodoxy, and misfortune from following heresy." [55] His successor repeated this injunction, promising that "through contentment with one's occupation, blessing would be obtained." [56]

Traditional views of rebellion in general and of peasant rebellion in particular were followed well into the period of Imperial China's final collapse. In fact, had it not been for the conviction of educated men that China's best interests lay in restoring Confucian benevolent despotism rather than in an anti-traditional rebel movement, the Taiping, that collapse might have come half a century earlier. Leading students of that rebellion argue that one of the basic reasons for its defeat was the alienation of the educated class.[57] Tseng Kuo-fan, the leading suppressor of the Taipings, revealed the antipathy of conservative scholars:

[54] Chao Yi, "Huang Ch'ao and Li Tzu-ch'eng," in *Nien-erh Shih Ch'a-chi* (Notes to the Twenty-Two Histories) (Taipei: Shih-chieh Shu-chu, 1958), chuan 20, vol. 2, pp. 277–78, 521 ff.
[55] Cited in C. K. Yang, *Religion in Chinese Society* (Berkeley: University of California Press, 1961), p. 227.
[56] *Ibid.*, p. 228.
[57] E.g., Eugene P. Boardman, *Christian Influences upon the Ideology of the T'ai-p'ing Rebellion* (Madison: University of Wisconsin Press, 1952), p. 126; and Hsiao Yi-shan, *Ch'ing-tai T'ung-shih* (General History of the Ch'ing Period) (Taipei: Shang-wu Yin-shu Kuan, 1963), vol. 3, pp. 296 ff.

Never until these latter days have such things been—no, not from the days of creation. At such unorthodox teachings, our Confucius and Mencius must be weeping bitterly in Hades. Shall any scholar, then, or any able to read, fold his arms in his sleeves and sit in peace? . . . [Even the late Ming peasant rebel] Li Tzu-ch'eng arriving at Ch'u fou [a locality sacred to Confucius] did not desecrate the sacred temple. [Chang] Hsien-chung worshipped the god of literary emolument. . . .[58]

Aside from the additional reaction here to Christian iconoclasm, it is clear that such men as Tseng Kuo-fan were following essentially traditional assumptions of the legitimacy of the ruling dynasty and the errors of rebellion.

MODERN NONCOMMUNIST VIEWS

While the traditional distrust of revolt helped to prolong Ch'ing rule, mounting internal and external challenges soon brought a fresh look at the nature of rebellion in general and of the Taipings in particular. Modern Chinese thinkers, forced by the impact of the West to come to terms with the Chinese past, correctly saw the Taiping movement and the Imperial reaction to it as an epitome of many of the problems raised by the confrontation of the West with their heritage; problems of the possibility of reform of an ancient system, of the historical role of the élite and of the masses, and of a "revolutionary tradition" in Chinese history.

A leading sinologist has traced five stages in the evaluation of the Taipings: (1) during the nineteenth century, marked by a "destruction or censorship of historical relics and documents and by an attitude of contempt for the insurgents"; (2) a "rather uncritical praise of the rebel cause" by early Chinese nationalists such as Sun Yat-sen; (3) the discovery of new materials and the stimulation of new approaches during the 1920s and 1930s; (4) an analysis of these new materials

[58] Cited in Boardman, op. cit., p. 124.

and the elaboration of the new interpretations; and (5) after
1950, the "division of scholarly opinion into two rival political groups. On the one side are the scholars in continental
China who honor the 'T'ai-p'ing revolution' . . . as a fore-
runner of their own revolution and praise its leaders for their
sound policies and exemplary conduct. . . . On the other
side are the scholars in Formosan China who tend either to
ignore or condemn the 'T'ai-p'ing rebellion.' " [59]

These changes of attitude, of course, have reflected the
dramatic political changes in modern China. Where nineteenth-century historians described tragic scenes of burning
and massacre perpetrated by the rebels and condemned their
unorthodox and vulgar institutions and writings, Chinese
revolutionaries of the turn of the century looked on the Taipings with the sympathy of fellow outcasts. Sun Yat-sen allegedly was influenced as a boy by stories of Taiping leaders
and liked to think of himself as a second Hung Hsiu-ch'uan,
the Taiping Heavenly King. Later he considered the Taiping
program as a precursor of his own socialistic ideas. He wrote:

> [The principle of people's livelihood] Min-sheng Chu-yi
> is nothing other than equalization of wealth; by this I
> mean the rich cannot oppress the poor. But several dec-
> ades before there was someone else who had already put
> the Min-sheng Chu-yi into practice. He was Hung Hsiu-
> ch'uan. The system initiated by him, such as state con-
> trol of workers, state ownership of all things, is a com-
> plete economic revolution and is just the equalization of
> wealth as advocated by present day Russia.[60]

---

[59] Teng Ssu-yu, *Historiography of the T'ai-p'ing Rebellion* (Cambridge: Harvard University Press, 1962), pp. 42–44. The communists
are by no means entirely favorable in their interpretations of all Taiping
activities, but recent noncommunist studies of the Taipings have tended
to be far more critical of rebel performance and skeptical of the egalitarian claims of Taiping documents. E.g., see Vincent Y. C. Shih, *The
Taiping Ideology* (Seattle, University of Washington Press, 1967), pp.
436–49, 489–92, and Franz Michael, *The Taiping Rebellion* (Seattle:
University of Washington Press, 1966).

[60] Cited in Vincent Shih, "Interpretations of the T'ai-p'ings by Non-
Communist Writers," *FEQ*, May 1951, p. 250. The interpretation of
the Nationalists as continuers of the work of the Taipings was prevalent

On the other hand, perhaps recognizing that the Taipings may not have carried out their idealistic programs, Sun also wrote, "Hung knew only of the ethnic issue and knew nothing of the rights of the people. He knew only of monarchy and knew nothing of democracy." [61] The primary appeal of the Taipings to Chinese nationalists was as an "ethnic revolution" of the Chinese against the Manchus, a theme still approved by many leading Chinese scholars, noncommunist as well as communist.[62] Chiang Kai-shek early approved of the patriotism of the Taipings, whom he called "restoration troops" and a "revolutionary army." He wrote:

> In the past our forefathers, Hung and Yang, rose in the southeast to overthrow the Ch'ing dynasty; though they failed and were defeated, their ethnic consciousness has flourished and become a great monument to our history.[63]

As Chiang became increasingly embroiled in the struggle for power with those more radical than himself, he began to question the desirability of praising the Taipings. He stressed instead a selection of the works of Tseng Kuo-fan and Hu Lin-yi, two of the most important of the Confucian opponents of the Taipings, whose sayings Chiang described as "the voice of true experience in governing men." [64]

By 1932 the transition of the attitudes of the ruling group of the Kuomintang from praising the Taipings as the forerunners of the Nationalist revolution to praise of the suppressors of the Taipings was complete. The patriotism of the Taipings continued to have a place in Nationalist historiography, since, according to Chiang, Tseng Kuo-fan fought not to save the alien Manchus but to "save the teachings of several

as late as 1927. See Cyrus H. Peake, *Nationalism and Education in Modern China* (New York: Columbia University Press, 1932), p. 187.

[61] Cited in Shih, "Interpretations of the T'ai-p'ings . . . ," p. 250.

[62] E.g., Hsiao Yi-shan and Chien Yu-wen.

[63] Cited in Shih, "Interpretations of the T'ai-p'ings . . . ," p. 250. The preface cited here was dated 1928, although the book in which it appeared was not published until 1935.

[64] See Mary C. Wright, "From Revolution to Restoration: The Transformation of the KMT Ideology," *FEQ*, August 1955, pp. 518–19.

thousand years";[65] but there was complete condemnation of
the social ideas of the Taipings. In fact, the previously revolutionary Kuomintang adopted the traditional view of rebellion. The official history of the Nationalists declared that
Taiping thought was "contrary to the spirit of Chinese culture, of which the Kuomintang was the true revolutionary
carrier." [66] Chiang stated in 1933 or 1934:

> We must know from looking at five thousand years of
> Chinese history that bandit disturbances [*fei luan*] were
> frequent, but regardless of the dynasty, no murderous,
> marauding local bandits [*t'u fei*] were able to succeed.
> Especially [must this be true] of the present bandits in
> Kiangsi, the so-called CCP who like previous bandits
> such as the Red Eyebrows, Yellow Turbans, Huang
> Ch'ao and Li Ch'uang are extraordinarily cruel, foot-
> loose [*hsia liu*] and bestial. . . .[67]

After 1928, of course, Chiang represented the government
in power and could only frown on all "disruptions," of which
there were many. Thus, the earlier sympathies of Sun Yat-
sen, Chiang Kai-shek, and other leading Nationalists could be
readily explained in terms of identification, since they too had
been rebels against the status quo. After coming to power
Chiang and others identified themselves with the traditional
views of Chinese statesmen regarding rebellion against the
state.

The efforts of the Nationalist government to invoke the
sanction of legitimacy for their own rule and to link the communists with the worst of the peasant rebel tradition in Chinese history has been continued. During the war Chiang
maintained that the Chinese government traditionally had

[65] *Chiang Chung-cheng Ch'üan-chi* (Collected Works of Chiang Kai-
shek) (Shanghai: Min-tzu Ch'u-pan She, 1937), vol. 2, fifth pien, p. 6.
[66] Cited in Wright, *op. cit.*, p. 521.
[67] Chiang Kai-shek, *Lu-shan Hsün-lien Chi* (Collected Training
Speeches Given at Lu Shan) (n.p., 1933–34), vol. 1, p. 200. An interesting specific parallel was drawn by Chiang Kai-shek when, during the
course of the Communist Long March, he predicted the destruction of
Mao at the very site of the annihilation of the forces of the Taiping
leader, Shih Ta-k'ai.

been magnanimous to its subjects and cited Sun Yat-sen's statement, "The Chinese people had long had great freedom and it was not necessary for them to fight for it." [68] He noted that the Chinese communists used the methods of armed bandits in Chinese history,[69] and in 1956 he elaborated:

> The Chinese Communists have combined on the one hand the ruthlessness and inhumanity of Huang Ch'ao and Chang Hsien-chung, the two most notorious brigands in Chinese history, and on the other, the modern techniques of terrorism and enslavement as perfected by the Soviet Imperialists. Therefore their crimes against our country and our people have surpassed those committed by others in the earlier dynasties.[70]

A standard Nationalist textbook put the negative interpretation of rebellion more subtly:

> There is one phenomenon in Chinese history that is worth paying attention to. That is that our own people's culture often advances in periods of peace [where] European history often has spirit of struggle . . . and transitional periods are produced out of turmoil. Looking at Chinese history from this view, then, Chinese history seems to be dark and without progress. Chinese history also has its larger scale struggles raised by the lower classes, but unfortunately these usually were chaotic sacrifices, without meaning of epochal progress. Rather it was not that China was without progress but that China's progress usually occurred under conditions of peace and advanced steadily [rather than as a result of revolutions].[71]

Finally, an extreme example of Kuomintang propaganda shows the complete contrast of communist and noncommu-

---

[68] Chiang Kai-shek, *China's Destiny* (New York: Macmillan Co., 1947), p. 210.
[69] Chiang Kai-shek, *Soviet Russia in China* (New York: Farrar, Straus and Cudahy, 1957), p. 60.
[70] Cited in *China Post* (Taipei), October 10, 1956, p. 3.
[71] Ch'ien Mu, *Kuo-shih Ta-kang* (Outline of National History) (Shanghai: Shang-wu Yin-shu Kuan, 1944), p. 11.

nist views. Seeking to show that the communists are descend-
ants of the outlaw tradition in Chinese history, it briefly out-
lines the rebellions of the Yellow Turbans, Huang Ch'ao, Li
Tzu-ch'eng, and Mao Tse-tung, concluding that these "bandit
leaders" were equally cruel, treacherous, and selfish.[72] In the
section on Mao a grisly picture shows the communist leader
standing over a pile of skulls, brandishing the sword of Chang
Hsien-chung and a gun marked "Made in Russia." The accompanying text states, "After all, what sort of man is Mao
Tse-tung? He is the blood descendant and filial son of the
Yellow Turbans, Huang Ch'ao, Li [Tzu-ch'eng], and Chang
[Hsien-chung]." [73] The communists agree with the conclusion but, understandably, not with the interpretation.

SOVIET AND EARLY CHINESE
COMMUNIST INTERPRETATIONS

Long before the Bolshevik Revolution, certain Russian historians, following their European counterparts, began to emphasize the role of the masses in history.[74] After 1917 Soviet
historiography "first of all tried to find new content in facts
which were already well known, interpreting them in the
light of the class struggle, which up to that time had supposedly remained unnoticed or not understood." [75] Yet most

---

[72] Shen Hui and P'an Hsia, *Ku-chin Liu-k'ou Ho-chuan* (Biographies
of Ancient and Modern Bandits) (Taipei: Shanghai Yin-shua-ch'ang,
1951), p. 13.

[73] *Ibid.*, p. 5. Other less polemical writings on Taiwan give a better
balanced picture of the peasant rebellions but still present them largely
as disasters. For instance, Kuo T'ing-yi wrote in 1955, "not much could
be said either [for the Taiping leaders'] political knowledge or common
sense. The only asset they had was their adeptness in intriguing and
scheming and in the use of unscrupulous tactics." Kuo T'ing-yi, "The
Totalitarian Rule of the T'ai-p'ing Heavenly Kingdom," *Annals of
Academia Sinica*, no. 11, part 1, 1955, p. 211.

[74] See Herbert E. Bowman, "Soviet Literary and Historical Scholarship," in C. E. Black (ed.), *The Transformation of Russian Society*
(Cambridge: Harvard University Press 1960), p. 376.

[75] Shteppa, *op. cit.*, p. 22.

early Marxist historians, as opposed to the Leninists and social revolutionaries, applied this emphasis on the class struggle almost entirely to the modern labor movement rather than to the historical role of the "dark people." Pokrovsky and other early Soviet historians treated peasant movements in history as isolated local occurrences and were particularly skeptical of the four great Russian peasant movements.[76] Soon, however, Lenin's policies and the need for more tangible historical roots than were offered in Pokrovsky's dry economic materialism brought an increased emphasis on the historic role of the Russian peasantry, especially on the uprisings led by Bolotnikov (1606–07), Razin (1667–71), Bulavin (1707–08), and Pugachov (1773–75).

This tendency to place greater stress on human factors in history was evident from the early 1920s, and in the 1930s was carried another step with growing stress on national heroes of the governing class as well as on the masses. Following the fall from grace of the Pokrovsky school in 1934, Party leaders attacked the earlier handling of the Russian peasant movements. Pokrovsky supposedly neglected the peasant movements in his early writings, distorting them as "Cossack-peasant risings," but then, toward the end of his life, went to the opposite extreme and overpraised their organization and chances of victory.[77]

Stalin and his ideologists sought to hold historians to a communist balance in the study of the peasant movements, stressing both their significance and their ultimate dependence on proletarian leadership. In 1932 he stated:

> We Bolsheviks have always taken an interest in such [Russian peasant rebels as] . . . Bolotnikov, Razin, Pugachov, and so on. We regard the deeds of these individuals as a reflection of the spontaneous rebellion of the

---

[76] See Leo Yaresh, "The 'Peasant Wars' in Soviet Historiography," *American Slavic and East European Review*, October 1957, pp. 247–248; and Anatole G. Mazour, *Modern Russian Historiography* (Princeton: D. Van Nostrand Company, 1958, 2d ed.), pp. 192–93.

[77] M. Nechkina, "The Uprising of Razin and Pugachov in the Conception of M. N. Pokrovsky," *Protiv Istoricheskii Kontseptsii M. N. Pokrovskogo* (Moscow, 1939), pp. 247, 265; see also pp. 244–46, 256, 260, 263, 274–75.

peasantry against feudal oppression. . . . But of course no analogy can be drawn here between them and the Bolsheviks. . . . Peasant uprisings can be successful only if they are combined with uprisings of the workers and if they are led by the workers.[78]

From the 1930s, then, the prevailing Soviet view became that one must not neglect the role of the masses in history, but neither could one interpret the activities of the masses in such a way as to make them independent of the leadership of the "advanced classes." [79] The dilemma of avoiding either overpraise or minimization of the peasant wars has been the most consistent theme in both Soviet and Chinese historiography of the peasant wars, but, relatively speaking, the Soviets have emphasized the negative and Chinese historians the positive side of the equation.

Following World War II, the tightening of Soviet ideological controls meant renewed emphasis on the theory as well as the practice of class struggle. The death of Stalin greatly accelerated the retreat from overemphasis on the role of the leader to concern with the role of the masses. Even before Stalin's death there was a considerable increase in literature on the peasant movements.[80] Some Soviet historians soon went too far in characterizing the revolutionary qualities of the peasant wars as entirely "progressive" and were charged with overemphasizing the class struggle at the expense of economic factors.[81] One, B. F. Porshnev, was charged with ex-

[78] J. V. Stalin, "Talk with the German Author, Emil Ludwig," *Works* (Moscow: Foreign Languages Publishing House, 1955), vol. 13, p. 112.

[79] K. F. Shteppa, *Russian Historians and the Soviet State* (New Brunswick: Rutgers University Press, 1962), pp. 137, 154, 163, 192, 361. See also Klaus Mehnert: *Stalin Versus Marx: The Stalinist Historical Doctrine* (London: George Allen and Unwin, 1952).

[80] See Yaresh, *op. cit.*, pp. 253–54. A work on the German peasant war of 1525 won the Stalin prize in 1947 and stressed the revolutionary effects if not intent of this movement. See M. M. Smirin, *Narodnaya Reformatsiya Thomasa Muntzer i Velikaya Krestyanskaya Voina* (The People's Reformation of Thomas Muntzer and the Great Peasant War) (Moscow: Akademiya Nauk, 1955, 2d ed.), p. 46.

[81] See Leo Yaresh, "The Problem of Periodization," in C. E. Black (ed.), *Rewriting Russian History* (New York: Vintage Books, 1962), pp. 72–73.

aggerating the role of peasant revolts and underestimating the primacy of material forces. Porshnev had maintained that the "peasant struggle against exploitation . . . determined the development of feudalism," a position which in fact is essentially the same as that taken by most Chinese communist writers on this question. But his Russian critics point out that Porshnev ignored the role of the bourgeoisie in the defeat of feudalism and made the class struggle determine the development of productive forces rather than the other way around.[82] Another critic gets to the real point of Party objections to an overfavorable view of peasant struggle when he wrote that Porshnev presented

> a populist point of view . . . by picturing the peasant struggle against feudalism as a movement in which the labor principle began to predominate over property . . . B. F. Porshnev *brings into question the historical necessity of the hegemony of the proletariat in relation to the peasantry* in the Socialist Revolution.[83]

This problem of the degree of revolutionary potential which should be recognized for the peasant class has also dominated recent Chinese debates on the nature of the peasant wars. Significantly, the prevailing Chinese view stresses the role of the class struggle of the peasantry at least as much as did Porshnev, and it is the detractors of the peasant wars who are condemned rather than their exaggerators, as has usually been the case in the Soviet Union.[84]

---

[82] Leo Yaresh, "The 'Peasant Wars' in Soviet Historiography," pp. 255–56.

[83] Cited in Shteppa, *op. cit.*, pp. 196–97. Emphasis supplied.

[84] For a recent Soviet discussion of the nature of the Russian peasant wars, see V. V. Mavrodin *et al.*, "On the Characteristics of the Peasant Wars in Russia," V*oprosy Istorii* (Problems of History, hereafter VI), no. 2, 1956. Among other Soviet articles on the question of the peasant wars, two are of special interest. One summarized views of the peasant movements of the middle ages for the benefit of high school teachers, while the other reported on the experimental teaching of the history of the Taiping Rebellion in a Leningrad high school. See S. D. Skazkin, "Peasant Wars Against the Exploiters in the Middle Ages," *Prepodavaniye v Shkole* (Teaching in the Schools), no. 3, 1952; and G. M. Linko, *et al.*, "On a Teaching Theme: Peasant War in China for the Eighth Grade," *Propodavaniye v Shkole*, no. 1, 1953.

Soviet historiography touches on most of the questions regarding the communist evaluation of the struggles of the peasant class which we will examine in our analysis of Chinese communist views. However, Chinese communist historiography of the peasant wars has played a far greater role in the intellectual life of the Chinese nation after 1949 than has been the case in the Soviet Union, first of all because of the pertinence and availability of the materials. The Chinese have records of this type of phenomenon for a period of over two thousand years, and, furthermore, connections between this "revolutionary tradition" and the Chinese revolution seem much closer than the relation of the Russian peasant revolts to Lenin. It would not be too much to say that the Chinese communist treatment of the Chinese peasant revolts has played much the same role that the treatment of the European labor movement has played in Soviet historiography. The Chinese peasant movements were the most striking forerunners of Chinese communism, in the same way that the labor movement of the nineteenth century in the West preceded the rise of Bolshevism. Moreover, China not only lacked a significant labor movement in modern times which could serve as the genesis of the communist movement, but also had not had a revolutionary bourgeois period as in Europe. The peasants therefore were the only candidates for a revolutionary working class in the long history of China.

A second reason for the predominant concern of Chinese communist historiography with the historical peasant wars is the tremendous emphasis the Party places on the inculcation of the concept of struggle. The study of the peasant movements provides the most obvious historical documentation for this concept.

Nevertheless, the development of the historiography of the Chinese peasant wars really gained momentum only during the 'forties, and particularly after 1949. This of course reflected the shift from nationalist goals of the war period to an increasing stress on social revolution. Moreover, before the time when communist victory appeared imminent, leading Marxist historians were more concerned with demonstrating the progression of history toward communism than with demonstrating the historical existence of the class struggle. As the prospects of communist victory began to improve, increasing attention was directed toward establishing the revolutionary tradition of the Chinese communists. This was a natural development reflecting the needs of the Party, first to establish faith in the future and then to secure its own legitimacy.

Chinese historians who did deal with the peasant wars before 1949 were concerned primarily with researching and imparting factual information rather than with using the history of the peasant wars as ammunition for the theory of the class struggle. This was partly a reflection of relative freedom from Party dictation, but more so of the preoccupation with other issues such as the problem of the nature of Chinese society. Other reasons for the reluctance of Marxist historians to write histories of the peasant revolts before 1949 may have been an awareness of the theoretical problems involved and a shortage or unavailability of source materials. During 1923–27 and 1937–45 the united front with the Nationalists dictated against undue stress on the class struggle, while at other times the KMT forbade discussion of such subjects as class war.[85]

In any case, most senior Chinese Marxists seemed to prefer to write about ruling-class subjects rather than about lower-class rebels. The historical themes of Kuo Mo-jo, for instance, concern traditional heroes, the "emperors, ministers, and generals" of Chinese history. Aside from a 1928 poem[86] and a pamphlet on Li Tzu-ch'eng's capture of Peking in 1644,[87] Kuo did not discuss the peasant revolts until 1959 and then obviously in response to an editor's demand.[88] Other senior

[85] See Wang Yü-ch'uan, "The Development of Modern Social Science in China," *Pacific Affairs*, vol. 2, no. 3, 1938, pp. 358 ff.

[86] See *Kuo Mo-jo Hsuan-chi* (Selected Writings) (Peking: K'ai-ming Shu-tien, 1951), vol. 1, pp. 103 ff.

[87] Kuo Mo-jo, *Chia-shen-nien San-pai-nien-chi* (Commemoration of the 300th Anniversary of Chia-shen Year) (Peking: Jen-min Ch'u-pan She, 1954), reprint of 1944 article.

[88] Kuo Mo-jo, "The Historical Processes of the Chinese Peasant Revolts," *SSP*, pp. 48–54.

Marxist historians, such as Fan Wen-lan, Lü Chen-yü, and Chien Po-tsan, have all tended to treat the peasant wars with caution. The impression is strong that these men, being primarily theorists, were before 1949, and are still, closer to the classical Marxist view of the conservatism of the peasantry and the primacy of economics over the class struggle. By contrast, the more revolutionary Chinese Party leaders always gave great attention to the peasants and their class struggle. Like the Bolsheviks, they could put the needs of the revolution ahead of theoretical consistency, both with respect to the evaluation of the peasantry and the primacy of the class struggle.[89]

The reticence before 1949 of the older Chinese historians to speak of class war in Chinese history becomes clear in a perusal of historical literature of the period. The first article on peasant movements in Chinese history listed in Chinese communist bibliography of modern periodical literature[90] was published in 1919. Several others date from the 'twenties, and by the 'thirties there were several score, but most of these were written by noncommunist historians. Furthermore, the great majority were simple narrative accounts rather than theoretical discussions of a particular uprising. Among the better-known historians who described specific peasant revolts before 1949, including Lo Erh-kang, Wu Han, Li Wen-chih, and even T'ao Hsi-sheng, this straightforward narration is particularly evident. Only occasionally

[89] Actually, senior communist historians like to claim a long-standing concern for preaching the gospel of class struggle. Thus, a leading historian listed studies of the peasant revolts in second place among the efforts of Chinese Marxist historians before 1949. These were (1) to prove that Marxism applied not only to the West but to China, which went through a similar historical progression, (2) to stress the history of the masses and of peasant revolts, (3) to refute the view that feudalism ended in the Chou dynasty and that modern China was already capitalist, (4) to reveal the content of imperialist aggression against China, and (5) to periodize modern Chinese history after the Opium War. In fact, however, the related first and third themes received by far the most attention before 1949. Liu Ta-nien, *op. cit.*, *KMJP*, July 22, 1953.

[90] *Chung-kuo Shih-hsueh Lun-wen So-yin* (Index of Articles on Chinese Historical Studies) Peking: K'o-hsueh Ch'u-pan She, 1957, 2 vols.), vol. 1, pp. 227–29.

does one read that the revolt under consideration was an example of class struggle.[91]

Most important, in the 1930s the few works which did generalize about peasant movements in Chinese history were written not by the "orthodox" Marxists but by the "false" Marxists who took what later were condemned as "Trotskyist" views. At least three of the four best-known books and many of the general articles written on the subject before the Sino-Japanese War argued that the cause of the many peasant revolts in Chinese history was the position of commercial capital in China. The proponents of this interpretation held that the rise of commerce in the later Chou dynasty led to decisive increases in land concentration and usury which in turn set off peasant wars from the Ch'in dynasty onward.[92]

They based their arguments on classical Marxist descriptions of the effect of the introduction of a money economy into a natural self-sufficient economy. Engels wrote that this economic development, which was believed to have taken place in China in late Chou times, was "always associated with a more or less rapid revolutionization of the former mode of distribution . . . [with] the inequality of distribution among the individuals and therefore the antagonism between rich and poor becoming more pronounced." [93] The result was a great increase in vagabondage and the possibilities of class warfare.[94] For proponents of the theory that traditional China was a "merchant capitalist society," the great

---

[91] Among these were Hsieh Kuo-chen's 1925 article on revolts of some household servants or "slaves" in the late Ming. See "Investigation of a Ming Slave Revolt," in Hsieh Kuo-chen, *Ming-Ch'ing chih chi Tang-she Yun-tung K'ao* (Investigations of Political Society Movements of the Ming and Ch'ing Period) (Shanghai: Shang-wu Yin-shu Kuan, 1934), p. 276; and Chang Yin-lin's 1937 study of a Sung rebellion, "The Revolt of Wang Hsiao-po and Li Hsun in Szechwan, 993–5: An Unsuccessful Communist Movement," *Ch'ing-hua Hsueh-pao* (Tsing Hua Journal), vol. 12, no. 2, 1937, p. 315. Neither Hsieh or Chang was a communist at the time, although their approach in these articles was close to the prevailing interpretation.

[92] Cf. the discussion of the Asiatic mode of production and the nature of ancient Chinese society in Chapter 2.

[93] Engels, *Anti-Duhring*, p. 168.

[94] See Marx and Engels, *The German Ideology*, p. 51.

increase in the exploitation of the peasants in the first millennium before Christ was a perfect explanation for the commencement of large-scale peasant movements from the Ch'in onward.

The influence of the theory of commercial capitalism is especially evident in the books published before 1949. A 1928 book by an important early communist, Ch'en Kung-po, who soon broke with the Party and received a Master's degree at Columbia University, New York, in 1924, seems to have been the first by a Chinese Marxist to deal specifically with the peasant revolts.[95] He stressed economic determinism and the rise of commercial capitalism and paid little attention to any theoretical analysis of the class struggle. Two books published in 1933 by Ts'ai Hsueh-ts'un and Hsueh Nung-shan are much more specific in their elaboration of the connections between the peasant movements and commercial capitalism. Ts'ai sought to refute the views of Kuo Mo-jo and others that although the reforms of Shang Yang and Ch'in Shih Huang-ti (fourth and third centuries B.C.) abolished feudalism in name, feudalism in its economic sense continued to exist. If so, he argued, and if one ignored the rise of merchant capitalism during the Chan Kuo period, then there was no way to understand the peasant wars which occurred from the Ch'in onward.[96]

Similarly, Hsueh Nung-shan stated that it was superficial simply to assert that the uninterrupted progress and development of the Chinese peasant wars was a necessary product of feudal economy and government and landlord exploitation, since this does not raise the heart of the problem, which was why Chinese peasant wars began earlier and occurred with greater frequency and intensity than elsewhere. This, Hsueh said, was due to the "early prevalence of commercial capital" manifested in usury and unfair market exchanges extorted

[95] Ch'en Kung-po, *Chung-kuo Li-shih-shang te Ke-ming* (Revolutions in Chinese History) (Shanghai: Fu-tan Shu-tien, 1928). At the time Ch'en was associated with noncommunist leftist groups.

[96] Ts'ai Hsueh-ts'un, *Chung-kuo Li-shih-shang te Nung-min Chan-cheng* (The Peasant Wars in Chinese History) (Shanghai: Ya-tung Shu-tien, 1933).

by the merchants and, subsequently, in increased land concentration. Hsueh concluded that it is not logical to say that the peasant revolts are a product of a simple natural economy (feudalism). Rather, their cause lay in the undermining of the natural economy by the influences of commercial capitalism.[97] Many anti-communist historians and politicians of the early 1930s also subscribed to the "Trotskyist" explanation of Chinese social history. Thus, an apparent sympathizer with the "left" Kuomintang used this Marxist theory to advocate attention to Sun Yat-sen's principle of "people's livelihood." Otherwise, he warned, there would be another peasant war led by the "communist bandits." [98] Another writer subscribed to the theory of commercial capitalism, which he traced back to Karl Radek's theories of Chinese history.[99] Although he believed that this theory provided a basic explanation for the Chinese peasant wars, he argued that in fact the peasant wars were secondary in importance to conflicts within the government class and that therefore greatest attention should be paid to the affairs of the governing classes.[100] The chief editor of the largest single collection of articles and documents on modern Chinese social history published during

[97] Hsueh Nung-shan, *Chung-kuo Nung-min Chan-cheng chih Shih te Yen-chiu* (Study of the History of Chinese Peasant Wars) (Shanghai: Shen-chou Kuo-kuang She, 1933, 2 vols.), vol. 1, p. 1. I have been unable to see a fourth book of this period on the subject, which is, Fan Ti-jui, *Chung-kuo Ku-tai Nung-min Yun-tung* (Peasant Movements in Ancient China) (Shanghai, 1938).

[98] Wang Li-ching, "Analysis of the Peasant Wars in Chinese History and the Road for the Solution of the Peasant Problem," *Chung-kuo Ching-chi* (Chinese Economy), vol. 1, no. 1, April 1933.

[99] Karl Radek, who was associated with Trotsky's faction, wrote voluminously on problems of contemporary China when he was director of Sun Yat-sen University in Moscow, 1923–27. Pokrovsky and most communist historians of the 1920s emphasized the role of commercial capitalism in pre-modern societies. G. Safarov's 1928 book, the first on the class struggle in Chinese history, and other works also followed a similar line of argument.

[100] Liang Yuan-tung, "The Forms of Struggle in Chinese History," *Shih Ti Shih* (Historical and Geographical Knowledge), vol. 5, no. 15, 1936; abstracted in *Shih-ti She-hui Lun-wen Chai-yao Yueh-k'an* (Abstract Monthly of Articles on History, Geography and Sociology), vol. 2, no. 9, p. 3. See also T'ao Hsi-sheng, *Chung-kuo She-hui yü, Chung-kuo Ke-ming* (Chinese Society and Revolution) (Shanghai: Hsin Sheng-ming Shu-chü, 1929), preface.

the Republican period also was an exponent of the theory of commercial capitalism in China.[101] It should be noted that neither Marx nor such Chinese "Trotskyists" as T'ao Hsisheng denied that the existence of "merchant capitalism" precluded a "feudal mode of production." Furthermore, unlike the theory of Oriental society, the theory of commercial capitalism stressed the role of the class struggle. However, it certainly complicated "feudal economic relations," and accordingly, orthodox "Stalinists" decided to discourage further discussion of the theory of commercial capitalism in China after the mid-1930s.

Although all the theories holding that traditional China was dominated by a pre-capitalist or Asiatic mode of production rather than by feudalism were condemned,[102] their arguments have continued to influence the historiography of the peasant wars. This is not surprising, since they in fact account for much in the history of Chinese society that is not explainable in terms of "feudalism."

General histories by more orthodox Marxists published before 1949 describe the class struggle, but only as one of many historical factors. In a book published in 1937, Teng T'o, editor of *Jen-min Jih-pao* from 1953 to 1958 and one of the foremost victims of the purges of 1966, described the rebellions more as products of natural disasters rather than of class struggle.[103] In the 1941 edition of *Chung-kuo T'ung-shih*

[101] Li Chi (chief ed.) for Chung-kuo Li-shih Yen-chiu She, *Chung-kuo Nei-luan Wai-huo Li-shih Ts'ung-shu* (Collected Books on the History of China's Internal Disruptions and Foreign Disasters) (Shanghai: Shen-chou Kuo-kuang She, 1936–47, 36 vols.). See Kwok, *op. cit.*, pp. 162–68, for discussion of other writings of the type in the 1930s.

[102] Hence, Chao Li-sheng, the first prominent student of the peasant wars to be branded a rightist under the new regime, also devoted a large place to the influences of commercial capitalism. See Chao Li-sheng and Kao Chao-yi, *Chung-kuo Nung-min Chan-cheng Shih Lun-wen Chi* (Collected Articles on Chinese Peasant Wars) (Shanghai: Hsin Chih-shih Ch'u-pan She, 1955), p. 13. Despite criticisms of these theories, there are increasing indications that the Chinese communists are increasingly discussing the content, if not the name, of the various theories of Oriental society. See especially Chapter 9.

[103] Teng Yun-t'e (Teng T'o), *Chung-kuo Chiu-huang Shih* (History of Chinese Disaster Relief) (Shanghai: Shang-yin Yin-shu Kuan, 1937), p. 144. According to Lü Chen-yü (*Shih Lun Chi*, p. 37, note 2), Teng

Chien-pien (A Simple General History of China) the highest-ranking communist among the historians, Fan Wenlan, stressed the fact that the old histories neglected the masses, while he, on the contrary, would show the "iniquities of the governing class," but he is still relatively cautious in extolling the peasants. In his 1954 preface to the revised edition of this work (page 3), he is far more emphatic about the role of class struggle and explains that the theory of the class struggle is the key to historical research, though at the same time he warns against oversimplification.[104]

Other senior Marxist historians such as Lü Chen-yü, Chien Po-tsan, and others also devote more space and emphasis to peasant revolts in revised and expanded versions published after 1949, but they, more than the post-liberation generation of historians, continue to treat these movements in the perspective of other developments in Chinese history. In the "cultural revolution" of the mid-1960s, Chien especially was attacked for just this "neglect of the people's history." [105] The same more cautious approach in the use of the concept of the class struggle was found before 1949 even in those histories intended for popular consumption.[106]

The older communist historians themselves clearly regard discussions of peasant wars as a relatively new subject. Lü

---

was a defender of "orthodox Marxism" in the 1930s, but became a leading victim of the "cultural revolution" of 1966. Critics attacked Teng's alleged slanders of the peasant rebellions in this book. See *SCMM* 541, citing *CKCN*, June 16, 1966.

[104] According to Albert Feuerwerker and S. Cheng, *Chinese Communist Studies of Modern Chinese History* (Cambridge: East Asian Research Center, Harvard University, 1961), p. 8. Chou Ku-ch'eng, in the 1939 edition of his *Chung-kuo T'ung-shih* (General History of China, page 2), spoke of Marx's theory that "history was the history of the class struggle . . . as only a view of history" and not "the substance of history." In his 1955 edition this is significantly changed to read, "history in the process of [class] struggle."

[105] E.g., see Ch'i Pen-yü *et al.*, "Comrade Chien Po-tsan's Historical Stand Must be Criticized," *JMJP*, March 25, 1966, p. 5; and "Comrade Chien Po-tsan's Anti-Marxist Historical Viewpoint," *JMJP*, April 23, 1966, pp. 5 and 6.

[106] E.g., Ching Chih, *Chung-kuo Li-shih* (Chinese History) (Shanghai: Tu-shu Sheng-huo, 1939); Yin Ch'i-min, Fan Wen-lan, *et al.*, "Lectures on Chinese History," serialized in *Ch'ün Chung* (Masses) (Chungking, May 30, 1944).

Chen-yü wrote in the preface (page 3) to the 1961 reprint of his *Chung-kuo She-hui Shih Chu Wen-t'i* (Problems of Chinese Society) that, in addition to the old problems of the Asiatic mode of production and of periodization which had been discussed in the 1940 edition of the book, there were now "new problems" including the nature and role of the Chinese peasant wars.

Kuo Mo-jo, for many years the Director of the Chinese Academy of Sciences, wrote in 1945 that after thirty years' work on various problems relating to the laws of development of Chinese society, historians were "beginning to study" peasant revolts. Even this study was considered only as a key to one of the old problems, the question of why China's feudal society lasted for two thousand years instead of a few hundred as in Europe. "Why," he asked, "were there so many peasant revolts . . . and why did they always lose, or, if they won, why were they unable to change the social structure?" [107]

Kuo Mo-jo revealed in this article all too clearly the lingering mistrust of the role of peasant wars in Chinese history among the older Chinese Marxist historians. He wrote that one of the reasons Chinese society stagnated for so long was that the "uninterrupted wars [which clearly would include peasant unrest] killed the peasantry by the hundreds of thousands causing production to cease." [108] This line of reasoning is strikingly similar to the statements of anti-communist historians that Chinese history advanced only in times of peace, and similar statements were repeatedly criticized after 1949 when voiced by historians of lesser stature than Kuo.

Kuo's comment also contrasts strongly with Mao's statement, made six years earlier, that the peasant wars "alone formed the real motive force of historical development in China's feudal society" and were the "glorious revolutionary tradition and splendid historical heritage" of the Chinese people. [109] Such effusive statements about the "class struggle of the peasants" are found in the works of non-Party histori-

[107] Kuo Mo-jo, "Historical Studies in War-Time China," VI, vols. 5–6, 1945, p. 184.
[108] *Ibid.*, p. 185.
[109] "The Chinese Revolution and the CCP," *SWMTT*, vol. 3, pp. 74 and 76.

ans only when it became clear which way the political tide was moving.

More strictly propagandistic treatments of the Chinese peasant movements began to appear on the eve of the communist triumph.[110] In the preface to one such book by Sung Yang, Fan Wen-lan indicated what was to come. He warned that unless Chinese intellectuals recognized the place of the masses, there would be no place for them in the "new China":

> For us intellectuals, finding who were the masters of history is of first importance. Because when one discovers the masters of history, he also finds the masters of present society. Once we recognize this and always honestly serve [the masses], then and only then can the intellectuals find their bright and happy future.[111]

During these years Mao kept up with historical work to some extent, no doubt both from his well-known love of history and because of his belief in its theoretical importance. His interest in and attitude toward peasant rebels in history is revealed in an interesting aside by Wu Han, the former Vice Mayor of Peking, attacks on whom began the "Great Cultural Revolution" in late 1965.[112] Before 1949 Wu was the biographer of one of the two peasant rebels before Mao who were able to succeed to the throne of China. Wu wrote that Mao called him over one night (apparently about 1948) to criticize his treatment of a Yuan dynasty rebel, P'eng Ying-yü. Mao reputedly felt that such a steadfast fighter of the peasant class would not have sold out to the government as Wu had implied in his first consideration of the evidence. Wu states that, on looking into the sources further, he found Mao's assumption to be correct, since P'eng had been killed by gov-

---

[110] E.g., Pai T'ao, *Chung-kuo Nung-min Ch'i-yi te Ku-shih* (Stories of Chinese Peasant Revolts) (Harbin: Kuang-hua Shu-tien, 1949).

[111] Fan Wen-lan, preface to Sung Yang, *Chung-kuo Nung-min Keming Yun-tung Shih-hua* (Talks on the History of Chinese Peasant Revolutionary Movements) (Tientsin: Tu-che Shu-tien, 1949).

[112] See Chapter 10.

ernment forces some years later.[113] Whether true in all details or not, this story shows Mao's view of the way the Chinese peasant wars should be handled: that is, that they should be exemplars of the theories of class loyalty and class struggle. According to another report of one of Mao's infrequent interviews from this period, he also thought of himself as the leader of "the latest—and the last—of the many peasant revolutions that run through . . . Chinese history. He spoke with intimate knowledge and with compassion of the revolts." [114]

Before 1949, although Mao and other Party leaders stressed both the contemporary and the historical role of the Chinese peasantry, historians generally chose to concentrate on the theoretical implications of the nature and development of Chinese society. Certainly the Marxist historiography of the 1930s and 1940s represented a drastic change from traditional concepts, but the change was from a concern with the personal attributes of the rulers to attention to the economic attributes of the society. After 1949 there was a return to a consideration of personal attributes, but this time to the characteristics of "the people." This change reflected political needs. It was necessary to find a more positive historical role for the masses which the government claimed to represent and from which the Party claimed to have emerged.

[113] Wu Han *et al.*, *Tsen-yang Kai-tsao* (How to Reform) (Hong Kong: Ho-tso Shu-tien, 1950), pp. 50–52.

[114] Mark Gayn, "Peking Has a Yenan Complex," *New York Times Magazine*, January 30, 1966.

PART TWO

Communist Analysis of the Chinese Peasant Rebellions

CHAPTER FIVE

Causation, Leadership, and Organization

EMPHASIS on the class struggle and on the historical role of the peasant class greatly accelerated after 1949, although for the first decade of communist rule most studies were devoted to a factual study of some one or group of the twenty-odd major peasant revolts mentioned above[1] and described in the appendix. Then from about 1958, following intensified ideological debate, most publications have concentrated on general theoretical problems rather than on factual questions in the interpretation of the peasant movements.[2] These theoretical discussions reveal very clearly at least a three-way split within Chinese communist interpretations of the peasant movements, mirroring the contradictory elements which have existed throughout the Marxist historiography of

[1] See Chapter 4.

[2] According to the bibliography appended to SSP, 272 of 425 articles published on the subject of the peasant wars between 1949 and mid-1961 were devoted to studies of specific revolts. However, general theoretical discussions far outnumbered specific studies, 52 to 34 in 1960 and 59 to 12 in the first six months of 1961. This ratio increased further in the mid-1960s. The greater stress on the "glorious revolutionary tradition" of the Chinese people is clearly related to growing Chinese nationalism and Peking's advocacy of peasant-based revolution.

the problem. They similarly reveal the developing emphasis
from Marx to Lenin to Mao to the present generation of
Chinese theorists, toward more emphasis on struggle in general and on the class struggle of the peasantry in particular.

The majority of mainland historians stress the revolutionary consciousness and potential of the peasants in history
much as Mao stressed the role of the peasantry in the contemporary revolution. This majority represents the first of
three schools of opinion and writes the most enthusiastic interpretations of the history of the peasant wars. At the
"right" extreme a small group of predominantly senior historians, most of whom were denounced in the "Great Proletarian Cultural Revolution" of the mid-1960s, repeat warnings
from classical Marxism about the dangers of this "fairly universal leftist tendency" to "irresponsibly exaggerate" the
"subjective" revolutionary consciousness and the "objective"
role of the peasant masses.[3] Finally, there is a middle group
of Chinese historians who seek to balance the revolutionary
and reactionary sides of the "dual nature" of the peasantry in
their presentations.

The problems in the interpretations of the history of the
peasant movements, which have preoccupied the above-mentioned groups of writers on the subject, include the following,
in order of their presentation: (1) the background and causation of the frequent periods of rural unrest in Chinese history;
(2) the roles played by the rebel leaders in relation to the
masses of their followers and the social composition of the
movements; (3) the organizations and government established (in Chapter 5); (4) the programs, goals, and ideology
of the rebels (in Chapter 6); (5) their relations with religious
and secret societies, their ideological consciousness and attitudes toward the emperor (in Chapter 7); (6) the "function" or effects of the rebellions, and (7) their evolution and
development from more spontaneous to more organized forms
of protest (in Chapter 8); (8) the nature of the "anti-feud-
alism" of the Chinese peasant movements, (9) the causes of
their failure, and (10) those features which are held to dis-

[3] See Chapter 10.

tinguish the Chinese peasant movements from similar phenomena in other countries (in Chapter 9). Finally, the important role these discussions play in the ideological education of the Chinese people is analyzed in Chapter 10.

THEORIES EXPLAINING THE
CAUSATION OF THE
PEASANT REVOLTS

1. ECONOMIC (FLOODS, LAND COND.)
2. MORAL (CONDUCT OF RULER)
3. CLASS

Concern with the problem of the causes of social unrest is as old as Chinese philosophy itself. The first and still a popular theory of causation linked mass discontent with economic want. Chinese philosophers and statesmen from the middle of the first millennium before Christ stressed the necessity of economic well-being for the maintenance of order.[4] Parallel to this theory of economic causation, however, the idea that natural and social misfortune was somehow caused by the conduct of rulers also appeared very early in Chinese thought. This theory of "moral causation" became dominant after the overthrow of the Ch'in by 206 B.C. appeared to confirm its reasoning[5] and was summarized in the common saying "the

---

[4] Thus, Mencius (III, 3, translated in Legge, *The Four Books*, p. 611), wrote that "if they [the people] have a certain livelihood, they will have a fixed heart," while Han Fei specifically stated that disorder was due to want and deprivation (see Lin Mou-sheng, *Men and Ideas*, p. 113). This belief that the cause of social unrest was to be found in economic shortages was codified in such expressions as "the ancients said 'when starvation and cold arrive, even [sage rulers like] Yao and Shun would not be able to prevent the growth of banditry in the country.'" Cited in Yang Lien-sheng, *Studies in Chinese Institutional History* (Cambridge: Harvard University Press, 1963), p. 183.

[5] Hence, Chia Yi, Ssu-ma Ch'ien, Tung Chung-shu, and other influential Han thinkers blamed the inhumanity of Ch'in rule for its downfall. Tung Chung-shu, for instance, sought to show that the decisive increases in the abuses of the rich together with government pressures and misrule were the causes of the unrest of the Ch'in and early Han. See de Bary, *et al.* (eds.), *Sources of the Chinese Tradition*, p. 233. Wang Mang, traditionally the second victim in Imperial times of the rule that misgovernment engenders its own fall, is alleged to have admitted that natural disasters and deprivation alone were insufficient

officials force the people to rebel" (*kuan pi min fan*). An Imperial decree of 1799 put the case in extreme terms: "Revolts are due solely to the insatiable avarice of the local officials who suck the peasants dry." [6] Most statements of the causes of social unrest also mentioned economic factors—several thousand natural disasters have been noted in the long history of Imperial China[7]—but these, too, implicated the government because the emperor was supposed to mediate between heaven and earth.

Considerable evidence supports the theories of both economic and moral causation,[8] and most modern noncommunist historians combine the two, stressing one or the other factor.[9]

sort of
dumb
or
reductio?

---

explanations for the widespread rebellions of his reign. See H. H. Dubs's translation of Pan Ku's *History of the Former Han Dynasty*, vol. 3, p. 418.

[6] Cited in Wang Yü-ch'uan, 'The Rise of Land Tax and the Fall of Dynasties in Chinese History," *Pacific Affairs*, vol. 9, 1936, p. 219.

[7] Even the communist writer Teng Yun-t'e (Teng T'o), who counted 1,035 droughts and 1,037 floods in the period from 206 B.C. to 1936, concluded that all peasant revolts were "forced by natural disasters and years of famine." See his *Chung-kuo Chiu-huang Shih*, p. 144. Many other independent scholars of the Republican period followed this line of reasoning and would have agreed with Hsiao Yi-shan that the "source of all rebellion" lay in the population–landsqueeze cycle. See Hsiao Yi-shan, *Ch'ing-tai T'ung-shih* (General History of the Ch'ing Period) (Taipei: Shang-wu Yin-shu Kuan, 1963, 5 vols.), vol. 3, pp. 35–36. See also Hsiao Kung-ch'uan, *op. cit.*, p. 200. Chalmers Johnson (*Peasant Nationalism and Communist Power* [Stanford: Stanford University Press, 1962], pp. 15–17) and others, on the other hand, deny that poverty in the village was the decisive factor in Chinese rebellions.

[8] One leading Western historian, Teng Ssu-yü, emphasizes misgovernment and political corruption as the "fundamental cause" of rebellion. See Teng Ssu-yü, *New Light on the History of the Taiping Rebellion* (Cambridge: Harvard University Press, 1950), p. 37. Also Teng Ssu-yü, "A Political Interpretation of Chinese Rebellions," *Tsing Hua Journal of Chinese Studies*, September 1958.

[9] Many stress social and economic factors, especially the relationship of population to land, conditions of land ownership, and the effects of natural disasters. Virtually all modern noncommunist scholars mention a combination of these causes, often expressed in the formula "natural disasters plus government exploitation equals peasant rebellion." See T'ao Hsi-sheng as cited by Wang Li-ching in *Chung-kuo Ching-chi*, vol. 1, no. 1, April 1933, p. 2. Vincent Shih (in "Some Red Chinese Rebel Ideologies," *T'oung Pao*, no. 44, 1956, pp. 170 and 206) speaks of the "usual reasons for rebellious activities such as government corrup-

To these theories of causation, communist historians characteristically have added emphasis on the social and class manifestations of the economic structure. In comparison with the Western stress on the causative role of ideas, the traditional Chinese concept that social unrest was due to economic want and misgovernment accorded fairly well with Marxist theories of causation, although the starting points of the two of course were fundamentally different. Consequently, mainland historians borrow more heavily from traditional theories in discussing causation than in discussing other problems in the history of the peasant movements.

Engels gave perhaps the clearest explanation of the classical Marxist theory that changes in the economy are the ultimate cause of human action:

> In every society which has appeared in history, the manner in which wealth is distributed and society divided into classes or orders is dependent upon what is produced, how it is produced, and how the products are exchanged. From this point of view the final causes of all social changes and political revolutions are to be sought, not in man's better insight into eternal truth and justice, but in changes in the modes of production and exchange. They are to be sought not in the philosophy but in the economics of each particular epoch.[10]

In fact, in Chinese communist more than in Soviet and far more than in nineteenth-century Marxist writings, "man's better insight" often does replace economic factors as the "final cause of social change." Mao insisted that the ideas of Marxism-Leninism played a causal role in the Chinese revolution only because "China's social conditions called for it," [11] but

---

tion, land concentration, and natural calamities" and wrote that "with these factors, economic, political, and natural combined, rebellions would be a matter of course." See also Hsiao Kung-ch'uan, *op. cit.*, pp. 467–71.

[10] Engels, "Socialism, Utopian and Scientific," *MESW*, vol. 2, p. 136. See also Engels, *The Peasant War in Germany*, pp. 38 ff. At times, however, Engels assigns the decisive role to ideas in the organization of revolt. E.g., see *ibid.*, p. 53.

[11] Mao Tse-tung, "The Bankruptcy of the Idealist Conception of History," *SWMTT* (Peking ed.), vol. 4, p. 457.

the perception of exploitation itself rather than an emphasis on its economic and social roots has dominated Chinese communist ideology since the 1930s and 1940s. This stress on the human side of the equation, or on "voluntarism," has been abetted by voluminous traditional documentation of the abuses of "greedy officials" and the plight of the poor. A slight twist in the interpretation of the sources, and the "right of revolt" changes from a traditional warning to the government to a communist description of the power of "people's war." As a senior historian explained the outbreak of the first large-scale Chinese peasant movement, "the people's patience with tyrannical government is limited; past a certain point and no matter who is emperor, everyone will want to join in a life and death struggle against him." [12]

Besides this stress on popular initiative, mainland historians try to show that the causes of revolt operated along class lines: the "landlord class," because it controlled the economic base of the society, extorted surplus value from the labors of the peasantry, which in turn took up arms against this state of affairs. In Mao's words, "The ruthless economic exploitation and political oppression of the peasantry by the landlord class forced the peasants to rise repeatedly in revolt against its rule." [13] The peasants were also much more subject to natural disaster and material hardship than the wealthier landlords. In the communist scheme, not only was the landlord-controlled government to blame for social unrest —this could be the case also in traditional historiography— but misgovernment by the landlord class was a manifestation of the economic system itself and not merely of a decline of morality as in the Confucian system. The influence of Confucian "moral determinism" appears to reinforce Marxist "economic determinism" in the great Chinese communist stress on human exploitation as a cause of revolt.

The exact nature of "feudal exploitation" in China is trou-

[12] Chien Po-tsan, *Chung-kuo Shih Lun-chi* (Collected Essays on Chinese History) (Shanghai: Kuo-chi Wen-hua Fu-wu She, 1947), vol. 2, p. 153.
[13] "The Chinese Revolution and the CCP," *SWMTT*, vol. 3, p. 75.

blesome. In the 1930s, many Marxist-oriented writers placed great stress on the iniquities of what was termed "commercial capitalism." They described the development of an economy with extensive trade in agricultural products and handicrafts and the growth of a merchant class during the later Chou. According to this thesis, the growing power and wealth of the trading class, which controlled the sale and purchase of crops and products, led to a growing exploitation of the peasants, who were increasingly forced into debt at exorbitant interest and eventually had to abandon their land to become tenants or migrants. Merchants and successful land-owners, who were closely allied economically, were able to put much of their capital into acquiring new land. The peasants were increasingly forced off the land by an exploiting alliance of landlords, merchants, and usurers. These economic developments, together with the parallel political formation of an "absolute despotism" based on large-scale public works, were said to explain the frequency of the Chinese peasant wars and also why the first large-scale revolts broke out in 209 B.C.[14]

While these early Marxist theories explaining the causation of the Chinese peasant wars were condemned as Trotskyist variations of the theory of a special type of "Oriental society," [15] they exerted a profound influence on communist historiography. Most theoretical discussions of the peasant movements in the 1930s took this approach, and despite claims of success in the "struggle for the purity of Marxism," these arguments often are still presented in content if not in name. For instance, according to Chao Li-sheng, one of the earliest "post-liberation" specialists on the peasant wars, the persistence of communal remnants in classical times prevented the full development of slavery, while the later development of commerce, usury, and free alienation of land

[14] For an early statement of this theory see T'ao Hsi-sheng, *Chungkuo She-hui Hsien-hsiang Shih-ling* (Collected Miscellany on Chinese Social Phenomena) (Shanghai: Hsin Sheng-ming Shu-chü, 1931), pp. 205–18.
[15] They were condemned officially by the early 1930s in the Soviet Union and by the mid-1930s in China. For further discussion of the theories of Oriental society, and commercial capitalism, see Chapter 4.

formed the basis for an "absolutist Imperial government" quite different from its Western counterparts. Thus, while maintaining that China like other countries passed through the normal stages of production, Chao insists that those early economic and political developments explained the "especially difficult economic position and the especially oppressed political position of the Chinese peasantry and artisans." [16] He summed it up this way:

> The construction of an absolutist political superstructure on the basis of communal remnants increased the economic and political liabilities of the peasants and artisans, and the combination of feudal land relations with commercial and high-interest capital intensified the recurring bankruptcy of the peasants and artisans. In our view this was the most basic characteristic of old Chinese class society.[17]

While Chao himself was later condemned as a "rightist," the similarity of his arguments to the old theories of a special Asiatic mode was not one of the major accusations brought against him. Numerous other historians advance similar arguments, though seldom so explicitly.[18] One author wrote that the existence of a centralized despotism from the Ch'in on-

---

[16] Chao Li-sheng and Kao Chao-yi, *Chung-kuo Nung-min Chan-sheng Shih Lun-wen Chi,* p. 12. *Kao Chao-yi* is the wife of Chao Li-sheng.

[17] *Ibid.,* p. 14. Sun Tso-min, a student of Chao Li-sheng's and the most prolific writer on the subject of the peasant movements in the late 'fifties, follows this line of reasoning and argues that communal remnants and centralized despotism explained the slow development of Chinese feudalism. See Sun Tso-min, *Chung-kuo Nung-min Chan-cheng Wen-t'i T'an-su* (An Investigation into Problems of Chinese Peasant Wars) (Shanghai: Hsin Chih-shih Ch'u-pan She, 1956), preface.

[18] E.g., "Report on Kuangtung Historical Conference," *SCMP* 2514, citing *KMJP,* May 19, 1961; see also *SSP,* p. 503. A recent volume on the peasant wars never mentions "commercial capitalism," stressing rather the development of feudal land relations in classical China. However, the authors do emphasize the presence of communal remnants, which made ancient Chinese society "peculiar" if not "Oriental." See Ch'i Hsia *et al., Ch'in Han Nung-min Chan-cheng Shih* (History of the Peasant Wars of the Ch'in and Han), especially p. 3.

ward explained the fact that China early experienced peasant wars involving the entire country, despite the fact that Marx and Engels and Soviet historians conceived of this possibility only in the decadent last years of feudalism.[19] Numerous other examples also indicate the impatience of mainland historians with strict adherence to orthodox interpretations.[20] It is clear that writers use such terms as "feudalism" in order to present an image but bend the reality to allow for the "peculiarities of China."

The continued influence of various theories of "Asiatic society" is evident in a summary article on the subject of the peasant wars. It lists several varieties of explanation for the great frequency and intensity of Chinese peasant movements: (1) the great number of Chinese peasant revolts was due only to the long duration of feudalism, and therefore the causes in China, as elsewhere, were feudal economic and extra-economic pressures centered primarily on various forms of land rent; (2) the exploitation of the peasantry by the landlords, usurers, and merchants was unusually severe in China because of the early development of a landlord economy and the role of usurers and merchants; (3) the early appearance of a centralized absolutist state with corvée labor imposed throughout the empire; and (4) implicit in the last two arguments, "China was an ancient Oriental type of state with large-scale waterworks and other public-works projects mobilizing several hundred thousand peasants." [21] It is thus

[19] Li T'ien-tso, "The Problem of the Special Features of the Chinese Peasant Wars," *SSP*, p. 215.

[20] For criticisms of attempts to apply Marxist formulas to land-holding in Chinese history, see also "The Form of Land Ownership Under Feudal Society in China," *SCMP* 2479, pp. 21 ff., citing *KMJP*, March 11, 1961.

[21] Shih Shao-pin, "On the Discussion of Problems in the Peasant Revolutionary Wars in Chinese Feudal Society," *SSP*, pp. 502–3. This section of Shih Shao-pin's summary was not included in the version included in *LSYC*, no. 6, 1960, or in *JMJP*, November 11, 1960, presumably because of the open references to China's "peculiarities." Either policy changed between 1960 and the publication of the book in 1962, or, more likely, it was felt that the book published in only five thousand copies would be seen only by specialists, unlike the articles in official publications.

apparent that many mainland historians retain the content, if
not the name, of the theories of an "Asiatic mode" and of
"commercial capitalism" to explain the causes of the Chinese
peasant movements.

More orthodox communist theories of causation stress economic and extra-economic forms of exploitation. These supposedly derive from the basis of feudal relations, "feudal
ownership of the land and incomplete ownership of the producer." [22] Therefore, land rent was the principal form of economic exploitation.[23] Most Chinese historians maintain
that personal extra-economic exploitation in the form of duties owed by the peasant to the landowner or to the state, so
important in European feudalism,[24] were a major factor only
in the early periods of Chinese feudalism. Then the peasant
wars resisted attempts to enslave (*nu-li hua*) or enserf them
(*yi-fu hua*) and all types of dependency relations (*yi-fu
kuan-hsi*). Direct economic causes such as the increasing concentration of land ownership also existed throughout the feudal period but became more acute and the primary cause of
the peasant rebellions after the middle of the T'ang.[25]

Above all, Chinese communist historians argue that dispossession of the peasant from his land because of a recurring
concentration of land in the hands of the wealthy land-

---

[22] Chao Hsi-yen *et al.*, "Criticize Several Mistaken Views on the
Historical Function of the Peasant Wars, in [Sun Tso-min's] Book . . .
T'an-su," SSP, p. 409.

[23] E.g., see Jen Chieh, *Chung-kuo Nung-min Ke-ming Shih-hua*
(Talks on the Chinese Peasant Revolutions) (Peking: T'ung-su Tu-wu
Ch'u-pan She, 1956), p. 2. Wang Shou-yi ("Doubts About the Equal
Land Slogan of the Late Ming Peasant Army," LSYC, no. 2, 1962),
pointed out that at times onerous taxation was a greater burden than the
rent owed by the tenant to the landlord.

[24] Soviet historians argue that the extra-economic feudal obligations
owed by the serfs to the landowner were often more important causes
of discontent in Russian feudalism than direct economic exploitation.
For instance, Pokrovsky was accused of neglecting the extra-economic
duties of the serfs and exaggerating the role of land pressure in describing the causes of Pugachov's rebellion. See M. Nechkina, "The Uprising
of Razin and Pugachov in the Conception of M. N. Pokrovsky," in
Protiv Istoricheskii Kontseptsii M. N. Pokrovskogo, p. 26.

[25] See communist theories on laws of evolution of the peasant movements for further discussion of the changing nature of causation, Chapter 8.

lords and merchants was a fundamental manifestation of the exploitation leading to the peasant wars, and one which persisted so long as the feudal land system existed. As Chao Li-sheng put it, "a law of old Chinese class society . . . was that as the ownership of the land was gradually concentrated [into fewer and fewer hands], the workers of the land became ever more scattered [and had less and less land]." [26] One senior Marxist historian noted that the size and frequency of the Chinese peasant wars were closely connected to the problem of increasing concentration of land ownership, while another wrote that the dispossession of improvident farmers was the main cause of the Taiping revolt. [27] A recent major study of the peasant wars attempts to link such direct economic causation as the land problem with the extra-economic exploitation which was the "basic motif" (*chi-pen hsien-su*) of the Ch'in and Han peasant movements. [28]

Consideration of the land problem has also been important in noncommunist and traditional historiography. [29] Chinese

---

[26] Chao Li-sheng and Kao Chao-yi, *op. cit.,* p. 13.

[27] Chien Po-tsan, *Li-shih Wen-t'i Lun-ts'ung,* p. 113; and Hua Kang, *T'ai-p'ing T'ien-kuo Ke-ming Chan-cheng Shih* (History of the Taiping Revolutionary War) (Shanghai: Hai-yen Shu-tien, 1949), p. 196. Actually, the concentration of land holding was also central to the classical Marxist concept of class struggle. E.g., see Engels, *Anti-Duhring,* p. 168. See also LSYC Pien-chi Pu. (eds.), *Chung-kuo Li-tai T'u-ti Chih-tu Wen-t'i T'ao-lun Chi* (Collected Discussions on the Problem of China's Land System Through the Ages) (Peking: San-lien Shu-tien, 1957).

[28] Ch'i Hsia *et al., Ch'in Han Nung-min Chan-cheng Shih,* p. 13.

[29] According to Sorokin and Zimmerman (*Principles of Rural-Urban Sociology* [New York: Henry Holt, 1929], p. 460), "The main cause of farmer-peasant revolts and radical movements has always centered around land—its possession and distribution. . . ." In China, Tung Chung-shu (130 B.C.) felt that the concentration of land in the hands of great families was ruining the Han peasants. See H. Maspero, "Les Régimes Fonciers en Chine des Origines aux Temps Modernes," *Mélanges posthumes sur les religions et l'histoire de la Chine* (Paris: Etudes historiques, Civilizations du Sud, 1950), vol. 3, p. 157. On the other hand, some influential modern scholars, such as Liang Ch'i-ch'ao and Liang Shu-ming, maintained that the land problem of traditional China was not due to the concentration of ownership but the opposite, to the fragmentation of ownership due to equal inheritance and the lack of an hereditary aristocracy. See R. Scalapino and H. Shiffren, "Early Socialist Currents in the Chinese Revolutionary Movement," *JAS,* May 1959, p. 336; and Lyman Van Slyke, "Liang Sou-ming and the Rural Recon-

communist writers go further and maintain that the recurring concentration of land ownership was the leading manifestation of feudal exploitation and hence the most consistent single economic cause of the Chinese peasant wars. Because the landlord class owned the means of production, the land, they were able to control the primary producer, the peasant, living off his rent and charging exorbitant interest rates. The small peasant owner gradually went into debt and eventually lost his land because of high interest rates, marketing squeeze, and onerous taxes imposed by the merchants, usurers, and officials. Tenants were even worse off and subject to exorbitant rents of half or more of their crops. In recurring periods of Chinese history peasants by the hundreds of thousands fled their land to become "wandering people" (*yu min*) who formed the bulk of recruits for most peasant armies. This conception of Chinese social history is widely held by noncommunist as well as by communist writers. Full and partial tenancy certainly dominated rural labor conditions in many periods of Chinese history. But the formula, in so far as it attempts to speak of the landlord class exploiting the peasant class, obviously ignores the turnover from peasant to landlord and vice versa.[30]

---

struction Movement," *JAS*, August 1959, p. 464. Among other noncommunist scholars, Eberhard believes that it is impossible to prove that land concentration in conjunction with tax evasion by landlords, the heart of the theory of dynastic cycle, caused the overthrow of any dynasty. See W. Eberhard, *Conquerors and Rulers: Social Forces in Medieval China*, p. 54. Bielenstein would agree that evidence of land concentration as the cause of the decline of the former Han is inconclusive. He notes (*The Restoration of the Han Dynasty*, vol. 1, p. 93) the formation of large estates in the former Han but does not consider this development a basic cause of the social unrest at the end of the period. Hsiao Kung-ch'uan believes that the concentration of land ownership in fact decreased in the most depressed localities in modern China due to the losses suffered by the landlords as well as by the peasants. Hsiao, *op. cit.*, pp. 397–98. On the other hand, Fairbank and Reischauer tend to accept the damaging effects on the small farmer of increasing concentration of land ownership. E. O. Reischauer and J. K. Fairbank, *East Asia: The Great Tradition* (Boston: Houghton Mifflin Company, 1960), p. 120. Ho Ping-ti noted that normal institutional and economic factors worked against the small farmer (*Studies in the Population of China, 1368–1953* [Cambridge: Harvard University Press, 1959], p. 222) and accelerated the concentration of land ownership.

[30] E.g., Francis Hsu (*Under the Ancestors' Shadow* [New York:

Some communist historians also have objected to the over-simplification inherent in attributing the causation of rural mass movements merely to landlord monopoly of the land. A recent writer, for instance, argues that the land problem, although always present, was often not the most pressing question. Thus, he maintains that during the late Ming government taxation was a heavier burden on the peasants than rents owed to the land-owners. The peasant preferred to pay rent as a tax-exempt tenant rather than to pay the land tax as a small farmer.[31] Other mainland historians have called for greater attention to the complexity and variety of exploitation in the years preceding each major revolt.[32]

Yet, while the more responsible works have always listed a variety of causes,[33] the dominant theme and distinguishing feature of Chinese communist theories of causation is the assertion that all other factors are secondary to the class antagonisms between the landlord and peasant classes. The well-known historian Lo Erh-kang, following his indoctrination in the early 'fifties, wrote that in his "pre-liberation" detailing of the many causes of the Taiping rebellion he had obscured the "most fundamental cause . . . the struggle of the peasant class against the landlord class." Population pressure, land concentration,[34] the influence of Christianity, the encroach-

---

Columbia University Press, 1948], pp. 4–12, 278) maintains that few Chinese families preserved their wealth beyond three generations but rose and fell as the dynasties did.

[31] Wang Shou-yi *op. cit., LSYC,* no. 2, 1962, pp. 110–12.

[32] Ts'ai Mei-piao ("Discussion of Several Questions in the Debate on the History of the Chinese Peasant Wars," *LSYC,* no. 4, 1961, p. 71) reverts to the view that oppression plus economic want was the basic cause of the peasant wars.

[33] Fan Wen-lan, *Chung-kuo T'ung-shih Chien-pien* (1947 ed.), pp. 604–5, lists special conditions which applied in the northwest in the late Ming, including the flight of landlords with subsequent breakdown of controls in the area.

[34] In 1949 Lo had written that the pressure of population on the land was the greatest single cause of the Taiping rebellion. See Lo Erh-kang, "The Problem of Population Pressure Before the Revolution of the Taiping Heavenly Kingdom," *Chung-kuo She-hui Ching-chi Shih Chi-k'an* (Chinese Social and Economic History Review), vol. 8, no. 1, 1949, pp. 20–80. Available arable land per capita declined from about one-half acre in 1766 to about one-quarter acre in 1850.

ment of imperialism, natural disasters, the collapse of the government, and anti-Manchu feeling were also factors, Lo admitted, but they were isolated causes and secondary to the "decisive cause" of class antagonism.[35] Another historian of the Taipings, maintaining that every governing class presents its own historical view of causation, attempted to refute what he considered the two prevailing bourgeois views of the causes of the Taiping—namely, overpopulation and the influence of Christian ideas. Echoing a statement by Mao,[36] he argues that, since many other peasant revolts occurred in Chinese history when there was relatively little population pressure or religious influence, one cannot claim that these were the basic causes of the Taiping movement. The fundamental cause was class antagonism, born of increased feudal and imperialist oppression. Such factors as land concentration and the role of Christian ideas were only manifestations of this basic contradiction between the governing landlord class and the peasantry.[37]

Chinese communist historians, as most modern historians, discuss many casual factors, but, unlike noncommunist historians, they try to subsume all these factors under a hypothetical class contradiction between the working people and the propertied classes. Far more than their Western communist counterparts, they emphasize the misery of the people more than economic developments as the cause of revolt. They reveal a kind of "voluntarism" which considers peasant awareness of being exploited a more direct cause of revolt than underlying economic forces. Paradoxically, the Chinese communist position is closer to the nineteenth-century romantic view that revolt was due to the misery of the people than it is to the classical Marxist stress on the "bourgeoisie" as the driving force of the French Revolution.

[35] Lo Erh-kang, "Criticism of the Harms and Deceits of the Rightist Line in Science as Considered from the Point of View of Historical Studies," *KMJP*, August 28, 1957.

[36] See Mao Tse-tung, "The Bankruptcy of the Idealist Conception of History," *SWMTT* (Peking ed.), vol. 4, p. 452.

[37] Tai Yi, "On the Causes of the Outbreak of the Revolution of the TPTK," *KMJP*, January 11, 1961.

LEADERSHIP AND SOCIAL COMPOSITION OF THE CHINESE PEASANT MOVEMENTS

The thread of class analysis runs throughout communist historiography of the peasant movements, but it is especially marked in the discussion of the next problem, the question of the leadership and social composition of the revolts. Important Marxist concepts, concerning the relative roles played by individuals and by the masses in history, are also involved in this discussion.

At first sight, communist propagandists appear to have considerable ammunition for arguing that the Chinese mass movements were led by representatives of the lower classes. It is well known to all Chinese historians that the leaders of the first large-scale social unrest in 209 B.C. were farmhands and that the founders of the Han and Ming dynasties were commoners who fought their way to power after years of turmoil. On more careful consideration, however, it is apparent that the real dividing line between the leaders of the mass protest movements and the leaders of the government forces was that between commoners of various classes and officials of varying backgrounds and not between upper and lower economic classes. While some peasant movements in Chinese history were led by impoverished leaders of low social origin, more were led by men of middle social and economic rank whose distinguishing characteristic was not their poverty but their rebellious spirit. Indeed, many were relatively wealthy. While it is true that a successful scholar seldom joined a mass rebellion, many who failed to pass the Imperial examinations or were otherwise frustrated in their careers did. In fact, most noncommunist historians assume that some degree of education was necessary for the leadership of any enduring rebellion.[38]

[38] E.g., see Hsiao Kung-ch'uan, *op. cit.*, p. 477. Actually opposition to the government could be and sometimes was led by lowly members of

The first question in the communist treatment of the problem of such leadership concerns the relation of man to his environment, either collectively in the class struggle or individually as a rebel leader. The classical Marxists were ambiguous in their discussion of this and other complex issues. They assigned a completely revolutionary role to the oppressed class only in the ultimate revolution when the proletariat also led the development of a new stage of production. Previous transitional revolutions were led by a minority of proponents of the new order, the slave-owners, the feudalists, and the bourgeoisie rather than the lowest classes, although the masses might supply the force of the revolution. Engels pointed out that in earlier times social relations were complicated, and while the driving force of history may have come from the depths of society, the leaders of the new order were the "new middle class" struggling with the old mobility for supremacy.[39] Even in the proletarian revolution a key leadership role would be played by members of higher classes. According to the *Communist Manifesto*, "a small section of the ruling class cuts itself adrift and joins the revolutionary class."[40] Presumably Marx, Lenin, and most other communist leaders have thought of themselves in this light.[41]

There is further confusion in the Marxist classics over the relationship of the leader, of whatever class, to the economic forces of history and to the masses who were supposed to be the real "masters of history."[42] In the view of Marx and Engels, the masses were much less conscious of their historical role than they are made to appear in Chinese communist writings. Engels spoke of "the people" who could only comprehend "religious prophecy," while only "the initiated" could

---

society, but the construction of a new government required political knowledge, which was generally a monopoly of the scholar class in China.

[39] E.g., see Engels, *Anti-Duhring*, p. 24.

[40] *MESW*, vol. 1, p. 43.

[41] See Max Nomad, *Aspects of Revolt* (New York: Brookman Associates, 1959), p. 90.

[42] See M. M. Bober, *Karl Marx's Interpretation of History*, pp. 81–87; and Leo Yaresh, "The Role of the Individual in History," in C. E. Black (ed.), *Rewriting Russian History*, pp. 77–106.

understand "ultimate aims." [43] Therefore, "every social epoch needs its great men and when it does not find them it invents them." [44] Yet Marx and Engels are very explicit in insisting that the individual leader is limited to the conditions in which he finds himself: "men make their own history but they do not make it just as they please; they make it under circumstances directly encountered, given and transmitted from the past." [45]

Engels elaborated these theories of the role of men, particularly in relation to economic processes,[46] while G. V. Plekhanov, the founder of Russian Marxism, allowed a still greater role for the individual.[47] Lenin characteristically sought to explain the problem of the individual in terms of the class struggle:

> The theory of the class struggle . . . represents a tremendous acquisition for social science for the very reason that it lays down the methods by which the individual can be reduced to the social with the utmost precision and definiteness . . . in a word to the action of classes, the struggle between which determined the development of society. This refuted the childishly naive and purely mechanical view of history held by the subjectivists, who contented themselves with the meaningless thesis that history is made by living individuals. . . . [48]

Stalin even more characteristically elaborated on the role of the hero. Where Plekhanov spoke of the ability of the great man to hasten or retard the development of history, still the orthodox view, Stalin actually spoke of "changing" conditions: "It is people who make history, but they make it only to the extent that they correctly understand the conditions

[43] Engels, *The Peasant War in Germany*, p. 77.
[44] Marx, "The Class Struggles in France," *MESW*, vol. 1, p. 194.
[45] Marx, "Eighteenth Brumaire of Louis Bonaparte," *MESW*, vol. 1, p. 247. See also Marx and Engels, *The German Ideology*, pp. 14, 48.
[46] See especially *MESW*, vol. 2, pp. 392–93, 489, and 505.
[47] See G. V. Plekhanov, *The Role of the Individual in History* (New York: International Publishers, 1940), pp. 52, 60.
[48] V. I. Lenin, "The Economic Content of Narodnism," *Collected Works* (1960 ed.), vol. 1, pp. 410–11.

they found ready-made, and to the extent that they know how to change these conditions." [49]

The Chinese communists have modified the historical applications of these theories by placing relatively more stress on the role of the masses than on the role of either economic forces or individuals in history. The classical Marxists emphasized economic developments in the processes of history, Soviet theorists added a greater role for the individual, and the Chinese communists stress the historical role of "the people." All three ingredients are present and vary with each interpretation, but there has been a shift in emphasis in explaining the decisive factors of history. In the classical Marxist formula, "history creates heroes, heroes do not create history," and economic and social developments are clearly primary. But the so-called "needs of the masses" dominate Chinese communist historiography on this question. The hero is "produced from the needs of the masses" as well as from the needs of history, and presumably even the cult of the "Thought of Mao Tse-tung" is tied to the needs of the masses. Furthermore, the masses are the source of the development of production itself, the ultimate value in Marxist historiography.[50] The senior historian Lü Chen-yü elaborated on the significance of this approach for the student of history:

> History is made by the laboring people, . . . through their production struggles and class struggles. . . . Hence, the history of class society is the history of class struggle. Because of this we say, only from the class stand of the proletariat and the laboring people can [we] correctly recognize the position and function of the laboring people in history and how they create history, and, moreover, reveal how the exploiting classes throughout history used literate scholars to slander poisonously the laboring people.[51]

[49] Cited in Yaresh, *op. cit.*, p. 88.
[50] See Chang Hsiang-shan, *Jen-min Ch'ün-chung ho Ke-jen tsai Li-shih-shang te Tso-yung* (The Function of the Masses and the Individual in History) (Peking: Ch'ing-nien Ch'u-pan She, 1954), p. 46.
[51] Lü Chen-yü, "How to Study History," CKCN, October 6, 1961, p. 21.

Teng Hsiao-p'ing, the pre-"cultural revolution," First Sec-
retary of the CCP, restated the Marxist formula on the relation of leader to the masses but gave it a characteristic
emphasis on the latter:

> While recognizing that history is made by the people,
> Marxism never denies the role that outstanding individ-
> uals play in history. Marxism only points out that the
> individual role is in the final analysis dependent upon
> given social conditions . . . leaders emerge naturally
> from the midst of mass struggles and cannot be self-
> appointed. Unlike the leaders of the exploiting classes in
> the past, the leaders of the working class party [i.e., the
> CCP] stand not above the masses but in their midst.[52]

Such Chinese stress on the role of the masses clearly reveals
the recurring inconsistency between the economic-evolution-
ary and the social-revolutionary theories of Marxism, because
the mass movements often seemed to stand in the way of
historical progress.[53] Mao restated the classical Marxist theory that the evaluation of a government or leader depended
on whether he hastens or retards the forward evolution of history:

> The effect, good or bad, great or small, which the policy
> or practice of any Chinese political party produces on
> the Chinese people depends in the last analysis on
> whether it fetters or liberates their productive forces or
> whether and how much it helps to develop their produc-
> tive forces.[54]

Yet most mainland historians, whether consciously or not,
place the interests of "the people" and productive relations

[52] Teng Hsiao-p'ing, "Report on the Revision of the Constitution of
the CCP," in *Proceedings of the Eighth National Congress of the Chinese People's Congress* (Peking: Foreign Languages Press, 1956), p. 199.
[53] E.g., see Jung Meng-yuan, *Li-shih Jen-wu te P'ing-chia Wen-t'i*
(The Problem of Evaluation of Historical Persons) (Shanghai: Hua-
tung Jen-min Ch'u-pan She, 1954), pp. 26–32.
[54] Mao Tse-tung, "On Coalition Government," *SWMTT*, vol. 4,
p. 296.

ahead of the advancement of production and productive forces in evaluating important individuals in history. The assumption is that the economy advanced only if the lot of the masses was improved following government concessions forced by the rebellions. Unfortunately for this argument, improvements in the Chinese economy usually came, if at all, long after the slaughters of the major peasant uprisings. Therefore, the disruptions of rebellion initially brought only devastation, while long-term advances were due to complex forces. Thus, rebel leaders often appeared to retard rather than to advance the state of the economy.

The problem is especially acute in judging those government leaders who suppressed and oppressed the masses but advanced the cause of the state and the economy or in judging those peasant rebels whose very successes led to grave dislocations of the economy. Examples of the former type who have been reappraised in recent years are Ch'in-shih Huang-ti, Ts'ao Ts'ao, T'ang T'ai-tsung, and Yueh Fei.[55] The uprisings of the Yellow Turbans, of the late T'ang and Ming, and of the Taipings, which were accompanied and followed by widespread disruption, are examples of the latter type. If possible, the Chinese communist historians seek to harmonize the two components of the interests of the people and the interests of the economy by showing that the former was essential to the latter, and that only peasant wars forced improvements in both. That it is often not possible to prove this may be seen from discussion of the programs of various emperors and of such projects as building the Great Wall and the Grand Canal.

The evaluation of the "peasant rebels" who went on to found the Han and Ming dynasties involves all of these considerations. In both cases it was evident that these rebellions succeeded precisely because their leaders achieved the support of key upper-class groups, involving in the communist

[55] There has been a tendency since the middle 1950s analogous to the reappraisal of Ivan the Terrible and Peter the Great in Soviet historiography to reevaluate these government leaders. This question is discussed later in this chapter.

frame of reference a "sell-out" of the peasants to the landlords. Of course, these considerations of the limitations of the
revolutionary accomplishments of pre-modern rebels fit in
with the communist stipulation that only the proletariat
could lead the "liberation" of the working classes, but they
also make it evident that the more successful the rebel leader,
the more likely he was to betray alleged "peasant class
goals." [56]

Regarding the question of the class origins of the leaders of
"peasant rebellions," the Chinese communist historians seek
to distinguish the social origins or family background (*ch'u-
shen*) of the rebels from their "class attributes" (*chieh-chi
shu-hsing*) or the class which they served.[57] This is a relatively new development in mainland historiography, although
it is clearly based on statements in the Marxist classics dealing
with "far-sighted" members of the ruling class joining the
revolutionary class. In the early years after the communist
triumph, following other Party policies, historians were quite
rigid in treating historical figures according to their class origins. One of the first studies of the history of the peasant
wars took a negative view of all rebel leaders of landlord-class
origin, such as the Sui rebel leader Li Mi.[58] Later studies
criticized this approach as too artificial, no doubt because
there would be few "peasant leaders," not to speak of modern "proletarians," to discuss were it followed consistently.

Peasant leaders might come from any class so long as they
"served the peasant class." [59] In fact, this stress on the
"class attributes" of a leader provides a formula for the evaluation of extremely diverse figures, since the leader need not
remain attached to the class of his birth. For instance, Li Yen,

[56] See Chapter 8.

[57] E.g., see *SCMP* 2734, p. 5, citing *KMJP*, April 9, 1962; Sun Tso-
min, "Regarding the Book *Chung-kuo Nung-min Chan-cheng Wen-t'i
T'an-su*," *KMJP*, May 26, 1958; and Ts'ao Kuei-lin, "On Li Yen,"
LSYC, no. 4, 1964, p. 70.

[58] Wang Tan-ling, *Chung-kuo Nung-min Ke-ming Shih-hua* (Talks
on the History of the Chinese Peasant Revolutions) (Shanghai: Kuo-chi
Wen-hua Fu-wu She, 1952), p. 128. See also Tuan Wen-yuan, "Discussion of the Problem of Li Mi," *KMJP*, no. 9, 1953, p. 19.

[59] Sun Tso-min, *op. cit.*, p. 89.

the talented son of a high Ming official who became a key figure in the rebellion led by Li Tzu-ch'eng, was an example of a man of landlord-class origin supposedly switching to serve the peasantry in his mature life.[60] By contrast, the founder of the Ming dynasty was a poor peasant who, after his successful acquisition of power, adopted landlord-class attributes.[61]

After the resurrection of Ts'ao Ts'ao as a progressive historical figure by Kuo Mo-jo and other senior historians in 1959, this trend to recognize the place of important figures in Chinese history regardless of their "class stand" was accelerated. In 1961, Ch'en Yi even admitted that many top-ranking communists were not of working-class background.[62] By the mid-1960s, however, the pendulum swung in the other direction as a result of the "Great Proletarian Cultural Revolution."

All along, many younger historians continued to oppose a favorable evaluation of government leaders who were "butchers of the people," no matter what their other accomplishments. Articles explicitly attack Kuo Mo-jo for advocating the rehabilitation of Ts'ao Ts'ao, one of the suppressors of the Yellow Turbans,[63] and implicitly criticize the emphasis of Kuo and others on the role of such rebel leaders of governing-class origin as Li Yen.[64] They criticize those historians who seek to build patriotism by stressing the great generals and emperors or even the exemplary peasant leaders, since all these interpretations slight the role played by the masses.[65] A

---

[60] See Ts'ao Kuei-lin, "On Li Yen," *LSYC*, no. 4, 1964, pp. 153–72. Ts'ao praises Li as a representative of the most "progressive" of the four types of upper-class "intellectual" who might join a peasant rebellion.

[61] Ch'en Hsu-lu, *Lun Li-shih Jen-wu P'ing-chia Wen-t'i* (A Discussion of the Problem of the Evaluation of Personages in History) (Shanghai: Hsin Chih-shih Ch'u-pan She, 1956), pp. 20–22.

[62] See CNA 393, citing *CKCN*, September 1, 1961.

[63] Lin Yen-shu *et al.*, "Regarding the Discussion of the Evaluation of Ts'ao Ts'ao," *SHYK*, no. 9, 1959.

[64] E.g., Sun Tso-min, *op. cit.*, p. 51; and Chou Wei-min, "On the Problems of Ch'uang Wang's Entry into Peking," *KMJP*, November 24, 1960. In 1944 Kuo wrote a pamphlet on the three-hundredth anniversary of the fall of the Ming in which he concentrated almost entirely on the contributions of Li Yen to the late Ming rebellion. See Kuo Mo-jo, *Chia-shen-nien San-pai-nien-chi.*

[65] E.g., CNA 237, citing *JMJP*, May 16, 1958; Wang Hsing-ya,

leading argument in the anti-rightist criticisms of Chao Li-sheng was that Chao had given undue praise to the twelfth-century patriot Yueh Fei, since Yueh had suppressed the rebellion of Yang Yao as well as fought the invading Jurchen.[66] The weight given these contradictory tendencies varies in the works even of the same historian. There was an apparent effort after the late 1950s by older and more conservative historians to secure a place for the individual "governing class" regardless of such objections by more doctrinaire colleagues. Kuo Mo-jo explained in 1959:

> From the viewpoint of the new history, of course [we] must stress the writing of the activities of the laboring people, but as the past society was a class society, the activities of the ruling class also cannot be omitted.[67]

Chien Po-tsan and Lü Chen-yü warned historians against either going to the old extreme of slandering the masses or completely neglecting the governing class.[68] Fan Wen-lan was most explicit when he said that while proposals to do away with the "dynasties, kings, generals, and ministers" altogether

> seem to be very revolutionary, in fact [they] are subjectivist. A class society was formed by the ruling class and the exploited class standing in opposition to each other. If attention was devoted only to the activities of the masses of the people without reference to dynasties, kings, generals, and ministers, then the result would be

---

"Purge the Reactionary Hero-Centered Viewpoint from the Research and Teaching of History," *SHYK*, no. 10, 1958, p. 10; Liu Yao-t'ing *et al.*, "The Development of Historical Science in the Light of Ten Years of Struggle on the Intellectual Front," *SHYK*, no. 11, 1959, pp. 16–17; and Li Yin-nung, "On the Question of the Awareness of Feudal Governors of the Force of Peasant Revolutions," *Yang-ch'eng Wan-pao*, September 7, 1961.

[66] See Chapter 10.

[67] Kuo Mo-jo, "On Several Problems of Contemporary Historical Research," *HCS*, no. 4, 1959, and *KMJP*, April 8, 1959; and Lü Chen-yü, "How to Study History," *CKCN*, October 6, 1961.

[68] Chien Po-tsan, "Some Problems in Contemporary Historical Studies," *Hung Ch'i*, no. 10, 1959.

that in Chinese history only the peasant wars are left and the entire history would be eliminated.[69]

Earlier, Fan had criticized his own lack of attention to the outstanding generals and emperors of Chinese history.[70]

In the effort to resolve some of these difficulties in evaluating leaders in history, Wu Han suggested six criteria: (1) the interests of the people, (2) the development of production, (3) historical development as a whole, (4) influences on politics rather than on private lives, (5) class origins and attributes, and (6) relevance to the times.[71] The last point is explained as judging the men of history by the standards of their contemporaries rather than by today's standards.

Nevertheless, while mainland historians vary in their stress on one or the other of these criteria, the majority of them continue to emphasize the "interests of the people" in evaluating historical figures, even if it means going against the warnings of the other historians. Senior Party and academic leaders note that the development of economic production is more fundamental to the communist theory of history, but an alleged concern for the interests of the masses even at the apparent expense of historical development now dominates mainland historiography, as the "cultural revolution" attacks on Wu Han, Chien Po-tsan and others dramatized.

The emphasis on the masses is illustrated by the criteria recently used to define five categories of peasant rebels in Chinese history:

first, the isolated hero who never enters into the life of the masses;

second, the leader of a mass movement who has goals differing from the masses and who gives no help to the

---

[69] According to "Chinese Historians Meet in Peking in Commemoration of the 110th Anniversary of the Taiping," *SCMP* 2514, pp. 21–22, citing *JMJP*, May 31, 1961.

[70] Fan Wen-lan, *Chung-kuo T'ung-shih Chien-pien* (A Simple General History of China) (1961 ed.), Preface, p. 6.

[71] See "Talk Freely About and Evaluate Personalities," *SCMP* 2457, pp. 11–13, citing *KMJP*, January 15, 1961; and Wu Han, "On Appraisal of Figures of History," *SCMP* 2721, pp. 1–12, citing *JMJP*, March 23, 1962.

peasants [Liu Hsuan and Liu Hsiu of the rebellion against Wang Mang are cited in this category];

third, leaders whose goals differ from the goals of the masses but who contribute to the organization and campaigns of the mass movement [such as Sun En, c. 400; Li Mi, c. 616; and Sung Chiang, c. 1120];

fourth, leaders such as those in type three who help the peasants but for their own purposes, and who later are completely transformed into representatives of the feudalists such as the founders of the Han and Ming;

finally, the dedicated peasant leader who fights consistently for the peasants against the landlords [Huang Ch'ao and Li Tzu-ch'eng are included here, as presumably would be certain Red Eyebrow, Yellow Turban, Sung, Taiping, and other rebel leaders].[72]

It is evident that the primary distinction between the "dedicated" peasant leader and the others in this scheme is their lack of success, since victory was achieved only through coming to terms with certain power groups. Hence, many Chinese communist historians emphasize alleged loyalty to the masses even over contributions to economic growth. This voluntaristic tendency was accelerated by the intensification of the "cultural revolution" in 1966.

Though there is disagreement about the weight to be given to motivation and result,[73] most mainland historians stress the latter in judging the actions of a peasant leader. Thus, Sun Tso-min, the most voluminous writer on the subject during the latter 'fifties, considered that leaders rising from prominent or landlord families—such as Chang Chueh (A.D. 184), Li T'e (c. A.D. 300), Sun En and Lu Hsun (c. A.D. 400), Li Mi and Hsu Shih-chi of the Sui, Wang Hsien-chih and

---

[72] "Anhui University History Department Holds Discussion of Chinese Peasant Wars," *KMJP*, April 3, 1961. Similarly, Ts'ao Kuei-lin (*op. cit.*, *LSYC*, no. 4, 1964, pp. 170–71) lists four types of upper-class "intellectual" who might join a peasant revolt, ranging from the opportunist to the genuine sympathizer.

[73] The ideal is to account for both. E.g., see *SCMM* 268, p. 33, citing *Hung Ch'i*, June 16, 1961.

Huang Ch'ao of the late T'ang, and Li Yen of the late Ming —should be affirmed as leaders of peasant rebellions because they contributed to the goals of the peasantry.[74] Other rebels of noble descent who joined a peasant movement, such as Chang Erh and Ch'en Yü of the Ch'in, should not be so considered, not so much because their motives differed from those of the peasant masses, which was often the case with the first group of leaders, but because they harmed the peasant movement.[75] Presumably Sun, like the Anhui historian mentioned above, would consider leaders who not only served the peasant masses but came from peasant background as most exemplary. In this category he mentions Ch'en Sheng and Wu Kuang of the anti-Ch'in rebellions; Wang K'uang and Fan Ch'ung of the anti-Wang Mang rebellions; Tou Chien-te, Fang La, Chu Yuan-chang, and Li Tzu-ch'eng of the rebellions at the end of the Sui, Northern Sung, Yuan, and Ming dynasties, respectively; and the Taiping leaders Yang Hsiu-ch'ing and Li Hsiu-ch'eng.[76] Li Hsiu-ch'eng was one of the most frequently praised peasant rebels in Chinese communist historiography of the 1950s, but since the early 1960s he has been criticized for confession to Tseng Kuo-fan after torture. It is argued that to surrender to the enemy, even when the cause is apparently lost, is a betrayal of class integrity.[77] In the "cultural revolution" of the mid-1960s, "defense of the traitor" Li Hsiu-ch'eng became a principal criticism of the "revisionists." [78]

Regarding the class characteristics of peasant rebel leaders, mainland historians consider their weaknesses from the Marxist point of view but to a lesser extent than in Western Marxist historiography. Peasant qualities are considered the source of both the strength and weaknesses of the rebel lead-

[74] Sun Tso-min, *op. cit.*, p. 89.
[75] *Ibid.*, p. 92.
[76] *Ibid.*, p. 89.
[77] E.g., see articles in *KMJP*, December 20, 1956; *LSYC*, no. 4, 1963; no. 4, 1964; and nos. 5–6, 1964. For further discussion of the treatment of Li Hsiu-ch'eng see Stephen Uhalley, "The Controversy over Li Hsiu-ch'eng," *JAS*, February 1966, pp. 305–17.
[78] See Chapter 10.

ers. Thus, Li Tzu-ch'eng's virtues of loyalty and self-discipline are said to spring from his sharing the life of the peasantry, but at the same time his lack of vision and other shortcomings are also traced to his peasant mentality.[79] One historian reported that Huang Ch'ao's decadent morals were due to his origin among the petty urban traders.[80]

Turning to the class composition of the Chinese peasant movements, some mainland historians have noted the important role of men of middle-class origin in the Chinese peasant revolts,[81] but, understandably, these remarks have not gone much beyond their expression. Lü Chen-yü stated in 1961 that historians should realize that

> within a class there are several layers, such as the big, mid, and small landlords within the landlord class. Slaveowners, feudalists, and capitalist classes also had several dissimilar layers, and within each layer also several different organizations and groups. In oppressing and ruling the people these groups are consistent but within them there are contradictions. . . . Thus the study of classes and society must also analyze these [governing class contradictions]. Besides the two opposed classes and their dissimilar layers, there are also middle groups who, while wavering, are a very important force though they have connections with the exploiters and sometimes with the exploited classes.[82]

[79] E.g., see Li Wen-chih, "The Late Ming Peasant Revolutionary Leader, Li Tzu-ch'eng," in Li Kuang-pi and Ch'ien Chun-hua (eds.), *Chung-kuo Li-shih Jen-wu Lun-ts'ung* (Compilation of Discussions on Chinese Historical Figures) (Peking: San-lien Shu-tien, 1957), p. 123.

[80] Weng Ta-tsao, *Huang Ch'ao Lun* (On Huang Ch'ao) (Shanghai: Shang-wu Yin-shu Kuan, 1950), p. 61.

[81] Of course, this is not a new observation. For instance, a writer using Marxist interpretations observed the important role of the "heterodox intellectuals" in the peasant wars. See Ku Ch'en, "The Role of Mass Power in History," *Hsin Sheng Ming* (New Life), vol. 3, no. 1, 1930, p. 1.

[82] Lü Chen-yü, "How to Study History," CKCN, October 6, 1961. In his general history Lü also noted the role played by middle and small landlords in the peasant movements. See Lü Chen-yü, *Chien-ming Chung-kuo T'ung-shih* (A Simplified General History of China) (Peking: Jen-min Ch'u-pan She, 1961), pp. 428, 549. See also Lü Chen-yü,

The authors of the second major post-1949 work on the peasant wars emphasized the broad social composition of the Chinese mass movements. This was a natural development, they felt, given the exploitation of all groups by the Oriental state. They saw an evolution in the ability of the leaders to cope with the changing social composition of the peasant movements.[83] Leading historians have noted the important role played by "disillusioned intellectuals" in the Taiping movement,[84] and a Soviet writer compared the role of these "lower ranks of feudal intellectuals" to that of the lower clergy in the medieval European peasant movements.[85]

Nevertheless, the tendency to stress the "peasant" in peasant rebel leadership has prevailed. Those who have given attention to the role of nonpeasant members in the peasant wars have been criticized for maximizing the role of the gentry in the successes achieved during these movements.[86] Party leaders have always stressed the role of the poorest layers of rural society, the "semiproletariat" and the "lumpenproletariat," [87] even though Mao has recognized the existence

---

"Historical Science Must be Developed on the Basis of Comrade Mao Tse-tung's Thought," *LSYC*, no. 5, 1960, p. 22.

[83] Chao Li-sheng and Kao Chao-yi, *Chung-kuo Nung-min Chan-cheng Shih Lun-wen Chi*, pp. 14–15. Wang Tan-ling wrote the first major study of the subject.

[84] E.g., Fan Wen-lan, *Chung-kuo Chin-tai Shih* (History of Modern China) (Peking: Jen-min Ch'u-pan She, 1961), vol. 1, p. 151.

[85] F. B. Belyelubsky, "On the Social Character of the Taiping Leadership," *NAA*, no. 1, 1963, p. 96.

[86] E.g., Sung Hsi-min and Wang Hsin-yeh, "A Criticism of One of the False Views of Chao Li-sheng on the Question of the Peasant Wars," *WSC*, no. 12, 1958, pp. 48–49. The authors note among other things that Chao Li-sheng attributed least success to the "purest" of the first three peasant wars, the Yellow Turbans.

[87] See Mao Tse-tung, "Analysis of the Classes in Chinese Society," *SWMTT*, vol. 1, pp. 17–18, 20. Actually there is some evidence that the so-called "middle peasants" were in fact more active politically than their poorer countrymen in the modern Chinese revolution. According to a sympathetic Western observer of the land reform carried out in communist areas in the late 1940s, a developing class consciousness was strongest among "new middle-class peasant cadres. Among the poor peasants . . . there were varying outlooks. Some were still apathetic, others had at least become eager to follow the example of their more advanced and energetic fellows." See David and Isabel Crook, *Revolu-*

of as many as eight layers of the peasantry.[88]

Communist analysis of the social composition of the masses of the peasant movements corresponds to their treatment of the question of leadership. While in specific cases they note considerable diversity of composition and ill-defined class distinctions, they tend to resolve such refinements into the usual generalization of peasants against the landlords. The authors of one of the most extensive Chinese communist treatments of the problems of classes in Chinese society wrote that despite the great complexity and changing forms of traditional social structure, class antagonisms between the exploiter and the exploited were common to ancient as well as to modern society. "Within the ranks of feudal society, no matter how complicated," they continued, "the feature of exploitation of the absolute majority of peasants by the landlord class (both state and private) was always evident." "Because of this," they added, "even though there was no legal distinction between the commoner peasant and the commoner landlord, the 'rank' of commoner should be divided into . . . the upper minority of landlords and the lower majority of direct producers. The exploited classes who were tied to the land as 'bound peasants' and the mean people who had lost their freedom" engaged in all forms of class struggle, from flight and evasion to armed struggle.[89] The most important group within the latter class was the "wandering people" who fled their normal rural occupations to indulge in vagabondage and banditry and who formed a ready-

---

tion in a Chinese Village, Ten Mile Inn (London: Routledge, 1959), p. 170.

[88] Big and small landlords, peasant landlords, semi- or part-landowners, sharecroppers, poor peasants, farm laborers, rural artisans, and elements déclassé (wandering people). See Mao Tse-tung, "Analysis of the Various Classes of the Chinese Peasantry and Their Attitudes Toward the Revolution," cited in Schram, *The Political Thought of Mao Tse-tung*, pp. 172–77. See also Mao's 1931 study of a Kiangsi hsien, *Mao Tse-tung Hsuan-chi* (Selected Works of Mao Tse-tung) (Mukden: Tung-pei Shu-tien, 1948), pp. 75–92.

[89] Hou Wai-lu et al., (eds.), *Chung-kuo Ssu-hsiang T'ung-shih*, vol. 4, part 1, pp. 37–38, 44.

made pool for rebel armies throughout Chinese history.[90]

A recent article summarizes the prevailing view of the social composition of the peasant movements:

> Although the basic mass of the peasant war was the peasantry, because the target of the revolution was a despotic dynasty . . . therefore the masses participating in the revolution often included workers, urban poor, and even small shop managers, intellectuals, and mid and small landlords. They formed a united front of the middle and lower layers of society *led by the peasant class*.[91]

In short, Mao's policy of a united front of all groups under the supposed leadership of the proletariat is applied to the analysis of the history of feudal China, but with the peasantry replacing the proletariat in the commanding position.

The classical Marxists would agree on the principle of a common front against the reactionary forces of society,[92] and Lenin applied the idea of a temporary common front of rich and poor specifically to revolution in the countryside.[93] However, neither Marx, Engels, nor Lenin would allow the peasant class the leading position in such an alliance. Where the Chinese communist historians speak of "a united front of the middle and lower layers of society led by the peasant class" in feudal China, Western Marxists, if they alluded to such a common front at all, would place the bourgeoisie in the lead of the struggle against feudalism. This change in Marxist historiography is not surprising, since presumably there was no bourgeoisie in China capable of leading an antifeudal revolution.[94] As in the bourgeois-democratic and so-

[90] See T'ao Hsi-sheng, *Chung-kuo She-hui Hsien-hsiang Shih-ling*, pp. 211–19.

[91] Shih Shao-pin, "On the Discussion of Problems in the Peasant Revolutionary Wars in Chinese Feudal Society," *SSP*, p. 503. Emphasis supplied.

[92] See Marx and Engels, *The German Ideology*, p. 41.

[93] See V. I. Lenin, "To the Rural Poor," in *Alliance of the Working Class and the Peasantry*, pp. 66–67.

[94] Only in the late Ming rebellions has there been some discussion of a potential alliance between such "incipient bourgeois" leaders as Huang

cialist revolutions, the peasantry in effect becomes the "revolutionary class" by default.

Some leading historians have warned against an exaggeration of the possibilities of a peasant-led united front in feudal China. Thus, Chien Po-tsan objected to the statements of some historians that Li Tzu-ch'eng achieved a real united front with such intellectuals as Li Yen and with the developing urban and economic forces of the late Ming. Rather, only the proletariat is capable of achieving such a united front, he wrote.[95] Other critics of the prevailing "leftist" view of the peasant wars, at least before the purges of the mid-1960s, maintained that the weaknesses of the peasant class, on the one hand, necessitated the use of landlord gentry for planning and administration and, on the other, were responsible for the peasants' inability to prevent the corruption and sabotage inherent in gentry participation.[96]

Finally, we may note again that Chinese communist definitions of class are purposely vague. As Mao said, "by the broad masses of the people is meant all those who are oppressed . . ."[97] or, in contemporary context, all those who follow Party leadership.[98] Therefore, class war in Chinese history is defined in the broadest possible terms, as the struggle of the oppressed against their oppressors, a "struggle for the

---

Tsung-hsi and Ku Yen-wu and the peasant revolutionaries Li Tzu-ch'eng and Li Yen. However, it is explained that there was little possibility of this occurring because of the anti-rebel bias of the Confucian-trained scholars. In any case, since 1959 or 1960 Party theorists have silenced discussion of incipient capitalism in China, presumably because of the threat to the current theories of imperialism and the role of the Communist Party. See also Chapter 8.

[95] Chien Po-tsan, *Li-shih Wen-t'i Lun-ts'ung*, p. 134.

[96] E.g., see Wang T'ien-chiang, "The Class Composition of the Local Officials of the TPTK," *LSYC*, no. 3, 1958.

[97] Mao Tse-tung, "On the Question of the National Bourgeoisie and the Enlightened Gentry," *Selected Works* (Peking ed.), vol. 4, p. 207. Stuart Schram (*The Political Thought of Mao Tse-tung*, pp. 170–71) has included a translation of an article of 1919 in which Mao, following the influence of Li Ta-chao, calls for a "great union of the popular masses" of all classes to achieve national ends.

[98] See Mao Tse-tung, *On the Correct Handling of Contradictions Among the People* (Peking: Foreign Languages Press, 1960), p. 8.

liberation of enslaved labor." [99] Furthermore, a particular class is defined according to the way it is treated. Thus, if in the Ch'in peasants were treated like slaves, they can be called "virtual slaves," and a mass rebellion a "slave revolt." [100] Similarly, various oppressed groups in Chinese history are equated with the peasantry and included in the composition of the peasant wars. Moreover, historians note changes in the social composition of Chinese peasant wars with time. One stated that dispossessed peasants were the basic force of the peasant wars but admitted that the status of this group varied according to the society of the time.[101] Most historians saw the social composition of the peasant movements evolving to include more complex social strata following economic developments after the T'ang dynasty.[102] Others, however, have argued that landlords played a greater part in the earlier rebellions than in those after the T'ang.[103]

THE ORGANIZATION OF
THE PEASANT MOVEMENTS

The question of whether or not the peasant rebels were able to establish their own peasant government is the third topic of considerable discussion in the mainland historiography of the peasant wars. The question raises problems of the degree of organization attained by the rebels and the degree

[99] Wu Yü-chang, *Chung-kuo Li-shih Chiao Ch'eng-hsu Lun* (Discussion on the Processes of Teaching Chinese History) (Shanghai: Hsinhua Shu-tien, 1950), p. 1.

[100] E.g., see Ho Tzu-ch'uan, "Ch'in Shih-huang," *HCS*, no. 4, 1959. Jung Sheng ("Ideas on the Most Fundamental Difference Between Slaves and Serfs," *WSC*, no. 2, 1958) attempts to use Marxist theory to distinguish between slaves and serfs in ancient China.

[101] Chao Li-sheng and Kao Chao-yi, *op. cit.*, p. 148.

[102] E.g., P'an Te-shen, "On the Function, Characteristics and Nature of the Peasant Revolts and Wars in the Later Period of Chinese Feudal Society," *SSP*, p. 197.

[103] E.g., Kao Min, "Tentative Discussion of the Question of the Laws of Development of the Peasant Uprisings and Wars in Our Country's Feudal Society," *SSP*, pp. 146–47.

— could peasants organize themselves?

to which that organization represented the class interests of the peasants.

The classical Marxists were unequivocal in their belief that the peasantry was unable to represent its own interests. Marx wrote that the French peasants were

> incapable of enforcing their class interests in their own name. . . . They cannot represent themselves, they must be represented. Their representative must at the same time appear as their master, as an authority over them. . . . The political influence of the small holding peasants therefore finds its final expression in the executive power subordinating society to itself.[104]

Yet, only an influential minority of Chinese historians supports these classical Marxist views which appear to slight the revolutionary potential of the peasant class. This minority maintains that the organizations set up by the Chinese peasant rebels were only reflections of the "feudal government," since the superstructure of the society, including political forms, was necessarily determined by the economic base of the time.[105]

The majority of Chinese historians contend that, on the contrary, Chinese peasant movements could and often did establish political organizations, which temporarily represented the peasant class, although all concede that prior to the emergence of the proletariat such "governments" sooner or later became instruments of the ruling class. This majority view is in turn split between the middle position that the peasant rebel political organizations were only "temporary structures [set up for the purpose] of military struggle," [106] and the argument that the Chinese peasants actually established their own class government. Proponents of the latter view cite numerous "short-lived peasant governments," culminating in the Taiping movement, which allegedly carried

[104] Karl Marx, "The Eighteenth Brumaire of Louis Bonaparte," *MESW*, vol. 1, p. 334.
[105] See Shih Shao-pin, *op. cit.*, *SSP*, p. 509.
[106] *Ibid.*

out anti-feudal revolutionary policies through a "fairly complete" government organization.[107] Because of the weaknesses of the peasant class rooted in their property-owning instincts, these "peasant governments" necessarily copied feudal forms and eventually were transformed into feudal governments. But in the initial processess of their struggle against the landlord class they carried out policies in the class "interests of the peasants" and merited the name "peasant government." [108]

The leading spokesmen of the traditional, negative Marxist view of the organizational achievements of the peasants deny that the leaders of the revolts represented the immediate political interests of the peasants. Sun Tso-min wrote that the rebellions of Huang Ch'ao and Li Tzu-ch'eng "clearly show that the peasant leaders transformed [their outlook] . . . they no longer represented the class stand of the peasants, they represented the class stand of the landlords, and finally after the victory of the revolt [they] became new feudal emperors, established another feudal government, and began to protect the order they had created." [109] A writer named Ts'ai Mei-piao stated this view most strongly when he wrote that there could not be even a "temporary peasant class government," since in the "feudal period" there could only be "feudal government." He argued that this was amply proven by the rebel use of feudal forms and titles.[110] Soviet and "revisionist" Chinese historians such as Chien Po-tsan also hold this position.[111]

[107] E.g., see Shih Tse, "On the Government of the TPTK Revolution," *KMJP*, June 17, 1964.

[108] Shih Shao-pin, *loc. cit.*, p. 510.

[109] Sun Tso-min, *op. cit.*, p. 26. See also Sun Tso-min, "A Tentative Discussion of the Nature of Li Tzu-ch'eng's Ta Hsun Government," *HCS*, no. 3, 1962.

[110] Ts'ai Mei-piao, "Discussion of Several Questions in the Debate on the History of the Chinese Peasant Wars," *LSYC*, no. 4, 1961, pp. 76–80.

[111] E.g., see L. V. Simonovskaya, *Velikaya Krestyanskaya Voina v Kitai, 1628–1645*, p. 94; Chien Po-tsan, "Some Tentative Ideas on the Handling of Several Historical Questions," *KMJP*, December 22, 1961. For other examples of criticisms of the affirmation of peasant governments, see "What Was the Function of the Peasant Wars in History?"

Indicative of the greater influence of the "leftist," more radical interpretation has been the great number of criticisms,[112] culminating in that of Chien Po-tsan and others in 1966,[113] of such skeptical views denying the existence of "peasant governments." Among better-known historians arguing that the peasants could and did set up organizations representing their class interests are Pai Shou-yi, Ning K'o, and Ho Tzu-ch'uan. Pai stated that "time and again [the peasant revolts] overthrew the landlord government and time and again temporarily established their own governments";[114] and Ning elaborated that "after the peasants overthrew the feudal government, they were able to establish peasant governments representing their class interest through peasant dictatorships." [115] Ho explained that many rebellions in Chinese history established "peasant governments which served the interests of the peasantry and proposed slogans clearly in the interests of their own class." [116]

Others cite Mao's discussion of the Hunan peasant governments. While admitting that Marx had denied that the peasantry could organize themselves as a class and that Mao's remarks on the Hunan peasant associations concerned the peasantry in the modern proletarian-led revolution, these authors nonetheless insist that "under certain conditions the peasantry was a class and so could organize its own govern-

Wen Hui-pao (Shanghai), June 9, 1959; and Ch'i Li-huang, *op. cit.*, *LSYC*, no. 3, 1962.

[112] E.g., see *T'ien-chin Shih-fan Ta-hsueh Li-shih hsi*, "Regarding the Heated Controversy over the Problem of the Laws of Development of the Chinese Peasant Wars," *SSP*, pp. 467–72; see also articles discussing "peasant government": *WSC*, no. 12, 1958; *KMJP*, March 17, 1958, September 20, 1960, November 7 and 23, 1961; *Wen Hui-pao* (Shanghai), July 6, 1959; *SHYK*, no. 6, 1960; and *LSYC*, no. 1, 1962.

[113] E.g., see Ch'i Pen-yü *et al.*, "Comrade Chien Po-tsan's Historical Views Must be Criticized," *JMJP*, March 25, 1966, p. 5; and Shih Shao-pin, "Resolutely Support the Direction of the Revolution in Historical Science," *JMJP*, March 27, 1966, p. 5. See also articles in *JMJP*, June 14, 1966, p. 3.

[114] Cited in Ts'ai Mei-piao, *op. cit.*, *LSYC*, no. 4, 1961, p. 77.

[115] *Ibid.*

[116] Cited in HCS (eds.), "On Questions of the Nature, Function, and Distinguishing Characteristics of the Peasant Wars in Chinese History," *SSP*, p. 488.

ment. . . . This could not exist for long . . . and the peasantry could not organize a [viable] government, but under certain conditions they could temporarily establish their own government." [117]

Ch'i Hsia, formerly one of the foremost exponents of the negative view of the organizational qualities of the peasant revolts,[118] yielded to the criticisms of his more enthusiastic colleagues at a conference discussion in early 1960. He declared that his earlier views that the

> peasant wars could not establish a peasant government . . . were wrong. The peasants' revolutionary struggles not only would abolish the system of feudal exploitation but would change their own political system . . . and though they did not achieve this goal, they tried. . . . [Thus] to deny the "peasant governments," established in certain peasant wars, is to undervalue the function of the peasant revolutionary struggles.[119]

To resolve the contradictions between negative classical Marxist views and enthusiastic Chinese views of the organizational abilities and achievements of the pre-modern peasantry, many mainland historians seek to distinguish between a "revolutionary peasant government" and a true "peasant class government." [120] Although the latter were forced to borrow feudal ideas and forms, they still represented the class interests of the peasants, albeit not to the extent achieved in more modern revolutionary governments.[121] In any case, many writers argue that there was no question that Chinese peasant revolts such as the Taiping established their own government, illustrated by their armed organization, local adminis-

[117] Fang Chih-kuang *et al.*, "Discussion of Several Problems in the History of the Peasant Wars in China's Feudal Society," *SSP*, p. 135.
[118] See T'ien-chin Shih-fan Ta-hsueh Li-shih hsi, *op. cit.*, *SSP*, pp. 465–66.
[119] Ch'i Hsia, "On the Question of the Nature of the Chinese Peasant Wars," *SSP*, pp. 62–63.
[120] E.g., Li T'ien-tso, "The Problem of the Special Characteristics of the Chinese Peasant Wars," *SSP*, pp. 226–27.
[121] Hsueh-shu Tung-t'ai column, "Discussion of Several Problems in the History of the Chinese Peasant Wars," *JMJP*, May 18, 1962.

tration, and some degree of execution of revolutionary policies. The real question, therefore, was not the existence of
such governments, Marx to the contrary, but the reasons for
their failure and transformation into instruments of the
"feudal governing class." [122]

These conflicting views illustrate both the artificiality and
the significance of the historiography of this subject. On the
one hand, the arguments revolve around semantics more than
content, since all agree that sooner or later prior to the communist revolution the governments ceased to represent the
peasant class; but, on the other hand, this and similar questions are considered "matters of principle," since the arguments and terminology employed are held to reveal whether
or not the historian has adopted the "class stand of the
people." [123]

[122] See "What was the Function of the Peasant Wars in History?"
Wen Hui-pao (Shanghai), June 9, 1959; and Wu Yen-nan, "On the
Question of Goals and Peasant Governments in the Peasant Revolts and
Wars," *SHYK*, no. 6, 1960.
[123] Wu Ch'uan-ch'i, "One Cannot Say the Peasant Wars Are Exten-
sions of Feudal Landlord Class Policies," *KMJP*, April 3, 1964, p. 2.

CHAPTER SIX

Slogans and Ideology

WHILE the degree of emphasis varies considerably in all communist discussions of the history of the peasant movements, there is greatest disagreement over the nature of rebel ideology. Differences of interpretation in the consideration of this and related problems range from a generally negative appraisal of the intellectual perception of the pre-modern peasant to considerable enthusiasm for the motivation and ideology of the peasant rebel. The former position is unquestionably closer to the classical Marxist view of the peasantry, but the latter view prevails in mainland China.

Where the Marxist classics treated the goals of the historical peasant movements at all, they assumed at most a negative consciousness on the part of the rebel leaders—a sense of opposition, not of commitment.[1] Even Mao saw the function of historical mass movements more in "objective" than

[1] Engels, in his study of the German peasant war of 1525, credited the positive aspects of Muntzer's program to the plebeian (urban pre-proletariat) composition of the peasant movement and portrayed its expression in religious terms. Engels, *The Peasant War in Germany*, pp. 59 ff. Lenin, as reflected in his adoption of a program of land redistribution in 1906, considered the peasant's demand for land his only positive goal. See his "The Agrarian Programme of Social Democracy in the First Russian Revolution, 1905–07," *Collected Works*, vol. 13, p. 295.

in "subjective" terms, more in the impact of the rebellions on the governing class than in the development of a revolutionary consciousness of injustice among the peasantry. The younger generation of Chinese communist historians go further and see positive ideological content in the Chinese revolutionary tradition.

Although no Chinese communist historian equates the ancient peasant movements with the modern revolutionary movement, many assign them qualities which European Marxists reserved for bourgeois and plebeian revolutionaries. Soviet historians affirm the positive nature of peasant wars,[2] but apologize for the limited ideology of the peasants.[3] By contrast, most Chinese historians stress the goals of the peasant leaders as a principal manifestation of their revolutionary nature. This stress on a positive ideology provides another example of the progression from Marx through the Russians to the Chinese in the appraisal of the revolutionary qualities of peasant movements.

As the intensification of the "cultural revolution" in the mid-1960s dramatized, many prominent historians do not accept the majority stress on the positive qualities of the peasant wars. Those who continue to argue more orthodox and skeptical views of peasant ideology maintain that although the antagonistic contradiction between the peasants and the landlords was the primary source of tension in feudal society, the peasants were not and could not have been aware of this opposition in class terms. They were aware of exploitation by

---

[2] E.g., M. M. Smirin, *Narodnaya Reformatsiya Thomasa Muntzer i Velikaya Krestyanskaya Voina*, p. 46.

[3] Some Soviet historians also note the positive aspects of peasant rebel demands for "land and freedom" and other manifestations of "peasant ideology, dreams, and thoughts." E.g., V. V. Mavrodin *et al.*, "On the Characteristics of the Peasant Wars in Russia," VI, no. 2, 1956, pp. 70–71. But there has not been anything like the same degree of emphasis on the positive side of rebel ideology as there has been in mainland Chinese historiography. Recently there is some evidence that the Chinese materials have aroused a renewed Soviet interest in premodern revolutionary ideologies. For instance, the editors of the journal *Problemy Vostokovedeniye* (no. 1, 1960, p. 56) called attention to the "enormous significance" of research on such egalitarian slogans as appeared in the peasant revolts of the Sung period.

their own landlord but not of the landlord system of exploitation.[4] The conservatives stress the limited goals of the rebels
and their ultimate reliance on landlord-class ideas and organization.[5]

Although these views are consistent with classical Marxism,
they have been subjected to considerable criticism as "slanders of the peasant class." Critics contend that the peasant
rebels did not merely attempt to acquire or preserve their
own small property but also demanded a change in the "system of feudal exploitation," the overthrow of the landlord-
class government, and an advance in their own social, economic, and political position.[6]

Among the majority[7] of mainland historians who adopt
this more favorable view of peasant mentality, some have
stated that the "rich revolutionary spirit" of the peasant rebels included the vague notion of establishing "a society where
there is no exploitation of man by man," [8] that the more
advanced peasant wars had "ideals alternative to a feudal
government," [9] and that "for thousands of years" the peasants sought the abolition of inequalities rooted in economic
classes.[10] Others have written that "egalitarianism was not
only a form of peasant thought but at the same time tended
towards a kind of social system," [11] and that the demand for
an "ideal society" based on the concept of "universal har-

[4] Chien Po-tsan, according to Hsueh-shu Tung-t'ai column, *JMJP*,
November 18, 1961. Sun Tso-min and Ts'ai Mei-piao are the leading
exponents of a more negative view of the peasant rebel ideology.

[5] Ts'ai Mei-piao, for instance, noted that many peasant leaders re-
quested Confucian scholars to teach them, since "they believed that
'before undertaking a big enterprise one should consult a sage.'" Ts'ai
Mei-piao, "Discussion of Several Questions in the Debate on the History
of the Chinese Peasant Wars," *LSYC*, no. 4, 1961, p. 80.

[6] T'ien-chin Shih-fan Ta-hsueh Li-shih hsi, "Regarding the Heated
Controversy over the Problem of the Laws of Development of the Chinese Peasant Wars," *SSP*, pp. 459–63.

[7] See *ibid*., pp. 459–60.

[8] Yang K'uan, "On the Function of the Revolutionary Ideology of
the Chinese Peasant Wars and Its Relation with Religion," *SSP*, p. 339.

[9] *Ibid*., p. 324.

[10] Ch'i Hsia *et al.*, *Ch'in-Han Nung-min Chan-cheng Shih*, p. 19.

[11] Hsiang Yang, "On Two Problems in the Chinese Revolutionary
Wars," *KMJP*, no. 4, 1962, p. 11.

mony" always existed in the ideology of the Chinese peasant revolts, developing from a demand for communal ownership of property in the earlier periods to demands for equal land-holding after the T'ang.[12]

One of the leading exponents of this enthusiastic appraisal of the Chinese peasant wars listed five types of goals sought by the rebels: (1) the overthrow of the reigning dynasty; (2) the right to free ownership of land; (3) the easing of enslavement or enserfment binding the peasant to the landlord; (4) an easing of heavy labor and military duties, or corvée; and (5) the abolition of the economic and legal privileges of the ruling class.[13] In short, although all mainland historians admit that the programs of the peasant rebels could not be realized without communist leadership, most argue, in a way that goes beyond classical Marxist guidelines, that "the revolutionary significance of this kind of struggle should not be minimized."[14]

Several factors are involved in the general Chinese communist interpretation of the ideology of the peasant rebels. First, the discussion of the alleged peasant rebel ideology is derived from a relatively small number of slogans and statements which communist historians presume to manifest the wishes of the inarticulate masses throughout the centuries. Implicit in the communist handling of this problem is the belief that only they, as representatives of the working class, know the real wishes of the masses, while traditional and bourgeois historians were either ignorant of these ideals or consciously concealed and distorted them. This type of interpretation also assumes the sincerity of the rebel slogans, although their

[12] E.g., Wang Ssu-chih, "On the Question of the Nature of the Peasant Wars," *SSP*, pp. 159 ff. According to others, the peasant demands changed from opposition to onerous government corvée and close ties to one's master in earlier periods to opposition to inequalities in status and landholding after the T'ang.

[13] Pai Shou-yi, "The Characteristics of the Peasant Wars in Chinese History," *HCS*, nos. 8 and 9, 1960, as summarized by Smolin, "The Discussion by Chinese Historians on the Question of the Peasant Revolts in the Period of Feudalism," *NAA*, no. 2, 1962, p. 193.

[14] Jung Sheng, "Tentative Discussion of Some Special Characteristics of Ming and Ch'ing Peasant Class Struggles," *SSP*, p. 17.

appeal proves popular support for the ideas expressed, regardless of the real aims of the leaders.

Another key assumption in the communist analysis of rebel ideology is the assertion that the different motivation of the rebels made their proposals different in kind from similar statements and ideas found in classical philosophy and also in the proposals of various "feudal" governments. Chinese historians note the origin of peasant thought in "governing-class philosophy," but they maintain that "government reforms," such as those of Wang Mang and Wang An-shih and the "equal field" systems, were meant to perpetuate the regime, while the peasant programs, on the contrary, were used to attack existing rule.[15] Where members of the Sung ruling class would help the poor, contemporary Sung rebel slogans would abolish the distinction between rich and poor.[16] Therefore, mainland historians argue that where governing-class proposals to ameliorate glaring inequalities were intended only to preserve political power, similar rebel demands were used in the struggle against the government and were designed to win power for the laboring class, which alone could effect a really new order.

The most obvious methodological difficulty in evaluating Chinese claims of a positive rebel ideology in history is the inadequacy of source materials dealing with this aspect of the revolts. While an extensive literature exists for the economic and political background and military campaigns of the rebellions, prior to the era of the Taipings there is only secondary and fragmentary mention of the rebels' own beliefs. These references consist primarily of scattered and fragmentary rebel slogans and speeches, reported by historians who invariably wrote from the point of view of the government and

---

[15] E.g., Hou Wai-lu, "The Development of the Peasant Wars and Their Programs and Slogans in Early and Late Periods of Chinese Feudal Society," *SSP*, pp. 26 and 29. See also *HCS* (eds.), "On the Questions of the Nature, Function, and Distinguishing Characteristics of the Peasant Wars in Chinese History," *SSP*, p. 497.

[16] Ning K'o, "The Question of Spontaneity and Consciousness of the Chinese Peasant Wars," *SCMM* 311, p. 37, citing *Hung Ch'i,* April 1, 1962.

without intimate knowledge of the rebel leaders. It is virtually impossible to know what weight should be given to the fragmentary hints of a sense of "peasant justice"—whether to assume, as do even some communist historians, that they represented merely rebel attempts to gain recruits and sympathy,[17] or whether they represented more basic ideals.

Some of the slogans which the mainland historians advance as proof of peasant ideals of justice must be mentioned as background for our analysis of the communist interpretations.[18] Hou Wai-lu classifies the egalitarian content manifested in these statements according to whether they implied a better distribution of the property already possessed by the rebels or whether they implied confiscating the surplus property of the rich to relieve the poor.[19] A third and most common category of slogan simply reflects a negative protest against abuses of the government rather than a positive program.[20]

In the first great peasant war led by Ch'en Sheng and Wu Kuang (209 B.C.), the complaint "Are kings, nobles, generals, and ministers a race of their own?" (*wang hou chiang hsiang, ch'i yu chung hu?*) is cited to show peasant opposition to hereditary privileges but is, of course, also well within the Confucian tradition.[21] Rebel slogans promising rewards and

[17] Sun Tso-min, "A Tentative Discussion of the Nature of Li Tzu-ch'eng's Ta hsun Government," *HCS*, no. 3, 1962; and Sun Tso-min, "The Question of the Blows of the Chinese Peasant Wars Against the Feudal System," *SSP*, p. 117.

[18] Many of these slogans are discussed in the following articles: Vincent Shih, "Some Chinese Rebel Ideologies," *T'oung Pao*, 44, 1956 (included also in his book, *The Taiping Ideology*); and Yuji Muromatsu, "Some Themes in Chinese Rebel Ideologies," in A. F. Wright (ed.), *The Confucian Persuasion*. Norman Cohn's *The Pursuit of the Millennium* (New York: Harper Torchbook, 1961) provides interesting comparative material for medieval Europe. See also Arthur Christensen, *L'Iran sous les Sassanids*, pp. 311 ff.

[19] Hou Wai-lu, *op. cit.*, *SSP*, p. 35.

[20] Many mainland historians would agree with the statement made by T'ao Hsi-sheng in 1934 ("Various Revolts in Sung Times," *Chung-shan Wen-hua Chiao-yü-kuan Chi-k'an*, vol. 1, no. 2, 1934) that middle- and upper-class rebels revolted against the government, while the poor revolted because of egalitarian hopes.

[21] This was pointed out in a recent article by Ts'ao Yung-nien, "On

decrying the abuse of the Ch'in government are better known.[22]

The simple office titles and term of greeting ("great man") of the Red Eyebrows (A.D. 18–27), and their legal principle "If a man killed another, he is executed; if he wounds another, he must give compensation" [23] are cited to show peasant protest against the unequal "feudal laws of the early Han." The latter phrase is clearly based on the principles of Mo Ti and the Legalists, advocating equal punishment for all, regardless of social rank.[24] The fact that the Red Eyebrows, like other rebels of the time, also named their own emperor is attributed to landlord influences or to "peasant monarchism," while their popularity is supposedly proven by a refrain of the time to the effect that "I would rather meet the Red Eyebrows than [the Wang Mang general] T'ai-shih." A similar slogan appeared in 1944 when Honan peasants reportedly stated, "We would prefer to be slaughtered by the Japanese than to endure the tyranny of [the Kuomintang] General T'ang En-po."

Communist historians have frequently interpreted the title

---

the Slogans of Ch'en Sheng and Wu Kuang," *KMJP*, August 14, 1963. The Western scholar Vincent Shih, from whom the following translation is taken (*loc. cit.*, p. 157), concluded that this statement "struck at the root of the idea of rule by birth. . . . However, this should not be construed to mean that they believed in equality for all; or that they aimed at the abolition of social classes. It was merely an expression of a personal desire to be equal with those in power. . . . But inasmuch as Ch'en Sheng did not accept birth as a principle in political or social stratification, his idea was truly revolutionary." Bielenstein, however, believes that this statement and others may have been only literary devices used by traditional historians (*The Restoration of the Han Dynasty*).

[22] Ch'en Sheng reportedly said, "If I become rich and famous, I will not forget the rest of you" (*kou fu kuei, wu hsiang wang*); "the world has long suffered under Ch'in" (*T'ien hsia k'u ch'in chiu yi*); and "attack the unrighteous and punish the violence of Ch'in" (*fa wu tao, chu pao ch'in*). See B. Watson, *Records of the Grand Historian of China*, pp. 19–20.

[23] See Hans Bielenstein, *The Restoration of the Han Dynasty*, vol. 1, p. 138.

[24] Hou Wai-lu (*op. cit., SSP*, pp. 26–27) pointed out that a similar expression is described in the *Lu-shih Ch'un-ch'iu* as a Moist principle of law.

of the influential text (*T'ai-p'ing ching*) used by the Yellow
Turban rebels (184) as the "Book of Great Equality." Recently, however, many mainland historians, as well as most
noncommunist historians, regard this as a distortion of the
original meaning of the term *t'ai-p'ing*. Many now hold that
the book was a conservative influence rather than an instiga-
tion to revolt.[25] Nevertheless, mainland historians advance
evidence of certain welfare measures, if not of egalitarian proposals, as evidence of an intensified peasant struggle for justice in the late Han.[26]

[25] E.g., see *ibid.*, p. 28, for the interpretation of the egalitarian intent
of the *T'ai-p'ing ching*. According to a summary article carried in Hsueh-
shu Tung-t'ai column, *JMJP*, December 15, 1960, Yuan Liang-yi, Hsu
Chih, Yang K'uan, and Lü Chen-yü agreed with Hou Wai-lu that the
T'ai-p'ing ching expressed the ideals of the peasant class. Fan Wen-lan,
Jung Sheng, and Ch'i Hsia (*Ch'in-Han Nung-min Chan-cheng Shih*,
pp. 158 ff.) disagree, while Wang Ming maintains that the work was a
composite one containing both progressive and reactionary ideas. See
also Ho Ch'ang-ch'ün, "On the Slogans of the Yellow Turban Peasant
Uprising," *LSYC*, no. 6, 1959, pp. 33–40. Hsiung Te-chi (*LSYC*, no. 4,
1962) agrees that the *T'ai-p'ing ching* was a composite work but, like
Jung Sheng, contends that it was entirely reactionary and thus transformed the Five Pecks of Rice movement in Szechwan from a revolutionary to a reactionary movement. Hsiung believes the document had
no connection with the Yellow Turban movement led by Chang Chüeh.
However, *Chien-ming Chung-kuo Ssu-hsiang Shih* (Simplified History
of Chinese Thought) by Yang Jung-kuo [Peking: Chung-kuo Ch'ing-nien
Ch'u-pan She, 1962], pp. 61–63) follows Hou Wai-lu's interpretation.
Timoteus Pokora ("On the Origins of the Notions T'ai-p'ing and Ta-
t'ung in Chinese Philosophy," *Archiv-Orientalni* vol. 29, no. 3, 1961, p.
451) of the Czechoslovakian Academy of Sciences maintains that egalitarian ideals were important in Han popular Taoism and influenced not
only the Yellow Turbans but Han Confucianism. However, Paul Michaud ("The Revolt of the Yellow Turbans," *Monumenta Serica*, 1958,
p. 52), a recent Western student of the Yellow Turbans, argues that
there is, in fact, insufficient evidence to establish the identity and hence
the real content of the original texts of the Yellow Turbans. Vincent
Shih ("Some Chinese Rebel Ideologies," *op. cit.*, pp. 166–67) explained
that some Western historians also misinterpreted the term "t'ai-p'ing" as
"making equal what is unequal." Rather, it should read "to each his
due," implying acceptance of one's status and of an unequal social stratification.

[26] Communist historians emphasize the programs of mutual aid and
criticisms of the rich by the contemporary Szechwan peasant rebellion
which also broke out in A.D. 184 and lasted for thirty years or more. See
references to this in *SSP*, pp. 325 and 488; and Liu Ch'üan, "A Tentative
Discussion of the Question of the Goals of the Chinese Peasant Upris-

Certain isolated slogans from the period of the Northern and Southern dynasties and the Sui have also been mentioned in this connection.[27] However, in line with the problem of the role of the class struggle in early feudalism and in the absence of many clear-cut slogans for the period, most mainland historians do not stress aspects of positive peasant ideology before the late T'ang. They argue that the peasant movements of the early feudal period were primarily negative protests against specific government and individual abuses, such as the corvée and the personal restrictions imposed by the lord on his tenant or serf.

Most communist historians believe that after the middle of the T'ang, a "kind of conscious opposition" and a more "purposeful struggle waged against the feudal system" were manifested in the peasant movements.[28] The growing class-

---

ings," *KMJP*, September 17, 1959. However, recent interpretations take a more reserved view of the late Han rebel program. E.g., Ch'i Hsia, *op. cit.*, pp. 185–86. For Western views, see Howard S. Levy, "The Bifurcation of the Yellow Turbans in Later Han," *Oriens*, nos. 13–14, 1960–61, pp. 251–55. See also Levy, "Yellow Turban Religion and Rebellion at the End of the Han," *Journal of the American Oriental Society*, no. 76, 1956; W. Eichhorn, "Description of the Rebellion of Sun En and Earlier Taoist Rebellions," *Mittelungen des Institutes für Orientforschung*, no. 2, 1954, p. 330; and R. A. Stein, "Remarques sur les mouvements du Taoisme Politico-Religieux au 2e Siècle ap. JC.," *T'oung Pao* no. 50, 1963.

[27] For instance, some mainland historians also refer to the egalitarian ideals of another dissident state set up in Szechwan a century later. They cite the *Chin Shu* biography of one of its leaders, Li T'e, which speaks of the "equal opening of land" (*K'en-t'ien chün-p'ing*). Chao Li-sheng and Kao Chao-yi (*Chung-kuo Nung-min Chan-cheng Shih Lun-wen-chi*, p. 41) do not think this movement derived from the earlier Five-pecks-of-rice movement, and they stress proposals for legal reform and other factors expressing the idea of "a certain egalitarian . . . utopian society." Yang K'uan (*op. cit.*, SSP, p. 325) calls the "open equal land" policy the "first proposal for equalizing land" advanced by Chinese rebels. Other writers, however, doubt the validity of these assertions. E.g., Ta Jen, "Huang Ch'ao's Revolt Also Raised the Land Problem," *KMJP*, no. 4, 1961, p. 12. In fact, the land proposal presumably would affect only newly opened lands. For the Sui peasant revolts, historians are able to note anti-government slogans designed to rally support against the Sui, but there is no evidence which can be construed to show alternative social ideals.

[28] E.g., see Shih Shao-pin, "On the Discussion of Problems in the Peasant Revolutionary Wars in Chinese Feudal Society," *SSP*, p. 502.

consciousness of the peasants was revealed in the slogans and programs manifested in the peasant uprisings from the late T'ang on, which supposedly show a progression in kind in peasant ideology from concern with more personal questions to fundamental social and economic problems.[29]

The great revolt (874–84) led by Wang Hsien-chih and Huang Ch'ao is considered transitional in this regard. Historians cite the personal seal of Ch'iu Fu (revolted 859), bearing the characters for "equality," and the titles taken by Wang Hsien-chih, "Heaven-appointed equality general" (*t'ien-pu p'ing-chün ta-chiang-chun*), and Huang Ch'ao, "heaven-storming, protecting-equality general" (*ch'ung-t'ien t'ai-pao chun-p'ing ta chiang-chun*),[30] as the first indications of rebel concern with the fundamental issues of social and economic inequality.[31]

---

[29] Some noncommunist scholars acknowledge that new social and economic problems from the Sung onwards might have influenced the social unrest of the time. Muramatsu (*op. cit.*, p. 242) notes a "kind of cumulative change that took place in rebel ideologies over the centuries." However, he also demonstrates (*ibid.*, p. 259) that most of the late T'ang and Sung rebel leaders, including all of those discussed below, were, in fact, led not by impoverished peasants but by well-to-do traders, smugglers, or landlords, and therefore their egalitarian slogans were insincere. There were social and economic grievances which were reflected in the Sung equality slogans, but the leaders were attempting to exploit rather than correct these grievances. Communist writers, however, attempt to show that some efforts were made to carry out the egalitarian programs in many of these revolts, and when this was the case the leaders, whatever their backgrounds, represented the peasant class. Earlier Chinese Marxist studies sought to show that the poor peasants and not middle-class elements were responsible for the "egalitarian" slogans in the Sung. E.g., this was the argument of the "renegade" T'ao Hsi-sheng, "Various Revolts in Sung Times," *Chung-shan Wen-hua Chiao-yü Kuan Chi-k'an*, vol. 1, no. 2, 1934.

[30] The *Tzu-chih T'ung-chien*, as cited by Hu Ju-lei, "The Historical Function of the Late T'ang Peasant Wars," *LSYC*, no. 1, 1963, p. 117. See also Jung Sheng, *op. cit.*, *SSP*, p. 2; and Pai Shou-yi, "Special Characteristics of the Peasant Wars in Chinese History," *SSP*, p. 240. The *Hsin T'ang-shu*, according to Levy (*The Biography of Huang Ch'ao* [Berkeley: University of California Press, 1961], p. 14), omits the phrase "protecting equality" from Huang Ch'ao's title. At least one author maintains that Huang Ch'ao also proposed land redistribution. See Ta Jen, *op. cit.*, *KMJP*, April 12, 1961.

[31] The late T'ang rebels were aware of and probably were inspired by the earlier T'ang "equal field system" which had disintegrated in the eighth century.

Mainland historians cite the treatment of the rebellion of Huang Ch'ao along with that of the Red Eyebrows and of Chang Hsien-chung,[32] as prime examples of the distortion and slander of the peasant revolts in traditional historiography. They charge that the bad reputation of Huang Ch'ao is due to the class bias of the traditional historian, since, in the words of Sung historians, the late T'ang rebels "hated the officials in particular and killed as many of them as they could," while "the wealthy families were all expelled in a barefoot condition." Yet the same historians, the communists emphasize, were forced to admit that "when the bandit [Huang Ch'ao] saw improverished people, he handed out gold and silk to them." [33]

One of the primary sources cited by communist historians as proof of an alleged peasant concern with the injustices of "feudal China" is the statement of Wang Hsiao-po, who revolted against the Sung in Szechwan in 994. He is reported to have stated, "I hate the inequality between rich and poor, now I will level it [the inequality] for you" (*wu chi p'in-fu pu-chün, chin wei ju chün-chih*). According to the same source, Wang's successor Li Hsun sought to carry out this principle by confiscating the surplus property of the rich and distributing it to the poor.[34] There is some discussion about the pos-

<hr/>

[32] For communist refutations of the slanders against Huang Ch'ao see Ta Jen, *op. cit.*; Chou Pao-chu, "Discussion of a Problem in the History of the Late T'ang Peasant War," *SHYK*, no. 6, 1959; Ho Lin-t'ien, "How to Look on the Two Mistaken Traditions Concerning Huang Ch'ao and the Boxers," *Hsiao-hsueh Chiao-shih*, September 1954; Teng Kuang-ming, "A Tentative Discussion of the Late T'ang Peasant Uprisings," *LKP*; and Yang Chih-chiu, "The Great Uprising of Huang Ch'ao," *LKP*.

[33] See Levy, *op. cit.*, pp. 28, 73–74.

[34] *Sheng-shui Yen T'an-lu* (Collected Talks on the Swallows of the Sheng River), chüan 8, and *Meng-ch'i Pi-t'an* (Notes Taken at Meng Ch'i), chüan 15, cited in Su Chin-yuan and Li Ch'un-p'u (eds.), *Sung-tai San-tzu Nung-min Ch'i-yi Shih-liao Hui-pien* (Collection of Sources on the Three Sung Peasant Uprisings) (Peking: Chung-hua Shu-chü, 1963), pp. 57 and 60. Chang Yin-lin, although not a communist, gave an early Marxist interpretation of this revolt in "The Revolt of Wang Hsiao-po and Li Hsun in Szechwan: An Unsuccessful Communist Movement," *Ch'ing-hua Hsueh-pao* (Tsinghua Journal), vol. 12, no. 2, 1937, pp. 315–35. This interpretation is disputed by the East German scholar

sible religious origins of Wang Hsiao-po's statement deploring inequality, but most mainland historians deny any religious connections with the revolt.[35]

Similar statements describing the activities of Chung Hsiang and Yang Yao in Hunan and Hupeh (suppressed 1135), together with the programs of the late Ming and Taiping rebels, form the principal exhibits for proponents of a revolutionary peasant ideology. A contemporary source states that Chung Hsiang told his followers, "The [present] law which distinguishes between the noble and the commoner and between the rich and poor is not a good law. If I am able to carry out a law, then the noble and commoner, the rich and poor will be made equal" (*fa fen kuei-chien p'in-fu, fei shan-fa yeh; wu hsing fa, tang-fa teng kuei chien, chün p'in-fu*). Although Chung Hsiang himself was a wealthy landlord, we are told that "small people" around Tung T'ing Lake, Hunan, flocked to join him, and they plundered and burned government yamens and killed officials, scholars, monks, sorcerers, and medicine men. The shocked recorder of these deeds reported that the rebels excused these actions by "calling bandit soldiers gentlemen and by saying the national law was an iniquitous law, [while] killing men was [a means] of carrying out the [new] law and plunder was [a means of] equalization" (*wei tzei-ping wei yeh-erh, wei kuo-tien wei*

W. Eichhorn ("Towards a History of the Uprising of Wang Hsiao-po and Li Hsun in Szechwan," *Zeitschrift für Deutschen Morgenlandischen Gesellschaft*, vol. 105, 1955), who maintains that the egalitarian statements in this movement were directed against the Sung government by Szechwan landlords and not against the wealthy by the poor. Ikeda Makoto ("Rebellion in the Szechwan District in the Early Sung Period," *Rekishigaku Kenkyu*, 152, July 1951) confirms that the revolt was primarily due to Sung exploitation of the Szechwanese. Nevertheless, this would again appear to be a question of the sincerity of the rebel leader rather than of the meaning of the statements which do specify inequalities between "rich" and "poor." Therefore, it seems reasonable to suppose that Wang's slogan and Li's actions did in fact reflect tensions between widely separated economic classes, whether or not they were advanced sincerely or for purposes of mobilization against the Sung.

[35] Chiang Yi-jen, "Regarding Several Questions in the Sung Peasant Revolt Led by Wang Hsiao-po, Li Hsun, and Chang Yu," *LSYC*, no. 5, 1958, p. 55.

hsieh-fa, wei sha-jen wei hsing-fa, wei chieh-ts'ai wei chün-p'ing).[36] According to a Soviet historian, these statements showed the "dreams of peasants for a life of primitive equality and justice and their struggles to liquidate poverty and injustice." [37] Be that as it may, the statement is a striking example of astute early rebel propaganda attempting to reverse the orthodox frame of reference.

There has been considerable comment and confusion over a statement by Fang La (revolted 1120–22), the characters for which are *fa p'ing-teng wu yu shang-hsia.* Depending on where the comma is placed, this statement can read "the law is equal and there is no high or low" or, if the negative *wu* is placed with the first four characters, "the law is unequal and there is high and low." [38] Earlier communist interpretations, predictably, followed the former interpretation.[39] Recently an article pointed out that the original source in fact stated that Fang La twisted a Buddhist text having the former meaning to say that inequality was to be expected.[40] Modern noncommunist interpretations support the latter view,[41] and, in any case, communist historians no longer cite this

[36] Hsu Meng-hua, *San-ch'ao Pei-meng Hui-pien* (Collections on Negotiations with the Northern Dynasties During the Three Reigns), chuan 137, cited in Su Chin-yuan and Li Ch'un-p'u (eds.), *Sung-tai San-tzu Nung-min Ch'i-yi Shih-liao Hui-pien,* pp. 224–25.

[37] G. Ya. Smolin, "Peasant Uprising Under the Leadership of Chung Hsiang and Yang Yao," *PV,* no. 1, 1960, p. 60. Elsewhere Smolin also notes that Chung Hsiang fought other peasant gangs, now described as "vagabond bandits." See his *Krestyanskoye Vostaniye v Provintsiakh Hunan i Hupeh, v* 1130–1135 (Peasant Uprising in the Provinces of Hunan and Hupeh from 1130 to 1135), pp. 57 and 69.

[38] Chuang Chi-yü, Chi-le pien in *Shuo Fu,* cited in Vincent Shih, "Some Chinese Rebel Ideologies," p. 175.

[39] E.g., Ch'ien Chün-hua and Ch'i Hsia, "Fang La's Uprising," *LKP,* p. 193.

[40] Feng Chih, "Did Fang La's Revolt Promulgate Slogans of Equality?" *KMJP,* September 29, 1960.

[41] Shih, *op. cit.,* p. 175; and Kao Yü-kung, "A Study of the Fang La Rebellion," unpublished Harvard University Ph.D. dissertation, 1962, p. 96. See also Kao Yü-kung, "The Fang La Rebellion," *HJAS,* no. 24, 1962–63. A third possible interpretation of this passage seems conceivable, that is that Fang was attacking Sung law as inconsistent with Buddhist ideals, and the historian described this sentence out of context as a distortion of the original Buddhist recommendation of equality.

phrase but other reports of Fang La's activities, such as
"when new members are very poor, the others would generally contribute small sums to their support . . . people and
things are used without distinction and they speak of themselves as one family." [42] In short, according to Hou Wai-lu's
definitions,[43] Fang La's rebellion is still cited as an example
of the lower form of "peasant communal ideals" of mutual
aid but no longer as an example of attempts to redress economic inequality by force.

Certain slogans advanced by dissident Buddhist secret societies during the chaotic years at the end of the Yuan dynasty
are also cited by communist writers as evidence of peasant
ideals. Part of the Buddhist sutra "The Descent to Earth of
Maitreya" described a utopia in which "all people big and
small shall be equal, there being none treated differently"
(*jen-min ta-hsiao chieh t'ung yi hsiang, wu jo kan chih ch'a
pieh yeh*).[44] Communist historians interpret such statements
as proof of the people's grievances against the landlords as
well as against the Mongol overlords, and minimize the religious implications.[45] A popular refrain of the time has been
translated:

[42] Cited in Shih, *op. cit.*, p. 174.

[43] See this chapter, above.

[44] Cited in Wang Ch'ung-wu, "On Ming T'ai-tsu's Revolt and the
Changes in His Policies," *Chung-yang Yen-chiu Yuan, Li-shih Yü-yen
So* (Academia Sinica), vol. 10, 1948, p. 60.

[45] Mainland historians continue to debate the relative importance of
the ethnic and socio-economic causes of the Yuan revolts. E.g., Tu Lieh-
yuan ("On the Nature, Development, and Two Stages of the Late Yuan
Revolutionary Struggles," *Hsi-pei Ta-hsueh Hsueh-pao* [Journal of
North-West University], no. 3, 1957, p. 124) criticizes those who
neglect the ethnic issue in their emphasis on class struggle in the history
of the anti-Mongol revolts. Similarly, Wang Ch'ung-wu, a leading authority on the Yuan who remained on the mainland, wrote in 1954, as
he had in the 1940s, that the racial contradiction with the Mongols was
the leading source of unrest in the 1350s. On the other hand, like Meng
Ssu-ming, another Yuan scholar of the Nationalist period, he recognized
that the revolt began (1351) over social and economic problems. See
Wang Ch'ung-wu, "On the Development and Historical Function of
the Late Yuan Peasant Revolts," *LSYC*, no. 4, 1954, pp. 87 ff.; and
Meng Ssu-yuan, "The Social and Class System of the Yuan," *Yen-ching
Hsueh-pao* (Journal of Yenching University), no. 16, 1938. Among
Western scholars, Shih (*op cit.*, p. 19) concedes that the anti-Yuan

Heaven sends the army of the White Lotus to destroy injustice. [Formerly] the unjust killed the refractory. [Now] those who do not submit kill the unjust. Only after destroying the unjust will there be great equality.[46]

By the late Ming, according to many mainland historians, economic developments were approaching conditions of incipient capitalism.[47] In the Marxist scheme of things such conditions would invariably influence the ideology of the Chinese rebels, but Party theorists no longer allow historians to make too much of the problem of incipient capitalism because of the threat of such an interpretation to current claims of China's progress from a backward, feudal heritage. If China had been moving toward capitalism on its own, the present explanations of the necessity for revolution, of the role of "imperialism," and of China's leadership of the emerging nations would be unnecessarily complicated.

Again, the materials of Chinese history strain at the confines of official dogma. On the one hand, revolts such as those of Yeh Tsung-liu and Teng Mou-ch'i (1442–49) and of Liu T'ung and Li Yuan (1466–71) are said to show new economic demands reflecting social and economic developments.

---

rebels raised some economic as well as ethnic issues, but he believes they directed their propaganda against the unequal economic position held by the Mongols and not toward a redistribution of wealth as had some of the Sung rebels. F. W. Mote thinks that such texts as the utopian passage cited above reflected a potentially revolutionary ideology, though in the process of trying to realize their goals, the rebels were forced to modify or abandon traditional ideas.

[46] L. A. Borovkova, "The Uprising of the Red Troops and the Rise of Chu Yuan-chang," *NAA*, no. 2, 1961, p. 94. The text reads: *t'ien ch'ien mo-chün sha pu-p'ing, pu-p'ing jen sha pu-p'ing jen, pu-p'ing jen sha pu-p'ing che, sha chin pu-p'ing fang t'ai-p'ing*. Cho Keng lu, chüan 27, cited in Pei-ching Ta-hsueh Chung-wen Hsi (eds.), *Chung-kuo Li-tai Nung-min Wen-t'i Wen-hsueh Tzu-liao* (Literary Materials on the Peasant Question in Chinese History) (Peking: Chung-hua Shu-chü, 1959), p. 107.

[47] See *Chung-kuo Tzu-pen Chu-i Meng-ya Wen-t'i T'ao-Lun Chi* (Collected Essays on the Problems Relating to the Roots of Chinese Capitalism), compiled by the Chinese History Teaching and Research Section of China's Peoples University (Peking, 1957).

The former were among the most important of some seventy-seven so-called "miners' revolts" of the middle Ming and supposedly involved for the first time significant numbers of urban plebeians as well as peasants, while the latter manifested supposedly new economic demands in the struggle to open up restricted lands.[48]

On the other hand, orthodox historians criticize efforts to attribute too great an advance in peasant ideology in the late Ming. Among the criticisms of historian Shang Yueh was the charge that he attributed the late Ming egalitarian slogans to the growing influences of incipient capitalism. Rather, orthodox interpreters maintain, these slogans were products of changes within feudalism and not of new forces, of quantitative and not qualitative changes.[49]

In any case, the ideology of the peasant rebels is said to have reached a new stage of development by the late Ming. Some writers state that the egalitarian ideals of the peasants developed from a concern for the equalization of movable property in the Sung to demands for equal landholding in the Ming.[50] According to this view, the proposal of Li Tzu-ch'eng and Li Yen for the "equalization of land and the avoidance of taxes" (*chün-t'ien mien-liang*) was the first such

[48] See Li Lung-ch'ien, "The Events and Characteristics of the Revolts of Yeh Tsung-liu and Teng Mou-ch'i in the Ming, Cheng-t'ung Period," *LKP*, pp. 227 ff.; Lai Chia-tu, "The Great Peasant Revolt of Liu T'ung and Li Yuan in the Ching-hsiang Mountains in the Mid-Ming," *LKP*, pp. 249–50; and Li Lung-ch'ien, "A Tentative Discussion of the Resistance Struggles of the Ming Miners' Movement," *SHYK*, no. 3, 1959, p. 34. According to a Japanese study (Miyazaki Ichisada, "Peasant Riots in Chinese History with Special Reference to the Affair of Teng Mou-ch'i," *Toyoshi Kenkyu*, vol. 10, no. 1), Teng Mou-ch'i, who called himself the "leveling prince" (*Ch'an-p'ing wang*), did exhibit a high degree of class-consciousness. See also Shih, *op. cit.*, p. 204; and Muramatsu, *op. cit.*, p. 260.

[49] Liao-ning Ta-hsueh Li-shih hsi, "Criticize the Mistaken Viewpoint of Shang Yueh on Rural Class Relations and Peasant Wars of the Ming-Ch'ing," *KMJP*, July 21, 1960; and P'an Te-shen, "On the Function, Characteristics, and Nature of the Peasant Revolts and Wars in the Later Period of Chinese Feudal Society," *SSP*, p. 194.

[50] E.g., Chang Shih-te and Wu T'ing-tung, "The Special Characteristics of Chung Hsiang and Yang Yao's Peasant Revolt," *LSCHWT*, 1958, no. 3 (March).

clear program advanced by the Chinese rebels. Li Tzu-ch'eng called himself "Great General Claiming Justice for Heaven" (*Fen t'ien ch'ang-yi ta yuan-shuai*).[51] Other late Ming rebel slogans, such as "equal buying and selling" (*p'ing-mai p'ing mai*) are also cited as evidence of enlightened rebel policies.[52]

The key issue in the evaluation of the ideology and alleged "search for peasant justice" in the late Ming rebellions (1627–45), as in the case of the Taipings, is the degree to which their slogans were carried out and, hence, the real intentions of the leaders. In both cases there are numerous statements attesting the rebels' destruction of the rich and some attesting their help of the poor, but, as one would expect, there is little if any evidence of systematic execution of an equal-land policy. In the case of Li Tzu-ch'eng's revolt, some historians argue that local records recently discovered in Shantung, which speak of the rebels "taking from the rich to help the poor" (*ke-fu chi-p'in*), prove rebel redistribution of land.[53] Other historians, however, maintain that the redistribution applied only to movable property, while the main content of Li Tzu-ch'eng's program was directed against the burdensome Ming taxes.[54] There is also much discussion of the

[51] Muramatsu, *op. cit.*, p. 262.

[52] Jung Sheng, *op. cit.*, *SSP*, p. 18.

[53] The source in question is Ting Yao-kang, *Ch'u-chieh chi-lueh*. For communist accounts, see Jung Sheng, *op. cit.*, *SSP*, pp. 10–12; Hsieh Kuo-chen, "Notes of Materials on the Function of the Late Ming and Early Ch'ing Peasant Revolts," *LSYC*, no. 3, 1962, p. 145. Other articles complain of a lack of sources with which to evaluate the "equal field" slogans of Li Tzu-ch'eng or emphasized the breakdown of the rebel morale and programs in 1644. E.g., see Li Wen-chih, "The Late Ming Peasant Revolutionary Leader, Li Tzu-ch'eng," in Li Kuang-pi and Ch'ien Chün-hua (eds.), *Chung Kuo Li-shih Jen-wu Lun-ts'ung*, p. 116; and Li Kuang-pi, "The Great Peasant Revolt of the End of the Ming," in Li Kuang-pi (ed.), *Ming Ch'ing shih Lun-ts'ung* (Collected Discussions on Ming-Ching History) (Wuhan: Hupeh Jen-min Ch'u-pan She, 1957), p. 116.

[54] Wang Shou-yi, "Doubts About the Equal Land Slogan of the Late Ming Peasant Army," *LSYC*, no. 2, 1962. Sun Tso-min (*op. cit.*, *HCS*, no. 3, 1962) and Ts'ai Mei-piao (according to *SCMM* 308, p. 34) also doubt the reliability and interpretation of key sources for the Ming rebellions and warn against an exaggeration of the revolutionary qualities of the late Ming revolts. Nevertheless, in line with the prevailing "leftist" appraisal of the peasant wars, the majority of historians

role of Li Yen, the son of a prominent government official, in the devising of Li Tzu-ch'eng's program.

The communists' main concern with Chang Hsien-chung, a rebel contemporary of Li Tzu-ch'eng and an archvillain in pre-communist historiography, is to refute so-called "slanders" of traditional historians. They also point out that Chang, though to a less extent than Li, redistributed property for the benefit of the poor and exempted taxes.[55]

The beliefs of the White Lotus rebellion of the late eighteenth century, including ideals of communal ownership and equality, are advanced as "simple egalitarian ideology" by one historian.[56] However, few other articles have supported this thesis, and some have attacked it.[57]

There is no disagreement among communist historians about the egalitarian nature of various Taiping proposals, but there is an enormous difference of opinion as to their "progressiveness" in the light of the conditions of the time and the degree to which they were carried out. The former problem concerns the degree to which such Taiping policies as the land program were influenced by and favored the growth of capitalism. Most mainland writers describe the Taiping rebellion as an "old-style peasant movement [against feudalism] 'flavored by' varying degrees of a bourgeois-democratic revolution." [58] The relation of the Taipings to the allegedly de-

---

continue to emphasize all evidences of "peasant justice" in the Ming as in other periods. For instance, Liu Chung-jih questioned Wang Shou-yi's negation of the "equal land policy" (*LSYC*, no. 5, 1962).

[55] E.g., Li Wen-chih, *op. cit.*, pp. 148 and 162; and Hsieh Kuo-chen, "Notes of Materials on the Function of the Late Ming and Early Ch'ing Peasant Revolts," *LSYC*, no. 3, 1962, p. 145. James Parsons ("The Rebellion of Chang Hsien-chung as an Example of the Internal Disturbances in China During the Late Ming Dynasty," unpublished University of California Ph.D. dissertation, 1954, pp. 122, 147, and 154) confirms that Chang did redistribute some property.

[56] Yang K'uan, "A Tentative Discussion of the Features of the White Lotus Teaching," *KMJP*, March 15, 1961.

[57] E.g., Shao Shun-cheng, "Secret Societies, Religion, and the Peasant Wars," *SSP*, p. 379.

[58] See articles in Ching Yen and Lin Yen-shu (eds.), *T'ai-p'ing T'ien-kuo Ke-ming Hsing-chih Wen-t'i T'ao-lun Chi*. Seven views on the nature of the Taipings presented in this book are summarized by L. P.

veloping anti-imperialism of the Chinese people is also an issue, though the Taiping rebellion is considered to have been directed primarily against the internal landlord class, rather than against the foreign powers.

As for the content of Taiping thought, a translation of part of the Taiping land proposals (1853) reveals their high degree of utopianism:

> All land shall be classified into nine categories . . . the distribution of land is made according to the size of the family, irrespective of sex. . . . [According to] the nine categories . . . all lands under Heaven shall be farmed jointly by the people under Heaven. If the production of food is too small in one place, then move to another where it is more abundant. All lands under Heaven shall be accessible in time of abundance or famine . . . in this way the people under Heaven shall all enjoy the great happiness given by the Heavenly Father, Supreme Lord, and August God. Land shall be farmed by all; rice eaten by all; clothes worn by all; money spent by all. There shall be no inequality and no person shall be without food or fuel. . . . In the empire none shall have any private property and everything belongs to God, so that God may dispose of it. In the great family of Heaven every place is equal and everyone has plenty. This is the edict of the Heavenly Father, Supreme Lord, and August God who especially commanded the T'ai-p'ing True Lord to save the world.[59]

Hsiao Kung-ch'uan, like most Western commentators on the Taipings, doubts that the rebels ever effected significant parts of this program,[60] yet he translates part of a contempo-

---

Delyusin, "Review of Research on the TPTK," *NAA*, no. 5, 1962, p. 184.

[59] Cited in J. C. Cheng, *Chinese Sources for the T'ai-p'ing Rebellion, 1850–1864* (Hong Kong: Hong Kong University Press, 1963), pp. 39–40.

[60] See *ibid.*, p. 38; and Hsiao Kung-ch'uan, *Rural China: Imperial Control in the Nineteenth Century*, p. 183. Vincent Shih contrasts the high-handed behavior of Taiping leaders and their anti-peasant bias with

rary account which many communist writers cite to prove opposite conclusions:

> They distributed clothing and other articles (which they
> had previously looted elsewhere) to poor people of the
> countryside. They made it generally known that they
> would in future exempt all taxes for a period of three
> years. . . . The rebels never indulge in killing in the vil-
> lages. . . . But they plunder most thoroughly house-
> holds in which families of officials, their private secretar-
> ies, or yamen clerks and runners have sought shelter, as
> well as residences of gentry families. They slaughter the
> occupants and burn down the buildings. . . .[61]

Mainland historians themselves are still widely split on the
question of how much of the Taiping land program was carried out. Lo Erh-kang, the best-known scholar of the Taipings
now in China, argued in the 1930s that the rebels did carry
out a "communal system" at least in the army and in areas
under their immediate control, although they did not extend
it because of the exigencies of their struggle.[62] In 1950 Lo
noted that the land system was "put into practice" around
Nanking.[63] Five years later Lo wrote that Taiping systems,
including the communal treasury, operated to the benefit of
the poor in the early part of the rebellion but later were undermined by corruption and declining morale and were never
fully realized.[64] Lo's continued uncertainty as to how to handle this aspect of the Taiping movement is revealed in his
statement that although the Taiping land system was "uto-

---

the pronouncements of Taiping propaganda. Thus the "Land System
of the Heavenly Dynasty" (cited above) belittled the social status of the
peasantry. See Shih, *The Taiping Ideology* (Seattle: University of Washington Press, 1967), pp. 50–51.

[61] Cited in Hsiao Kung-ch'uan, *op. cit.*, p. 142.

[62] Lo Erh-kang, *TPTK Shih-kang* (Outline History of the TPTK)
(Shanghai: Shang-wu Yin-shu kuan, 1937), pp. 95–96.

[63] Teng Ssu-yü, *Historiography of the Taiping Rebellion*, p. 64, citing Lo Erh-kang, *TPTK te li-hsiang-kuo* (Ideal State of the TPTK).

[64] Lo Erh-kang, *TPTK Shih Shih-k'ao* (Investigation of Events in
the History of the TPTK) (Peking: San-lien Shu-tien, 1955), pp. 204,
209, 226–28.

pian and unrealizable," the rebels "did carry out a kind of field-to-the-tiller policy," at least in the early years.[65] Following Party directives not to overestimate the achievements of the Taipings,[66] in 1957 Lo declared that earlier versions of one of his works had exaggerated the "progressiveness" of the Taipings.[67] The preface of the work in question had stated that the Taipings would "abolish landlord ownership," [68] an intention which the Chinese communists reserve for the "vanguard of the proletariat."

Thus, the problem of the degree of execution of the land program and other Taiping policies is still unresolved but is generally said to depend on the area and the period involved. Three types of Taiping land programs have been defined: first, in a few places the landlord holdings were confiscated and distributed to the poor as well as to Taiping officials; second, tenants were allowed to take over land deserted by the former owners; and, third, in most areas the old systems of landlord-tenant relations were continued as before.[69] There was no "fixed land system" in practice, but some revolutionary redistributions were effected when conditions allowed. Significant parts of the communal-treasury system were carried out in the early years of the Taiping rebellion, and the land law intended to extend this principle to forms of landholding. Since, however, the orders of the Taiping leaders were not implemented by local officials, the rebels later com-

[65] *Ibid.*, p. 205.

[66] "Remember the 100th Anniversary of the Revolution of the TPTK," *JMJP* editorial, January 11, 1951; and Fan Wen-lan, "Remember the 105th Anniversary of the Revolt of the TPTK," *JMJP*, January 11, 1956.

[67] A. Feuerwerker and S. Cheng, *Chinese Communist Studies of Modern Chinese History*, p. 79.

[68] Lo Erh-kang, *TPTK Shih-kao* (A Draft History of the Taiping Heavenly Kingdom) (Peking: K'ai-ming Shu-tien, 1951), preface, p. 1. This, in fact, was the orthodox interpretation at the time. E.g., see Fan Wen-lan, *TPTK Ke-ming Yun-tung* (The TPTK Revolutionary Movement) (Singapore: Hsin Min-chu Ch'u-pan She, 1948).

[69] Ts'ao Kuo-she, "Discussion of the Land and Tax Policy of the T'ai-p'ing T'ien-kuo," *Chung-shan Ta-hsueh-Hsueh-pao* (Journal of Sun Yat-sen University), no. 9, 1959. See also V. Shih, *Taiping Ideology*, pp. 230, 234, 237, 489–92.

promised with the gentry, who alone were able to administer the newly won territories.[70]

The prevailing view, then, is that the Taipings had revolutionary ideas but were unable to work them into a system or to carry them out with any consistency. They were revolutionary in intent but at best utopian or even reactionary in content.[71] A Soviet article attempts to summarize various views of the problem.[72] The author agrees with the general interpretation that Taiping programs of distributing empty lands and lightening taxes were progressive but not, as earlier writers held (including Lo Erh-kang and Efimov), evidence of "land-to-tiller" policies. He also subscribes to the prevailing Chinese view that the Taiping policies became less revolutionary in the process of administrating conquered areas. He believes that the Taipings carried out their policy of the communal treasury for all property from 1850 to 1853 and then proclaimed the land system which would have expanded this principle to land-holding. Since their orders were not implemented by local officials, the Taiping leaders soon compromised with the gentry, who alone were able to administer the newly won territories. Nevertheless, he felt that the Taiping movement undermined the position of the biggest landlords and benefited the poor.[73]

Communist historians naturally seek to deny Christian ori-

[70] See V. P. Ilyushechkin, "Agrarian Policies of the Taipings," *NAA*, no. 4, 1962, pp. 98–106; and Lung Sheng-yun, "On the Land Policy of the TPTK," *LSYC*, no. 6, 1963, for recent summaries of interpretations of the Taiping land program.

[71] The Taiping program would be reactionary according to communist theory insofar as it obstructed the development of capitalism in China. For a summary of the three positions taken on the nature of the Taiping land program, see *SCMP* 2479, p. 19, citing *KMJP*, March 10, 1961. See also Tu Te-feng, "On Several Questions in the T'ai-p'ing Heavenly Land System," in Ching Yen and Lin Yen-shu (eds.), *T'ai-p'ing T'ien-Kuo Ke-ming Hsing-chih Wen-t'i T'ao-lun Chi* (Collected Articles on the Nature of the TPTK Revolution), p. 293 ff.; Li Wen-chih, "The Function of the Revolution of the TPTK in the Transformation of the Feudal Productive Relations," *KMJP*, January 16, 1961; and Mou An-shih, *T'ai-p'ing T'ien-kuo*, p. 422.

[72] Ilyushechkin, *op. cit.*

[73] For a discussion of the last point, see Li Wen-chih, *op. cit.*, *KMJP*, January 16, 1961.

gins for Taiping ideology, arguing instead that social and class cleavages were the basis of the Taiping ideals. Fan Wen-lan in 1948 allowed some place for Christian as well as indigenous utopian ideals in Taiping ideology,[74] but now, in the emphasis on class antagonisms and the inroads of imperialism, there is little room for these considerations. There is some support among noncommunist historians for the view that Christianity was a less important source of Taiping ideology than certain parts of the native tradition.[75]

Through the middle of the 1950s, most writers stressed the revolutionary side of the Taiping program, although all acknowledged that no such sweeping revolution could succeed prior to the emergence of the proletariat. The weaknesses of the peasant class and the inevitable failure of the Taipings were stressed in important anniversary articles appearing in *JMJP* in 1951 and 1956,[76] but it was not until the late 1950s that most writers toned down their praise of the revolutionary qualities of the Taipings.[77]

The recent restraint in the evaluation of the Taipings contrasts with the opposite tendency in the treatment of earlier peasant revolts and may be explained by the proximity of the Taipings to the communist-led revolution. All Chinese are

---

[74] Fan Wen-lan, *TPTK Ke-ming Yun-tung*, p. 29. In his influential *History of Modern China* (*Chung-kuo Chin-tai shih*, 1961 ed., vol. 1, p. 151), Fan also described the Taipings as "a peasant class anti-feudal war" whose greatest significance lay in "proposing for the first time four great revolutionary slogans [arguing for] political, economic, racial, and sexual equality." After the recent attention to peasant rebel egalitarianism from the Sung on, it is doubtful if Fan would still speak of the Taipings as the "first" to propose egalitarian slogans.

[75] See Teng Ssu-yü, *Historiography of the Taiping Rebellion*, p. 75, citing Hsieh Hsing-yao on this point. See also E. P. Boardman, *Christian Influences upon the Ideology of the T'ai-p'ing Rebellion*.

[76] See *JMJP*, January 11, 1951, and January 11, 1956.

[77] E.g., the changing statements of Lo Erh-kang, see Chapter 10. For other cautious appraisals of the revolutionary qualities of the Taipings see articles by Lung Sheng-yun, *LSYC*, no. 2, 1958; by Wu Yen-nan, *SHYK*, no. 10, 1958; by Ch'i Lung-wei, *KMJP*, November 12, 1959; by Wang Hsin-pang, *KMJP*, September 1, 1960; and by Shen Yuan, *LSYC*, no. 1, 1963. Others continue to stress revolutionary aspects, e.g., see Hsu Hsi-ming, *LSYC*, no. 9, 1959; Ho Jo-chün, *SHYK*, no. 5, 1958; and conference on Taipings reported in *KMJP*, June 7, 1961.

aware of the significance of the Taiping movement, and there is no longer the need to dramatize its egalitarian proposals as is the case with the earlier peasant revolts. Rather, the danger is that Party uniqueness may be questioned by too great attention to the revolutionary qualities of the Taipings. Therefore, mainland historians are more careful to stress the inevitable failure of the Taipings than they are in the case of the earlier peasant movements. These can be praised in order to establish the "glorious revolutionary tradition" of the Chinese people without threatening the monopoly of correct leadership by the communists.

Most writers insist that while the Taiping revolt coincided with and helped to launch a new stage in Chinese history, it nevertheless belonged to the "old-style" peasant wars. The same considerations apply to the Nien and the Boxer revolts. The former are viewed as gaining their real significance by extending the Taiping movement into north China, and the latter as a peasant war directed against imperialism. Some writers attribute signs of new ideological content to the peasant movements occurring after the fall of the Manchus in 1911 but before 1919. However, the supposed manifestation of this in the slogan "strike the rich to help the poor" [78] occurred also in earlier revolts, including the one in 1903–04.[79] Therefore, the May Fourth Movement of 1919 and the founding of the Chinese Communist Party two years later mark the real dividing line between peasant movements of the "old and new type" in mainland historiography. Only with the arrival of communist leadership could peasant utopias begin to approach realization.

There are immense difficulties in evaluating the historical significance of the fragmentary evidences of rebel ideology enumerated above. The slogans, programs, and other evi-

[78] Advanced during the peasant revolt of 1912 in parts of Honan, Hupeh, and Anhui, this slogan had a "certain new content of struggle" and a "democratic revolutionary flavor," according to one author. See Lai Hsin-hsia, "On the Peasant Revolt led by Pai Lang in the Early Republic," *LKP*, pp. 454 and 459.

[79] Lai Hsin-hsia, "A Tentative Discussion of the Great Peasant Revolt of the Late Kuang-hsu Reign in Kwangsi," *LKP*, p. 427.

dence cited by communist historians to demonstrate an alleged peasant concept of justice are too fragmentary to permit more than the vaguest generalizations. Moreover, leading noncommunist students of the same materials draw quite different conclusions, specifically regarding the intellectual origins and political significance of rebel mentality. They consider rebel ideology not a refutation but a continuation of traditional ideals.

Nonetheless, although rebel slogans reflect traditional Chinese thought, they also challenge aspects of Imperial Confucianism. While popular resistance to social and economic abuses had less immediate effect than the occasional reform attempts within the government, they influenced continuing admonitions against various forms of injustice and demonstrated the existence of a spirit of protest which has been as much neglected in noncommunist studies of Chinese history as it has been exaggerated by the communists. Some of these materials will force greater attention to the tradition of protest in Chinese history than has yet been given in noncommunist historiography.

Leaving aside the implications of the materials on peasant ideology for Chinese historiography in general, it is evident that their interpretation presents great problems in the light of Marxist historiography. The first concerns the role of religion in the origin, formation, and organization of peasant rebel ideology.

CHAPTER SEVEN

Religious Attitudes

THE role of religion in the formation of rebel ideology has been another controversial subject. The classical Marxists maintained that religious wars were essentially class wars and, conversely, that class wars often took religious forms. Engels stated that "revolutionary opposition" to feudalism in medieval Europe "appeared only as an opposition to religious feudalism" and the "class struggles of that day were clothed in religious shibboleths." [1] Marx apparently believed religious ties to be a precondition of social unrest in Oriental society. He wrote that the Taipings like "all Oriental movements . . . had a religious coloration." [2] Yet, while recognizing the appeal of religious forms and ideals, Marx and Engels also attacked religion as the "opiate of the people" in so far as it turned men's minds from the problems of this world to the hereafter. Again a contradiction in the writings of the masters became a source of great confusion for the interpretations of the students. On the one hand, all class struggles of the feudal period in the West and "all Oriental

---

[1] Engels, *The Peasant War in Germany*, pp. 57 and 54. See also Karl Kautsky, *Communism in Central Europe in the Time of the Reformation* (New York: Russell and Russell, 1959 reprint).

[2] Cited in K. A. Wittfogel, "The Marxist View of China," *The China Quarterly*, no. 11, pp. 6–7.

movements" assume religious forms, and the masses can be aroused only by religious prophecy; but, on the other, religion dulls the revolutionary consciousness of the people and is "bunk" and "primitive nonsense." [3]

Traditional China lacked the sort of organized church and religious domination of life which, according to Engels, explained the religious forms taken by the European anti-feudal movements.[4] However, popular religions and primarily religious concerns obviously existed in China, as in Europe, and in this sense some communist historians apply relevant statements of the classical Marxists on religion to Chinese history. Their discussions are reminiscent in many ways of the debates between Christian reformers and conservatives.

Some mainland historians attempt to resolve the contradiction between positive and negative Marxist comments on religion by distinguishing the religion of the upper classes from the religion of the rebellious commoners. According to this argument, the latter transform the religious tenets used by the governing classes from an instrument of ideological control into a weapon against the governing class. Religious beliefs which seek to inculcate submission are an "opiate," but religious beliefs advocating social justice clearly are not.

The first general history of the peasant wars published in China after 1949 adopted this approach. It explained the origin and nature of the Yellow Turban ideology:

> in the processes of popularization of the superstitious theories [which "the reactionary governing class used to paralyze the resistance of the oppressed peasantry," these theories] were gradually transformed into a weapon of mass resistance against the governing class.[5]

Developing this line of reasoning, other Chinese historians maintain that, far from being especially rebellious, the Chinese peasant was loath to revolt because of the dominance of the feudal ideology which preached acceptance of one's lot.

---

[3] Engels, "Letter to C. Schmidt," *MESW*, vol. 2, p. 494.
[4] Engels, *The Peasant War in Germany*, pp. 55 ff.
[5] Wang Tan-ts'en, *Chung-kuo Nung-min Ke-ming Shih-hua*, p. 85.

Therefore, superstitious and religious practices were necessary to incite revolt.[6]

The forceful presentation by Yang K'uan in the early 1960s of these theories linking peasant wars with a "revolutionary form of religion" greatly stimulated discussion of this subject.[7] He wrote:

> The use of religion in the peasant wars in Chinese history has its special features, but the adoption of primitive religious ideals of equality and justice . . . and their organization along mutual aid and communal lines basically corresponds to the use made of heretical religion in the European peasant revolts.[8]

Such uses of religious ideas were possible because the primitive religions had been the "faith of the enslaved and oppressed," and, therefore, the religious demands for equality and justice accorded with the social and class demands of the oppressed peasantry.[9] It was natural that the peasants should fight fire with fire and employ religious forms to oppose the power of the feudal church in Europe and of Confucian ideology in China.[10] Religious forms had positive significance for the organization and ideology of the peasant movements. Yang, however, argued this was true only because such religious beliefs accorded with the "revolutionary demands" of

[6] Sun Tso-min, *Chung-kuo Nung-min Chan-cheng Wen-t'i T'an-su*, p. 83. Sun here follows the lead of his teacher Chao Li-sheng. See Chao Li-sheng and Kao Chao-yi, *Chung-kuo Nung-min Chan-cheng Shih Lun-wen-chi*, pp. 10–16. Among better-known historians, Ts'en Ch'ung-mien acknowledges the necessity of religious and superstitious forms for organization and propaganda, especially in the earlier periods. See Ts'en Ch'ung-mien, "How to Regard the Laws of Development of Our Country's Peasant Wars," *SSP*, pp. 56–57.

[7] For summaries of some of these discussions, see *JMJP*, August 25, 1960; and *SSP*, pp. 497–98 and 511–12.

[8] Yang K'uan, "Another Discussion of the Functions of Revolutionary Thought in the Chinese Peasant Wars and Its Relation with Religion," *SSP*, p. 358.

[9] *Ibid.*, p. 355; and Yang K'uan, "On the Function of Revolutionary Ideology in the Chinese Peasant Wars and Its Relation with Religion," *SSP*, p. 327.

[10] *Ibid.*, p. 332; and Yang K'uan, "Another Discussion . . . ," *SSP*, p. 354.

the peasant wars. He believed that those who maintained that all religions are the "opiate of the people" fail to note the distinction between the "primitive religions of the enslaved and oppressed" and the religions employed by the governing classes to keep their subjects in submission. According to Yang and like-minded theorists, the origin of peasant revolutionary thought is to be found in the processes of class oppression, but revolutionary thought is, of necessity, clothed in popular religious forms.[11]

Many mainland historians trace the origin of principles of higher justice in the Chinese peasant movements not to religion as such but to certain ethical ideals of Confucianism, Moism, Taoism and Buddhism and to the ideals of the "well-field system" and of the Great Harmony.[12] They argue that although many of these ideals originated in philosophical theories of the upper classes, their interpretation by the peasants differed fundamentally from the prevailing interpretations of Imperial China. This was to be seen in the different motivation of the government, which called on "heaven" and carried out reforms in order to retain power, whereas the rebels did so as a means of achieving social justice.[13]

Despite the apparent plausibility of such arguments, there are basic inconsistencies in saying that the religions of the upper and lower classes were different in kind. Not only is the attempt to draw this kind of ideological class division subject to all the difficulties of social analysis for pre-modern society, but there is also a methodological trap for the communist historians in these arguments. If it is maintained that the his-

---

[11] *Ibid.*, pp. 362–64. Yang also has written on the role of religion in the Yellow Turban revolt (see "On the *T'ai-p'ing Ching*," *Hsueh-shu Yueh-k'an*, no. 9, 1959) and of the White Lotus (*KMJP*, March 15, 1961). See also *JMJP*, January 26, 1961, for a summary of Yang's views on religion.

[12] Hou Wai-lu, "The Development of the Peasant Wars and Their Slogans in Early and Late Periods of Chinese Feudal Society," *SSP*, p. 26. See also Hou Wai-lu (ed.), *Chung-kuo Li-tai Ta-t'ung Li-hsiang* (The Great Unity Ideal in Chinese History) (Peking: K'o-hsueh Ch'u-pan She, 1959).

[13] According to the editors of *HCS*, "On the Question of the Nature, Function and Distinguishing Characteristics of the Peasant Wars in Chinese History," *SSP*, p. 497.

torical function of religion, like all ideology, is secondary to economic and social considerations and that therefore the peasant rebels merely used religion as a weapon in their social struggle,[14] the same argument would apply to the egalitarian slogans advanced during the peasant wars. If rebel leaders merely used religion for organizational purposes without really believing in the religious precepts involved, the same might be true of their use of the egalitarian slogans. Precepts and slogans would simply be weapons used in the struggle for power and not evidence of social contradictions between the rich and poor.

Another group of historians, arguing a middle position between those who stress and those who deny the role of religion in the Chinese peasant movements, acknowledge the important part of religion in some Chinese peasant movements but emphasize the primacy of class antagonisms in the formation of rebel ideology in general.[15]

The majority of Chinese historians go still further and dispute those who represent the classical Marxist view that religion is essential to the organization of a mass movement in feudal times. They point out that some peasant rebellions in Chinese history which had no significant religious connections, such as the late T'ang and Ming rebellions, developed as rapidly as those which did. The prevailing Chinese view is that religion could play a positive role in the initial organization of rebellion, but that religious characteristics depend on more fundamental social contradictions. Furthermore, most mainland historians believe that because of the inherently

14 The studies of H. J. Wiegand (*A Close-Up of the German Peasant War* [New Haven: Yale University Press, 1942], p. 8) and of Vincent Shih ("Some Chinese Peasant Rebel Ideologies," *T'oung Pao*, 44, 1956, p. 192) support the thesis that the rebels of Germany and China, respectively, utilized religious beliefs as much as they were stimulated by them. See also Yuji Muramatsu, "Some Themes in Chinese Rebel Ideologies," in Arthur F. Wright (ed.), *The Confucian Persuasion*. E. Sarkisyanz has studied the influences of Buddhism on certain Asian rebellions. See his *Buddhist Backgrounds of the Burmese Revolution* (The Hague: Martinus Nykoff, 1965).

15 Jung Sheng, Lung Sheng-yun, and Ho Ling-hsiu, "Tentative Views on the Relation Between Peasant Wars and Religion in China," *SCMP* 2370, pp. 10–11, citing *JMJP*, October 17, 1960.

negative characteristics of religion, superstition and quietism eventually replaced the revolutionary drive of the heretical religions.[16] They admit that religion played some organizational role in the peasant movements but argue that this role was not essential. Furthermore, they contend that the negative qualities of religion offset whatever value the "heretical religions" might have had in the organization of the masses.[17] Therefore, the function of religion could be at most organizational. It did not enhance revolutionary consciousness.[18]

Shao Hsun-cheng of the Peking University history department has been the strongest spokesman of the view minimizing the role of religion in the Chinese peasant movements. He maintains that the Chinese peasant wars differed fundamentally from the European peasant movements, since they opposed the government and not the established church. In China political and spiritual affairs were separate spheres of life, and, therefore, protests against the government need not involve religion.[19] He denies that a revolutionary people's religion can be distinguished from a reactionary ruling-class religion, and he stresses the fact that such great peasant wars as those at the end of the T'ang and Ming dynasties had no significant religious connections at all.[20] In short, according

[16] Even the proponents of the necessity of religious origins for all rebel ideology admit the negative characteristics of religion once a certain stage of the rebellion has been reached. E.g., see Yang K'uan, "On the Function . . . ," *SSP*, p. 338.

[17] E.g., Ch'en Chia-cheng and Lung Te-yü, "On the Relation Between the Ancient Chinese Peasant Wars and the 'Four Authorities,' " *SSP*, p. 264.

[18] E.g., Cheng T'ien-t'ing, according to "Tientsin Historians Discuss Some Questions in the History of the Chinese Peasant Wars," *SCMM* 308, p. 33, citing *LSYC*, no. 1, 1962. Others seek to distinguish religion itself from movements for religious reform. Religion is reactionary in content, but efforts to reform religion had their positive side. Thus, popular religion, as well as governing-class religion, is normally "reactionary," but when infused with a spirit of reform, it could serve progressive purposes. See Liang Jen-kan, "Religious Reform Was the Ideological Form of the Ancient and Medieval Class Struggles," *KMJP*, December 22, 1960.

[19] Shao Hsun-cheng, "Secret Societies, Religion, and the Peasant Wars," *SSP*, pp. 371–72.

[20] *Ibid.*, pp. 369–70, 373.

to Shao, one should not exaggerate the religious exterior in understanding the revolutionary content of the peasant wars.

Similarly, Shao gave a negative appraisal to the role of secret societies in the history of Chinese peasant revolts. Although they did serve to organize large groups of peasantry, their patriarchal and local nature served to confuse the class ideology of the membership. Frequently, as during the Taiping rebellion, these features of the secret society hindered rather than assisted the formation of a broad united front of the exploited against the exploiters. Those secret societies which advanced most rapidly, as did the T'ien-ti Hui, did so because they developed their class interests and the principles of mutual help.[21] Therefore, Shao wrote, although religion and secret societies were sometimes used to organize the masses, the real force of these movements came from the demands of the peasants against the landlords and the government.[22] A recent student of the White Lotus and T'ien-ti Hui societies in the late nineteenth century also concluded that secret societies were "backward organizations which could not find a way out for the oppressed masses," but he felt that they should be affirmed as an important organizational component of the anti-imperialist and anti-feudal struggles of the late nineteenth century.[23]

The above-mentioned theoretical complexities are presumably the reason for the relative paucity of studies of the important place of religion and the secret societies in the Chinese peasant movements. Nearly all mainland historians admit their organizational function. Yet there have been few concrete studies, mainly confined to a few articles on the Yellow Turbans, the White Lotus, and some nineteenth-century societies.[24]

[21] *Ibid.*, pp. 378 ff.
[22] *Ibid.*, p. 383.
[23] Wang T'ien-chiang, "The Secret Societies of the Latter Half of the Nineteenth Century," *LSYC*, no. 2, 1963, pp. 97, 100.
[24] According to some historians, secret societies in China go back to pre-imperial times. See Nieh Ch'ung-ch'i, *Erh-ch'ien-nien Lai Mi-hsin chih T'uan* (Two Thousand Years of Secret Societies) (n.p., n.d.); B. Favre, *Les Sociétés Secrètes en Chine* (Paris: Maisonneuve, 1933); and W. P. Morgan, *Triad Societies in Hong Kong* (Hong Kong: Government Printing Office, 1960).

REVOLUTIONARY CONSCIOUSNESS

The most crucial consideration in the treatment of the ideology of peasant rebels concerns the degree to which the peasants themselves were conscious of revolutionary goals. Over this issue mainland historians are most widely split and the departure from classical Marxism is most clearly revealed.

The majority of mainland historians take what has been criticized as a "fairly universal leftist tendency" in their "irresponsible exaggeration" of the revolutionary qualities of the Chinese peasant movements.[25] They glorify the ideology of the peasant rebels to an extent which goes well beyond the limits set by most Western Marxist historians, ascribing to them such revolutionary goals as "a fervent wish of thousands of years for a society where there is no exploitation of man by man." [26] Others, closer to the orthodox Marxist insistence on the weaknesses of pre-modern rebel movements, contend that the peasant wars were always "a simple spontaneous struggle against feudal exploitation . . . [and] opposed only the individual landlord, official, or . . . emperor . . . and that the peasants had no way of understanding that their oppression was not simply an individual matter but was [rooted in] the whole feudal economic system." [27]

The debate between exponents of these conflicting views centers on the emphasis on the degree to which the peasant movements acted consciously or spontaneously.[28] No com-

[25] Sun Tso-min, *Chung-kuo Nung-min Chan-cheng Wen-t'i T'an-su,* p. 2. See also Sun Tso-min, "The Use of Historicism and Class Viewpoint in the Research on the History of Our Country's Peasant Wars," *JMJP,* February 27, 1964.

[26] Yang K'uan, "On the Function . . . ," *SSP,* p. 339.

[27] Ch'i Hsia, "On Several Problems in the Late Sui Peasant Uprising," *LKP,* p. 110.

[28] This distinction is central to the debate over the primacy of "subjective" (i.e., class consciousness) or "objective" (conditions of work) factors in the determination of class, a discussion which is also prominent in Western sociology. E.g., see Oscar Glantz, "Class Consciousness and Political Solidarity," *American Sociological Review,* vol. 23, August 1958, pp. 375–76.

munist historians maintain that the rebels were wholly conscious of revolutionary goals, since this could be true only of the modern communist-led revolution, nor do any say that the Chinese peasantry was entirely unconscious of "feudal" injustices. These shadings of emphasis are significant, however, since they determine the final evaluation of the class struggle in pre-modern times. The question was recently summarized:

> How to understand and expound correctly the relationship between spontaneity and consciousness of peasants' wars in such a way that the peasants' revolution is not regarded as a proletarian one, on the one hand, and the revolutionary character of the peasants' wars is not disparaged, and the dividing line is not blurred between the peasants and landlords on the other. Such is a very complicated and difficult question.[29]

In short, Chinese historians wish to stress the revolutionary qualities of the Chinese peasantry, but they are constrained by Marxist theory from giving the pre-modern peasantry the characteristics of the modern proletariat.[30]

Certainly the problem of confusing the conservative peasantry with the revolutionary proletariat never arose for Marx and Engels. Regarding the specific question of consciousness of revolutionary tasks, Marx wrote that this could develop only in the last stages of a given mode of production when man became aware of the "one-sidedness" of his working conditions and moved from a class simply opposing the prevailing mode of production to a "class for itself" and advocating a new mode of production.[31]

[29] Ning K'o, "The Question of Spontaneity and Consciousness of the Chinese Peasant Wars," *SCMM* 311, p. 43, citing *Hung ch'i*, April 1, 1962.

[30] As we have repeatedly seen, the Marxist classics as well as the Chinese communists mention both the revolutionary and backward aspects of the "dual nature" of the peasant mentality. Yet the shift from the emphasis on the latter by Western Marxist historians to Chinese emphasis on the former is unmistakable.

[31] See Karl Marx, *The Poverty of Philosophy* (Moscow: Foreign Languages Publishing House, n.d.), p. 166; and Marx and Engels, *The German Ideology*, p. 71. In the former book Marx is speaking of the

In the case of late feudalism, they believed this awareness would be led by representatives of the bourgeoisie and not by the peasantry. In contrast to current Chinese descriptions, Engels described a relatively passive medieval peasantry which, "although gnashing their teeth under the terrible burden, were nonetheless difficult to rouse to revolt." [32] Moreover, according to Engels, the egalitarian slogans advanced during the peasant revolts were not components of a positive program but were only symbols of protest, launched by a "class which was as yet undeveloped." [33] While he spoke of "theoretical enunciations corresponding with these revolutionary uprisings of a class not yet developed" (e.g., the Anabaptists, Munzer, the Levelers, Babeuf), which would "abolish class privileges" or even "class distinctions themselves," [34] Engels stressed, above all, the appropriateness of reform for the times. He wrote that even early socialist panaceas "were foredoomed as utopian; the more completely they were worked out in detail, the more they could not avoid drifting off into pure phantasies." [35]

The most important point in the classical Marxist treatment of ideology, in addition to the insistence that ideas derive from economic and social conditions, is the related assumption that ideas be judged according to their appropriateness for a given stage of production. Marx, Engels,

---

development of the proletariat from the early bourgeois period when it was "already a class as against capital, but not yet for itself," to the later bourgeois epoch when the proletariat developed a positive revolutionary consciousness "for itself." Mao comments on this development in stages of class knowledge in "On Practice," *SWMTT*, vol. 1, pp. 288–89.

[32] Engels, *The Peasant War in Germany*, p. 52.

[33] See Engels, *Anti-Duhring*, pp. 24 and 123.

[34] Engels, "Socialism, Utopian and Scientific," *MESW*, vol. 2, p. 121. See also V. I. Lenin, "Two Utopias" (1912) in *Selected Works in Two Volumes* (Moscow: Foreign Languages Publishing House, 1950), vol. 1, pp. 306–11.

[35] Engels, "Socialism, Utopian and Scientific," *MESW*, vol. 2, p. 121. It is true that elsewhere Engels attributed a revolutionary potential to ideas, which is surprising for one of the founders of materialist historiography. See *ibid.*, pp. 117–18; and *The Peasant War in Germany*, pp. 53, 59, 77, and 78.

Lenin, and Mao have all praised egalitarian ideas in so far as
they "express the aspirations of" the peasants but attacked
them in so far as they did not accord with the economic
needs of the time. All premature idealism is utterly insignificant, they explained.[36] In his consideration of the German
peasant war Engels stated:

> The worst thing that can befall a leader of an extreme
> party is to be compelled to take over a government in an
> epoch when the movement is not yet ripe for the domi-
> nation of the class which he represents, and for the reali-
> zation of the measures which that domination implies.
> . . . He is compelled to represent not his party or his
> class but the class for whose domination the movement
> is then ripe [i.e., the peasantry represented the bour-
> geoisie].[37]

According to Marx and Engels, the actions of lower-class rebels prior to the proletarian revolution tend to be not only
unconscious of revolutionary goals but are likely to play into
the hands of the governing class or of the rising middle class.

Lenin denied the ability of the pre-modern peasantry to be
aware of the systematic causes of oppression and hence to
oppose the feudal system as such.[38] Like Marx and Engels,
he was quite specific in establishing the appropriateness of a
given program to its time.[39]

[36] See especially Marx and Engels, *The German Ideology*, pp. 29–
30. See also Engels, *Anti-Duhring*, pp. 119–23, and "On Social Relations in Russia," *MESW*, vol. 2, pp. 49–50.

[37] Engels, *The Peasant War in Germany*, pp. 138–39.

[38] V. I. Lenin, "To the Rural Poor," in *Alliance of the Working
Class and the Peasantry* (Moscow: Foreign Languages Publishing House,
1959), p. 32.

[39] E.g., see V. I. Lenin, "The Agrarian Program of Social Democracy
in the First Russian Revolution, 1905–07," *Collected Works* (1962
ed.), vol. 13, p. 237. However, this is not to imply that Lenin ignored
pre-modern ideologies. He wrote that the struggles of the oppressed
"even for a hopeless cause . . . [were] necessary for the sake of the
further education of these masses and their training for the next struggle." Lenin, "Preface to the Russian Translation of Marx's Letters to
Kugelmann," in *Marx, Engels, Marxism* (Moscow: Cooperative Publishing Society, 1934), p. 97. Moreover, under "an exceptionally favor-

Mao also, for all his praise of the "objectively" revolutionary qualities of the peasantry, has condemned the backwardness of peasant ideology in history. He wrote:

> The extreme poverty and backwardness of the peasants, resulting from such ruthless exploitation and oppression by the landlord class, is the basic reason why China's economy and social life has remained stagnant for thousands of years.[40]

In his report on the Hunan peasant movement, Mao noted that "in China, culture has always been the exclusive possession of the landlords, and the peasants had no access to it." [41] Furthermore, peasant ideology was limited by the "four kinds of authority—political authority, clan authority, theocratic authority, and the authority of the husband." [42] He rejected "peasant egalitarianism":

> Absolute equalitarianism can be traced back to an economy of handicrafts and small peasant farming at its source . . . not only is absolute equalitarianism merely an illusion of the peasants and small proprietors in the days when capitalism or private property has not been abolished, but even in the days of socialism material things will be distributed on the principle "from each according to his ability, to each according to his work." [43]

---

able combination of circumstances," Lenin spoke of "tremendous peasant initiative, revolutionary energy, class consciousness, organization and . . . creative energy of the people." "Agrarian Program of Social Democracy," *Collected Works* (1962 ed.), vol. 13, pp. 345–46.

[40] Mao Tse-tung, "The Chinese Revolution and the Chinese Communist Party," *SWMTT*, vol. 3, p. 75.

[41] Mao Tse-tung, "Report of an Investigation into the Peasant Movement in Hunan," *SWMTT*, vol. 1, p. 56.

[42] *Ibid.*, p. 45. For a summary of the recent discussions on what Mao meant by these "four authorities," see *KMJP*, December 24, 1960; and Ch'en Chia-cheng and Lung Te-yü, *op. cit.*, *SSP*, pp. 263–78.

[43] Mao Tse-tung, "Rectification of Incorrect Ideas in the Party," *SWMTT*, vol. 1, p. 111. In 1948 Mao told cadres that the communist program of equal land distribution was only a temporary expedient: "We support the peasants' demand for equal distribution of land in order to help arouse the broad masses of peasants speedily to abolish the system

True to the classical Marxist tradition, Mao stressed the evolution of class knowledge and class consciousness from early to later stages of development. He echoed Marx's discussion of the transition of the proletariat from early negative opposition to the old order to a self-conscious "class for itself" in the late bourgeois epoch. Similarly, he traced the development of the "Chinese people's knowledge of Imperialism." [44]

Nevertheless, Mao Tse-tung and other Chinese communist theorists have credited the Chinese peasantry with a degree of consciousness and organizational ability in the contemporary revolution which go far beyond statements by Marx and Engels and which were at most hinted at in Lenin's writings. More important to our study, many of the earlier reservations of Mao about the ideology of the peasant class have been brushed aside in recent writings by mainland students of the Chinese peasant wars. In the last few years, varying degrees of conscious opposition to the feudal system have been assigned to the peasant rebels by the majority of historians in a way which goes far beyond the statements of the classical writers and even of Mao himself.

There are several approaches to the problem of revolutionary consciousness in the peasant revolts. Some of the most influential historians, notably Kuo Mo-jo and Hou Wai-lu, have sought to resolve the contradiction between attributing "a certain degree of consciousness" to the rebels and classical Marxist statements, by maintaining that this consciousness appeared only in the declining period of feudalism when men might become aware of restrictive working conditions according to the Marxian scheme. After the middle of the T'ang, peasants moved from hazy conceptions of basic rights and opposition to the corvée to demands for equal rights with the feudal governing class and, during the Ming, to demands for

---

of ownership by the feudal landlord class, but we do not advocate absolute equalitarianism. Whoever advocates absolute equalitarianism is wrong." ["Speech at Conference of Cadres," *SWMTT* (Peking ed.), vol. 4, pp. 235–36.] Of course, Mao was speaking of the contemporary revolution and, like Lenin, he considered egalitarianism progressive in the struggle against feudal ownership of land.

[44] See Mao Tse-tung, "On Practice," *SWMTT*, vol. 1, pp. 288–89.

equal distribution of land.[45] While this interpretation is consistent with the Marxist concept of historical evolution, it poses the peasantry and not the bourgeoisie and plebeians as the leading class in the struggle against feudalism, and it describes a revolutionary ideology considerably in advance of comparable developments in Europe. Moreover, most Chinese historians deny that the history of the Chinese peasant wars can be divided into two periods, roughly corresponding to an unconscious earlier stage of opposition to feudal abuses and a post-T'ang stage of "a certain degree of conscious opposition to the feudal system." They contend that the latter was present throughout the history of Imperial China.

More fundamental arguments have arisen over the degree of consciousness attained by peasant rebels. While all mainland historians obey the Marxist injunction that only the proletarian movement is fully conscious of its revolutionary tasks, and while peasant wars were essentially a "kind of spontaneous revolutionary movement," there are wide variations of opinion as to the amount of peasant-class "self-consciousness" permitted within this formula. One historian defined this consciousness:

> Long confronted with their bitter life and the brutal exploitation and oppression by the landlord class, the peas-

---

[45] Hou Wai-lu, *op. cit.*, *SSP*, pp. 25 and 31; see also Hou Wai-lu, "Historical Characteristics of the Peasant Wars of the T'ang and Sung," *HCS*, March 1964.

Mainland historians often stress the fact that revolutionary consciousness was raised not only in the course of thousands of years of struggle against feudal masters but also within the course of each revolutionary period. Hence, Chien Po-tsan (*Chung-kuo Shih Lun-chi*, vol. 2, p. 149) explained that Ch'en Sheng and Wu Kuang, despite their poverty and lack of experience, were able to lead the first great rebellion in Chinese history because of their increasing anger at the exploitation of the Ch'in. This made conditions ripe both for revolt and for their leadership. Ts'en Ch'ung-mien (*SSP*, p. 55) and others have noted that the revolutionary consciousness of the peasant rebels is raised during the process of struggle, and Kuo Mo-jo told China Youth that the Taiping leaders Yang Hsiu-ch'ing and Li Hsiu-ch'eng were "lowly laborers who [were] able to become able leaders because the time was ripe and because of their education in the processes of revolution." See Kuo Mo-jo, "Genius and Hard Work," *SCMM* 323, p. 15, citing *CKCN*, June 29, 1962.

ants would inevitably develop a certain knowledge (although it was obscure, superficial and even distorted knowledge) of their lot and develop their class consciousness. This found expression on the one hand in their hatred for the landlord class and the feudal system and, on the other, in their eager longing for liberation and happy life. From this, the peasants developed a strong demand for revolution and, proceeding from their class position and historical position, formed naive egalitarianism and naive ideas of equality.[46]

The proponents of a more enthusiastic appraisal of the peasant wars in Chinese history maintain that not only did peasant movements have an objectively revolutionary function but that "under certain conditions [the peasants] formed a class"[47] and expressed a "certain degree of [revolutionary] consciousness."[48] They argue that the peasant rebels did express ideals which surpassed the feudal thought of the time and "gradually acquired a class knowledge of the mutual opposition between rich and poor and between noble and base."[49] Although the peasants did not have knowledge of the fate of their struggle, they did have a consciousness of their revolt in the sense of having definite goals and plans. Therefore, the peasant movements were not just blind attacks against feudal abuses, as stated by some Chinese historians, but were directed against the entire feudal system of exploitation.[50]

Where orthodox Marxist interpretations admitted at most a negative consciousness of opposition by the peasants, the prevailing view in Chinese communist historiography attributes to the peasants a certain positive, albeit hazy, revolutionary consciousness. One writer expressed the tension between

[46] Ning K'o, *op cit., SCMM* 311, p. 34.
[47] "Opening of Discussion of Problems of Peasant Wars in Chinese Feudal Society by Historical Circles," *KMJP*, September 20, 1960.
[48] Ning K'o, *op. cit., SCMM* 311, p. 34.
[49] "Some Problems in the History of the Peasant Wars," *KMJP*, November 7, 1961.
[50] E.g., see Pai Shou-yi, "On the Discussion of the Nature of the Peasant Wars in Chinese Feudal Society," *SSP*, p. 185.

this interpretation and the classical Marxist view in the following words:

> Of course, in feudal society pure peasant wars were all spontaneous, but following the developments of feudalism and the changes in material life, did not the nature of the peasantry change [*nung-min tzu-shen shih-fou yeh tsai pien-hua ne*] . . . was there not a certain consciousness within the spontaneity? [51]

Criticisms, especially in the early 1960s, of exaggerations of the revolutionary quality of the peasants wars by such leading historians as Kuo Mo-jo,[52] Fan Wen-lan,[53] and Chien Po-tsan suggested that senior theorists were concerned about the theoretical implications of this type of interpretation.[54] Chien warned that "the peasants opposed feudal oppression and exploitation but did not and could not oppose feudalism as a system." They opposed individual landlords but not the landlord class, the emperor but not the Imperial system.[55] Sun Tso-min, the most voluminous writer in the mid-1950s on the subject of the peasant movements, stresses, in a manner consistent with Mao's statements, the "objectively revolutionary" historical function of the peasant revolts but denies that they had any "subjective revolutionary consciousness." [56] Ch'i Hsia is another prominent historian who long denied to the peasants any significant degree of conscious op-

[51] Tien-chin Shih-fan Ta-hsueh Li-shih hsi, "On the Heated Discussion of the Problem of the Laws of Development of the Chinese Peasant Wars," *SSP*, p. 464.

[52] Kuo Mo-jo, "On Several Problems of Contemporary Historical Research," *HCS*, no. 4, 1959, and *KMJP*, April 8, 1959.

[53] See "Chinese Historians Meet in Peking . . . ," *SCMP* 2514, pp. 21-22, citing *JMJP*, May 31, 1961.

[54] See the criticisms of B. F. Porshnev in Soviet historiography in Chapter 4.

[55] Chien Po-tsan, "Tentative Views on the Handling of Several Historical Problems," *KMJP*, December 22, 1961. As early as 1952 Chien warned against an exaggeration of the revolutionary nature of the peasant revolts. See Chien Po-tsan, *Li-shih Wen-t'i Lun-ts'ung*, p. 134.

[56] See especially Sun Tso-min, "The Question of the Blows of the Chinese Peasant Wars Against the Feudal System," *SSP*, p. 109.

position to the feudal system either in early or later periods.[57]

Finally, in 1961 it seemed that the Party was swinging its weight behind the representatives of views stressing the more backward aspects of the historical peasant movements in a manner similar to its earlier restraining comments on the Taipings.[58] This seemed the implication of the above remarks and of the most negative appraisal of peasant rebel ideology published up to that time, which restated Mao's basic position, itself an advance on classical Marxist statements, but which stopped well short of the attitudes expressed in the earlier tide of articles praising the revolutionary consciousness of the peasant movements. The author Ts'ai Mei-piao wrote:

> This kind of opposition [movement] propelled history forward and became the true force of historical development, but the peasant rebels did not and could not imagine this. That the peasant revolts struck at the feudal governments of the time and propelled the development of social production was the objective result of the uprisings but was not their preconceived plan . . . only with the coming of the proletariat was it possible to know one's class position and self-consciously carry out the class struggle.[59]

Despite the conformity of this position with orthodox Marxist views of the class struggles of the peasants in history, it soon became clear that in fact the Party was at least temporarily favoring the more enthusiastic appraisals of the historical peasant movements. It later was revealed that these debates, and the shifts in their emphasis, both reflected and influenced the struggle between the "Maoists" and the "revi-

[57] E.g., Ch'i Hsia, "On Several Problems in the Late Sui Peasant Uprisings," *LKP*, p. 110.

[58] See end of Chapter 6.

[59] Ts'ai Mei-piao, "Discussion of Several Questions in the Debate on the History of the Chinese Peasant Wars," *LSYC*, no. 4, 1961, p. 62. Ts'ai later repeated these views. See "More on Several Problems in the History of the Chinese Peasant Wars," *HCS*, no. 11, 1962.

sionists" in the top echelons of the Party.[60] But well before
the intensification of the "cultural revolution" in 1966 the great
majority of historians continued to oppose the more conservative and orthodox views of the peasant movements. Throughout they criticized by name the "second-string" spokesman of
this view, most notably Ts'ai Mei-piao, Sun Tso-min, Ch'i
Hsia,[61] and, from the cultural revolution of 1966, the more
influential Wu Han, Chien Po-tsan, and others.[62] About 1960
Sun Tso-min and Ch'i Hsia reflected the pressures of the
leftist criticism by substantially modifying earlier, more negative conclusions. Sun conceded that at times the peasant
rebels did develop a "certain class knowledge" and obtained
"glimpses of a new order," although he continues to deny
that they were conscious of opposing the feudal system as
such.[63] Ch'i Hsia confessed to having too negative a view of
the peasant revolts:

> My mistaken views on this problem were due to superfi-
> cial methodology but primarily they were due to the fact
> that [I] had not thoroughly reformed my capitalist class
> world view and standpoint or purged the "emperor, gen-
> eral and minister" system of historiography. This made it
> impossible to investigate creatively the peasant wars with
> a revolutionary world view and to praise creatively the
> revolutionary struggles of the peasants.[64]

A little later Ch'i was accused of going to the other extreme
and of exaggerating the revolutionary consciousness of the

---

[60] See Chapter 10.

[61] E.g., see references in *SSP*, pp. 130–31, 456, and 462 ff.; in
SCMM no. 308, pp. 33–36, citing *LSYC*, no. 1, 1961; in *CHYC*, nos.
3 and 5, 1964; and Wu Ch'uan-ch'i, "We Cannot Say the Peasant
Wars Are a 'Continuation' of Feudal Landlord Policies," *KMJP*, April
3, 1964; and T'ang Yu-yuan, "Regarding Some Questions on the Class
Contradictions in China's Feudal Society," *LSYC*, nos. 5 and 6, 1964,
pp. 43–54.

[62] E.g., see "Comrade Chien Po-tsan's Anti-Marxist Historical Viewpoint," *JMJP*, April 23, 1966. For a summary of criticisms of Wu Han,
see *JMJP*, April 10, 1966, pp. 5–6. See also Chapter 10.

[63] Sun Tso-min, *op. cit.*, *SSP*, p. 189.

[64] Ch'i Hsia, "On the Question of the Nature of the Chinese Peasant
Wars," *SSP*, p. 72.

Ch'in and Han peasant wars.[65]

In addition to the far larger numbers of writers favoring a revolutionary interpretation of the peasant movements, another evidence of high sanction of this radical view of history was the publication of an extreme statement of the revolutionary qualities of the peasant rebels in the Party journal, *Red Flag*, no doubt in part in answer to Soviet criticisms of the Chinese model of a rural-based revolution.

Quotations from this article reveal the tension between the precepts of Marxism and the Chinese effort to utilize peasant wars to establish the revolutionary tradition. Since the article also sums up the prevailing view of the significance of the peasant revolts, it provides a useful commentary on the discussion of current views of peasant ideology:

> . . . Peasant wars of the old type were indeed spontaneous revolutions. The degree of consciousness on the part of the revolutionary peasants could not go beyond the limit of spontaneity. It is certainly not right and is anti-historical to overlook this point, to exaggerate the consciousness of the peasants of feudal society as if it were the same as the consciousness of the proletariat of today. But it must also be realized that the gradual growth of peasants' revolutionary thought and their consciousness in the struggle was also very valuable. This is a glorious tradition of the Chinese people and is a precious historical legacy. This is also the foundation on which the peasants were able to accept the leadership of the proletariat and Marxist-Leninist education during the period of the New Democratic revolution and radically raised their class consciousness.[66]

If for the sake of stressing the spontaneity of peasants' wars the certain degree of consciousness manifested by

[65] Chu Ta-chün *et al.*, "Criticism of the History of the Ch'in-Han Peasant Wars," *LSYC*, no. 4, 1963, pp. 74–75.

[66] Ning K'o, "The Question of Spontaneity and Consciousness of the Chinese Peasant Wars," *SCMM*, no. 311, p. 43, citing *Hung Ch'i*, no. 7, April 1, 1962.

the peasants in their struggles and the gradual increase in this consciousness are negated altogether, then it would mean going to the other extreme of disparaging the revolutionary quality of the peasants.[67]

PEASANT MONARCHISM

A final debate on the question of the mentality of the peasant rebels revolves around the degree to which the rebels were thought to oppose the Imperial system of government. Mainland historians follow three different lines of emphasis, with the majority opposing what is actually the traditional Marxist view of this problem.[68] Engels early noted that

> The Russian people . . . has true enough, made numerous isolated peasant revolts against the nobility and against individual officials, but never against the tsar, except when a false tsar put himself at its head, and claimed the throne. . . . The tsar is on the contrary the earthly god of the Russian peasant.[69]

Lenin noted the faith of the people in the "tsar's mercy," [70] while Stalin used the term "tsarist" to describe Russian peasant rebels who "came out against the landlords, but were in favor of a 'good tsar.' " [71]

The Chinese historians have conducted extensive discussions on the real meaning of the term "tsarist" or "monarchist" (*hung-ch'üan chu-yi*). In general, it is considered a sort of "peasant monarchism," wherein the peasants were unable to conceive of any alternative to seeking salvation from the

---

[67] *Ibid.*, p. 34.

[68] For a summary of mainland views on this subject, see Shih Shao-pin, "On the Discussion of Problems in the Peasant Revolutionary Wars in Chinese Feudal Society," *SSP*, p. 504.

[69] Engels, "On Social Relations in Russia," *MESW*, vol. 2, p. 59.

[70] V. I. Lenin, "To the Rural Poor," in *Alliance of the Working Class and the Peasantry*, p. 84.

[71] J. Stalin, "Talk with the German Writer Emil Ludwig," *Works*, vol. 13, p. 115. See Chapter 4.

emperor. According to a 1956 Soviet definition, in the Russian peasant wars

> The battle is not against tsarism and for a republic [but] for an autocracy headed by a "good, wise tsar." This was typical naive monarchism, the basis of which was the patriarchal structure of the Russian countryside.[72]

Those who argue that the Chinese peasant rebels, no less than those of other countries, exhibited this trait of mind point to the fact that all successful Chinese rebels aspired to become king or emperor. As Marx said, they were unable to represent their own interests without appealing to established rulers or political conventions, and this was a natural consequence of the "feudal system." [73] Therefore, this group of Chinese historians maintains that, characteristically, "in feudal society the peasants opposed only the feudal landlords and corrupt officials but protected the good emperor." [74] Many cite the rebels against Wang Mang, all of whom chose heirs of the Han line, as examples of "monarchism" in Chinese history.[75] Others point out that Chinese rebels often protected not only the "good emperor" but good officials.[76]

Other proponents of the place of "monarchism" in the his-

---

[72] V. V. Mavrodin *et al.*, "On the Characteristics of the Peasant Wars in Russia," *VI*, no. 2, 1956, p. 69.

[73] Marx, "The Eighteenth Brumaire of Louis Bonaparte," *MESW*, vol. 1, p. 334.

[74] Pei-ching Ta-hsueh Chung-wen-hsi (eds.), *Chung-kuo Li-tai Nung-min Wen-t'i Wen-hsueh Tzu-liao*, p. 396. Sun Tso-min and the earlier Ch'i Hsia are the principal representatives of this traditional Marxist interpretation, as they are on many other questions. See *SSP*, p. 465. Wu Han among others also favors it. See *SSP*, p. 497.

[75] Tung Chia-tsun, "On the Question of Monarchism," *SSP*, p. 281.

[76] E.g., Ch'i Hsia, *op cit.*, *LKP*, p. 110; and Li Wen-chih, "The Late Ming Peasant Revolutionary Leader, Li Tzu-ch'eng," in Li Kuang-pi and Ch'ien Chün-hua (eds.), *Chung-kuo Li-shih Jen-wu*, p. 111. Among noncommunist scholars, Hsiao Kung-ch'uan (*Rural China: Imperial Control in the Nineteenth Century*, p. 435) cites an interesting example of nineteenth-century rioters continuing to respect the imperial institution even as they bitterly opposed local branches of the government. Yuji Muramatsu ("Some Themes in Chinese Rebel Ideologies," in A. F. Wright [ed.], *The Confucian Persuasion*, p. 263) notes rebel concern for the "good ruler."

tory of the Chinese peasant wars maintain that one cannot properly distinguish the protection of the rebel leader who has taken the title of emperor—i.e., the "good emperor"—from the protection of the "good" ruling tsar, as was the case in Russian history. They point out that by the time the rebel leader had taken a royal title, he usually had been transformed from a representative of the peasant class into a representative of the landlord class.[77]

Advocates of an emphasis on "peasant monarchism" in the history of the Chinese peasant movements note that such a mental attitude would be consistent with Mao's stress on "feudal" political ideas which were one of the "four great cords that have bound the Chinese people and particularly the peasants."[78] They might also have noted Mao's confession that when he was still a student, "I was not yet an anti-monarchist; indeed I considered the Emperor as well as most officials to be honest, good and clever men. They only needed the help of K'ang Yu-wei's reforms. I was fascinated by accounts of the rulers of ancient China. . . ."[79]

Yet the fact that many dynasties were overthrown by the force of peasant movements has led many mainland historians to dispute the applicability of the statements about "tsarism" by Engels and Stalin for the history of the Chinese peasant wars. Many try to resolve this dilemma by maintaining that the Chinese peasant revolts departed from the letter but not from the spirit of the European examples. Thus, Chien Po-tsan and others argue that peasant opposition to the reigning emperor must be distinguished from opposition to the

[77] Tung Chia-tsun, *op. cit.*, SSP, pp. 282–83.

[78] Mao Tse-tung, "Report of an Investigation into the Peasant Movement in Hunan," *SWMTT*, vol. 1, p. 45.

[79] Edgar Snow, *Red Star over China*, p. 121. It is also interesting to note some attitudes of previous rebel leaders toward their predecessors. Chu Yuan-chang supposedly saw himself as a second Han Kao-tzu, the only other peasant rebel who succeeded in founding a new dynasty. See Chao Yi, *Nien-erh Shih Cha-chi* (Notes on the Twenty-two Histories), chüan 32. Chang Hsien-chung, the scourge of late Ming times, is reported to have most admired the dashing aristocratic general Hsiang Yü who, like Ch'en Sheng and Han Kao-tzu, revolted against the Ch'in. See Parsons, "The Rebellion of Chang Hsien-chung as an example of the Internal Disturbances in China During the Late Ming Dynasty," p. 176.

Imperial system. Because of the "peculiarities" of China, the peasant rebels often did oppose the reigning emperor, but in the feudal period they could not conceive of an alternative to the Imperial system itself.[80] In short, "peasant monarchism" existed in the history of the Chinese peasant movements but was weaker than elsewhere.[81] There was no servility toward the reigning emperor as in Russian and Japanese history, but the feudal peasants could not conceive of an alternative system to monarchism in "feudal China" any more than elsewhere. As Ts'ai Mei-piao explained:

> The Chinese peasantry could not establish their own class government, and could only live under the feet of the "good emperor." In this respect the Chinese [experience] resembled the Russian. [But the Chinese peasants] time and again opposed the dark imperial government . . . and in this respect differed from the Russian peasantry. . . . Why was this? . . . The answer must be sought not simply in the mentality and wishes of the peasantry but in the special points of Chinese society and economy.[82]

Implicit in these arguments, and even more in the denials by some historians that any kind of "peasant monarchism" existed in Chinese history, is the assumption of qualitative differences between the beliefs of the exploiting and exploited classes. As in the treatment of peasant religious beliefs, communist writers portray ruling-class beliefs about the sacredness of the throne as devices to perpetuate power, but the exploited are said to have turned these beliefs into weapons against their masters.

Ning K'o argued that "peasant monarchism" existed in Chinese as it did in European feudalism but that it differed from "landlord monarchism." He admits that many Chinese rebels, such as some in the Sui and middle Ming periods,

---

[80] According to Hsueh-shu Tung-t'ai column, *JMJP*, November 18, 1961.

[81] Ch'en Chia-cheng and Lung Te-yü, *op. cit.*, p. 265.

[82] Ts'ai Mei-piao, *op. cit.*, *LSYC*, no. 4, 1961, p. 81.

"continued to recognize the highest position of the [reign-ing] feudal emperor," and that most either declared them-selves emperor or king or invoked the example of past dynas-ties. In this sense, monarchism was a "universal phenomenon of scattered self-sufficient feudal economy," but in China more than elsewhere the peasants used this belief as a weapon against the reigning emperor. "Peasant monarchism" should not be denied, according to Ning, but still less should it be emphasized, since this attitude was secondary to class considerations just as "royalist slogans" were secondary to the "egalitarian slogans." [83] He considered that popular Chinese attitudes toward the emperor differed from those in such countries as Russia and Japan, since in China the masses early recognized the exploitive nature of the Imperial system and realized that the emperor was not sacred but could be, and often was, overthrown.[84]

If the majority view on this question attempts a compro-mise between denial and affirmation of the existence of "peasant monarchism" in the Chinese peasant revolts, some mainland historians depart still further from the orthodox view. Pai Shou-yi maintains that the references in the Marxist classics to "monarchism" were intended only as descriptions of the Russian peasant revolts. The Chinese peasant move-ments, by contrast, merely used "monarchism" as a form of struggle:

> [They] not only opposed the landlords, nobles and cor-rupt officials, but also ceaselessly opposed the emperor. [They] not only turned the struggle against the local feudal government but also against the highest repre-sentatives of the landlord class—the imperial court. The history of the peasant wars, which overthrew the Ch'in, Han, Sui, T'ang, Yuan and Ming dynasties, eloquently explains this point. . . . The Chinese peasant wars

---

[83] Ning K'o, "The Question of Monarchism in the History of the Chinese Peasant Wars," *SSP*, pp. 259–60. Yang Yao (1130–35) is cited as one example of a successful rebel leader who did not take an imperial title.

[84] *Ibid.*, pp. 261–62.

differed from the Russian peasant wars and never manifested "monarchism." [85]

Another historian points out that the concept of the Mandate of Heaven[86] and not any illusions about the reigning monarch explained the adoption of dynastic titles and precedents by the Chinese peasant rebels. He wrote:

> The history of the Chinese peasant wars proves that in periods of great armed antagonism between the peasant and the landlord classes, the peasants (with few exceptions) did not harbor illusions about the reigning monarch but wished to overthrow the reigning Emperor, seize the government and become masters of their own fate.[87]

[85] Pai Shou-yi, "Special Characteristics . . . ," *SSP*, p. 240. For other recent statements supporting these views, see *SSP*, p. 215 and 472; *JMJP*, May 18, 1962; and *SCMM*, 308, p. 34, citing *LSYC*, no. 1, 1962.

[86] For a discussion of the relation of the concept of the Mandate of Heaven and the Chinese peasant revolts, see Ts'en Ch'ung-mien, "How to Regard the Laws of Development of Our Country's Peasant Wars," *SSP*, p. 56.

[87] Wang Ssu-chih, "On the Question of the Nature of the Peasant Wars," *SSP*, pp. 168–69.

CHAPTER EIGHT

Function and Evolution

GIVEN the priority in Marxist historiography of demonstrating the evolution of history toward communism, the manner in which the class struggle advanced this progression is in many ways the most crucial of the topics discussed in the mainland treatment of the peasant wars. It is the ultimate criterion and starting point for the discussion of all the other problems in the history of the peasant wars.

Mao early emphasized this aspect in his 1939 statement that the "class struggles of the peasants . . . alone formed the real motive force of China's historical evolution," [1] while

---

[1] Mao Tse-tung, "The Chinese Revolution and the CCP," in S. Schram, *The Political Thought of Mao Tse-tung*, p. 191. In the revised edition of his work (*SWMTT*, vol. 3, p. 76), Mao's statement is brought more into line with the orthodox Marxist theory of historical evolution by saying that the peasant revolts "alone formed the real motive force of historical development in Chinese feudal society." However, even in the amended version Mao's emphasis on the role of the peasantry gives a new twist to the classical Marxist conception of historical forces. According to traditional Marxist theory, "revolutions are the locomotives of history" (Marx, "The Class Struggle in France," *MESW*, vol. 1, p. 217), but these revolutions were the epochal upheavals led by the ascendant class, which in the case of the feudal period was the emergent bourgeoisie and the plebeians. Mao's formula thus raises many questions for the interpretation of Chinese history, and for the whole

the first great debate[2] on the evaluation of the peasant movements concerned "the function of the peasant wars" (*nung-
min chan-cheng te tso-yung*), or the question of how the
peasant movements advanced the development of the society
and the economy. All discussions of the subject mention the
problem, but from 1956 onward there was considerable controversy over its proper interpretation, and this in fact
marked the real beginning of active debate over the role of
the peasant movements in Chinese history.[3]

Leading Marxist thinkers have always stated that "revolution is the driving force of history," [4] but they did not elaborate on how this was accomplished. Mao explained that the
peasant movements advanced the history of Chinese feudalism because "each of the major peasant uprisings and wars
dealt a blow to the existing feudal regime and to some extent
furthered the development of the productive forces of society." [5]

Starting from Mao's statement, the early "post-liberation"
interpretation of the "function of the peasant wars" stressed
the concessions wrung from an unwilling government by the
rebels, which improved productive relations (*sheng-ch'an
kuan-hsi*) or working conditions, which in turn allowed the
development of the dynasty's productive forces (*sheng-ch'an
li*) or of its economy.[6] From the late 1950s, however, and

---

problem of the relation of the theory of class struggle to the theory of
economic development.

[2] There was a lesser debate about the role and nature of the "peasant
class leader" in 1953, but the discussion lapsed after that year.

[3] See articles listed in the bibliography appended to *SSP*, pp. 534–35.

[4] Marx and Engels, *The German Ideology*, p. 29.

[5] Mao Tse-tung, "The Chinese Revolution and the CCP," *SWMTT*,
vol. 3, p. 76. The original version of this passage stated "each peasant
uprising," omitting the word "major" (Schram, *op. cit.*, p. 191), a distinction of some importance. See this chapter, below.

[6] E.g., see Chien Po-tsan, "On the Peasant Wars of Ancient China"
(1951) in *Li-shih Wen-t'i Lun-ts'ung*, pp. 110 ff.; and Sun Tso-min,
Chung-kuo Nung-min Chan-cheng Wen-t'i T'an-su, pp. 10 ff. An ideal
example from Russian history of this process would be Tsar Alexander's
explanation of the emancipation of the serfs: "It is better that [the
reform] should come from above than from beneath." Lenin cites this
example, commenting, "At last the government yielded, fearing a general uprising of all the peasants." *Collected Works*, vol. 6, p. 424.

especially during the "cultural revolution" of the 1960s, there were increasing criticisms of such an interpretation—that the main function of the peasant wars was to force the government to improve the working conditions of the peasants. Some charged that this approach ignored the deeper currents of history in favor of a "new theory of the dynastic cycle," [7] and others feared that it gave too much credit to the ruling class and not enough to the masses.[8] Others felt it oversimplified a complex phenomenon and contributed to a new cyclical theory of Chinese history—"peasant revolts, concessions, improved productive relations followed by advances in productive forces, stagnation, decline, and renewed peasant revolts." [9]

Accordingly, recent interpretations of the function of the peasant movements stress not only government concessions for the improvement of working conditions but also the peasants' struggle for production and their general influence on the society of the time. These included teaching and expanding the experience of class struggle for the benefit of later generations,[10] influencing progressive philosophers and writers such as Mencius, Tung Chung-shu, T'ao Yuan-ming, Tu

[7] E.g., Ch'i Hsia, "Regarding the Research on the History of Our Country's Peasant Wars," *JMJP*, December 4, 1956; and Liu Yao-t'ing *et al.*, "The Development of Historical Science in the Light of Ten Years of Struggle on the Intellectual Front," *SHYK*, no. 11, 1959, p. 17.

[8] See discussions of this point in *JMJP*, March 16, 1966; *KMJP*, January 12, 1966, and November 3, 1965; *SSP*, pp. 407 ff. and p. 508; *SCMP* 2446, pp. 5–6, citing *KMJP*, January 6, 1961; *LSYC*, no. 4, 1963, pp. 171–72; and *Yang-ch'eng Jih-pao* (Canton), September 7, 1961.

[9] See Hsueh-shu Tung-t'ai column, "Chien Po-tsan Discusses the Problems of the Chinese Peasant Wars," *JMJP*, November 18, 1961. Chien concluded that one "cannot describe the peasant wars only by one law." Chien Po-tsan, "Tentative Views on the Handling of Several Historical Problems," *KMJP*, December 22, 1961. In fact, Chien's 1961 criticisms exactly described his own discussion of the peasant wars a decade before. See Chien Po-tsan, *Li-shih Wen-t'i Lun-ts'ung*, pp. 110 ff. In 1966 Chien's denouncers strongly condemned his handling of the peasant wars. E.g., *JMJP*, March 25, April 23, and June 14, 1966.

[10] See "Some Academic Problems Discussed at the Annual Meeting of the Kuangtung History Society," *SCMP* 2446, p. 6, citing *KMJP*, January 6, 1961.

Fu, Lo Kuan-chung, Li Chih, and Huang Tsung-hsi,[11] advancing new forms of production,[12] and helping to forge better relations between the minority races of China.[13]

Some historians distinguish between the "direct" political function of the peasant revolts to overthrow the existing dynasty and their "indirect economic function" to "give the new dynasty a lesson," thereby forcing it to better working conditions.[14] All are agreed that the economic forces of any given period are determinant of social change but that when the economy reaches a certain stage of crisis, revolt is necessary to clear the way for further change.[15] Thus, they seek to link the role of the class struggle with economic evolution.

The most troublesome questions in the discussion of the functions of the peasant wars fall into two general areas: the role of those peasant movements which seemed to have either no effect or an adverse effect on their time, and their role at different stages of the development of Chinese feudalism. The latter question will be discussed in the next section of this chapter, under the general topic of the evolution of the Chinese peasant movements.

Mainland historians are widely split on the degree to which smaller revolts, or those which appeared to be followed by decline rather than by progress, should be credited with advancing the course of history. It is easy to praise the anti-Ch'in, Sui, and Yuan revolts, since the great Han, T'ang, and Ming dynasties could be said with some justification to have

[11] See SSP, pp. 397 ff., 440 ff., 490–93; and Pei-ching Ta-hsueh Wen-hsueh hsi (eds.), *Chung-kuo Li-tai Nung-min Wen-t'i Wen-hsueh Tzu-liao*, p. 396.

[12] E.g., see Ts'en Ch'ung-mien, "How to Regard the Laws of Development of Our Country's Peasant Wars," SSP, pp. 59–60.

[13] See HCS (eds.), "On the Questions of the Nature, Function and Distinguishing Characteristics of the Peasant Wars in Chinese History," SSP, p. 491.

[14] E.g., see "What Was the Function of the Peasant Wars in History?" *Wen-hui-pao* (Shanghai), June 9, 1959; and "Discussion of Problems in the Peasant Wars in Our Country's Feudal Society," KMJP, June 20, 1962.

[15] E.g., Liang Tso-kan, "Oppose Vulgar Interpretations of the Principle 'Class Struggle Is the Motive Force of Social Development,'" KMJP, May 24, 1956.

been their result. However, the evaluation of such large-scale revolts as those of the late Han, T'ang, and Ming, of the Taipings, and of many smaller revolts, all of which were followed by adverse conditions, poses difficulties for the Marxist, whose first loyalty must be to demonstrate historical progress.[16] One group of historians argues that only those peasant revolts which actually overthrew the existing dynasty played a progressive role in Chinese history.[17] Some go further and argue that even if the rebels did overthrow the old dynasty, if they did not bring about the formation of a new dynasty and chaos ensued, then one could not credit such uprisings with a progressive function, although the bad effects of such periods of disruption should not be blamed on the peasant revolts but on the government which caused them.[18]

This stress on successful revolt has proved a controversial and somewhat embarrassing interpretation. One of the most consistent criticisms of "slanders" of the peasant rebels has been of the implication, inherent in such an approach, that the peasant revolts increased the misery of the people. Not only "bourgeois historians," but communist historians are accused of this offense.[19] Even Fan Wen-lan was taken to task for saying that militarist secessions and chaos followed the revolt of the Yellow Turbans.[20]

[16] Kuo Mo-jo's 1945 statement (*VI*, vols. 5–6, p. 184) that "uninterrupted wars killed peasants by the hundreds of thousands causing production to cease" illustrates this dilemma. (See Chapter 4.)

[17] See Shih Shao-pin, "On the Discussion of Problems in the Peasant Revolutionary Wars in Chinese Feudal Society," *SSP*, p. 509.

[18] E.g., see Yin Hsiang-hao, "One Cannot Confuse the Question of Dark Periods of History and the Function of Peasant Revolts," *KMJP*, June 21, 1956; Wang Yi, "On Several Problems in the Evaluation of the Peasant Wars," *KMJP*, July 19, 1956; and Jen Chi-yü, *op. cit.*, *SSP*, p. 402.

[19] See Sun Tso-min, "The Battle of Ch'u-Han," *KMJP*, May 10, 1956. The well-known historian Ch'en Yin-ch'ueh was criticized for neglecting or slandering the class struggles of the peasants (see *KMJP*, November 10, 1958; *LSYC*, no. 12, 1958; and *SHYK*, no. 11, 1958), as was Chou Ku-ch'eng (*KMJP*, November 10, 1958, and December 25, 1958; see also *SCMM* 439, citing a criticism of Chou in *Hung Ch'i*, nos. 17–18, 1964).

[20] Ma K'ai-liang, "An Example of a Capitalist Class Idealist Histori-

Most mainland historians feel compelled by the facts of Chinese history to admit that the function of the peasant revolt "varied according to the size of the blow it struck at the reactionary governing class. Those peasant revolts that overthrew the feudal dynasty had a large function, while the function of the revolts which were suppressed was smaller." [21]

Yet even this distinction arouses considerable debate,[22] and many writers maintain that one cannot exclude certain peasant revolts, just because they failed, from the universal law that "each peasant uprising . . . changed the productive relations of society and . . . furthered the development of the productive forces of society." [23] Sun Tso-min, the most prolific writer on the subject, criticized those who said that conditions became worse instead of better after certain revolts, and he argued that even relatively small uprisings, such as those led by Wang Hsiao-po (993–94), Chung Hsiang (1130–35), and T'ang Sai-erh (1420), advanced the development of Chinese history.[24]

Most historians agree that every peasant revolt advanced the deeper currents of history regardless of immediate appearances. "Every people's armed struggle propelled historical progress, although the peasants could not understand that," and although the function of the class struggle depended on its place in the feudal period, as one writer put it.

---

cal Outlook," *Jen-wen K'o-hsueh Tsa-chih* (Magazine of Human Sciences), no. 5, 1958, p. 26.

[21] "Discussion of Problems in the Peasant Wars in Our Country's Feudal Society," *KMJP*, June 20, 1962.

[22] See Ch'i Hsia, *op. cit.*, *JMJP*, December 4, 1956.

[23] Mao Tse-tung, "The Chinese Revolution and the CCP," original version, cited in Schram, *The Political Thought of Mao Tse-tung*, p. 191.

[24] Sun Tso-min, *Chung-kuo Nung-min Chan-cheng Wen-t'i T'an-su*, pp. 16–17, 35–37. See also Sun and Fan Hsueh-yi, "Correctly Evaluate the Function of Peasant Uprisings in Chinese History," *KMJP*, April 12, 1956. Actually, Sun was criticized in turn for distorting the facts pertinent to these uprisings. For instance, it was pointed out that the concessions Sun claimed had been a result of the uprising of Wang Hsiao-po in fact had been granted prior to the revolt. See Ning K'o, "Some Ideas on . . . [the above article]," *KMJP*, June 7, 1956.

One cannot ignore the unsuccessful class struggles, he continued, since the crucial question was not the apparent success or failure of the undertaking but the stage of development of society. He concluded:

> . . . the basic content [of the function of the peasant uprisings] is that in periods of conformity of productive relations and productive forces, class war propels the development of productive forces while in periods when they do not conform, class war destroys the fetters of the old productive relations and opens the way to advance of productive forces. Because of this in any period, and regardless of form, class struggles were the motivation of social development.[25]

Examples of improvements in the economic and social conditions of the time, on which all communist historians can agree as proof of the progressive function of the peasant movements, include (1) an alleged reduction in slavery in the early Imperial period, (2) more lenient early Han tax and legal regulations, (3) new forms of land and tenancy relations and a lightened burden of corvée and military duties after the Han, (4) the ending of the power of the old aristocracy and then of militarists after the Tang, (5) improvements in the tax structure in the T'ang and Ming, (6) the opening of new lands and the development of new economic forms in the Ming and Ch'ing. Communist historians argue that all of these improvements were due in some measure to government fears of further peasant uprisings or to the blows of the peasant revolts themselves.

Finally, mainland historians argue that a function of the peasant revolts was to better the relations between the various races of China. Since "racial oppression is rooted in class oppression," the various races cooperated against their common class enemy and thereby forged a better union of the people of China, according to this view.[26] The problem of

[25] Liang Tso-kan, "A Brief Discussion of the 'Dark and Chaotic Periods' in History," *KMJP*, August 16, 1956.

[26] E.g., Wu Yen-nan, "On the Historical Function of the Chinese Peasant Revolts and Wars," *SSP*, p. 451; and Lü Chen-yü, cited in *HCS* (eds.), *op. cit.*, *SSP*, p. 491.

the role of the minority races in the class struggle of "feudal times" involves the whole question of "just" and "unjust" war. Wars are defined as "just if they oppose oppression [either domestic or foreign] and advance historical development" and unjust if they do not.[27] Unfortunately, as we have seen, the ending of oppression did not necessarily further historical evolution.[28] Racial conflicts are held to be a product of class society and will presumably disappear together with class society. Peasant uprisings hastened this process and improved relations among the various races of China during the millennia preceding the socialist revolution.

It is held that in all these ways the peasant revolts improved the "productive relations" or working conditions of their time and thus enabled the further development of society. Aside from the dubiousness of many of these claims, which would have to be examined in specific cases, there are also evident inconsistencies in the arguments from the Marxist point of view, most notably the apparent contradictions between economic progress and social disruptions referred to above and the meshing of the theory of the class struggle and the theory of historical evolution, our next topic.

EVOLUTION AND DEVELOPMENT

Because of the "peculiarities of Chinese conditions," the question of historical evolution is a particularly thorny one for the Marxist theorist whose basic concepts were derived

[27] See Lü Chen-yü, "Historical Science Must be Developed on the Basis of Mao Tse-tung's Thought," *LSYC*, no. 5, 1960, p. 26.

[28] Examples of confusion over this point can be seen in the discussions of the Sui revolts. For instance, Ch'i Hsia ("On Several Problems in the Late Sui Peasant Uprisings," *LKP*, p. 115) criticized the alliance of the rebel Liu Hei-ta with the Turks against the newly founded T'ang as reactionary because it retarded the development of the T'ang state. Yet elsewhere (*ibid.*, p. 103) he praised the struggles of the peasants against the Sui Korean expeditions. An even more glaring inconsistency was the earlier praise of Yakoob Beg's revolt against the Ch'ing but later denunciations of Beg as a "running dog of the British imperialists." See Kuo Ying-te, "Correction of My Former Mistaken Evaluation of Yakoob Beg," *KMJP*, June 21, 1956.

from Western history.[29] There are the obvious inconsistencies relating to the development of a "slave" and then a "feudal" society in ancient China. Not only is there a question as to the existence of such economic modes of production, but in terms of the development of the class struggle many striking incongruities arise.

Slave society was the most exploitive mode of production, and consequently the class struggle should have been most marked at that time. Stalin was aware of the theoretical complications following from this when he wrote that in the feudal epoch "exploitation is nearly as severe as it was under slavery . . . [consequently] class struggle between the exploiters and exploited is the principal feature of the feudal system." [30] It follows that the class struggle should have been more intense in the slave period, but the fact is that in China there were no "slave" revolts at all in the Shang and Chou periods comparable to the "peasant rebellions" which broke out from the beginning of the "feudal period." [31] Some historians attempt to get around the absence of the class struggle in the transition from slavery to feudalism by contending that the revolts against the Ch'in, Wang Mang, and the later

[29] A limited example, which illustrates the confusing effect of the different data with which the European and Chinese Marxists must work, is the question of the evolution of land rent. The progress from rent in labor, to rent in kind, to rent in money was a basic consideration in the studies of the founding fathers of Marxism, but in China all three forms have existed simultaneously or at least in a different sequence. Such differences in social and economic history naturally lead to considerable confusion when Chinese Marxists apply formulas designed for Western conditions. That these concepts often prove inapplicable in the West as well is, of course, another question.

[30] J. Stalin, *Dialectical and Historical Materialism*, p. 423.

[31] Mainland historians admit that slave revolts in the Mediterranean world were more conspicuous than in the "Eastern countries," thus providing a contrast with Chinese claims to a "unique tradition of peasant revolts." See Chou Tzu-ch'iang, "The Class Struggle in the Transition Period Between Slavery and Feudalism in China," *LSYC*, nos. 5 and 6, 1964, p. 134; Yang K'uan, "On the Historical Function of the Class Struggle in Ch'un-ch'iu Chan-kuo Times," *WSC*, no. 8, 1954; T'an Pi-t'ao, *Wai-kuo Shih K'o-pen* (Text of the History of Foreign Countries) (Shanghai: K'ai-ming Shu-tien, 1950), p. 44; and Tung Chia-tsun, *Chung-Kuo Nu-li She-hui Shih* (History of Chinese Slave Society) (Canton: She-hui Hsüeh-she, 1955), pp. 73–74.

Han, depending on where the author marked the transition to feudalism, were slave revolts.[32] Other historians mention revolts of the Chou period, such as that against King Li (842 B.C.) and the semi-legendary "bandit Chih" of Chan Kuo times.[33] Most Chinese historians, however, ignore this question and clearly avoid the problem of the role of the class struggle in the transition from slave to feudal society, since it has no solution. In short, the one period of ancient Chinese history where both communist and noncommunist historians agree there was a real revolution, either to "feudalism" in the case of the Marxists or from feudalism to the Imperial order in the case of non-Marxists, is the only period which has no verifiable mass rebellions. By contrast, the next fifteen hundred years, when there should have been no "social revolution" according to the classical Marxist view of historical evolution, were full of mass revolts. Conversely, despite these disruptions, "Chinese feudalism" endured for two millennia.

Similar problems arise in the effort to integrate the interpretations of the peasant revolts with the periodization of modern history and the transition from "feudalism" to a "semi-feudal, semi-colonial" China in the nineteenth century. For instance, there is the problem of the role of the peasant wars in encouraging the "roots of capitalism" after the middle of the Ming.[34] Then in the nineteenth century

[32] E.g., Chang Heng-shou ("A Tentative Discussion of the Nature of Society in Han Times," *LSYC*, September 1957), who placed the transition from slave to feudal in the middle of the Han after the revolt of the Red Eyebrows. Wang Ssu-chih *et al.* ("Discussion of the Nature of Han Society," *LSYC*, no. 1, 1955, p. 31) also take this position. Many Soviet and some Chinese historians contend that the slave system gave way to feudalism only after the later Han and the revolt of the Yellow Turbans. E.g., L. Pozdnyeva, "Revolts of the Slaves and Poor," in V. V. Struve (ed.), *Drevny Vostok* (Ancient East) (Moscow: Uchpedgiz, 1958), p. 235.

[33] E.g., see Yang K'uan, *op. cit.*, *WSC*, no. 8, 1954; and Chou Tzu-ch'iang, *op. cit.*, *LSYC*, nos. 5 and 6, 1964. The "Ts'ang T'ou army," which fought with Ch'en Sheng against the Ch'in, is also considered a "slave army."

[34] Supposedly this development was cut short first by the incursion of the Manchus and then by that of the imperialists. See Ch'i Hsia, "On the Question of the Nature of the Chinese Peasant Wars," *SSP*, p. 73;

the greatest peasant movement in history, the Taiping, occurred not at the end of "feudalism" but in the beginning of the new stage ushered in by the arrival of the "imperialist" powers. The other peasant revolts of the late nineteenth and early twentieth centuries are also interpreted as "old-style, anti-feudal" class wars, although with an increasing anti-imperialist content, culminating in the Boxer movement. Therefore, the beginning of the "new democratic revolution" in 1919 and the communist triumph in 1949, and not the end of "feudalism," are the real dividing lines in the periodization of the history of the Chinese peasant movements. Revolts before the twentieth century were supposedly evolving to ever greater intensity, but, deprived of communist leadership, they were condemned to the habitual weaknesses of the "old-style" peasant wars. After the communist triumph in 1949, all future revolts against the government would automatically be reactionary, since for the first time in history the majority and working class was also the governing class.

Another basic "peculiarity" in the role of the peasant wars in historical evolution derives from China's unique pattern of political history, especially its two thousand years of dynastic rise and fall. In the historiography of the subject the cyclical pattern of Chinese history determines in significant ways the interpretation of the function of the peasant movements. Their role depends on their place within each dynasty, and whether they occurred in the prosperous early years or the decadent last years of a dynasty, in much the same way that the role of class struggle in Western Marxist historiography depended on its position in the development of each stage of production. In Chinese communist historiography the class struggle is said to end or improve restrictive productive relations at the end of each dynasty, enabling the development of productive forces in the next dynasty, in the same manner that the social revolution was held to bring on the transition from a given stage of production to another in Western Marxist historiography.

---

and Chao Li-sheng and Kao Chao-yi, *Chung-kuo Nung-min Chan-cheng Shih Lun-wen Chi,* p. 153. See also Chapter 6.

The tendency to describe Chinese history in the framework of traditional cyclical formulas has been repeatedly criticized on the mainland. We are told that in the 1930s many Chinese Marxists mistakenly followed Safarov's cyclical explanation of the development of Chinese society.[35] More recently there have been protests against the treatment of the peasant wars in terms of the dynastic cycle. As one writer put it, if one merely narrates the cycle of

> . . . land concentration, feudal class oppression, and exploitation inducing peasant revolts which in turn enable the economy to develop until there is again a concentration of land and more oppression and peasant uprisings . . . is this not the [old] historical cycle? [36]

Another article charged that as of 1959, although much progress had been made in the historiography of the peasant wars, many mainland historians "still have not changed the dynastic system of teaching." [37]

Despite the incompatibility of Marxist theories of historical evolution with the theory of the dynastic cycle, the Chinese communists have decided to go along at least with the outward symbolism, if not with the content, of the traditional periodization of Chinese history. This will undoubtedly remain the case until such time as more fundamental problems of the timing of "Chinese slavery and feudalism" are solved. Not until then will mainland historians be likely to drop the terminology of the dynasties and periodize Chinese history according to the proper Marxist socio-economic formation. Although leading Chinese historians admit the similarity of the oppression–peasant-war cycle to the old "dynastic system," they argue that this alternative is necessary at

[35] Lü Chen-yü, *Shih Lun-chi*, p. 32.

[36] Ch'i Hsia, *op. cit.*, *JMJP*, December 4, 1956. See also Chi Wen-fu, "Profoundly and Thoroughly Observe the Viewpoint of the Class Struggle in Historical Research," *SCMP* 2500, p. 11, citing *KMJP*, April 28, 1961.

[37] Liu Yao-t'ing *et al.*, "The Development of Historical Science in the Light of Ten Years of Struggle on the Intellectual Front," *SHYK*, no. 11, 1959, p.17.

the moment and perhaps is preferable in any case to dry Marxist formulas of succeeding stages of production. The fact is that most influential mainland historians still prefer more colorful indigenous forms.

On the other hand, mainland historians reject the content of the "dynastic system" of traditional historiography in so far as it deals only with the rise and decline of the governing class, and they attempt to relate these events to broader studies of economic and social factors and, above all, to the class struggle.[38] They seek to retain key aspects of both Marxist and traditional periodization, in effect using a form of the dynastic cycle, but one which is modified to show a constant progression up the two-thousand-year plane of Chinese feudalism. This approach might be described as "an evolving peasant-war cycle."

The evolution of the peasant wars themselves, from early to late periods of Chinese feudalism, is another side of the question of their role in pushing the evolution of history. We recall that the connection of productive relations to productive forces is the most fundamental question in the interpretation of the role of the class struggle within the Marxist scheme of historical evolution. The class struggle must force changes in productive relations or working conditions of the time, after these begin to impede the development of the productive forces of the economy. In the early stages of any given mode of production, however, the productive relations, newly revised as a result of the social revolution ending the old epoch, are in accord with the new economy. Therefore, there is no place for this most obvious role of the class struggle in the early period of any given mode of production. Only after the further development of the economy should there again be a need to shatter outmoded productive relations.

The problem of the function of the class struggle at such times is particularly acute in China, where the "early feudal

---

[38] See Chien Po-tsan, "On the Question of Overthrowing the Dynastic System of History," *KMJP*, March 28, 1959; also carried in *HCS*, no. 3, 1959. See also articles on the subject in *HCS*, no. 4, 1959; and *JMJP*, April 8, 1959.

period" extended over many centuries and yet was marked by numerous large-scale peasant wars. If these class struggles are held to oppose the feudal system, then—since feudalism was still progressive as against slavery—the early peasant movements would in fact be reactionary.

One group of historians tries to resolve this question by dividing the history of the Chinese peasant wars into two basically different periods. They argue that when productive relations accorded with the productive forces in early feudalism, the function of the class struggle was to advance production by direct economic methods such as the opening of new lands. The early peasant-class struggles therefore did advance the feudal economy, and they did not attack productive relations which were still in accord with the economic needs of the time. While the proponents of this interpretation admit that the early peasant revolts also opposed the feudal system of exploitation, they argue that the peasants came out against the basis of restrictive productive relations, attacking social and economic inequalities only after feudalism began its decline.[40]

This distinction between the function of the peasant movements in early and late feudalism was given great impetus by the comments of Kuo Mo-jo in connection with the reevaluation of Ts'ao Ts'ao in 1959. Kuo argued that the Yellow Turbans could not have raised the land problem as some maintained, because such a fundamental aspect of feudal productive relations did not and could not become a leading concern of the peasants for another thousand years.[41] Hou Wai-lu and others expanded on this argument, seeking to prove that the peasant wars prior to the T'ang opposed government excesses but came out directly against productive re-

[40] E.g., see Liang Tso-kan, *op. cit.*, *KMJP*, August 16, 1956; and discussions of this question in *KMJP*, September 20, 1960, and *SSP*, pp. 187–88 and 508.

[41] Kuo Mo-jo, "The Processes of Historical Development of the Chinese Peasant Revolts," in *SSP*, p. 50. There were earlier references to a rising consciousness in the processes of the long anti-feudal wars (e.g., see Yang Wei-min and Jen Shu-ming, "The Uprising of Wang Hsiao-po and Li Hsun in the Early Northern Sung," *LKP*, p. 159), but this theme was greatly stimulated by the articles of Kuo and Hou.

lations only afterward.[42] These arguments are based largely
on the assertion that the slogans and programs of the peasant
revolts after the T'ang showed a new sense of opposition to
social and economic inequalities, the bases of the system of
feudal exploitation.[43] As Hou Wai-lu put it:

> . . . following historical development, the peasants'
> feelings of injustice also developed from lower to higher
> forms. They [the Chinese peasant rebels] passed from
> slogans and programs of religious principle . . . from
> wild illusions of resistance to poverty and demands for
> human rights to opposition to special land rights and to
> advocating egalitarian ideals, following step by step from
> the long, exhausting experiences of struggle. . . . [Thus]
> the history of the Chinese peasant wars had clearly
> different characteristics in the early and later periods of
> feudalism. . . .[44]

Others agreed that there was a basic change in the slogans
and programs of the peasant rebels before and after the
T'ang, but they felt that a more meaningful change was the
transition from opposition to the feudal state before the T'ang
to opposition to the landlord class in general after the T'ang.[45]

Another approach to the dilemma of explaining "anti-
feudal" revolts when feudalism was still progressive is the
effort to subsume the motivation of early peasant wars, such
as those of the Han, under an attack on the remnants of

[42] Hou Wai-lu, "The Development of the Peasant Wars and Their
Slogans in Early and Late Periods of Chinese Feudal Society," *SSP*, pp.
25 ff.; and Hou Wai-lu, "The Historical Characteristics of the Peasant
Wars of T'ang and Sung," *HCS*, no. 4, 1964. See also articles by Jung
Sheng, "Tentative Discussion of Some Special Characteristics of the
Ming-Ch'ing Peasant Class Struggles," *SSP*, pp. 1 ff.; and Kao Min, "A
Tentative Discussion of the Question of Stages of Development of the
Peasant Uprisings and Wars in Our Country's Feudal Society," *SSP*,
pp. 140 ff.

[43] See Chapter 6.

[44] Hou Wai-lu, *op. cit.*, *SSP*, pp. 25–26.

[45] Kao Min, *op. cit.*, *SSP*, p. 145; and Wu Yen-nan, "A Tentative
Discussion of the Characteristics of the Peasant Revolts of the End of
the Sui and T'ang," *SHYK*, no. 11, 1959.

slavery.[46] In other words, when the peasant revolts of early feudalism did seem to attack basic working conditions or productive relations, these attacks are interpreted as directed against the restrictive relations of the earlier period rather than against those of ascendant feudalism.

Some Chinese communist historians maintain that revolts of the early Imperial period actually strengthened the feudal system of the time.[47] This was because in helping to advance feudal economy, the peasant movements strengthened the basis or rule of the governing class.[48] As one writer put it, the peasant wars

> . . . in the early period of feudal society propelled the forward development of feudal society while later they hastened the decline of the feudal system and created favorable conditions for the growth of capitalist roots.[49]

Their function in the early period, then, was to "advance the feudal productive forces" of the time,[50] and one historian even denied that the lot of the peasants (their productive relations) was improved as a result of their struggles in the early period of feudalism. Rather, they were progressively enserfed throughout the Han and later.[51]

While consistent with Marxist theory, these efforts to divide the history of the Chinese peasant wars sharply between those of early feudalism and those of later feudalism are less consistent with the facts of Chinese history. They are still less consistent with the propaganda aims of the Chinese commu-

---

[46] E.g., Ch'i Hsia *et al.*, *Ch'in Han Nung-min Chan-cheng Shih*, pp. 196 ff.

[47] E.g., see discussion by Fang Chih-kuang *et al.*, "Discussion of Several Problems in the History of the Peasant Wars in China's Feudal Society," *SSP*, pp. 123 ff.

[48] Shih Shao-pin, *op. cit.*, *SSP*, pp. 508–9. This interpretation frequently has been made in Soviet historiography of the peasant wars. See Leo Yaresh, "The 'Peasant Wars' in Soviet Historiography," *American Slavic and East European Review*, vol. 16, no. 3, October 1957.

[49] Li Yin-nung, "On How to Understand Chairman Mao Regarding the Function of the Peasant Revolts," *SSP*, p. 439.

[50] Fang Chih-kuang *et al.*, *op. cit.*, *SSP*, p. 129.

[51] Wu Yen-nan, *op. cit.*, *SSP*, p. 443.

nists, who would prefer to present the peasant class as always opposed to feudalism.

Accordingly, although many mainland historians admit that the early peasant revolts in effect helped the governing class by strengthening the economic base of feudalism, they stress much more the "subjectively" anti-feudal intent of all peasant rebels.[52] They attack the arguments that the early-feudal peasant revolts strengthened feudalism as "reactionary," citing similar debates in Soviet historiography.[53]

The most effective and an increasingly used argument advanced to deal with the dilemma of the role of the peasant wars in early feudalism is the distinction between improving the economic base of feudal society, which is said to have been the function of the pre-T'ang peasant revolts, and striking at the feudal system of exploitation, which all peasant revolts supposedly did. Proponents of this view attack those who confuse the two and say that the early peasant revolts strengthened feudalism as a whole. All peasant revolts attacked the feudal system of exploitation throughout the feudal period.[54] Therefore, the early peasant movements may have helped to strengthen the feudal economy, but, like the later peasant revolts, they also attacked feudal exploitation. Some proponents of this view contend that those who deny the ability of the class struggle to affect productive forces in the early period are guilty of economic determinism, since the masses would have to await the development of the economy to resume their struggles.[55]

Chinese preference for the proposition that all revolts against exploitation are progressive, regardless of the requirements of historical evolution, is illustrated in the course of several discussions of the problem. In these debates early

[52] *HCS* (eds.), *op. cit.*, *SSP*, pp. 492–93.

[53] Jung Sheng, *op. cit.*, *SSP*, p. 5.

[54] E.g., Pai Shou-yi, "Special Characteristics of the Peasant Wars in Chinese History," *SSP*, p. 173. See also T'ien-chin Shih-fan Ta-hsueh Li-shih hsi (eds.), "Regarding the Heated Controversy Over the Problem of the Laws of Development of the Chinese Peasant Wars," *SSP*, pp. 426–33.

[55] T'ien Ch'ang-wu, "Is It Historical Materialism or Is It Economic Determinism?" *KMJP*, May 14, 1964, p. 3.

statements by various writers that the early peasant revolts could only have strengthened feudalism were criticized and eventually reversed in favor of the proposition that all peasant revolts were anti-feudal. For instance, the prominent writer Ning K'o, who was introduced as having done "comparatively much" research on the history of the peasant wars, was forced by criticisms to change from the position that the function of the peasant revolts varied according to their occurrence in early or late feudalism, to the admission that there was no real break in the development of the peasant movements until the nineteenth century.[56] In other words, all peasant wars were anti-feudal according to prevailing mainland historiography, the logic of Marxist dialectics to the contrary.

Other opponents of the view that there was no real distinction between the function of the peasant wars of the early and late periods of "Chinese feudalism" attack the argument that the slogans and programs of the early rebels were different in kind from those of the later feudal period, showing a progression from earlier unconscious opposition to personal exploitation to later conscious opposition to the system of feudal exploitation. They point out that even in the classic of poetry *Shih Ching*, a poem of the early first millennium before Christ questions the justice of nobles obtaining luxuries without work,[57] and that the first peasant rebel leaders questioned the monopoly of important posts and advanced slogans calling for equal laws. Furthermore, the Yellow Turbans raised the land problem, and, therefore, despite the arguments of Kuo Mo-jo, early peasant revolts in China were conscious of more than the mere desire to overthrow the dynasty.[58] The peasant revolts from the Ch'in to the T'ang

---

[56] See "Discussion of Problems in the Peasant Wars in Our Country's Feudal Society," *KMJP*, June 20, 1962. For a similar episode see "Some Academic Problems . . . ," *SCMP* 2446, p. 7, citing *KMJP*, January 6, 1961.

[57] Pei-ching Ta-hsueh Wen-hsueh Hsi (eds.), *Chung-kuo Li-tai Nung-min Wen-t'i Wen-hsueh Tzu-liao*, p. 397.

[58] Liu Ch'üan, "A Tentative Discussion of the Question of the Goals of the Chinese Peasant Uprisings," *KMJP*, September 17, 1959; and

as well as of later periods demonstrated their demands for an "ideal society" which was anti-feudal, and they sought the "communal ownership of goods" and later of land.[59] Just as Marx stated that the proletariat struggled against the bourgeois class even in the early capitalist period, so did the Chinese peasants attack early feudalism.[60]

It is evident that mainland historians differ considerably in their interpretations of the periodization and evolution of the peasant revolts. As Maxists, all agree that there was a steady advance in the forms and objects of class struggle throughout China's long feudal period,[61] but they disagree as to whether these developments added up to basic differences and, if so, as to the nature of the differences. Even the divisions among groups of mainland historians which occur in the discussion of other problems of interpretation do not apply here. Where in other discussions older historians tend to oppose the more radical interpretations of younger scholars, in the debates over the evolution of the peasant revolts senior theorists also split into several groups. Kuo Mo-jo and Hou Wai-lu are the leading exponents of the view that there was a substantive change in the function and nature of the peasant wars before and after the T'ang, but Lü Chen-yü and others argue that all, and not just the later, peasant revolts were anti-feudal and concerned throughout Chinese history with such basic problems as land-holding. At the other extreme, Chien Po-tsan and a few others doubt that the peasants ever opposed feudalism as a system.[62] Although the latter view is close to classical and

---

Wu Shih-mo, "Did the Peasant Class Strike the Feudal System and Demand the Establishment of a New Social System or Not?" SSP, pp. 77 ff. For a discussion of the slogans of the early revolts, see Chapter 6.

[59] Wang Ssu-chih, "On the Question of the Nature of the Peasant Wars," SSP, pp. 160–65.

[60] See HCS (eds.), op. cit., SSP, p. 492.

[61] For instance, Pai Shou-yi spoke of a development in size, duration, organization, and ideology of the Chinese peasant revolts (see Smolin, "The Discussion by Chinese Historians on the Question of the Peasant Revolts in the Period of Feudalism," NAA, no. 2, 1962, p. 95). Hou Wai-lu (op. cit., SSP, pp. 40–41) described this growth in size and intensity.

[62] HCS (eds.), op. cit., SSP, pp. 489–90.

even Leninist views of the nature of peasant opposition to feudalism, it represents a "rightist" deviation in the context of current Chinese political life and has been increasingly attacked during the 1960s.

Paradoxically, some of the Chinese historians who take the dimmest view of the peasant revolts support the seemingly more radical interpretation that all Chinese peasant movements struck at the feudal system.[63] Similarly, many of the more enthusiastic proponents of the revolutionary qualities of the peasant revolts uphold the view that the early peasant movements strengthened rather than weakened early feudalism.[64] The result is that most Chinese historians compromise between these two interpretations and maintain that the peasant revolts always opposed exploitation but constantly evolved toward higher forms of struggle, especially after the T'ang, when they became anti-feudal in effect as well as intent.[65]

Besides the two-stage theories of the evolution of the class struggle in "feudal China," there are also more detailed attempts to periodize the history of the Chinese peasant wars. If all agree there was some evolution of the forms of the peasant revolts and most believe this evolution should be divided into two stages, others make three or four divisions in the development of the peasant movements. These are fixed primarily according to the demands of the peasant rebels and the stages of feudal society.[66]

Those historians who favor a periodization of the history of the peasant revolts into three stages hold that the peasants during the Han or, according to some, down to the T'ang fought primarily for their personal right of existence, against the remnants of slavery and enserfment and against the government corvée and land policies, while by the late T'ang and Sung they fought for equal property, and in the Ming and

[63] E.g., Sun Tso-min, "The Question of the Blows of the Chinese Peasant Wars Against Feudalism," *SSP*, pp. 105 ff.

[64] E.g., Wu Yen-nan, *op. cit.*, *SSP*, pp. 422–24. See also discussion in *KMJP*, September 20, 1960.

[65] E.g., Jung Sheng, *op. cit.*, *SSP*, pp. 4–5.

[66] See Shih Shao-pin, *op. cit.*, *SSP*, pp. 505–7.

Ch'ing they fought against the entire system of landlord-class exploitation.[67] Those who favor a division in the history of the peasant wars into four periods speak of changes in the principal contradictions of each period: between the peasants and the state in the Han; between the peasants and the noble landlords in the period of division and in the T'ang; between the peasants and the rising private landlord class with their expanding system of tenancy in the Sung and Yuan; and between the peasants and all the feudal classes in the Ming and Ch'ing.[68]

Still other debates concern the evolution of a specific peasant war, particularly after the reigning dynasty had been overthrown, as in the case of the struggles against the Ch'in, Wang Mang, the Sui, the Yuan, and the Ming. All mainland historians agree that a peasant movement represented the interests of the peasant class as long as it fought oppressive government, but they disagree in their analysis of the class struggle after the overthrow of the existing government, when the needs of society seemed to call for a restoration of order and a resumption of economic development. This question is further complicated since, according to Marxist theory, any viable political form of organization was bound to reflect the feudal base of society in the feudal period and any peasant revolt was bound to be transformed into a feudal government sooner or later.

In recent years historians have disputed some earlier interpretations which held that once the existing government was overthrown, the peasant movement automatically became reactionary in the ensuing struggle for power.[69] All agree that

[67] *Ibid.*, p. 506.

[68] *Ibid.*, pp. 506–7. See also Liaoning Ta-hsueh Li-shih hsi, "The Nature and Characteristics of the Chinese Peasant Wars," *SSP*, pp. 103–04; and Fang Chih-kuang *et al.*, *op. cit.*, *SSP*, p. 125. See also discussions on this question in *KMJP*, September 20, 1960; and in *Yang-ch'eng Jih-pao* (Canton), June 2, 1959.

[69] See Wang Tan-ts'en, "Regarding [my book] *Chung-kuo Nung-min Ke-ming Shih-hua*," *KMJP*, August 22, 1953; Ch'i Hsia, *op. cit.*, *LKP*, p. 112; and Shang Yueh, *Chung Kuo Li-shih Kang-yao* (Hong Kong: San-lien Shu-tien, 1957), p. 174. See also the discussion in *KMJP*, September 20, 1960; and Ch'i Hsia, *op. cit.*, *JMJP*, December 4, 1956.

in these circumstances a peasant movement did undergo a certain transformation—feudalists usually entered the movement either by invitation or by deception, or the movement was used by landlord groups merely as an instrument of dynastic change. But most feel that one should never speak of the class struggle as reactionary, regardless of its stage of development. They argue, therefore, that a "war of feudal unification" conducted after the overthrow of the old dynasty represented only a new stage of the peasant war, not a transformation of the nature of the peasant war from progressive to reactionary.[70] Many writers sought to solve this dilemma in the case of the anti-Sui revolts by claiming that the revolts which continued after the founding of the T'ang continued to play a progressive role despite their prolongation of disruption because they continued to force concessions from the early T'ang government.[71] This argument is also applied to the revolts against the Ch'in, Wang Mang, and the Mongols.

Many historians argue that, in fact, the function of the peasant revolt was greatest when the revolt involved such a transformation from an "anti-feudal war" to a "war of feudal unification." [72] This question obviously presents difficulties in the historian's explanation of how opposition to the government changed to the attempt to form a new government by suppressing rival peasant movements. The necessity at some stage in the process of revolt to stop destruction and get on with construction is evident. Yet it is obviously difficult for the Marxist historian to explain that what was progressive at first could become reactionary a little later and vice versa. As one historian admitted, this was an obvious contradiction, but in his view it could be resolved only by the complete triumph of communism, since that would end the necessity

[70] See *KMJP*, September 20, 1960.

[71] E.g., Chao Li-sheng and Kao Chao-yi, *op. cit.*, pp. 76–77; Sun Tso-min, *Chung-kuo Nung-min Chan-cheng Wen-t'i T'an-su*, p. 29; and Wu Feng, "On the Class Struggle and Internal Governing Class Struggles in the Early T'ang," *HCS*, no. 1, 1962; and Chi Chien, "The Relation of the Late Sui Peasant Uprisings with T'ang T'ai-tsung's 'chen kuan' Government," *KMJP*, May 30, 1953.

[72] Chao Li-sheng and Kao Chao-yi, *op. cit.*, p. 80.

of all future revolt.[73]

As in the case of the role of the class struggle at the beginning of the feudal epoch, there is no real answer in Marxist historiography for the role of the class struggle within the lesser cycle of the dynasty. In both cases, working conditions are theoretically conducive to further historical development in early periods, and there is no ready explanation for the role of the class struggle at these times.

[73] *Ibid.*, pp. 82–83. Different interpretations, of course, are given to revolts occurring after the founding of the People's Republic. See Chapter 10.

CHAPTER NINE

Characteristics and Causes of Failure

FOLLOWING descriptions of communist interpretations of the background, organization, ideology, and development of the Chinese peasant movements, we may consider some communist conclusions.

The three different interpretations of peasant rebel ideology in general and of the degree of consciousness manifested in the Chinese peasant revolts in particular—those denying any conscious opposition to the feudal system as a whole, those arguing that such consciousness did develop but only in the later period of Chinese feudalism, and those which maintain that peasant revolts throughout the history of Chinese feudalism consciously opposed the system to one degree or another—are summarized in the debate on "the nature [*hsing-chih*] of the Chinese peasant wars." These discussions center on "the nature of the peasants' opposition to feudalism."

The classical Marxist view, stressing the conservative mentality of the peasantry, is most strongly stated in the view of a small group of mainland historians who maintain that the Chinese peasant wars never opposed the feudal system in its

entirety but only the abuses of individual officials and landlords. The defenders of this view are almost entirely members
of the older generation of Marxist historians.[1]

Criticisms of their views on this and related issues
launched the "Great Proletarian Cultural Revolution," and
even before the mid-1960s the great majority of lesser-known
and presumably younger historians argued that this view un-
derestimates the class struggles of the Chinese peasants,
which were anti-feudal in both intent and effect. The inference is that the generation of historians trained since 1949
and joined also by a few lesser-known older historians[2] have
carried the progression in the Marxist treatment of historical
peasant movements to another stage. They have projected
into history Mao's enthusiastic portrayal of the contemporary
Chinese peasantry in a way which accords with current Chinese pronouncements but very little with traditional Marxist
views of the subject. The Chinese peasant rebels may not
have been able to carry out advanced political programs, they
argue, but they made the attempt.[3] The peasants' political
élan, born of working-class conditions, took precedence over
their conservative, property-owning instincts. They were a
really revolutionary, anti-feudal class, even if their struggles
were "spontaneous" rather than "conscious" prior to the
emergence of the proletariat.

The third view of this subject, which holds that the Chi-

---

[1] E.g., Chien Po-tsan and Wu Han, both of whom were sharply
criticized in the mid-1960s (see Chapter 10). Even before the "cultural
revolution" only Sun Tso-min, Ts'ai Mei-piao, and several others among
the younger generation espoused the negative view of the peasant wars,
which we are told is held by "very few." See G. Ya. Smolin, "The Discussion By Chinese Historians on the Question of Peasant Revolts in
the Period of Feudalism," *NAA*, no. 2, 1962, pp. 92–93; and Shih
Shao-pin, *op. cit.*, *SSP*, pp. 500–501. Fan Wen-lan, Kuo Mo-jo, Hou
Wai-lu, and Lü Chen-yü generally take compromise views in discussions
of the subject.

[2] E.g., Ch'i Pen-yü, Shih Shao-pin, Pai Shou-yi, Ning K'o. Li Kuang-
pi.

[3] E.g., see Pai Shou-yi, "On the Nature of the Peasant Wars in
Chinese Feudal Society," *SSP*, pp. 173–86; and Wu Shih-mo, "Did the
Peasant Class Strike the Feudal System and Demand the Establishment
of a New Social System, or Not?" *SSP*, pp. 77–87.

nese peasant movements moved from opposition to unequal legal and land-holding patterns only after the middle of the T'ang, seems to represent the best compromise between prevailing Chinese views of the peasant movements and Marxist orthodoxy.[4] However, most mainland historians maintain that the Chinese peasant movements opposed the feudal system throughout the history of Imperial China.

The debates of the 1960s over the relation of "historicism" and class viewpoint in historical work also mirror the divergent interpretations of the nature of the peasant revolts. In these discussions the few historians who take a more cautious view of the peasant revolts tend to stress "historicism" or a greater allowance for the complexities and limitations of historical circumstance, while the more radical historians stress the preaching of the "class viewpoint" in historical writings. Accordingly, Sun Tso-min, even before the "cultural revolution" one of the few who still defended the more skeptical and cautious view of the peasant revolts, wrote that "in the past there appeared in the studies of some comrades of the history of the peasant wars unhistorical tendencies in the exaggeration of the [revolutionary] consciousness of peasant rebel leaders." [5] Sun repeated, as he had many times in the past, the classical Marxist arguments to the effect that the conservative, property-owning nature of the peasantry was at least as basic as its revolutionary, working-class nature and that this was revealed in the history of the Chinese peasant wars as well as in Western history.

Yet most people in the debates on "historicism," as in other historical discussions, attacked all efforts to question

[4] Championed by Kuo Mo-jo and Hou Wai-lu.

[5] Sun Tso-min, "The Use of Historicism and Class Viewpoint in the Research on the History of Our Country's Peasant Wars," *JMJP*, February 27, 1964. See also Sun, "Is It Supporting Class Analysis or Destroying Class Analysis?" *CHYC*, no. 4, 1964, pp. 61–70. In his 1956 book, *Chung-kuo Nung-min Chan-cheng Wen-t'i T'an-su*, Sun had already decried what he called the "universal leftist tendency" to exaggerate the peasant revolts. At least one writer did come to the defense of the views of Sun and of Ts'ai Mei-piao, but he did not mention Sun by name. See Chi-Tun-yü, "Is the Theory of Two Types of Revolution Economic Determinism?" *CHYC*, no. 5, 1964, pp. 51 ff.

the anti-feudal nature of the Chinese peasant wars. They attempted to refute the distinction drawn by Chien Po-tsan, Sun Tso-min, Ts'ai Mei-piao, and a few others between "objective" struggle against the feudal government and the "subjective" consciousness of that struggle. Where the conservative interpretation of the peasant movements holds that acts of resistance did not imply knowledge of the goals of resistance, the radical interpretation denies that the peasant could oppose the landlord government without some awareness of what they were fighting. Proponents of this view contend that the rebel slogans revealed some knowledge of political goals and that therefore the Chinese peasant revolts were antifeudal in intent as well as in practice. Above all, the enthusiastic interpreters of the peasant revolts contend that while one should not beautify (*mei-hua*) the peasants, a tendency criticized by the conservatives, the opposite tendency of finding fault (*ch'ou-hua*) with the peasant class is a far more serious error and a "matter of principle." [6] The class line stressed in the "cultural revolution" shows the importance of this "principle."

Nevertheless, even representatives of this most radical interpretation, who hold that the Chinese peasant revolts were always anti-feudal, attempt to show the development of the class struggles of the peasants from lower to higher forms of opposition and at the same time to draw a clear distinction between the most advanced peasant wars and the modern proletarian-led communist revolution.

[6] Wu Ch'uan-ch'i, "We Cannot Say the Peasant Wars Are a 'Continuation' of Feudal Landlord Policies," *KMJP*, April 3, 1964. See also articles and discussions of this issue in *KMJP*, May 14, 1964, p. 3, and June 21, 1964, p. 1; *LSYC*, no. 6, 1963; *HCS*, no. 4, 1964; *CHYC*, no. 3, 1964, pp. 16–34, 84–85; and *CHYC*, no. 6, 1964, pp. 43 ff. For a summary of articles on the general question of "historicism" see *SCMP* 3162, pp. 15–21, citing *KMJP*, January 18, 1964; and *URS*, vol. 32, no. 25, September 24, 1963, p. 1.

CAUSES OF FAILURE

In the crudest explanations of the reasons for the failure of the various peasant movements, communist historians simply repeat Mao's formula that in the absence of an "advanced political party" and such "correct leadership as is given by the proletariat and the Communist Party today, the peasant revolutions invariably failed."[7] In fact, in pre-modern times it was difficult at best for the rebel leader to imagine a truly revolutionary program or, if he did, in the absence of modern communications and propaganda techniques, to win the support necessary for its execution. Yet, rather than analyze the reasons for this, most communist studies of the peasant movements are content to rest on the classical Marxist statements of the inherent weaknesses of the peasant class.

Engels stressed lack of unity and coordination as the principal cause of the defeat of the German peasant war of 1525.[8] This organizational weakness, according to Engels, stemmed from the conservatism and inherent lack of vision of the peasant class. Similarly, Lenin described the failure of a Russian peasant movement of 1902 as due to its lack of political consciousness and consequent inability to prepare or pose political demands. All these failings demonstrated the necessity of proletarian leadership and propaganda.[9] Prevailing Soviet interpretations continue to stress organizational weakness rooted in the limitations of the peasant class as the leading cause of the inevitable failure of peasant movements in history.

The Chinese communist analysis of the causes of defeat of the peasant wars has gone through several stages of evolution. According to Kuo Mo-jo, this problem first came under intensive discussion during the war years, when historians

[margin annotation: cf. Hinton's "well's eye view"]

[7] Mao Tse-tung, "The Chinese Revolution and the CCP," *SWMTT*, vol. 3, p. 76.
[8] Engels, *The Peasant War in Germany*, pp. 154–55.
[9] See V. I. Lenin, "To the Rural Poor," in *Alliance of the Working Class and the Peasantry*, p. 183.

sought the reason for the "stagnation" of Chinese feudalism for two thousand years. Why had there not been a successful indigenous revolution capable of ending Chinese feudalism before the advent of the West? [10] Prior to 1949, leading "leftist" historians advanced several categories of reasons for the inevitable defeat of the various rebellions, including tactical and strategic mistakes and the strength of opposing forces. By the early to mid-1950s, however, orthodox interpretations relegated all such causal factors to a position secondary in importance to Mao's dictum that the peasant revolts failed because of the lack of "an advanced political party" or of "correct leadership such as is supplied by the CCP today." [11] At times there has been more elaborate and sophisticated analysis of the errors of the peasant rebels.[12]

These trends can be illustrated by the treatment of the causes of the failure of the Taiping movement. In 1937 Lo Erh-kang, whose interpretations of the peasant revolts have generally been in line with the views of orthodox communist historians, wrote that the Taiping rebellion, like many Chinese peasant revolts before it, was bound to fail so long as it refused to compromise with existing power groups. This was because the rebels alienated the educated classes, whose services they most needed, because of their disruptions of the social and economic order. Lo believed that the rebels could have won the support essential to victory only if they had modified their religious beliefs and ceased their struggle— clearly impossible conditions.[13] Lo also mentioned the mistakes of the Taiping leaders and the limitations of their ideology.[14]

[10] Kuo Mo-jo, "Historical Studies in War-time China," VI, nos. 5–6, 1945.

[11] "The Chinese Revolution and the CCP," *SWMTT*, vol. 3, p. 76. Actually, the lack of "advanced class leadership" was mentioned as the chief cause of the failure of the Taipings at least as early as 1932. See Teng Ssu-yü, *Historiography of the Taiping Rebellion*, p. 82.

[12] E.g., see report of a high school class discussion of reasons for the failure of the revolt against the Ch'in led by Ch'en Sheng and Wu Kuang, *LSCH*, no. 3, 1959, pp. 47 ff.; and discussion in *KMJP*, September 20, 1960.

[13] Lo Erh-kang, *T'ai-p'ing T'ien-kuo Shih-kang* (Outline History of the TPTK) (Shanghai: Shang-wu Yin-shu Kuan, 1937), pp. 100–103.

[14] *Ibid.*, pp. 103–6.

In 1947 Fan Wen-lan wrote in his influential *History of Modern China* that the determinant cause of the failure of the Taiping movement was the mistaken ideology of its leaders. This in turn derived from the tendencies of the peasant class toward cliquism, conservatism, and hedonism.[15] The superior strength of the reactionary alliance between the Ch'ing and the imperialist powers is also mentioned, but elsewhere Fan wrote that the leading powers were too busy with the Crimean War and other activities to have intervened effectively had the Taipings succeeded in the 1850s.[16] In these early interpretations Fan mentioned the absence of correct class leadership as a cause of the Taiping defeat, but he did not stress it.

Then, in the 1950s the Party decreed a more explicit approach to the problem of why pre-modern revolts necessarily failed. On the one-hundredth anniversary of the beginning of the Taiping revolt, *Jen-min Jih-pao* stressed Mao's statement that the fundamental cause of the failure of the revolt was the absence of "advanced class leadership." [17] Fan himself repeated this emphasis in a similar article five years later,[18] and the theme has been continued, though with more subtlety. The leading role of the imperialist powers is also stressed far more in the current orthodox treatment of the causes of failure of the Taipings than was the case before the 1949–51 period.

In the early 1950s and during the anti-rightist campaigns, when a less sophisticated approach to Marxist theory prevailed, many writers, especially if they were writing for a popular audience, also stressed the machinations of the landlord class in causing the defeat of the peasant rebels. Whenever relatively large numbers of landlords were present in the

---

[15] Fan Wen-lan, *Chung-kuo Chin-tai Shih*, pp. 151–54; and Fan Wen-lan (ed.), *TPTK Ke-ming Yun-tung* (The Taiping Revolutionary Movement) (Hong Kong: Hsin Min-chu Ch'u-pan She, 1948), p. 69.

[16] Fan Wen-lan, in *TPTK Ke-ming Yun-tung Lun-wen chi* (Peking: San-lien Shu-tien, 1950), pp. 1–5.

[17] "Remember the Hundredth Anniversary of the Revolution of the TPTK," *JMJP*, January 11, 1951.

[18] Fan Wen-lan, "Remember the One Hundred and Fifth Anniversary of the Revolt of the TPTK," *JMJP*, January 11, 1956.

"peasant armies," as in the anti-Ch'in, anti-Wang Mang revolts, subsequent treacheries were invariably blamed on the influence of "landlord-class elements." The gentry was even alleged to have sent its agents into the peasant armies to corrupt their leaders and sabotage their efforts. This was the interpretation of the "feudal states' restorationists" who infiltrated Ch'en Sheng's forces and of the Liu family in the revolts against Wang Mang.[19] Thus, the communist historians are faced with an obvious dilemma in their treatment of the role of the educated upper classes in the success or failure of the uprisings. If the gentry was alienated and did not participate, the revolt could not succeed. If it did participate, its pernicious class influences were supposed to harm the cause of the peasants.

By the 1960s there were efforts to allow for greater historical complexity in the treatment of the rise and fall of the peasant movements.[20] Under the prevailing emphasis on the revolutionary qualities of the peasant revolts, the tendency is to stress that the basic feature of the peasant movements was not that they inevitably failed but that they alone pushed forward the development of Chinese history.[21] Others have observed that the point is not to deny the failures and limitations of the peasant rebellions in Chinese history but to learn from their mistakes.[22]

In addition to the factors mentioned above as causes of rebel failure—the lack of advanced class leadership and the inherent weaknesses of the peasant class, the infiltration and sabotage by class enemies, and the mistakes of the rebel leaders themselves—the most commonly mentioned cause of defeat is what Mao called the "roving insurgent mentality" (*liu-k'ou chu-yi*) of the peasant rebels. It is said to derive from

---

[19] E.g., see Chuang Wei, *Chung-kuo Nung-min Ch'i-yi te Ku-shih* (Stories of the Chinese Peasant Uprisings) (Shanghai: Hua-tung Jen-min Ch'u-pan She, 1952).

[20] See Mou An-shih, *T'ai-p'ing Tien-Kuo*, pp. 420–39.

[21] Tien-chien Shih-fan Ta-hsueh Li-shih hsi (eds.), *op. cit.*, SSP, p. 474.

[22] Lung Sheng-yun, "On the Question of Prejudice in Research Work on the History of the TPTK," *KMJP*, March 3, 1958.

the political weaknesses of the peasant class and is defined as mere wandering with "the view that base areas are neither necessary nor important" and as the libertarian "wish to go to the big cities and indulge in eating and drinking." [23] Mao particularly criticized the traits of the "old-style peasant wars" as no longer permissible under present conditions.

Vagabondism is clearly related to the key role of the "wandering people" (*yu min*) in the Chinese peasant movements.[24] Yet while the Chinese communists generally praise this Chinese version of the lumpenproletariat,[25] the "vagabondism" of the roving insurgents has also been called the leading "feature of all Chinese peasant uprisings and the cause of their defeat." [26] On the other hand, Lo Erh-kang

[23] Mao Tse-tung, "Rectification of Incorrect Ideas in the Party," *SWMTT*, vol. 1, pp. 114-15, and "Strategic Problems in Guerrilla War," *SWMTT*, vol. 2, pp. 135-36. In the original text of the former article Mao included Hung Hsiu-ch'uan as well as Li Tzu-ch'eng and Huang Ch'ao as leading examples of this tendency. See S. Schram, *The Political Thought of Mao Tse-tung*, p. 200. See also Mao Tse-tung, *On Guerrilla Warfare*, trans. S. B. Griffith (New York: Praeger, 1961), especially pp. 107-8 and 61-62. It is interesting to note that Tseng Kuo-fan also distinguished between "roaming bandits" like Shih Ta-k'ai and the Taipings operating from the base area of Nanking. See F. Michael, *The Taiping Rebellion*, p. 119.

[24] Certainly the role of the vagabonds in the history of the Chinese peasant revolts cannot be overestimated. They could be fitted nicely into Chinese communist theory if Western or "Trotskyist" schemes of periodization were adopted, since Marx and Engels (*The German Ideology*, p. 51) traced the rise in vagabondage to the decline of feudalism.

[25] Forming another contrast with traditional Marxist views. For Mao's praise of the *yu-min*, see Schram, *op. cit.*, pp. 176, 193, 196, 200; and Mao's "Hsing-kuo Tiao-ch'a," *Mao Tse-tung Hsuan-chi* (Mukden: Tung-pei Shu-tien, 1948), p. 90. Compare these remarks by Mao with Engels' criticism of the lumpenproletariat (*The Peasant War in Germany*, p. 23). Actually, the Chinese *yu-min* appeared to combine characteristics of the Western urban lumpenproletariat and the rural agricultural proletariat. Engels praised the latter as the "most numerous and natural allies" of the proletariat. *Ibid.*, pp. 24-25 and 59.

[26] Chien Po-tsan, "On Several Questions in the Evaluation of Historical Personages," *Li-shih Wen-t'i Lun-ts'ung*, pp. 134-35. See also Chao Li-sheng and Kao Chao-yi, *Chung-kuo Nung-min Chan-cheng Shih Lun-wen Chi*, pp. 145-47; Sun Tso-min, *Chung-kuo Nung-min Chan-cheng Wen-t'i T'an-su*, pp. 40-41; and Sun Tso-min, *op. cit.*, *KMJP*, May 26, 1958. T'ao Hsi-sheng was among the first to discuss the historical implications of the Marxist view of "vagabondism." See his

and others have lauded the highly mobile tactics of such rebel armies as the Nien,[27] and Hua Kang noted the similarity of certain Taiping and Red Army tactics.[28] Still others have attacked the descriptions of the free-wheeling behavior of Huang Ch'ao, Li Tzu-ch'eng, and other rebels as slanders of the working class.[29] Communist evaluation of the "roving insurgent mentality" or "vagabondism" of the rebels is obviously ambiguous.

Confusion on this question is due to historians' awareness of the contrast between the Marxist classics' derogatory criticism of the "vagrants" and their "vagabond mentality" and the obvious role of the "wandering people" in the history of the Chinese revolts.[30] Another source of confusion in the treatment of the question of "roving insurgency" arises from the terseness of Mao's own discussion of the problem. Although Mao sharply criticized the "vagabond mentality," he did not fully spell out the distinction between desirable mobile tactics in military operations and the fatal inability of the rebels to construct a permanent base of support.[31] Accordingly, Chinese historians who stress "vagabondism" as a leading weakness of the Chinese peasant revolts are called to task for misinterpreting Mao and confusing the tactics of guerrilla warfare with the mentality of preferring aimless destruction

---

Chung-kuo She-hui Hsien-hsiang Shih-ling (Shanghai: Hsin Sheng-ming Shu-chü, 1931), pp. 205–18.

[27] Lo Erh-kang, *Nien-chün te Yun-tung Chan* (The Mobile War of the Nien Army) (Changsha: Shang-wu Yin-shu Kuan, 1939). In his preface to a 1955 revision of this work, under the title *TPTK Hsin-chün te Yun-tung Chan*, Lo stated that he had studied the Nien originally, in part, to apply their tactical principles to the war against Japan.

[28] Hua Kang, *TPTK Ke-ming Chan-cheng Shih* (History of the Taiping Revolutionary War) (Shanghai: Hai-yen Shu-tien, 1949), p. 223.

[29] E.g., Chang Pao-kuang *et al.*, "The Problem of Vagabondism in the History of the Chinese Peasant Wars," *SSP*, p. 207.

[30] See remarks by Yang Chih-chiu on the vagrant origins of the T'ang rebel Chu Wen. "The Great Uprising of Huang Ch'ao, *LKP*, pp. 151–52.

[31] Elsewhere Mao seemed to call for more mobility rather than less, as when he criticized the Li Li-san line for trying to hold Changsha instead of "undertaking [it] as a temporary action." See E. Snow, *Red Star over China*, p. 161.

and enjoyment (*hsiang-lo chu-yi*). They point out that frequently the peasant movements had no choice but to become roving insurgents, since they were driven out of their old base area.[32]

Nevertheless, the "vagabond mentality" is still considered a leading manifestation of the low level of peasant-class political awareness. The prevailing interpretation holds that, although the Chinese peasant rebels were often driven by circumstances beyond their control to wander from place to place, they still should have devoted more attention to the problems of securing a revolutionary base. That they did not do so was because of the "roving insurgent mentality" of the rebels, rooted in the class characteristics of the wandering people.[33] This characteristic was considered particularly prevalent in the revolts of the Red Eyebrows, of the late T'ang and Ming dynasties, and of the Nien.

Thus, mainland historians do stress the weaknesses and inevitable failure of pre-modern peasant movements, and they stop short of admitting any really revolutionary accomplishments for the peasant rebels. At most a pre-modern peasant movement might set up a new feudal dynasty by compromising with the ruling class and selling out the alleged aspirations of the peasants. Yet the search for the establishment of a continuous tradition of class struggle in China has led communist historians, in the absence of any identifiable bourgeois or labor movements, to exalt the historical class struggles of the Chinese peasantry. In the process, they have gone well beyond the confines of classical Marxism as to what was considered possible for the pre-modern peasantry. The line of development in this aspect of Marxist historiography has

[32] E.g., Chang Pao-kuang *et al.*, *op. cit.*, *SSP*, p. 207; Chang Pin, "Some Ideas on the Book, *Chung-kuo Nung-min Chan-cheng Wen-t'i T'an-su*," *KMJP*, March 17, 1958; and Ch'en Ch'ang-yuan, "Several Questions about Sun Tso-min's *Chung-kuo Nung-min Chan-cheng Wen-t'i T'an-su*," *WSC*, no. 11, 1958, pp. 39–42.

[33] See Kung P'eng-chiu, "Investigation into the Mobile Tactics of the Late Ming Peasant Army," *LSCH*, no. 3, 1959, pp. 23–25; Teng Kuang-ming, "A Tentative Discussion of the Late T'ang Peasant Uprisings," *LKP*, p. 127; and Chao Li-sheng and Kao Chao-yi, *Chung-kuo Nung-min Chan-cheng Shih Lun-wen-chi*, pp. 145–47.

been a continuous one from Marx to Engels to Lenin to Mao and finally to the younger generation of Chinese historians.

CHARACTERISTICS

It is fitting to conclude with a brief description of what the communists term the distinguishing characteristics (*t'e-tien*) of the Chinese peasant wars, inasmuch as these writings show very well the use of certain very un-Chinese Marxist beliefs in behalf of Chinese nationalism.

Mao wrote in the oft-cited passage from "The Chinese Revolution and the CCP" that the "gigantic scale of such peasant uprisings and peasant wars in Chinese history is without parallel in the world," [34] and mainland historians consider the size and frequency of the Chinese peasant movements their first distinguishing characteristic.[35] This appears to have some justification in terms of statistics,[36] though its significance, of course, is open to question. Even if one divides the traditional figures by ten,[37] one still finds in Chinese historical writings numerous claims of mass movements of tens of thousands and several of hundreds of thousands. The

[34] "The Chinese Revolution and the CCP," *SWMTT*, vol. 3, p. 76.
[35] E.g., see Shih Shao-pin *op. cit.*, *SSP*, pp. 502–4; Li T'ien-tso, "The Problem of the Special Characteristics of the Chinese Peasant Wars," *SSP*, pp. 215–36; Pai Shou-yi, "Special Characteristics of the Peasant Wars in Chinese History," *SSP*, pp. 237–56; and Ku Feng, "Kuan Lu-ch'uan Discusses the Special Features of the Chinese Peasant Wars," *Nan-fang Jih-pao* (Canton), May 8, 1962.
[36] Some case studies of several medium-sized rebellions speak of peasant armies of a hundred thousand (James Parsons, "The Culmination of a Chinese Peasant Rebellion: Chang Hsien-chung in Szechwan, 1644–1646," *JAS*, May 1957, p. 389) and of 30,000–50,000 (Teng Ssu-yü, *The Nien Army*, p. 199). Other Western historians accept much larger figures for other rebellions of the Ch'in, Han, Sui, T'ang, Yuan, and Ch'ing.
[37] Assuming the wish of the government authorities to exaggerate the size of the rebel forces. See remarks attributed to Miyazaki Ichisada, *HJAS*, no. 2, 1937, p. 28; by Bielenstein, *The Restoration of the Han Dynasty*, vol. 1, p. 79, and vol. 2, p. 91; and by Reischauer and Fairbank, *East Asia: The Great Tradition*, p. 217.

Taiping army at its height is said to have numbered as high as three million. The most famous peasant movements of European and Russian history apparently seldom reached such proportions.[38] Moreover, in other societies peasant movements do not appear to have occurred with as great frequency or to have attained the geographical scope of the Chinese peasant movements.[39]

While Engels stated that "no general nation-wide" peasant rebellions occurred in Europe until the German peasant war of 1525,[40] mainland historians claim that many "national (*ch'uan-kuo*) peasant uprisings occurred throughout the history of Imperial China. Soviet historians also note on occasion evidence of the intensity of the Chinese peasant movements, and one wrote that "the uprising of the Taiping was the most powerful peasant revolt in the history of mankind." [41] Of course, they and most Chinese historians would deny that the Chinese peasant revolts were different in kind from similar movements elsewhere, but the Chinese communists do claim a "superior tradition" in terms of size and frequency of peasant movements in Chinese history.

A second related group of alleged characteristics of the Chinese peasant movements is considered to be their greater

[38] Vincent Shih, *The Taiping Ideology*, pp. 488–9. The Jacquerie were reported to have numbered some 100,000 when they rose in revolt in northern France in 1358 (see P. Boissonade, *Life and Work in Medieval Europe* [New York: Alfred A. Knopf, 1927], p. 327); the forces led by Thomas Munzer, 30–40,000 (Engels, *The Peasant War in Germany*, p. 109); and those led by E. Pugachev in Russia in 1773–74, 20–30,000 (M. Florinsky, *Russia: A History and an Interpretation* [New York: The Macmillan Co., 1953], p. 588; and B. H. Sumner, *A Short History of Russia* [New York: Harcourt, Brace & World, 1949], p. 160). Uprisings of the Muromachi period in Japan, the Middle East and in India may have been comparable in scope, but again one must be wary in dealing with the statistics of such movements. See G. Sansom, *A History of Japan, 1334–1615* (Stanford: Stanford University Press, 1961), vol. 2, p. 120.

[39] Barrington Moore attributes the great frequency and intensity of Chinese peasant revolts primarily to the lack of rapport between the peasantry and the upper classes. See his *Social Origins of Dictatorship and Democracy* (Boston: Beacon Press, 1966), pp. 201 ff.

[40] Engels, *The Peasant War in Germany*, p. 52.

[41] M. I. Baranovsky, "Anglo-American Capitalist-Suppressor of the Taiping Uprising," VI, no. 1, 1952, p. 106.

degree of organization and the broad base of participation in these movements. The reasons advanced for these characteristics are often similar to the arguments of the 1930s regarding the nature of traditional Chinese society. They start from the assumption of a despotic state which served to unite all opposition.[42] However, the belief that the "size, organization, and duration of the Chinese peasant movements were unique in world history" is meant to imply the innately revolutionary character of the Chinese peasantry[43] more than the peculiarly oppressive nature of the Imperial state. This is seen in the contention that the larger peasant movements all struggled for political power against the existing government, unlike the more aimless movements of other countries.[44]

A third set of characteristics of the Chinese peasant movements, according to mainland historians, was the greater militancy of their ideology. They argue that the clear political slogans and egalitarian programs, outlined in Chapter 6, revealed a high degree of class content. Moreover, they argue that this greater degree of class-consciousness was often manifested without the use of religious disguises, or that it imparted a more revolutionary outlook to the heretical religion than was the case in other societies.[45]

Another aspect of the more militant ideology of the Chinese peasant movements, according to most Chinese historians, was rebel willingness to oppose the existing emperor and not just "bad gentry" and officials. This characteristic is contrasted with rebel behavior in countries such as Japan and Russia, where, in Stalin's words, the peasants revolted against the "nobility and individual officials but never against the tsar." [46] As we have seen, the divisions of opinion which exist

[42] E.g., Shih Shao-pin, *op. cit.*, *SSP*, pp. 502–3; and Chao Li-sheng and Kao Chao-yi, *op. cit.*, pp. 11–12.

[43] E.g., Li T'ien-tso, *op. cit.*, *SSP*, p. 226; and Pai Shou-yi, "Special Characteristics . . . ," *SSP*, pp. 254–55.

[44] *Ibid.*, p. 237–39.

[45] *Ibid.*, pp. 247 ff.

[46] Joseph Stalin, *Works* (Moscow, 1955), vol. 13, p. 115. However, Engels (*MESW*, vol. 2, p. 59) noted that the Russian peasants did at times name their own pretender tsar, a fact which corresponds to the Chinese rebels' use of the concept of the mandate of heaven in naming their own candidates for emperor. See Chapter 7.

among mainland historians on the question of "peasant monarchism" follow the lines of argument over other questions of peasant rebel ideology. The prevailing view is that the Chinese rebels had fewer illusions about the exploitive nature of the monarchy than their counterparts elsewhere and were less restrained by "monarchist ideology." Although historians admit that the Chinese, like the Russian peasant rebels, named their own monarchist pretenders, this supposedly differed from landlord-class "monarchism." As in the rebel use of upper-class religion, a concept designed to discourage revolt was in fact changed in content and used by the rebels to oppose the government.

PATRIOTISM AND ANTI-IMPERIALISM

A final characteristic which portrays both the nationalist and class content in the historiography of this subject is the alleged "patriotic nature" of the Chinese peasant wars, both against nomadic invaders and in the past hundred years against "the imperialists." Fan Wen-lan early wrote that the peasants were the only true patriots of Chinese history. He argued that they often defended the fatherland while the rich either made their deals with the various barbarian conquerors or defended their interests out of base economic motives. Since the governing class put their economic interests ahead of patriotic values, their "patriotism," when it was evident at all, was inferior to the "patriotism" of the working class.[47] At times this formula brought complications, especially when an acknowledged governing-class patriot, such as Yueh Fei, suppressed popular rebellion as well as fought nomadic invaders,[48] but it also appeared apt for such periods as the

[47] Fan Wen-lan, introduction to *Chung-kuo T'ung-shih Chien-pien*, pp. 65–66. However, earlier in this 1954 essay (pp. 6–7) Fan criticized the neglect of the Han and T'ang conquests in the earlier version of his history. Compare this with Chien Po-tsan's 1959 criticism of unnecessary praise of the role of the minorities in Chinese history. See Appendix, note 76.

[48] E.g., see Chin Ying-hsi, "How Chou Ku-ch'eng Defends Ch'in

mid-seventeenth and twentieth centuries when domestic conservatives allied with aliens against native rebels.

Thus, mainland historians attempt to stress the class basis of patriotism,[49] although it is apparent that usually the peasants had no choice but to fight because they were too poor to flee foreign invasions. Furthermore, although class contradictions theoretically determined racial struggles, there were many possible combinations. As one statement put it, the struggles of the peasant class were "sometimes directed against the internal noble class and sometimes against a foreign governing class. At other times the peasantry supported the internal government against the foreign aggression and oppression and at others opposed both [forms of oppression] at once." [50]

The Yuan-dynasty revolts are variously interpreted as representing all of these possibilities, ranging from the earlier White Lotus revolts directed primarily against the feudal landlord class to the national liberation war led by Chu Yuan-chang against the Mongols.[51]

Pai Shou-yi speaks of three kinds of class racial war in Chinese history: (1) the cooperation of various races against a

Kuei, Favors Capitulation, and Calumniates Advocates of War," SCMM 439, p. 14, citing *Hung Ch'i*, nos. 17–18, September 1964.

[49] E.g., Li T'ien-tso, *op. cit.*, SSP, pp. 252–53. See also the criticism of Chao Li-sheng by Wang Hsing-ya, "The Reactionary Nature of Capitalist Class Rightist Chao Li-sheng's Research on the History of the Chinese Peasant Wars," WSC, no. 12, 1958, p. 46. Kao Yü-kung ("A Study of the Fang La Rebellion," unpublished doctoral dissertation, Harvard University, 1962, p. 26) points out that the Chinese peasant armies opposed the invaders only after incursions into China and consequent disruptions of peasant life. Furthermore, Kao argues this belated "patriotism" applied only to the peasant revolts of later Chinese history, particularly against the Mongols and Manchus. Muramatsu ("Some Themes in Chinese Rebel Ideologies," in Arthur Wright [ed.], *The Confucian Persuasion*, pp. 264 and 267) traces the first racial themes in the Chinese rebellions to the Sung but believes that by themselves they were never sufficient cause for revolt.

[50] LKP, postface.

[51] E.g., see Wang Ch'ung-wu, "The Development and Transformation of the Late Yuan Peasant Revolt and Its Historical Significance," LSYC, no. 4, 1954, pp. 87 ff.; and L. A. Borovkova, "The Uprising of the Red Troops and the Rise of Chu Yuan-chang," NAA, no. 2, 1961, pp. 89 ff.

common class enemy, such as supposedly occurred in the
sixth-century rebellions in north China and again in the Taiping movement; (2) wars in which varying degrees of class
and racial antagonisms operated simultaneously, such as the
Sung and Yuan revolts, which opposed both the landlords,
the Jurchen, and the Mongols; and (3) the class war which
transformed into a racial war, as in the case of the late Ming
and early Ch'ing rebellions.[52] Chao Li-sheng, Sun Tso-min,
and others speak of an evolution in the ability of the peasant
rebels to understand the relation of racial and class contradictions.[53]

In the nineteenth and twentieth centuries, another obvious
and very important manifestation of the patriotism of the
peasants, according to communist authors, has been the "anti-
imperialist struggles of the Chinese people." The exacerbat-
ing of tensions and problems within China by the coming of
the Western powers has long been recognized by noncommunist sinologists[54] and, not surprisingly, plays an important
role in communist historiography of the nineteenth-century
peasant movements.

Mainland historians date the beginning of the people's resistance to imperialism to the commencement of alleged
Western exploitation in the early nineteenth century. From
that date onward, there were two sides to China's modern
history, as one writer put it. On the one hand, there was constant "imperialist exploitation" and, on the other, the "glorious, tragic, and sacrificial struggle" of the Chinese people
against foreign invasion.[55] There was also the continued
struggle against "feudalism."

Most historians argue that internal contradictions be-

[52] Pai Shou-yi, "Special Characteristics . . . ," *SSP*, pp. 252–53.

[53] Chao Li-sheng and Kao Chao-yi, *op. cit.*, p. 17; and Sun Tso-min,
Chung-kuo Nung-min Chan-cheng Wen-t'i T'an-su, pp. 58–60.

[54] See Hsiao Kung-ch'uan, *Rural China: Imperial Control in the
Nineteenth Century*, pp. 408–10; and Fei Hsiao-t'ung, *China's Gentry:
Essays in Rural-Urban Relations* (Chicago: Chicago University Press,
1953), p. 116.

[55] Liu Yao-t'ing *et al.*, "The Development of Historical Science in
the Light of Ten Years Struggle on the Intellectual Front," *SHYK*, no.
11, 1959, p. 18.

tween the peasants and the landlords remained the primary contradiction in Chinese society through the Taiping period, being replaced as the primary contradiction by the people's struggle against imperialism only later in the nineteenth century, especially in the Boxer movement.[56] Hence, the Taipings were mainly anti-feudal and the Boxers mainly anti-imperialist.[57] In the twentieth century the internal and external contradictions alternated in importance until 1949, when the fight against imperialism again became and remained dominant.

As is evident, the establishment of the primacy of contradictions for any given period is another crucial but difficult question for the communist historian. Another example of the difficulties involved here and of the inconsistency of communist interpretations is the frequent denial of "external-influence" theories of causation, as in the case of attributing the fall of Imperial Rome to the "barbarian threat" rather than to internal decline.[58] Yet, of course, this is precisely what is done in blaming the fate of modern China primarily on "imperialist aggression" rather than on internal causes.

Despite the primacy of the contradiction with "feudalism" in the nineteenth century, the popular stress on anti-imperialism has led to an enormous emphasis on the anti-foreign aspects of the Chinese revolts from the 1840s onward. This emphasis is intended both to reveal imperialist exploitation and to raise Chinese "racial confidence" in their struggle against the West.[59]

Mainland historians describe the activities of the anti-Brit-

[56] See Jung Meng-yuan, *Chung-kuo Chin-pai-nien Ke-ming Shih-lueh* (Brief History of the Chinese Revolution in the Last One Hundred Years) (Peking: San-lien Shu-tien, 1954), pp. 24, 66; Fan Wen-lan, *Chung-kuo Chin-tai shih*, vol. 1, p. 329; Hu Cheng-ssu, "The Changes in Class Relations and Major Contradictions at the Time of the Opium War," *LSCHWT*, no. 8, 1958, p. 5.

[57] Liu Ta-nien, "What Did the Yi-ho T'uan Show?" *SCMP* 2341, p. 3, citing *JMJP*, August 30, 1960.

[58] See Chi Wen-fu, "Profoundly and Thoroughly Observe the Viewpoint of the Class Struggle in Historical Research," *SCMP* 2500, p. 11, citing *KMJP*, April 28, 1961.

[59] Liu Yao-t'ing *et al.*, *op. cit.*, *SHYK*, no. 11, 1959, p. 18.

ish corps in the Canton area in the 1840s and of various secret societies in subsequent years to prove that although the
"governing class" submitted to the powers, the Chinese people did not.[60] These interpretations, of course, define the
"people" to include some patriots of the ruling classes, sometimes even Lin Tse-hsu, the Imperial Commissioner charged
with solving the opium question in 1839.

While the Taiping rebellion is considered primarily an
"old-style" peasant war directed against the feudal landlord
class, its involvement with the imperialist powers is advanced
as proof of the Taipings' anti-imperialism. The Taipings convinced the Western powers of the "people's will to resist" and
thus helped to stave off the complete colonization of China.[61]
Western attempts to "strangle" the rebellion through such
devices as Ward's mercenary army and aid to the Manchu
government incurred the "blood debt of the Chinese people"
against imperialism.[62] Anniversary articles repeatedly advise
the remembrance and development of the "revolutionary and
anti-imperialist spirit" of the Taipings.[63]

Other late nineteenth- and early twentieth-century resistance movements allegedly reveal the intensification of anti-
imperialism and "people's patriotism" in China.[64] Under-

[60] See "The Anti-British Corps and the Sheng-p'ing Study Society,"
CKCN(P), February 17, 1956; T'ien Ju-kang, "The Resistance Move-
ment of the Foochow People Against the English Aggressors and the
Chinese Traitors in 1852," *KMJP*, July 4, 1957; and "Various Provinces
of China Compile Revolutionary History," *SCMP* 2525, citing NCNA
(Peking), January 19, 1961.

[61] Mou An-shih, *T'ai-p'ing T'ien-kuo*, p. 443.

[62] See Ting Yi, "American Aid to the Manchu-Ch'ing in Destroying
the Revolutionary Movement," *Ta Kung Pao* (Hong Kong), December
14, 1950; Hung Ch'i-hsiang, "America's First Aggressive Action Against
the Chinese Revolution," *Ta Kung Pao* (Hong Kong), May 3, 1951;
and Ching Wu, "The Alliance of the Imperialist and Feudal Forces
Which Ravaged China in the T'ai-p'ing Period," *KMJP*, May 12, 1955.

[63] See Ch'i Lung-wei, "The Spirit of Anti-Imperialism and Patriotism
of the TPTK," *KMJP*, January 5, 1961; and "The One Hundred and
Tenth Anniversary of the TPTK in the Shanghai Press," *SCMP* 2420,
citing NCNA (Shanghai), January 13, 1961.

[64] E.g., Li Shih-yueh, "Anti-Christian Movements in the Thirty
Years Before Chia-niu Year," *LSYC*, 1958, no. 6, pp. 1–15; and Li
Shih-yueh, "Features of the Anti-Christian Struggle After the Boxer
Movement," *KMJP*, July 9, 1959.

standably, communist writers praise the Boxer uprising as the prime example of a pre-communist "revolutionary movement of the Chinese people against foreign imperialism and its lackeys in China." It was the "last large-scale spontaneous peasant war in Chinese history" and was also the "first large-scale people's resistance to imperialism." [65]

Many mainland historians acknowledge the weaknesses of the Boxer movement, which "did not grow into a well-developed anti-Imperialist popular movement but on the contrary degenerated into an abnormal and unsound one and indeed ended in a miserable failure." [66] The Boxer movement had a "backward religious and superstitious organization" and was "only able to express its anger [against imperialism] in this backward superstitious form." [67] Most writers attribute these faults both to the deficiencies of all pre-communist peasant rebellions and to the actions of the reactionary gentry and government figures who infiltrated the movement and temporarily distorted the revolutionary consciousness of the rebels.[68]

Despite these reservations, communist historiography stresses the Boxer movement as a righteous "peasant-based Chinese people's anti-imperialist movement" [69] and as "one of the cornerstones of the great victory of the Chinese people fifty years later." [70] According to the now disgraced Wu Han,

[65] Chien Po-tsan, "The Yi-ho T'uan Movement," *LSCH*, no. 5, 1958, pp. 7 and 16.

[66] Hu Sheng, *Imperialism and Chinese Politics* (Peking: Foreign Languages Press, 1955), p. 133. Cf. Ch'en Tu-hsiu's views of the Boxers discussed in Chapter 2.

[67] Fan Wen-lan, *Chung-kuo Chin-tai Shih*, vol. 1, p. 329.

[68] Hu Sheng, *op. cit.*, pp. 135–36; Li Shih-yueh, "On the Nature of the Yi-ho T'uan Movement and Its Slogan 'Support the Ch'ing, Destroy the Foreigners,'" *KMJP*, October 27, 1960; and Liu Ta-nien, "What Did the Yi-ho T'uan Movement Show?" *SCMP* 2341.

[69] Chin Chia-jui, *Yi-ho T'uan Yun-tung* (The Boxer Movement) (Shanghai: Jen-min Ch'u-pan She, 1957), p. 28.

[70] Chou En-lai, as cited by Shih Ssu-ch'un, "On the Sixtieth Anniversary of the Yi Ho T'uan Anti-Imperialist Struggle," *LSYC*, no. 6, 1960, p. 13. This article is translated in *Political Information on Communist China*, no. 14 (*JPRS* 8312).

From a correct understanding of the significance of the Yi-ho T'uan movement, and from a correct narration of [their] activities . . . we can educate the broad masses to know that Imperialism is the mortal enemy of the Chinese people and of the world's people and that its nature did not and cannot change, [we can thus] reveal the barbaric and evil face of Imperialism and praise the great spirit of the Boxers' heroic, dare-to-die struggle against Imperialism and [thereby] strengthen the revolution of the broad masses against Imperialism and their realization that only through righteous struggle can one oppose unjust war and through armed struggle protect national and world peace.[71]

While, according to the prevailing view, the Boxer movement proved that "the peasants were the principal force in opposing Imperialist aggression" and the "carving up of China," [72] it also revealed the continuing struggle of the peasantry against the internal feudal reactionaries. The slogan "support the Ch'ing, destroy the foreigners" proposed in 1899 by some Ch'ing-influenced Boxer leaders only temporarily diverted a part of the Boxer movement from this task, while both before that date and after 1900 the peasants of north China continued their struggle against internal "feudalism." Another Boxer slogan, "Wipe out the Ch'ing, destroy the foreigners," supposedly proves this.[73]

The great emphasis on the anti-imperialist struggle of the Boxers is shown in the fact that the first volumes of source

[71] Wu Han, "On the True Nature of History," *KMJP*, December 3, 1960.

[72] Li Shih-yueh, *op. cit.*, *KMJP*, October 27, 1960; and Li Shih-yueh, "The Struggle Against 'Carving the Melon' of the People of Northeast China Before and After the Boxers," *SHYK*, no. 5, 1959.

[73] *Ibid.*; and Li Shao-chung, "[The Slogan] 'Support the Ch'ing, Destroy the Foreigners' of the Yi-ho T'uan," *KMJP*, February 16, 1956. However, Ku Yi-chun ("On Several Problems Regarding Ch'ing T'ing-pin's 'Wipe Out the Ch'ing and Destroy the Foreigners Revolt,'" *KMJP*, December 9, 1960) denies that the latter uprising was a part of the Boxer movement. For a discussion of these problems see Victor Purcell, *The Boxer Uprising* (London: Cambridge University Press, 1963).

materials issued by the Chinese communists for modern Chinese history were devoted to the Boxer movement. They were published in March 1951. One commentator stated, "Fifty years from now, when we read these materials, they can only make us increase our incomparable anger and hate at the Imperialist aggressors." [74] Another writer went so far as to say that

> . . . before the face of the righteous struggle of the Chinese people, the Imperialists tore up their mask of benevolent culture and launched the lowest and most barbaric, aggressive war in modern history.[75]

The intrusion of the powers into China assumes first importance in Chinese historiography:

> We stress the study of the anti-imperialist and anti-feudal revolutionary movements of the past century . . . during which the imperialist powers waged more than ten aggressive wars against China, more than twenty countries forced China to conclude unequal treaties and eight or nine powers kept garrisons, concessions, settlements and spheres of influence in China. . . . Studies of these events provide rich material for the patriotic education of our citizens.[76]

Since World War II the United States has, of course, replaced England and Japan as the leading imperialist nation in the eyes of Peking. Because "the nature of imperialism" does not change, America's role is read back into the nineteenth century. Leading articles contend that the role of America in the "suppression of the righteous struggle of the Boxers" reveals its "consistent hostility to the Chinese people." The celebrated Open Door policy is interpreted as motivated by the desire to "share in the looting of China" rather than as an effort to protect Chinese sovereignty. In all, Communist his-

[74] Yen Hsun, "Regarding Some Views on the Yi-ho T'uan," *KMJP*, January 20, 1955.
[75] Shih Ssu-ch'ün, *op. cit., LSYC*, no. 6, 1960, p. 19.
[76] Liu Ta-nien, "Historical Science in the New China," *LSYC*, 1962, no. 2.

torians charge the United States with over twenty "major aggressions" against China, from participation in the suppression of the Taiping and Boxer movements, to consistent aid for "reactionary" regimes from Yuan Shih-k'ai to Chiang Kai-shek.[77]

The Taiping and Boxer movements form an important part of the documentation for proving the "blood debt" owed the imperialists by the Chinese people, as does alleged patriotism of peasant rebels in inculcating the new "class nationalism." The oppressed of China and the world shall rise against their oppressors, who all happen to come from the imperialist nations, and "the encirclement of the cities by the rural areas" of Asia, Africa, and Latin America will determine the future of the world as it did the Chinese past.[78] Thus do historical studies, communism, and nationalism reinforce each other in China.

[77] E.g., see Liu Ta-nien, *Mei-kuo Ch'in-hua Shih* (History of American Aggression Against China), Peking, Jen Min Ch'u-pan She, 1951, and Ch'ing Ju-chi, *Mei-kuo Ch'in-hua Shih* (History of American Aggression Against China), Peking, Jen Min Ch'u-pan She, 1962.

[78] Lin Piao, "Long Live the Victory of People's War," *Peking Review*, September 3, 1965, p. 24.

CHAPTER TEN

Uses in Ideological Education

SPONSORS of the "Great Proletarian Cultural Revolution" lifted the curtain on their drama in November 1965 with attacks on Wu Han, the Vice Mayor of Peking and a respected senior historian. They accused his 1961 play, *Hai Jui Pa Kuan* (The Dismissal of Hai Jui), of using an historical analogy to attack Mao's policies, particularly the 1959 purge of defense minister P'eng Te-huai. Wu praised the sixteenth-century criticisms of imperial policy by the Ming official Hai Jui and rebuked the unjust dismissal of a loyal, if outspoken, minister. By implication Wu was attacking the ouster of P'eng Te-huai. In more theoretical terms, Wu and his colleagues on the Peking Party Committee allegedly neglected or distorted the theory of class struggle and the necessity of the dictatorship of the proletariat.[1] The use of this historical example to initiate the public phase of the "cultural revolution" demonstrates, among other things, the importance

[1] Lu Ting-yi, Chou Yang, and Teng T'o, among those mentioned in these pages, were criticized later in 1966 as responsible for these lapses in propaganda work.

Chinese continue to attach to the study of history. It and other academic exercises of the "cultural revolution" show equally the crucial role of the interpretation of class struggle in Chinese intellectual life.

In the interpretations of the history of the peasant wars, there have been many foreshadowings of the tensions revealed in the "cultural revolution." It is evident that not all Chinese communist historians—and this includes most of the senior generation[2]—are satisfied with the trend toward an ever more radical interpretation of the peasant revolts in Chinese history. Prior to the mid-1960s at least, the more conservative historians and theorists repeatedly warned against "irresponsible exaggerations" of the revolutionary consciousness and significance of the peasant wars. They have emphasized the necessity of not neglecting the history of the upper classes in stressing the historical role of the lower classes, and they have stressed the variety of historical conditions which preclude "discussing the [peasant revolts] only according to one law." [3] Proponents of this conservative view believe that "peasant leaders should be affirmed but not idealized or modernized to make them equal to the modern proletarian class leaders [in their revolutionary qualities]." [4] They would agree with Fan Wen-lan's statement that although

> . . . the theory of the class struggle is the basic line for the understanding of history, it is still difficult to explain history clearly. . . . If [one] only remembers [to use

[2] Including Kuo Mo-jo, Fan Wen-lan, Chien Po-tsan, and Wu Han among those formerly holding important positions, and such respected historians as Ch'en Yin-ch'ueh and Chou Ku-ch'eng. Sun Tso-min, Ts'ai Mei-piao, and Ch'i Hsia represent the younger generation among the "conservatives" but the great majority take a more class-oriented approach, and this tendency was confirmed in the "cultural revolution."

[3] Chien Po-tsan, "Tentative Views on the Handling of Several Historical Problems," *KMJP*, December 22, 1961. Similarly, former Minister of Culture Mao Tun wrote (*Chinese Literature*, no. 1, 1959, p. 209), "To try to use one formula to express the development of all literary trends past and present is foolish." Both Chien and Mao have been condemned for their views.

[4] Chien Po-tsan, *op. cit.*, *KMJP*, December 22, 1961.

the theory of] the class struggle and does not use concrete analysis, then one will make the most lively events
become dead forms.[5]

Yet, as this book and the "cultural revolution" testify, the
vast majority of historians trained since 1949 and many of the
middle generation[6] reject such reservations of the conservative
school as "smears" of the peasant rebellions and as "obscuring
the revolutionary ideology of the people." The inference is
strong that the generation of historians trained since 1949,
which by the late 1950s included over 90 percent of all
teachers of history,[7] has developed the teachings of its elders
in a way which is at once more radical in its stress on class
revolution and more Chinese in its emphasis on the peculiarly
revolutionary qualities of the Chinese peasantry. Led by Mao
Tse-tung and his supporters, the "orthodox left" sought to
make all Chinese give first priority to its radical class line in
the "cultural revolution" of the mid-1960s.

The development by the younger generation of the teachings of older Chinese Marxists appears analogous to Mao's
development of Leninism and to Lenin's own development
of classical Marxism. It suggests that the trend in the development of an ideology parallels the direction of a society. In
this case, that trend has clearly been to the "left" as Marxism
has moved eastward to countries in ever greater turmoil and,
in the case of China, as Marxism has been used to foster an
ever deepening social revolution.

The development of a more fundamentalist ideology by
younger historians is one evidence of a certain divergence between generations in communist China. It can also be argued
that this divergence is not so much between generations as
between propagandists and scholars, or between the ambi-
tious who play on revolutionary sentiments and the apolitical.
Even if this is the case, it is significant that a more revolu-

[5] Fan Wen-lan, *Chung-kuo T'ung-shih Chien-pien* (1961 ed.), preface, vol. 1, p. 11.

[6] Such as Pai Shou-yi and Ch'i Hsia following his confession in 1960.

[7] Only 451 of 4,793 higher-level history teachers were trained before
1949, according to Pai Shou-yi, "Aspects of Spring in the Historical
Fields," *KMJP*, October 15, 1959.

tionary theory is thought desirable and that most young historians work to supply it. The initiatives in these efforts, of course, come from senior policy-makers, as in the events of the mid-1960's, but young propagandists often go beyond their directives in constructing a revolutionary ideology. This suggests an interpretation somewhat different from the supposition that the younger generation is less militant than the older revolutionaries because it has not lived through the period of political struggle. Perhaps the youth of China are less committed to radical action than their elders, but they appear to be at least as committed to a radical theory. Or perhaps the connections between radical ideology and radical action are not direct. In any case, the split between doctrinaires and more flexible theorists implies tension between two groups among Chinese intellectuals, with the radical spokesmen in the ascendant. Most of the criticisms of backward thought appearing in the mainland press are signed by unknown, more militant, and presumably younger men.[8] By the mid-1960s they had clearly, if only temporarily, won the day, as Maoists in positions of power used precisely the activist class line as their principal weapon in the struggle against revisionism at home and abroad.

The ascendancy of ever more radical interpretations of the class struggle is mirrored in the involvement of the historiography of the peasant revolts in ideological education in communist China. Increasingly, the handling of the class struggle in history has become the principal criterion for judging the political correctness of academic writings, and increasingly it has been young enthusiasts who have attacked their elders for neglecting the role of class conflict in history.

The great importance of the historiography of the peasant revolts in mainland ideological reform was revealed in 1951 in the first major thought-reform campaign launched after 1949.

[8] This was less true in more scholarly publications such as *LSYC* than it was in the daily press, provincial publications, and more politically oriented journals such as *HCS* and *SHYK*. In 1966 *LSYC* was accused of having become an increasingly bourgeois journal since the early 1960s. See Shih Shao-pin, foreword to "Why Protect Wu Han," *JMJP*, June 3, 1966, p. 2. *LSYC* and virtually all cultural periodicals were suspended during the "Great Proletarian Cultural Revolution."

This movement for the political education of the intellectuals centered on the interpretation of the nineteenth-century educational reformer Wu Hsun and the supposedly unfavorable contrast between his activities and those of his contemporary and fellow townsman, the peasant rebel Sung Ching-shih, who worked "not to reform but to overthrow the feudal state." [9] The "Wu Hsun case" also revealed the sharpness of the departure of mainland interpretations from traditional Chinese views of rebels. It is not surprising to learn that even "some" of the "lower-level" Party cadres were confused by the preference for an obscure, formerly despised "peasant rebel" over a renowned reformer who also came of peasant stock. In the course of the "Great Proletarian Cultural Revolution" it was revealed that Chairman Mao himself had taken the leading role in the Wu Hsun case.

From that time onward, the most consistent theme in the ideological criticism of historians has been to charge denial or neglect of the class struggle in history.[10] This was the case in the attacks on such non-Marxist historians as Hu Shih, Liang Sou-ming, Ch'ien Mu, and others, and it has been the principal criticism against many of the historical publications appearing in China. In fact, the only writings which have escaped such criticism have been the enthusiastic generalizations of the history of the peasant wars by the more militant

[9] As one writer put it, "While other peasants were fighting the landlords to the death, Wu was kowtowing to the feudal landlord class." Chang Ch'i-chih, "The Biography of Wu Hsun Slanders Our Country's Peasant Revolutionary Struggles," in *Wu Hsun yü Wu Hsun Chuan P'i-p'an* (Canton: Hua-nan Jen-min Ch'u-pan She, n.d.), pp. 51–55. This article was originally carried in *KMJP*, May 24, 1951. See also "Report of Investigation of Wu Hsun and His Contemporary Peasant Rebel Leader Sung Ching-shih," *JMJP*, July 24, 1951; and Ch'en Pai-chen, "Peasant Revolutionary Hero Sung Ching-shih and His Black Flag Army," *JMJP*, July 24, 1952. This affair has been studied by Fox Butterfield, "The Legend of Sung Ching-shih: An Episode in Communist Historiography," *Harvard Papers on China*, no. 18, 1964, pp. 129–154.

[10] This tendency was applied to economics also when Sun Yeh-fang was denounced for stressing the contradictions between man and nature in the "building of socialism" over the class struggle between man and man. See *Peking Review*, October 21, 1966, p. 23.

authors. Not even Fan Wen-lan,[11] Kuo Mo-jo,[12] or, of course, Wu Han[13] has been exempt from these charges. Chien Po-tsan, vice president of Peking University and chairman of its department of history,[14] Hou Wai-lu, a vice director of the Academy of Sciences,[15] Liu Ta-nien,[16] Teng Kuang-ming,[17] and Ch'i Hsia,[18] among those figuring prominently in these pages, were denounced as "anti-communist" in the mid-1960s.[19] Earlier, the writings of less highly placed but prominent historians such as Ch'en Yin-ch'üeh,[20] Chou Ku-ch'eng,[21] Liang Yuan-tung,[22] Chang Shun-hui,[23] Hsieh

[11] Shih Shao-pin ("Why Protect Wu Han?" *JMJP*, June 3, 1966, p. 3) indirectly attacked Fan Wen-lan when he condemned the modern history institute, which Fan heads, and its journal *LSYC*. For an earlier example of criticism of Fan's interpretations, see Hsu Hsi-ming, "I Do Not Consider the Taiping Land System Reactionary," in Ching Yen and Lin Yen-shu (eds.), *TPTK Ke-ming Hsing chih Wen-t'i T'ao-lun Chi*, pp. 205–10.

[12] Kuo Mo-jo criticized himself in April 1966 (*CNA* 613, May 27, 1966) but managed to escape direct denunciations. His theories, especially as they touched on the rebellion of the Yellow Turbans, were called into question, as were Fan Wen-lan's, even in the late 1950s. See Chapter 8.

[13] An article in *JMJP* (April 10, 1966, pp. 5–6) summarized alleged errors in the writings of Wu Han since 1959. Wu began to be criticized as early as 1963 (see *SCMP* 3136, pp. 1–5, citing *JMJP*, December 24, 1963), and denunciations of him in November 1965 launched the "Great Proletarian Cultural Revolution." By 1966 there were criticisms of Wu in nearly every issue of relevant publications.

[14] Chien Po-tsan, as we have seen, has consistently been a leader of the relatively conservative interpretation of the peasant revolts. Some later criticisms of Chien are in *JMJP*, March 1, March 25, April 23, June 1, June 9, June 14, and December 15, 1966. The latter article, appearing in *Hung Ch'i* 1966, no. 15, has been translated in *SCMM*, no. 556.

[15] See especially the *New York Times*, December 3, 1966; *KMJP*, August 10, 1966; and *JMJP*, November 22, 1966.

[16] *JMJP*, January 8, 1966.

[17] *KMJP*, February 13, 1966.

[18] *SCMP* 3710, citing *KMJP*, May 18, 1966.

[19] See also Wang Chang-Ling, "Mainland Historians and the Great Cultural Revolution," *Issues and Studies*, vol. 3, no. 7, April 1967.

[20] See James P. Harrison, "The Ideological Training of Intellectuals in Communist China," *Asian Survey*, October 1965, p. 498.

[21] *Ibid.*; and Adam Oliver, "Rectification of Mainland China Intellectuals, 1964–1965," *Asian Survey*, October 1965, p. 482.

[22] See *CNA* 126, April 6, 1956; and Kuo Jen-min, "Tentative Dis-

Kuo-chen,[24] Wu Feng,[25] Sung Yun-piao,[26] Chang Ping-jen,[27] and many others have been repeatedly criticized for neglecting or distorting the "content of class struggle" in the history of the peasant revolts.[28] Ch'en Teng-yuan, an "old professor" at Northwest University, Sian, made the mistake, among others, of stating that "Chinese academic circles have not advanced since liberation."[29] In the anti-right campaigns he was accused of many historical errors but especially of distorting the history of the peasant wars by continuing to call rebel leaders and even some communist leaders "bandit chiefs"[30] and for "general hostility to the people's revolutions in history."[31] More general denunciations in the late 1950s of Shang Yueh, chairman of the department of history at People's University, for "cutting the foot of Chinese history to fit the shoe of West European historical theories" revealed the difficulties of "creatively applying the universal truths of Marxism-Leninism to the peculiarities of China."[32]

---

cussion of Several Problems in the Great Late Ch'in Peasant Revolt," *SHYK*, no. 7, 1958.

[23] Wei Fu-ch'ang, "Discussion of Problems in Professor Chang Shun-hui's *Chung-kuo Li-shih Yao-chi Chieh-shao*," *SHYK*, no. 6, 1960.

[24] See Liu Yi-nan, "Criticize *Nan-Ming Shih-lueh*," *LSYC*, no. 9, 1958, p. 62.

[25] E.g., T'ang Hsing, "Criticize Wu Feng's *Sui-t'ang Wu-tai Shih*," *LSYC*, no. 9, 1958.

[26] E.g., Ho Jo-chün, "Extirpate the Reactionary Capitalist Class Views of the Upper Level Modern Chinese History Text Edited by Sung Yun-piao," *SHYK*, no. 5, 1958.

[27] E.g., Wei Kan-chih, "Extirpate Capitalist Class Academic Views in the Teaching of Ancient Chinese History," *SHYK*, no. 9, 1958, p. 12.

[28] See Wang Hsing-ya, "Purge the Reactionary Hero-Centered Viewpoint from the Research and Teaching of History," *SHYK*, no. 10, 1958, p. 10.

[29] Ma Chang-shou, "Eliminate the Influence of Capitalist Class Historiography on Our Historical Circles," *Hsi-pei Ta-hsueh Hsueh-pao* (Jen-wen K'o-hsueh), no. 1, 1958.

[30] *Ibid.*; and Li Chih-ch'in, "Expose and Criticize the Capitalist Class Reactionary Historical Viewpoint of Ch'en Teng-yuan in the Teaching of Ancient History," *ibid.*, pp. 21 ff.; also articles in *ibid.*, no. 4, 1958. Actually Ch'en wrote a strong defense of the notorious rebel Chang Hsien-chung at this time, possibly in an effort to clear himself.

[31] See Ts'ai Mei-piao, "*Kuo-shih Chin-wen* [a book by Ch'en Teng-yuan] Should Be Criticized," *LSYC*, no. 11, 1958, pp. 21 and 23.

[32] See James P. Harrison, *op. cit.*, pp. 499–500.

Lei Hai-tsung, Huang Yuan-ch'i, Yang Hsiang-k'uei, and many other historians were denounced for more specific "anti-party" writings and actions during the anti-rightist movement of 1957–58.[33]

Neglect or distortion of the class struggle has been the chief accusation against several of the leading historians of the peasant revolts. Among these, however, prior to the mid-1960s, the only writer to be labeled a "rightist" himself, as against the many who have been accused of "rightist" or capitalist class ideas, was Chao Li-sheng. The distinction between "rightist" politics and "rightist" academic views in the criticisms of Chao corresponds to the accusations against many other "rightists" and suggests that attacks on Party policies rather than mistaken theories are a more serious cause of Party disfavor.

Chao was the most active discussant of the peasant revolts in the early 1950s and organized the first course at Shantung University devoted specifically to the subject. He wrote numerous articles[34] and, with his wife, the second major study of the peasant revolts to be published after 1949.[35] In these writings Chao admitted difficulties of theory and fact in his efforts to understand the history of the peasant revolts, but his book is one of the best available on the subject. He made an honest effort to present his materials in a manner consistent with Marxist theory, though he was clearly troubled by inconsistencies in the latter. For example, at one point he confessed the existence of an apparent contradiction between the Marxist theories of the necessity of economic progress and the theory of the class struggle which praises even revolts seeming to disrupt economic evolution.[36] Neither such statements nor the errors in historical interpretation of which he was accused, such as the glorification of the

[33] *Ibid.*
[34] Mostly carried in *WSC*, 1954–57.
[35] Chao Li-sheng and Kao Chao-yi, *Chung-kuo Nung-min Chan-cheng Shih Lun-wen chi.* The first comprehensive history of the peasant revolts published after 1949 was Wang Tan-Ts'en's *Chung-kuo Nung-min Ke-ming Shih-hua* (1952).
[36] Chao Li-sheng and Kao-Chao-yi, *op. cit.,* p. 84.

Sung patriot Yueh Fei at the expense of the contemporary rebel Yang Yao,[37] were the real reasons for Chao's persecution. Many other mainland historians have presented similar interpretations which have gone unchallenged.

More likely causes of the criticisms of Chao were hinted at in his attacks on government education policy in an article released in September 1956. At that time Chao allegedly confessed, among other things, to favoring "activist" students over the less "progressive," which he likened to "cultivating the rank and file of a robber gang," and to a general hatred of the CCP and its members.[38] Chao did not help his case by praising Shang Yueh's textbook as having fewer deficiencies than the general histories of Fan Wen-lan or Lü Chen-yü,[39] or by criticizing Fan Wen-lan's "superficial" acceptance of old slanders of an early fourth-century Szechwan rebellion.[40] There have also been criticisms of Chao's interpretations of the peasant revolts, particularly for calling the "pure peasant rebellion" of the Yellow Turbans less successful than the mixed landlord-peasant uprisings against the Ch'in and Wang Mang, for "slandering" Huang Ch'ao and Li Tzu-ch'eng by describing their concern for pleasure and looting, and for the already mentioned glorification of Yueh Fei at the expense of the Sung rebels.[41]

A student of Chao Li-sheng's at Shantung University, Sun Tso-min, carried forward Chao's efforts to interpret the history of the Chinese peasant revolts in a manner consistent

[37] See Wang Hsin-yeh and Sung Hsi-min, "Criticize One of Chao Li-Sheng's Absurd Theories . . . His Distortions and Slanders of the Peasants and Peasant Uprisings," *WSC*, no. 12, 1958, pp. 46–51; and Wang Hsing-ya, "The Reactionary Nature of Capitalist Class Rightist Chao Li-sheng's Research on the History of the Chinese Peasant Wars," *WSC*, no. 12, 1958, pp. 51–52.

[38] Chu Tso-yun, "Rightist Chao Li-sheng and the Struggle Between Two Roads Over the Direction of Our Higher Education Policy," *WSC*, no. 6, 1958, pp. 43–46.

[39] Chao Li-sheng, "Some Ideas on the Section of *Chung-kuo Li-shih Kang-yao* Devoted to the Peasant Wars," *WSC*, no. 3, 1955, p. 35.

[40] Chao Li-sheng and Kao Chao-yi, *op. cit.*, p. 41.

[41] Chu Tso-lun, *op. cit.*; and Chang Pao-kuang *et al.*, "The Question of the 'Four Authorities' in the History of the Chinese Peasant Wars," *SSP*, p. 207.

with classical Marxism. Indicative of the recent shift to simultaneously more radical and more Chinese interpretations, where Chao often stood to the left of his critics, his followers are today attacked for "rightist deviations." [42] Thus, Sun Tso-min is now the leader and one of the only representatives among younger historians of the more conservative school of interpretation. The trend to more radical interpretations of the peasant revolts appears to have occurred in the aftermath of the "One Hundred Flowers" movement along with the general shift to the left of Chinese communist policies. From 1958 onward, Sun, who had become the most voluminous contributor to the historiography of the peasant revolts, was under increasing attack for allegedly minimizing the revolutionary significance of the Chinese peasant revolts. Nonetheless, prior to the mid-1960s Sun was not personally branded a "rightist."

Already in a 1956 volume of essays Sun decried the "fairly universal leftist tendency" of the many historians who, in correctly "criticizing reactionary, governing-class, slanderous absurdities about the history of the peasant revolts . . . adopt a simplistic method of the other extreme" and "beautify" the history of the peasant movements. [43] Sun believed that the history of the Chinese peasant revolts was sufficient proof of their superior discipline and morale but that their

[42] For instance, Chao criticized those who interpreted early anti-T'ang revolts as "unprogressive" and believed this "rightist deviation" was a more serious error than the "leftist one" of denying the progressiveness of such emperors as T'ang T'ai-tzu and Li Shih-min. See Chao Li-sheng and Kao Chao-yi, *op. cit.*, p. 83. Similarly, in 1953 Wang Tan-ling's interpretation of the Sui revolts was criticized by conservatives who felt Wang adopted a "leftist" interpretation of the Sui rebels. See articles in *KMJP*, July 11 and September 19, 1953. In 1956 Sun Tso-min was himself attacked for the "leftist exaggeration" of overstressing the role of certain peasant revolts. His accuser was Ning K'o (*KMJP*, June 7, 1956), who by the early 1960s was one of the leaders of the radical interpretations of the peasant revolts. Thus, while most pre-1957 interpretations were criticized as too radical, after 1958 virtually all critics of the historiography of the peasant revolts attacked from the left charging "rightist deviations." In short, there was a radical shift to the left in interpretations of the peasant revolts after 1957.

[43] Sun Tso-min, *Chung-kuo Nung-min Chan-cheng Wen-t'i T'an-su*, p. 2.

deficiencies and mistakes should not be denied.[44]

Partly in reaction to the criticisms of the Hundred Flowers period and following the political demands of the time, mainland theorists increasingly considered such admittedly "objective" appraisals of the historical class struggles of the peasants as insufficiently committed to the cause of the working class. In 1958 a series of articles attacked the anti-peasant bias in Sun's 1956 book, concluding that Sun viewed the peasants as "stupid," since he (like the classical Marxists) stressed the inability of the peasants to see the causes of their suffering or to supersede the ruling feudal ideology. He was charged with slandering the "most revolutionary class before the proletariat" by minimizing the function, organizational ability, and ideology of the Chinese peasant revolts.[45] Perhaps more seriously, his critics attacked him for plagiarizing the views and lectures of "rightist" Chao Li-sheng.[46]

In 1960 the Shantung History Society and the Shantung branch of the Academy of Science convened a joint conference specifically to criticize the "erroneous views" of Sun Tso-min about the "backward nature of the peasant class." [47] Subsequently, Sun modified his views slightly, no longer denying the possibility of the rebels' temporarily establishing their own government and stressing the anti-feudal nature of all Chinese peasant revolts. But, unlike Ch'i Hsia, Sun refused to completely abandon his earlier reservations about the revolutionary aspects of the peasant revolts, either at the 1960 Shantung conference, which he attended, or later. In 1964 he reaffirmed the conservative view of the peasant revolts, citing in support the article by Ts'ai Mei-piao published in *LSYC* (no. 4, 1961).[48] Immediately, numerous spokesmen arguing for the supremacy of the theory of the class

[44] *Ibid.*, pp. 4–6, 28 ff.

[45] See articles by Chang Pin in *KMJP*, March 17, July 7, and August 4, 1958; by Ch'en Ch'ang-yuan, *WSC*, no. 11, 1958, pp. 39–42; Wang Ssu-chih, *SSP*, pp. 169–71; by Chao Hsi-yen *et al.*, *SSP*, pp. 407–22; and by Wu Yen-nan, *SSP*, pp. 440 ff.

[46] *KMJP* (eds.), note to Chang Pin, *op. cit.*, *KMJP*, August 4, 1958, p. 6.

[47] "Shantung Historical Circles Discuss Problems of the Chinese Peasant Wars," *KMJP*, October 11, 1960.

[48] Sun Tso-min, "The Use of Historicism and Class Viewpoint in the

struggle over "historicism" attacked Sun's "slanders" of the peasant rebels as a "matter of principle," because he "confused the role of the class war in history." [49]

As virtually the only young writer consistently to espouse in print the conservative view of the history of the peasant revolts, it seems strange that Sun did not invoke the comments of Fan Wen-lan, Kuo Mo-jo, and others who clearly supported his view of the peasant wars. The explanation probably lies in the fact that these historians and mainland editors were aware of Party favor for the more radical interpretation of the peasant revolts even before the outbreak of the "cultural revolution." The need for theoretical and historical support of Peking's current policies obviously outweighs the reservations of more responsible mainland historians. Therefore, not wishing to anger either the historical authorities with "guilt by association" or Party theorists by challenging current interpretations of the revolutionary role of the peasantry, Sun Tso-min almost alone continued to represent the conservative view of the role of the peasant class in history. By the time of the "Great Proletarian Cultural Revolution," his interpretations, despite their closeness to classical Marxist formulations, had been condemned as "revisionist" or even "anti-Marxist."

The historian of the peasant revolts in Chinese history best known outside the mainland probably is the Taiping scholar Lo Erh-kang. Because of his prestige and because he appeared to have accepted the new historiography, it may be useful to review his public record of ideological reform under the communists.

Prior to 1949 Lo took what he later called an "objectivist" view of the Taipings, under the illusion that history could be

Research on the History of our Country's Peasant Wars," *JMJP*, February 27, 1964. See also Sun, "Is It Supporting Class Analysis or Destroying Class Analysis?" *CHYC* 1964, no. 4.

[49] E.g., Wu Ch'uan-ch'i, "We Cannot Say the Peasant Wars Are a 'Continuation' of Feudal Landlord Policies," *KMJP*, April 3, 1964, p. 2; T'ien Ch'ang-wu, "Is It Historical Materialism or Economic Determinism?" *KMJP*, May 14, 1964, p. 3; and academic columns in *KMJP*, May 13 and June 21, 1964, p. 1, and in *CHYC*, no. 3, 1964, pp. 84–85, and no. 6, 1964, pp. 43 ff.

written independently of politics and class. By neither over-praising nor scolding the Taipings, as he put it in 1937, Lo hoped to avoid the "prejudices" both of traditional interpre-tations which described them as "long-haired bandits" and of the revolutionaries who regarded them as "people's heroes." Moreover, Lo expressed disdain for the "factually baseless theoretical propaganda" about the Taipings which emerged in the 1930s, an obvious reference to early communist inter-pretations.[50] At that time he thought of the Chinese peasant movements as "poor peasants' revolutions" which were doomed to failure unless they could come to terms with the scholar gentry, usually at the price of abandoning most of their goals.[51]

Soon after "liberation," Lo, along with most intellectuals on the mainland, became immersed in the intensive ideologi-cal reforms of the period. By the summer of 1952 he claimed to have realized the error of his earlier views, saying that "fundamentally there was no such thing as an objectivism beyond politics and class." Rather, the history of the Tai-pings would have to be written from the standpoint of "the people." [52] Also in 1952 Lo was made aware of Soviet inter-pretations of the Taiping and Nien revolts when the well-known Soviet sinologist Efimov visited China and stressed to Lo the "anti-feudal, anti-aggressor" nature of the nineteenth-century peasant movements.[53] Thereafter Lo stressed the common class basis of the Taiping and Nien movements.[54]

In a series of writings in the mid-1950s, Lo stated his desire for further ideological commitment. He stressed the anti-imperialist and class nature of the Taiping movement[55] and criticized his pre-1949 neglect of class analysis and study of events in isolation from the laws of history. "I did not see the woods for the trees" in my earlier historical studies, he wrote,

---

[50] Lo Erh-kang, *TPTK Shih-kang*, p. 2.

[51] *Ibid.*, pp. 100–101.

[52] Lo Erh-kang, "The Real Name of the Nien Chün," *An-hui Shih-hsueh*, no. 1, 1960, p. 11.

[53] See Lo Erh-kang, *TPTK Shih Shih-k'ao*, pp. 341 ff.

[54] Lo Erh-kang, "The Real Name . . . ," *op. cit.*

[55] See Lo Erh-kang, "Materials on the TPTK," *Wen-hui-pao* (Hong Kong), March 22, 1956.

and this "shows very well that historical workers, even if they are experienced and skilled researchers, cannot do their jobs well without the guidance of Marxism-Leninism." [56] He confessed to continuing inadequacy in "grasping the weapons of Marxism-Leninism" despite his desire to reform, and hence he pleaded for "help through criticism and self-criticism," the only means of advancing understanding.[57]

In the anti-right campaigns, Lo was one of the first non-Party historians to come to the defense of orthodox policy. He praised Party encouragement of historical research and the theoretical advantages of Marxist historiography, especially of the theory of class struggle, which enabled an understanding of the "decisive causes" in human history.[58] In the early 1950s Lo championed the revolutionary aspects of the Taiping land program, which, he argued, were partially carried out. In recent years he has defended the revolutionary consistency of the late Taiping leader Li Hsiu-ch'eng, maintaining that Li's confession after his capture was not a renunciation of the Taiping movement but was faked in order to gain time for fleeing remnants of the Taipings.[59] This view came in for special denunciation in the "Great Proletarian Cultural Revolution" as "defense of a traitor." There was an apparent comparison between Li Hsiu-ch'eng's "false confession" and the "false confessions" authorized by Liu Shao-ch'i to mitigate punishment of imprisoned communists during the war against Japan.[60] In both cases, it was argued, the

---

[56] Lo Erh-kang, "My Investigations in Writings on the History of the TPTK," *KMJP*, March 3, 1955.

[57] *Ibid.*

[58] Lo Erh-kang, "Criticism of the Harms and Deceits of the Rightist Line in Science as Considered from the Point of View of Historical Studies," *KMJP*, August 28, 1957.

[59] See articles of Lo Erh-kang and Ch'i Pen-yü on the evaluations of Li Hsiu-ch'eng's confession in *LSYC*, no. 4, 1963, and no. 4, 1964. The majority appear to disagree with Lo's interpretation of Li Hsiu-ch'eng's confession. E.g., see Chang Ch'i-chih, "Is It Historical Materialism or Subjective Idealism?" *CHYC*, no. 5, 1964, pp. 31–39; and articles in *LSYC*, nos. 5 and 6, 1964, pp. 1 ff. and 35 ff. See also Stephen Uhalley, "The Controversy over Li Hsiu-ch'eng," *JAS*, February 1966, pp. 305–317.

[60] E.g., see *JMJP*, January 8, 1967, p. 6. This assumption is supported by the fact that Ch'i Pen-yü, who initiated the criticism of Li Hsiu-

"revolution should have been upheld to the end" regardless of personal sacrifice.

Despite his efforts to use orthodox theory, Lo's writings have been criticized for "capitalist-class viewpoints" which fail to "satisfy the revolutionary emotions of the people." Specifically, some critics accuse Lo of ignoring the role of the masses by overemphasizing the achievements of rebel leaders, of exaggerating the importance of religious ideas in the motivation of the Taiping revolt, and of neglecting the anti-imperialist aspects of the nineteenth-century class struggles.[61] Nonetheless, Lo himself, no doubt because of his acknowledged willingness to undergo criticism and reform, has been spared the more frequent and vitriolic attacks made on some of his colleagues.

Prior to the "Great Proletarian Cultural Revolution" at least, in spite of or perhaps because of the intense intellectual pressures on the mainland, there have been relatively few wide-scale purges of historians involving dismissals or other tangible punishments. In the early years after "liberation," in the anti-rightist campaigns of 1957–58 and in the "cultural revolution" of the mid-1960s,[62] some historians were replaced, but it has been more common to "reform" those criticized through compulsory "re-education" or labor. The cases of historians, such as Lo Erh-kang, whose writings have been criticized but who personally have made the adjustments necessary to live with the new regime have been the norm. Where the inner ideals of some of these men no doubt still differ profoundly from the orthodox ideal, outward cooperation in word and deed has been the rule. Historians, like other mainland intellectuals, especially of the older generation, continue to present unorthodox views on occasion, but

---

ch'eng's confession (*LSYC*, no. 4, 1963), was an important associate of Ch'en Po-ta during much of the "Great Proletarian Cultural Revolution." See also *KMJP*, June 13, 1967, p. 4.

[61] E.g., Ch'en Hsueh-wen, "Problems in the Historical Viewpoint and Methodology of the *TPTK Shih-kao*," *KMJP*, February 19, 1959.

[62] More high-ranking historians, including Wu Han, Chien Po-tsan, and even Fan Wen-lan, were threatened in 1966 than in previous campaigns.

on the whole they have conformed.

The reasons for this general intellectual acceptance of basic Marxist premises on the mainland stem from a whole complex of intellectual, educational, and political factors. On the one hand, the spread of both Marxism and Chinese nationalism before 1949 and, on the other, the success of communist intimidation and indoctrination have provided a milieu favorable to the ideological purposes of the Chinese communists. The result has been apparent widespread acceptance of basic Chinese communist beliefs about the historical role of the masses and the class struggle, if not a complete conformity of inner belief. There have been disputes and genuine discussions, but by and large about interpretations of Marxism rather than denial of it. This was generally true even in the Hundred Flowers period, when Party policies and bureaucrats were attacked far more than Marxist theories.

The real significance of recent Chinese communist ideology therefore appears to be the emergence of an ever more militant ideology, championed by top leaders and by the great majority of those trained in Marxism since 1949. As seen from the historiography of the peasant wars, the champions of radical interpretations include perhaps even such older scholars as Lo Erh-kang and the great majority of younger historians. On the other hand, many of the men who learned their "academic" Marxism before 1949 are mistrustful of the currently prevailing interpretations of Chinese history. This has been particularly true since the turn to the left in late 1957 and suggests that the latest version of Maoism represents still another stage in the evolution of Marxism.

To be sure, there is much evidence of the resistance of the intellectuals to communist-directed ideological reform, not only during the Hundred Flowers and "cultural revolution" periods but throughout the history of communist rule. No doubt the noted novelist Pa Chin expressed common feeling when he wrote:

> I am a little afraid of those who, holding a hoop in one
> hand and a club in the other, go everywhere looking for

men with mistakes. Woe to him who comes across any
of these people. . . . Many (including myself) are
forced to be very cautious. In speaking and writing they
would rather say what others have said many times before and talk about them in as general terms as
possible.[63]

Nonetheless, such fear and resentment on the part of the
intellectuals is not really surprising, considering the magnitude of the commitment asked by the Party. In Chou En-lai's
words:

We want to liquidate entirely by this great cultural revolution all the old ideas, the entire old culture, all the old
habits and customs created by the exploiting classes in
the course of thousands of years to poison the people.
We want to create and form in the ranks of the broad
masses of the people the new ideas, the new culture, the
new habits and customs of the proletariat.[64]

The Party has claimed, perhaps justly, that "this great task
is . . . without any precedent in human history." [65]
The most significant aspect of mainland intellectual life to
the outside observer, if not to those involved, is not so much
its tension as the results of this tension. There is certainly increased resentment on the part of many, especially older intellectuals, but there is also at least the beginning of fundamental change in the beliefs of the Chinese people as a
whole. There are and have been ups and downs, passive and
open resistance to ideological reform, but there is no doubt
that a real revolution in values, under way for the past century, has been greatly accelerated and given new form by the
Chinese communists. Nowhere has this been more true than
in attitudes toward social conflict and the "class struggle."
That the Chinese communists have won widespread acceptance of the Marxist theory of class struggle can be argued

---

[63] Pa Chin, "Writers' Courage and Sense of Responsibility," *SCMM*
323, pp. 1–2, citing *Shanghai Wen-hsueh*, no. 5, 1962.
[64] As cited in the *New York Times*, June 19, 1966.
[65] *Peking Review*, no. 23, June 3, 1966, p. 5.

from the relative popular success of the presentation of the history of the Chinese peasant wars. Communist interpretations of the peasant revolts have presented a convincing picture for the use of polemicists, if not for objective historians, in which the Chinese peasantry appears to struggle against landlord oppression through the centuries but manifestly fails to win "liberation" prior to modern times. To be sure, the many contradictions and inconsistencies, repeatedly observed, have not assisted theoretical understanding even for communist students of the peasant revolts. But the popular readership, for which the discussions of fine points by leading historians are only preparatory, is more interested in general impressions than in the inconsistencies of various aspects of the theoretical framework. The point is that Chinese social history with its numerous mass movements does provide much convenient material for manipulation by communist propagandists.

However, before finally accepting the proposition that the communist presentation of the peasant revolts has been a popular success, factors qualifying or appearing to negate such an assumption should also be noted.

In addition to the fear of speaking out at all and to the constant differences of opinion over theoretical interpretations, there have been severe criticisms of the historiography of the subject. These have included charges of fragmentary, oversimple, or incorrect approaches and of inadequate grasp of source materials.[66] There have even been attacks on the "bias" favoring only those sources which speak well of a given peasant revolt. Hence, a Taiping historian criticized the "type of prejudice" which led Lo Erh-kang and others to "automatically accept materials favorable to the Taiping but to reject unfavorable materials as landlord class slanders." [67]

---

[66] E.g., see Ch'i Hsia, "Regarding Research on the History of Our Country's Peasant Wars," *JMJP*, December 4, 1956. There are numerous indications of the poor grasp of classical Chinese by younger historians, including misinterpretations and references to the paucity of students who can handle classical Chinese. See Chao Li-sheng and Kao Chao-yi, *op. cit.*, p. 3.

[67] Ch'i Lung-wei, "From the Inscription on . . . [a Taiping relic]

Furthermore, there are indications that not all Chinese accept the fundamental principle of the "justice" of the "people's" struggles against the governing class. This is seen in the occasional use of traditional terminology or points of view in mainland descriptions of the peasant revolts. The original script of the 1950 movie on Wu Hsun reportedly said of a nineteenth-century Shantung rebel that, like the late Ming rebel Li Tzu-ch'eng, he had no political ideas but only liked to kill.[68] Similarly, during the Hundred Flowers period a critic accused a Party cadre of being "rich in peasant rebel ideology" because he "decided arbitrarily and acted tyrannically." [69] Other historians apparently on occasion have continued to use such pejorative terms as *p'an-pien* and *tao-tsei* for peasant revolts and rebels.[70] The continued prevalence of "many reactionary, mistaken views" of such peasant rebels as Huang Ch'ao and the Boxers has been noted.[71] One professor was later taken to task for saying that the anti-Ch'in revolt led by Ch'en Sheng and Wu Kuang was due to the accident of floods rather than to the oppression of the governing class.[72] In the early 1960s a professor of ancient studies at Sun Yat-sen University denied that the theory of the class struggle was applicable at all to classical philosophy, since people became aware of this theory only after Marx. This episode became the subject of a new series of criticisms,[73] and such views may be widely held among certain intellec-

---

Discussing the Prejudice in the Present Research Work on the TPTK," *KMJP*, May 23, 1957. Defenders of orthodox historiography answered that the communist should indeed favor the working class, not denying earlier mistakes but learning from them.

[68] Chang Ch'i-chih, *op. cit.*, KMJP, May 24, 1951.

[69] *SCMP* 1575, citing NCNA (Lanchow), July 15, 1957.

[70] Wang Hsing-ya, *op. cit.*, SHYK, no. 10, 1958, p. 10.

[71] Ho Lin-t'ien, "How To Look on the Two Mistaken Traditions Concerning Huang Ch'ao and the Boxers," *Hsiao-hsueh Chiao-shih*, 1954, no. 9 (September).

[72] See Chien Po-tsan, "Oppose the Restoration of Capitalist Class Social Science," *JMJP*, July 15, 1958, and CNA 126, April 6, 1956.

[73] The professor in question was Liu Chieh. For representative criticisms see Chang Yu-lin, "The Method of Marxist Class Analysis and Historicism," *LSYC*, no. 3, 1963, pp. 27–44; "New Conflict in Academic Ideology," *URS*, vol. 32, no. 25, September 24, 1963.

tuals, but they are seldom stated openly in connection with
the study of social history. The ideas of the majority of the
"people" themselves change still more slowly.

As late as 1960 the leader of a group researching oral traditions about the Nien revealed that many old peasants inter-
viewed still thought of the Nien as "bandits who did not
leave any evil undone." Noting that "although after liberation the Party has done much work to restore the reputation
of the Nien," he concluded, "the thoughts of these old men
are still more or less incorrect," and "they make the Nien
into barbarians" in time-honored Chinese fashion.[74]

A summary of the same year described the academic reevaluation of the peasant revolts as far from complete:

> We must intensify our struggle against reactionary, his-
> torical studies both inside and outside China. The reac-
> tionary scholars of the Imperialists have always viciously
> slandered the history of our nation's peasant revolution-
> ary wars in order to serve their reactionary political pur-
> poses. Before liberation, the reactionary feudal, capital-
> ist, and comprador historians all distorted the history of
> the peasant's revolutionary struggles in every way. After
> liberation, although there have been no historians who
> would openly propagate reactionary historical views, the
> influence of such views still exists to a certain degree in
> certain writings. It includes the slandering of the peasant
> class, the beautifying of the landlord class, the minimiz-
> ing of the class struggle, the description of the peasant
> wars as most cruel and horrible, and the obliterating of
> the great historical functions of the peasant revolution-
> ary wars.[75]

---

[74] Chi Cheng-te, "The Collection and Editing of Traditional Stories
of the Nien," *JMJP*, September 15, 1960. Compare this account with
the professed communist esteem for popular oral history. According to
Lo Erh-kang (*op. cit.*, *Anhui Shih-hsueh*, no. 1, 1960, p. 11), the principal study of the Nien published since 1949 by Chiang Ti is "objectivist" and "influenced by the writings of the Ch'ing and landlord class."
See Chiang Ti, *Nien-chün Shih Ch'u-k'ao* (Preliminary Investigation
Into the History of the Nien Army) (Peking: San-lien Shu-tien, 1956).

[75] Shih Shao-pin, "On the Discussion of Problems in the Peasant
Revolutionary Wars in Chinese Feudal Society," *SSP*, p. 514.

Finally, in the intensification of the "cultural revolution" of the mid-1960s, a leading Party editorial complained:

> The bourgeois "authorities" in the field of historical studies . . . use their so-called historicism, i.e., the idealist conception of history, to oppose and adulterate the Marxist-Leninist teachings on class struggle. They stubbornly deny that the people are the motive force of world history, and they spare no effort to smear the working people and the peasant wars. . . . They eulogize only emperors, kings, generals, and prime ministers who rode roughshod over the people. They are the "royalists" in the field of historical studies.[76]

As stated, the innumerable criticisms of 1965 and 1966 of Wu Han centered on the alleged distortion of the class struggle in his 1961 play about a sixteenth-century reformer-official.[77] In praising reformers of the governing class, Wu, like the dramatist T'ien Han, Chien Po-tsan, and other prominent intellectuals criticized at the time, supposedly revealed his underestimation of and hostility toward the peasant revolts. These and other[78] criticisms significantly tipped off the full-scale purges of 1966, including those of the Director and Deputy Director of the Propaganda Department of the Party,[79] of a former editor-in-chief of *Jen-min Jih-pao* from 1953 to 1958,[80] and of the Chancellors of Peking, Nanking, and Wuhan Universities, among many others in cultural affairs.[81] Among prominent historians who had discussed the

[76] *JMJP* editorial, June 3, 1966, cited in *Peking Review*, June 17, 1966, p. 14.

[77] *Hai Jui Pa Kuan.* See CNA 606, April 1, 1966; and *JMJP*, April 10, 1966. See this chapter above.

[78] As those of Central Committee member Yang Hsien-chen, historian Chou Ku-ch'eng, and others. See Adam Oliver, "Rectification of Mainland China Intellectuals, 1964–65," *Asian Survey*, October 1965.

[79] Lu Ting-yi and Chou Yang. The connection of these men with P'eng Chen and Lo Jui-ch'ing and other high-ranking victims of the 1966 purge is uncertain.

[80] Teng T'o. In 1937 Teng, using the given name Yun-t'e, was the author of *Chung-kuo Chiu-huang Shih,* referred to in Chapter 2.

[81] Even Li Ta, President of Wuhan University and, with Mao Tse-tung and Tung Pi-wu, one of three surviving founding members of the

history of the peasant wars and who were denounced in the "Great Proletarian Cultural Revolution" were Hou Wai-lu, Sun Tso-min, Ts'ai Mei-piao, and Ning K'o.[82] With the exception of the latter, all these men followed moderate or conservative Marxist evaluations of the peasant rebellions. There were also criticisms of the higher-ranking Kuo Mo-jo, Fan Wen-lan, and Lü Chen-yü, and in later stages of the "cultural revolution," as Party and military leaders sought to recover a balance between leftists and rightists, Ch'i Pen-yü of the Central Committee's Cultural Revolution Committee, Wu Ch'üan-ch'i and other leftist interpreters of the peasant rebellions also came under fire.[83]

Despite evidence of persisting skepticism of the communist interpretations of the peasant revolts, there is much more evidence suggesting the deepening roots of the Chinese communist historiography of the subject. This seems evident in the voluminous writings of the younger generation of historians. These men, with very few exceptions, vary only in the degree of their enthusiasm for the revolutionary qualities of the peasant rebels. For every reference about continued doubts of the "progressiveness" of the peasant revolts, there are hundreds praising the "glorious revolutionary tradition of the Chinese people." General acceptance of the communist interpretations is also evident in the genuine indignation with which representatives of all mainland schools of interpretation attack traditional and bourgeois slanders of the peasant revolts.[84] Nor do the praises of the peasant revolts seem en-

---

CCP and a leading Marxist theorist since the 1920s, was denounced as "anti-Party."

[82] See above and Wang Chang-ling, *op. cit.* Li Shu, the editor of *LSYC* prior to its suspension in 1966, was condemned as an accomplice of Chou Yang's "anti-Marxist" clique. Li, Fan Wen-lan, Hou Wai-lu and others were accused of maintaining a stranglehold on this publication. The senior historian Lü Chen-yü allegedly committed the error of other followers of Liu Shao-ch'i: "confessing" to the Kuomintang while in prison in 1927 (CNA 683, November 3, 1967, p. 5).

[83] E.g., see CB 844, January 10, 1968, CNA 704, April 16, 1968, and CNA 709, May 24, 1968.

[84] E.g., see Liu Ta-nien, "What Did the Yi-ho T'uan Movement Show?" *SCMP* 2341, p. 5, citing *JMJP*, August 30, 1960.

tirely forced or dishonest, since their magnitude and enthusiasm would be difficult to engender by artificial means. Furthermore, the Chinese communist tendency to publish arguments counter to their own, demonstrated so vividly in the anti-right movement of 1957–58 and in the Sino-Soviet dispute, does not imply that there is great support for these opposing arguments. On the contrary, if that were so, it seems doubtful that such arguments—in this case, doubts about the historical progressiveness of the peasant revolts— would be given such a wide airing.

This is not to argue, of course, that the new interpretations of the peasant revolts has been a spontaneous or entirely voluntary development. There is certainly an awareness of the communist truism, "the lefter the better." Nevertheless, some degree of reinterpretation of the peasant revolts was inevitable with the modernization of Chinese thought. The communists have accelerated the pace of this reinterpretation and dictated its extremism. It therefore seems clear that there has been a fundamental shift in Chinese interpretations of "lower-class rebellions" in Chinese history. While some undoubtedly will continue to agree secretly that the peasant rebels were merely "murderous, marauding local bandits," [85] the vast majority of educated Chinese unquestionably accept them as the principal historical proof of China's "glorious revolutionary tradition." [86]

It may be fitting, in closing our discussion of the Chinese communist propagation of the theory of class struggle in history, to examine the distinctions drawn between the "righteous peasant revolutionary wars" of earlier times against feudalism and imperialism, and the "reactionary, monstrous crime" of rebelling against the new "people's government of China." [87]

Western observers occasionally have professed surprise that a government so manifestly authoritarian as the Chinese

[85] Chiang Kai-shek, see Chapter 4.

[86] Mao Tse-tung, "The Chinese Revolution and the CCP," *SWMTT*, vol. 3, p. 74.

[87] See "Put Down the Rebellion in Tibet Thoroughly," *JMJP*, March 31, 1959.

should constantly call to mind historical examples of rebellion against tyranny and the principle that oppression begets resistance. Why, after all, would a government that had won power continue to stress the ethic of struggle against constituted authority? There have been many examples in history of a government emphasizing peaceful obedience after itself winning power by violence, but seldom, if ever before the communists, of a tyrannical government continuing praise of resistance to tyranny.

In the first place, it is evident that the masses of the Chinese people are enmeshed in propaganda about the peasant wars in history to a much smaller degree than are the intellectuals.[88] This is, of course, a natural derivative of differing occupations, but it is perhaps also the Party's intention. Although the youth of China read praises of peasant struggles against oppression from grade school up,[89] most lengthy discussions of the subject appear in historical and cultural journals, in such papers as *Kuang-ming Jih-pao*, and in books and pamphlets of relatively small circulation. A smaller number of articles on the peasant wars appear in Party organs such as *Hung Ch'i* and *Jen-min Jih-pao*.

Nor have many movies and plays depicting pre-modern mass movements appeared on the mainland despite the attractiveness of the subject for pageantry, color, and political instruction.[90] Numerous movies and plays about Party-led

[88] On the other hand, the workers and peasants are constantly reminded of more recent struggles against twentieth-century exploiters of China and of the need for continued class struggle under the direction of the Party.

[89] In fact, up to one quarter or one third of the upper-level elementary school history curriculum for ancient China has been devoted to the history of the peasant movements. See Hsiao-hsueh Kao-nien-chi, *Li-shih Chiao-hsueh Shou-ts'e* (History Teaching Handbook for Upper Elementary School) (Shanghai: Shang-wu Yin-shu-kuan, 1951), pp. 22–23, There are numerous references to high school and college discussions of the peasant revolts. For two examples, see *LSCH*, no. 3, 1959, p. 47; and *SHYK*, no. 4, 1960.

[90] Ah Ying, *Li Ch'uang-wang* (The Dashing King Li [Tzu-ch'eng]) (Shanghai: Hsin-hua Shu-tien, 1949), was an early example of a play about a peasant rebellion. One movie, *Liu San-chieh* (Third Sister Liu), was an account of the exploits of a servant girl in mobilizing opposition to a particular landlord but depicted only a small-scale revolt, which

"people's struggles" against the warlords, the Nationalists, and the Japanese in modern times have appeared, but there is apparent reluctance to disseminate too widely accounts of armed insurrection against ancient governments which might be associated in the viewers' minds only with tyranny and hence possibly with the communist government. Accordingly, movies, plays, and popular literature set in traditional times, unlike articles oriented toward the political and intellectual élite, tend to deal more with government figures than with their rebellious subjects.[91] Criticisms of this state of affairs played a prominent role in the intraparty struggles of the 1960s.[92]

There might indeed be viewer identification with peasant rebels of the past. Kuangtung peasants reportedly looked for the magical return of the Taiping leader Hung Hsiu-ch'uan to lead resistance against the cooperativization of land in the mid-1950s.[93] Then, when the decline of material conditions on the mainland was reaching a danger point after 1959, *The White-haired Girl*, a famous communist play and movie depicting revolt against the difficult conditions of Kuomintang rule, was withdrawn from circulation in the villages lest audi-

---

was in fact resolved peacefully in the end. Thus, although there are references to many films based on "stories of the revolutionary past" (see *SCMP* 1692, citing *NCNA*, January 10, 1958), most of these are about communist-led revolts, while in historical dramas "the people like to see plays on the patriotism and democratism of ancient times . . . and to watch the bellicosity of outstanding personages of the feudal class." See "Three Thoughts on the Historical Drama," *JPRS*, May 8, 1962, citing *Hung Ch'i*, March 16, 1962.

[91] Most of the biographies in Wu Han (ed.), *Chung-kuo Li-shih Hsiao Ts'ung-shu* (Little Chinese History Library) (Peking: Chung-hua Shu-chü, 1958 *et seq.*), which is for popular consumption, deal with traditional favorites such as Lao Tzu, Ch'u Yuan, Lin Tse-hsu, and reappraised government figures such as Ts'ao Ts'ao. According to *Peking Review* (January 18, 1963), only two of twelve biographies were devoted to peasant rebels (Hung Hsiu-ch'uan and a leader of the "Resist the English Corps"). Actually, there were others (e.g., Ch'en Sheng, Fang La, and Li Tzu-ch'eng), but most do in fact deal with governing-class figures.

[92] E.g., see Ch'i Pen-yü, "Study History for the Sake of Revolution," *Hung Ch'i*, 1965, no. 13 (December 1965), pp. 14–22, translated in *SCMM* 506.

[93] According to reports of refugees to Hong Kong.

ences be incited by the equally bad conditions of the time.[94] Also beginning about this time there were numerous publications attempting to show that conditions were indeed much worse in former times than under communist rule. A series of campaigns to stress "the bitterness of the past in order to teach bitterness [against old enemies]" (*Yi-k'u Yin-k'u*) by study of the history of one's family, factory, and village (*San shih*) and by "telling stories of the revolution" (*chiang ke-ming ku-shih*) has continued this theme.[95]

Therefore, it is clear that the ideological lessons in the earlier history of the peasant wars in China are intended primarily for the intellectuals, while there may, in fact, be some hesitancy in spreading the idea of revolt against oppression among the population at large through the glorification of ancient peasant revolts. This has not been true, of course, where the communists can be shown to have led the revolt against internal "reactionaries" or against the "imperialists." Such examples from contemporary times are considered safer and more significant material for the inculcation among the masses of the theory of the class struggle than are stories of the ancient peasant wars.

Nevertheless, the extent to which the communists preach revolt against oppression, while directed primarily at the intellectuals, is still remarkable. This is not done without regard for the consequences, and therefore it reveals both the confidence and ideological commitment of the Chinese communists. Coming to power themselves through the mobilization of a peasant movement, they are well aware of the problems of controlling the peasantry, and they have moved decisively to do just that. This is undoubtedly the most important explanation for communist willingness to praise revolt against oppressive governments, although the effects of the "cultural revolution" may well force an eventual rethinking of the advisability of constant praise of revolt.

There have been sporadic revolts against the communist

[94] According to interview with refugee who left China in May 1962.
[95] See *China Survey*, January 15, 1966; and SCMM 378, pp. 17–20, citing CKCN, July 1, 1963.

authorities,[96] but nothing comparable to the large-scale movements of the past. Passive resistance is, of course, another matter.

Most observers feel that the communists have in fact altered the basic conditions in the villages of China which enabled the many large revolts in Chinese history.[97] The over-all lot of the peasantry may not have improved much, but some of the insecurities and inequities of distribution of the past have. Far more important, the communists have extended political controls to the grass-roots level much more effectively than had ever been done before. It is these practical measures of control which enable the communists to praise revolts against past oppression with minimum fear of their audience translating the suggestion of revolt into reality. They preach struggle against oppression but feel confident they can direct this "struggle" into the desired channel. The "cultural revolution" may well shake this confidence.

A third and theoretically important aspect of the communists' propagation of the value of struggle against oppression even after the establishment of their own authoritarian government is the insistence on the fundamental change in human relations which occurs with the communist revolution. For the first time in human history, the governing class is in theory also the working class and its government the representative of the absolute majority of the people. Therefore, the reactionary nature of revolt against communism would be as self-evident to the believing communist as the "justness" of revolt against all noncommunist governments. This distinction is, of course, an extension of the principle

---

[96] E.g., Shih Ch'eng-chih, *People's Resistance in Mainland China* (Hong Kong: Union Research Institute Press, 1956). In the difficult years 1959–62 there was increased opposition and revolt, but the situation did not get out of control. See references to rebels (*p'an fei*) in *Kung-tso T'ung-hsun*, nos. 1, 2, 4, 7, 14, and 21, January–May 1961. These are commented on by John Lewis, "China's Secret Military Papers," *China Quarterly*, April–June 1964, pp. 76–77; by Ralph Powell, "Politico-Military Relationships in Communist China," Washington: Department of State, 1963; and in *CNA* 510, p. 4.

[97] See Hsiao Kung-ch'uan, *Rural China: Imperial Control in the Nineteenth Century*, pp. 516–18.

already observed, that what was historically progressive at one stage becomes reactionary at another. Hence, revolt, like individualism and private ownership, is progressive under earlier social systems but reactionary under communism.

The "cultural revolution" does not refute the principle but rather, to the Maoist, arises from the fact that China is not yet fully communist. Mao has stressed since 1957, and driven home in the "cultural revolution," that class struggle persists under socialism, and communism will not be attained completely until the whole world is communist. Accordingly, the Maoists have again sponsored revolt against their enemies within China.

The great emphasis on the superiority of the political consciousness of the proletariat over all previous working classes, while treated in communist China differently than in the West, is another means of asserting the fundamental change in the course of history before and after the communist revolution.[98] Thus, from the moment of acquiring communist leadership in the 1920s, we are told, "the peasant movement threw off its [traditional] laws of development and appeared on Chinese soil with a completely new face."[99]

One interesting manifestation of the very different treatment given revolts against earlier governments and revolts against the communists is seen in the inversion of the terminology. Mainland descriptions of the Tibetan and other anti-communist revolts employ traditional pejorative terms for rebellion. "The war of betrayal and disruption" (*p'an-luan chan-cheng*) fostered by a few "traitorous bandits" (*mai-kuo tsei*) in Tibet, wrote *Jen-min Jih-pao* in 1959, has "betrayed the motherland and disrupted the unity of the country."[100] Secret societies within China similarly have been condemned

[98] E.g., see Feng Ting, *Kung-jen Chieh-chi te Li-shih Jen-wu* (Historical Tasks of the Working Class) (Shanghai: Hua-tung Jen-min Ch'u-pan She, 1953), pp. 9–10.

[99] Sung Yang, *Chung-kuo Nung-min Ke-ming Yun-tung Shih-hua* (Talks on the History of the Chinese Peasant Revolutionary Movements) (Tientsin: Tu-che Shu-tien, 1949), p. 55.

[100] See *China Reconstructs*, supplements of May and June 1959 issues, citing *JMJP*, March 31 and May 6, 1959.

for "sabotaging activities" and for "raping women and oppressing children." [101]

Thus, in a sense the interpretation of the peasant revolts has come full circle. Like its forerunners for two millennia, the present government of China excoriates those who do not accept its order, especially those foolhardy enough to take up arms against its authority.

Nevertheless, the communist praise of rebellion in history does represent a fundamental departure not only from traditional but from modern noncommunist views. For the vast majority of Chinese who think about their history at all, the belief in past class struggle appears sincere and a commitment to the idea of struggle against one's enemies in the present and future. This revolution in the interpretation of the past is one of the most striking aspects of modern Chinese intellectual history. Aspects of the interpretations may change, but commitment to the theory of the class struggle is likely to remain as long as Chinese communist rulers feel unsatisfied with present conditions.

[101] See An Ming, "Resolutely Hit the Sabotaging Activities of Reactionary Taoist Sects," *SCMP* 1092, pp. 17–20, citing *JMJP*, July 7, 1955.

CHAPTER ELEVEN

Conclusion

THE communist treatment of the peasant movements in Chinese history reveals important characteristics of Chinese communism as well as of contemporary Chinese intellectual life in general. These characteristics are an unprecedented commitment to the doctrine of class struggle, the adaptation of Marxism, and the close relation of ideology to politics. Certain observations on the content and success of the "new history" of the peasant revolts will also be noted.

The increasing emphasis by Chinese communists on struggle in general and on the class struggle of the peasantry in particular, as observed throughout this study, reflects the passage of Marxism from the established areas of Europe to the more unsettled and more agrarian East. A parallel development in Marxist theory, which represents another side of the evolution to a greater stress on the peasantry, has been the increased weight given to the historical role of "the people" in general. If classical Marxism stressed the economic evolution of history, or the "productive forces," the Chinese communists stress social revolution and human energy, or "productive relations" in history. They do so far more than the Russians, especially in recent years.[1]

[1] As in the theory of the revolutionary role of the peasantry, Lenin's

Both the economic and the human aspects are present in classical, Soviet, and Chinese theory, but there has been ever greater emphasis on the role of "the people," on human will, and on voluntarism,[2] until today in communist China the concept of "the people" is almost a religious one. The Chinese communists define "the people" as all who support Party policies, and the vagueness of the term is evident. Yet this broadening of classical Marxist class analysis, as well as the decreasing emphasis on economic determinism, has been a natural development in areas dependent on human initiative and on the cooperation of all classes, in the struggle to change the course of apparent historical evolution. The Leninist stress on the leading role of the revolutionary party is a feature of Maoism which is easily explained in terms of the self-appointed tasks of the Chinese Communist Party. Similarly, the unprecedented importance attached to ideology in Chinese communism derives from the necessity to defy "nature" and shape the country according to the wishes of the leadership. The fusion of old Chinese "moral determinism" with Leninist and Maoist voluntarism is dramatically demonstrated in a recent *Liberation Army Daily* editorial:

> About the relations of spirit and matter [one must say] that matter is primary and spirit is secondary. But this is said only about the genesis of thought, where matter comes first, then spirit. It is not true about the strength of the two. The strength of spirit is much greater than that of matter. . . . Therefore we pay great attention to ideological work. . . . The thought of Mao Tse-tung transforms man's ideology, transforms the fatherland. . . .[3]

---

work formed an intermediate stage in this development, although in some respects Chinese communist attitudes towards the peasantry and "the people" are more reminiscent of Russian populism than of Leninism. Similar views have been criticized as "populist" in the Soviet Union.

[2] This emphasis was already present in the thought of Li Ta-chao. See Maurice Meisner, "Li Ta-chao and the Chinese Communist Treatment of the Materialist Conception of History," *China Quarterly*, no. 24, October–December 1965. See also Chalmers Johnson, "Social Science in China Scholarship," *World Politics*, January 1965, p. 261.

[3] CNA 635, p. 7, citing *Chieh-fang Chün Pao*, May 28, 1966, p. 1.

Thus has Marxist materialism become Maoist idealism. "The people" and their awareness of oppression and of the need for revolution are stressed over the drier economic determinism of classical Marxism. The progression has been from class to Party to people.

The relation of theory to political need is evident in these changes in Marxist thought and is exactly reflected in the study of the class struggle in history. The historiography of the peasant wars shows equally the relation of academic discussion to current politics. Hence, the current radical interpretation of the Chinese past,[4] as seen in the stress on the most revolutionary aspects of the peasant revolts, intensified with the general shift to the left of Chinese communist policies after 1957. In mid-1958 there was a "predetermined release"[5] of certain materials designed to stimulate discussion of the peasant revolts, no doubt as part of the increased attention given to the political education of intellectuals in the wake of the Hundred Flowers episode. In the polemics with the Soviet Party over revolutionary strategy, the history of the Chinese peasant wars has been cited to show the feasibility of peasant-based revolutions in the East, while the proper handling of the theory of the class struggle has been one of the keys to the "cultural revolution" of the mid-1960s. Accordingly, Maoist policy clearly favors the radical view of the peasant revolts, since this view supports revolutionary propaganda even if it bears little resemblance to classical Marxist formulations on the subject.[6]

If the historiography of the peasant revolts has followed

[4] "Radical" here does not mean a denial of the value of Chinese history. On the contrary, recently there has been a parallel stress on great figures and themes in the Chinese past, which is reminiscent of developments in Soviet historiography of the 1930s, but there is generally greater stress on revolutionary aspects and especially on the class struggle in Chinese history.

[5] See G. Ya. Smolin, "The Discussion by Chinese Historians on the Question of the Peasant Revolts in the Period of Feudalism," NAA, no. 2, 1962, p. 192.

[6] The adoption of this approach and the criticism of classical Marxist arguments are perhaps analogous to earlier criticism of the "returned students" and "Stalinist dogmatists," who allegedly ignored Chinese conditions in the history of the Party.

Party initiatives, it has also reflected differences of opinion within the Party, as in the upheavals of the mid-1960s. In fact, policies toward the treatment of the peasant revolts, as toward treatment of the intellectuals and of Chinese tradition in general, portray the same schizophrenia between conservative and radical, right and left, that is evident in the entire history of the communist movement. To some degree, in China these differences reflect a tug of war between traditional values and Western intellectual antidotes fostered by many in the Party. To a greater degree, variant interpretations reflect differing approaches and differing needs at any given moment.

In the case of differences in the treatment of the peasant revolts, there is probably also a split on the basis of age as well as on the basis of conservative and radical temperament. Certainly the historians contributing the greatest volume and the most revolutionary interpretations of the peasant wars are unfamiliar names, and presumably younger students trained since 1949, while the older, better-known historians generally have been skeptical of the overwhelming stress on peasant class struggle. Such a divergence of generations could have many ramifications. Paradoxically, it could make academic control more difficult as generations well versed in communist classics are able to use the "weapon of Marxism" against their masters in much the same way that the Chinese communists try to do this against Soviet theorists. To a considerable extent, this has been the case in the "cultural revolution." The presence of radical young theorists suggests further that at the moment radical Party leaders are able to find numerous allies among the younger generation of historians who will work to support their policies with references to an alleged "revolutionary Chinese tradition." This in turn does not support hopes for greater moderation in the next generation of Chinese communist leaders.

The differences of opinion about theoretical interpretations repeatedly referred to throughout this study also reveal that Marxism can be a "two-edged sword," since its ambiguities can support a variety of interpretations. One can suggest

that in communist China scholars take advantage of this ambiguity to argue diverse positions as their only form of self-
expression. Accordingly, unanimity of interpretation on controversial topics can be achieved only through Party dictation.
But this is not likely. Rather, policy appears to be to allow
some diversity of interpretation of historical problems so long
as certain minimal guidelines are followed and the Maoist
theoretical position is not jeopardized.

Despite these differences of approach, there has been a
consistent stress in Chinese communist intellectual life on
the progressiveness of the class struggle as the primary force
of historical evolution. Moreover, in the historiography of
the peasant movements the consensus favors ever more radical interpretations. While some influential historians continue to warn against "unhistorical" approaches to the reconstruction of the past, and while continued variations of
emphasis are likely, it is certain that praise of historical and
contemporary class struggle will continue as long as the Party
backs revolutionary policies. Recent developments affirm this
continuing theme. As one writer put it, "Not to forget the
past means not to forget class struggle," [7] and a leading historian wrote that the "theory of class struggle . . . is the theoretical nucleus of historical materialism." [8] Among the problems of Chinese history, that of the evaluation of the peasant
revolts has been called "the most important." [9] If the ultimate goal of Marxist historiography is to demonstrate the inevitability of the progression of history toward communism,
Chinese historians stress the class struggle as the most essential means toward that goal.

Whatever the purposes of the Party in stressing the great
historical role of the peasant revolts, these interpretations
have and will have far-reaching effects on the general cultural
life of the nation and, indeed, on Chinese politics itself. Al-

[7] "Never Forget the Past," *SCMP* 3072, p. 5, citing *Kung-jen Jih-pao*,
September 8, 1963.
[8] Chi Wen-fu, "Profoundly and Thoroughly Observe the Viewpoint
of the Class Struggle in Historical Research," *SCMP* 2500, p. 10, citing
KMJP, April 28, 1961.
[9] Hsueh-shu Tung-t'ai column, *op. cit.*, *JMJP*, November 18, 1961.

though official interpretations may vary, the conception of Chinese social history is most unlikely to revert to pre-communist idealization of social harmony. Rather, it is likely that the tensions of recent intellectual and political life have convinced most Chinese that "struggle" is the normal, if not the most desirable and permanent,[10] condition of life. Thus, the historiography of the peasant wars has played an important role in the re-education of the Chinese people.

In evaluating the successes and failures of the historiography of the peasant revolts, the distinction between the investigation of historical truth and historical propaganda or education must be kept in mind. In the former area, the Chinese communists have not succeeded. They have made available a great amount of data, and they have raised many important questions concerning Chinese social history in general and the history of the peasant revolts in particular. They have discovered some new materials[11] and called attention to many other documents and references concerning peasant rebels. Yet the millions of words devoted to the subject have not furthered very much the understanding of this phenomenon in Chinese history. Many fundamental questions remain unanswered, including the real composition, goals, and actions of these movements. Even in terms of Marxist theory many of the most important questions are avoided, especially those relating to periodization, as in the role of the class struggle in the transition from "slavery to feudalism" and from "feudalism to semi-colonialism." Most important, the complexity of the historical phenomenon of the Chinese peasant revolts defies simple solution.

Concerning knowledge of history in the "new China," a leading playwright wrote, "the young generation has scanty historical knowledge, being misled by simplified thoughts and made disinterested in history . . . ,"[12] while a leading his-

---

[10] Of course, the Chinese communists follow the vision of the classical Marxists of an eventually harmonious and classless future.

[11] E.g., the discovery of a local record in Shantung supposedly proving the redistribution of property by the late Ming rebel Li Tzu-ch'eng and numerous sources on the nineteenth-century rebellions.

[12] T'ien Han, "Problems of Choosing a Theme," *URS*, vol. 25, citing

torian acknowledged that "some problems [in historical inter-
pretation] will have to wait for our children and grandchil-
dren to solve." [13] Moreover, it is apparent that many young
college-educated Chinese are unable to read the classical
language with ease. Perhaps most harmful of all, in historical
studies as in other areas, is the self-imposed isolation of China,
with virtually complete neglect of important advances in noncommunist sinology.[14]

In terms of the second criterion, however—the popularization of history and of Party policies through the study of history—it can be said that communist historiography of the
peasant wars is a great success. This is undoubtedly the most
important goal of Chinese communist historiography. As one
writer put it, "We should not interpret history only objectively. Studying the peasant wars, [we] must look first at the
anti-feudal nature and goals of the revolutionary peasants and
only later at other more objective considerations." [15] In
short, the desire to inculcate a belief in class struggle super-
sedes the desire to "investigate historical truth," though, like
their predecessors in Imperial China, most mainland historians believe these two goals reinforce each other. In fact, the
abundant traditional materials stressing government injustices as a cause of revolt, like the voluminous data on modern
imperialism, if read uncritically, do seem to support communist claims of the existence of the class struggle in Chinese
history.[16] Although these conflicts obviously pitted the ruled

---

Wen-yi-hsueh, no. 7, 1961. T'ien was strongly condemned in the "cultural revolution," as were many other popular writers.

[13] Pai Shou-yi, in *KMJP*, January 3, 1962.

[14] For instance, one finds acceptance of statistics in traditional histories which completely ignore work done on this subject in the West.
E.g., the statement that Wang Mang's policies caused the death of one
half the populace, as proven by Han population data. Ch'i Hsia, *Ch'in-
Han Nung-min Chan-cheng Shih*, pp. 87 and 126.

[15] T'ien Yu-ch'ing, cited by *HCS* (eds.), "On the Questions of the
Nature, Function and Distinguishing Characteristics of the Peasant
Wars in Chinese History," *SSP*, pp. 492–93.

[16] A statement about Soviet attitudes toward the class struggle in
history seems applicable to Chinese historiography of the peasant wars,
with peasant revolts substituted for workers' movements: "The class

against their rulers and hence were essentially political, there is no doubt that the average reader in communist China sees them in terms of class struggle, believing that the Chinese peasantry struggled for thousands of years against the abuses of the governing class and that ultimately their "liberation" had to await communist leadership. Hence, the historiography of the peasant wars has succeeded in its ideological function to the extent that it has made the communist seizure of power seem both inevitable and justified.

It may be said also that one historiographical tradition has been maintained: the inexhaustible energy with which the Chinese have pursued the writing of history and especially the writing of history in the service of the state. Nor has there yet been the degree of distortion and outright falsification of history that characterized so much of Soviet historical study. There has been selection and emphasis but not much crude cutting and fabrication except in the case of Party history,[17] perhaps as much because Party leaders have not felt this necessary up to now as because of any indigenous respect for history. It is also true, however, that the prodigious efforts to integrate the Chinese revolution with the Chinese tradition are understandable only in terms of a society attempting to come to grips with an immense historical legacy.

In terms of Marxist-Leninist-Maoist theory itself, the religion of contemporary China, there is evidence indicating its deepening roots in mainland historiography. This is especially noteworthy in many of the articles and writings of the younger generation. As popular history these works are at once more sophisticated and more radical in their interpretations than comparable writings of the early 1950s. They are certainly more Chinese. They are more sophisticated in showing greater skill in handling the complexities of history according to Marxist theory, at least prior to the "cultural rev-

struggle in the form of the workers' movement stood out so sharply that it was not necessary to invent or prove its existence." K. F. Shteppa, *Russian Historians and the Soviet State*, p. 167.

[17] E.g., the treatment of Ch'en Tu-hsiu and of Mao's role in the history of the CCP, and the criticisms of the historical roles in Liu Shao-ch'i and others in the "cultural revolution."

olution." They are more radical in their ever greater stress on the class struggle in theory, as if to compensate for its decline in practice. They are more Chinese in their stress on national achievements. Characteristically, these are all combined in the use of most revolutionary and untraditional theories in the interests of Chinese nationalism.

Therefore almost two decades of intensive ideological education in historical studies have been successful in inculcating a complicated body of historical theory, which has in turn trained new generations of intellectuals in the logic of the dialectic. The converse is not necessarily true: that it has convinced the Chinese historian that the dialectical interpretation of Chinese history is the only logical one. A method can be taught more easily than a belief, but the former inevitably influences the latter. Most important, in terms of content, the "new historiography" has succeeded in presenting the enormous historical legacy of China in terms suitable to the purposes of communist mass education. Chinese communist historiography may be termed a political and educational success, given the goals of the Party leaders.

These goals, above all, have been directed to showing that the strivings of mankind were the driving force of history and not deviations from the classical ideals of harmonious social relations. Therefore, the Chinese communists place maximum emphasis on the history of the peasant wars in order to inculcate a belief in the existence and efficacy of class struggle and the realization that "only through struggle is there a way out." [18] Mainland historians cite ceaselessly the protests of the Chinese peasantry for two millennia against "feudal exploitation" as proof of the "glorious revolutionary tradition of the Chinese people," and they call the historical experience of the peasant wars the "foundation on which the peasants were able to accept the leadership of the proletariat." [19] They stress the "revolutionary struggles" of the Chinese

[18] Su Hsing, "Ch'en Sheng, the First Leader of a Chinese Peasant Revolt," *CKCN*, no. 72, August 1951, p. 30.

[19] Ning K'o, "The Question of Spontaneity and Consciousness of the Chinese Peasant Wars," *SCMM* 311, citing *Hung Ch'i*, no. 7, April 1, 1962.

peasantry both "objectively," in so far as the peasant movements "alone formed the real motive force of Chinese historical development," [20] and "subjectively," in so far as the peasantry consciously aspired to replace feudal exploitation with a "peasant utopia." While some historians oppose the latter half of this equation as contrary to fact and to classical Marxist views, and while all obey the injunction that "pre-proletarian" mass movements inevitably failed, the prevailing Chinese view of the historical peasant rebellions is nevertheless one of enthusiastic approval. This tendency both influenced the form of the "cultural revolution" and was strengthened by it, although eventually a new reaction will inevitably set in.

The contrast between such communist praise and traditional Chinese vilification of rebellion has highlighted the depth of the revolution in values attempted by the Chinese communists and has been one factor necessitating the enormous attention given to this subject in ideological reform. This unprecedented orientation toward struggle in general and toward class struggle in particular has been fostered by the belief that for China to survive in the modern world, whether economically or politically, her people must honor competition and struggle in place of the traditional emphasis on harmony.[21] At the height of the "cultural revolution," Mao restated this commitment to struggle, with characteristic emphasis:

> Marxism consists of thousands of truths, but they all boil down to the one sentence, "It is right to rebel." For thousands of years, it had been said that it was right to oppress, it was right to exploit, and it was wrong to rebel. This old verdict was only reversed with the appearance of Marxism. This is a great contribution. It was through struggle that the proletariat learned this truth,

[20] Mao Tse-tung, "The Chinese Revolution and the Chinese Communist Party," *SWMTT*, vol. 3, p. 76.
[21] This theme runs through the history of Chinese communism from Ch'en Tu-hsiu on.

and Marx drew the conclusion. And from this truth there follows resistance, struggle, the fight for socialism.[22]

If the idea of struggle was originally a preeminently Western value, the Chinese communists now far outdo Western communists in its praises. Moreover, they do so by asserting that the class struggle was, and is, more intense in China and the poorer world than in the West. They contend that this was proved by the history of the Chinese peasant wars, which in frequency, size, and intensity were "without parallel in the world." [23] Hence, with double irony, the Chinese communists stress a Western and seemingly un-Chinese concept by maintaining that the class struggle was and is most severe in the Orient, an area largely excluded from formulations of Marx himself.

In addition, where Marx and Engels thought of the class struggle primarily in terms of the modern bourgeoisie and proletariat and Lenin developed the theory of a revolutionary peasantry in the modern revolution, the present generation of Chinese theorists have made the Chinese peasantry the most revolutionary class in Oriental history as well as in the modern revolution. In this they have been encouraged by, but in some areas have gone beyond, the writings of Mao Tse-tung himself. They have applied Mao's most enthusiastic writings on the contemporary peasantry to the study of the peasant wars in Chinese history. In short, since China lacked both a *bourgeoisie* and a *proletariat*, the peasant revolts in Chinese communist historiography have played a role comparable to that of the modern labor movement in Western Marxist historiography as the direct forerunners of the communist revolution.

Compared with Western and earlier Chinese approaches, the prevailing interpretation of the history of peasant wars is at once more nationalist and more radical in its class and revolutionary implications. It is more nationalistic in its stress on

[22] "Challenge the Old World," *JMJP*, August 26, 1966, cited in *Peking Review*, May 31, 1968, p. 3.
[23] Mao Tse-tung, *ibid.*

the peculiarly revolutionary qualities of the Chinese peasantry, and it is more radical in its unprecedented emphasis on class struggle. It therefore reveals both the chauvinism and Marxist fundamentalism of the Chinese communists. This simultaneous emphasis on Chinese uniqueness and on a revolutionary theory is significant because it shows that the Chinese communists believe that the best way to advance national interests is by stressing revolutionary heritage and commitment.

Sketches of Major Chinese Peasant Rebellions

THE ANTI-CH'IN REVOLTS
OF 209–208 B.C.

The first great popular revolt in Chinese history was initiated when two poor Honan farmers, Ch'en Sheng (or She) and Wu Kuang, led in rebellion a group of some 900 fellow conscripts delayed by floods on their way to duty at a government garrison in what is now Anhui province.[1] The first emperor of Ch'in had decreed the death penalty for such tardiness, and consequently Ch'en and Wu

> rose up from the paths of the fields and led a band of some hundreds of poor, weary troops in revolt against the Ch'in. They cut down trees to make their weapons, raised their flags on garden poles, and the whole world in answer gathered about them like a great cloud, brought them provisions, and followed after them as shadows followed a form. In the end the leaders of the entire east rose up together and destroyed the House of Ch'in.[2]

Actually, Ch'en and Wu's rebellion, said to have involved

[1] All place-names given in the following summaries refer to contemporary provinces and not to the historical names.
[2] Chia Yi, "Kuo ch'in lun," cited in Wm. Theodore de Bary et al. (eds.), *Sources of Chinese Tradition* (New York: Columbia University Press, 1960), p. 168. See also the account of the rebellion in Ssu-ma Ch'ien, *Shih Chi*, cited in Burton Watson (trans.), *Records of the Grand Historian of China* (New York: Columbia University Press, 1961), pp. 19–33.

several hundred thousand people in much of north China,[3] was weakened almost immediately by internal strife[4] and by poor organization and tactics[5] and was defeated by the Ch'in armies within six months. By then, however, other leaders had risen against the hated Ch'in, including the famous military aristocrat Hsiang Yü, who actually destroyed the dynasty, and Liu Pang, a commoner who finally succeeded in defeating Hsiang (202 B.C.) and founded the Han dynasty. In the communist historiography of these revolts, Ch'en Sheng and Wu Kuang are unanimously considered "true" peasant rebels, but the evaluation of Hsiang Yü, Liu Pang, and other rebel leaders varies according to the authors' interpretation of the social origins and subsequent actions of the leader in question.[6] The Ts'ang T'ou army which allied with Ch'en Sheng's forces rates special merit as a possible slave rebellion.[7]

[3] Statistics present a major problem. Traditionally, commanders in the field and historians exaggerated the size of rebel armies to dramatize the importance of their mission or the moral to be drawn from the uprising. Communist historians (as pointed out by Howard Levy, *Journal of Asian Studies* [hereafter *JAS*], August 1957, pp. 612–17) are quite inconsistent in often accepting traditional statistics exaggerating the size of a rebel army while denying similar exaggerations of rebel atrocities as slanders. Nevertheless, traditional and modern estimates mentioned in this study, even if reduced many times, still represent very large rebel forces. See Chapter 9 for further discussion of this point. In this chapter I have attempted to use the most reasonable estimates available, but these are tentative at best.

[4] Many communist authors often attempt to attribute these weaknesses to the infiltration of Chou aristocrats who wished to utilize the revolts against the Ch'in to restore their former positions; e.g., see Chien Po-tsan, "On the Uprising of Ch'en Sheng and Wu Kuang," in his *Chung-kuo Shih Lun-chi* (Collected Essays on Chinese History) vol. 2, pp. 155 ff.; and Ch'i Hsia, *Ch'in-Han Nung-min Chan-cheng Shih* (History of the Peasant Wars of the Ch'in and Han) (Peking: San-lien Shu-tien, 1962), p. 27.

[5] See Liu K'ai-yang, *Ch'in mou Nung-min Chan-cheng Shih-lueh* (Brief History of the Late Ch'in Peasant War) (Peking: Shang-wu Yin-shu Kuan, 1959), p. 97.

[6] Su Ts'ung-wu and Ch'i Hsia, "The Late Ch'in Peasant War," in Li Kuang-pi *et al.* (eds.), *Chung-kuo Nung-min Ch'i-yi Lun-chi* (Collected Discussions on the Chinese Peasant Uprisings) (Peking: San-lien Shu-tien, 1958), pp. 22–25.

[7] E.g., L. S. Perelomov, "On the Character of the Driving Forces of the War of 209–202 B.C. in China," *NAA*, no. 1, 1962, pp. 86–87.

THE REVOLTS AGAINST
WANG MANG, A.D. 18–27

The second great period of mass disturbances in Chinese history occurred in north and central China after the failure of Wang Mang's reforms and after a series of economic and political disasters. From A.D. 18 and 20, respectively, separate revolts of commoners broke out in Shantung and in Hupeh and after several years engulfed all the populous areas of China in the flames of civil war. The greatest of the peasant movements, known as the "Red Eyebrows," which came to embrace perhaps 300,000 rebels under the leadership of Fan Ch'ung, swept all before it prior to bogging down in aimless confusion after the overthrow of Wang Mang in A.D. 23.

The Red Eyebrows were only the largest of some fifteen rebel bands in north China, while in the south no less than three groups of commoners simultaneously revolted against the government of Wang Mang and were soon joined by members of the old Han ruling family. Some of these men succeeded in molding a more organized force out of the "Green Forest" and other peasant armies. After further internal strife and warfare, one of them, Liu Hsiu, went on to defeat the Red Eyebrows (A.D. 27), still other "peasant armies," and various Imperial contenders and restored the Later Han dynasty.[8] Typically, communist accounts portray this sequence of events as a seizure of the "fruits" of the peasant class struggle by representatives of the landlord class.[9]

---

[8] For a description of these rebellions, see Hans Bielenstein, *The Restoration of the Han Dynasty* (Göteborg: Elanders Boktryckeri, AB, 1953 and 1959, 2 vols.), especially vol. 2, pp. 40, 79–80, 83, 91, 94–95, and 113 ff.

[9] E.g., see Ch'i Hsia *et al.*, *Ch'in Han Nung-min Chan-cheng Shih*, pp. 107 ff.; Li Ting-fang, "The Revolts of the Red Eyebrows and Green Forest [Army]," *LKP*, p. 57; and Wu Su-chih, *Lu-lin-chün ch'i-i te Ku-shih* (Stories of the Uprising of the Green Forest Army) (Wuhan: Ch'un-yi T'ang, 1956), pp. 56 and 77.

THE REVOLTS AT THE END
OF THE EASTERN HAN

In A.D. 184 large-scale rebellions with important religious overtones erupted over much of China. In that year a Hopeh shaman and faith-healer, Chang Chüeh, promised the beginning of a new era and the end of a time of troubles in which the empire had been beset with court factionalism and oppression, foreign wars, famine, and plague. Chang and his cohorts preached a mixture of Taoist beliefs based on the controversial book, the *T'ai-p'ing ching*.[10] In February 184 he decreed an uprising of several hundred thousand followers, organized into thirty-six groups in eight provinces of China. This rebellion was crushed with great bloodshed after some nine months, but in the course of it another rebellion, involving the Taoist sect known as the "Five Pecks of Rice School," broke out in Szechwan, where it persisted for some decades. Other insurrections and general turmoil continued in east China for a few years after 184.[11] Despite the evident religious motivation behind these movements, the prevailing mainland interpretation considers them "peasant class wars" which utilized and transformed religious ideals for their own purposes in the struggle against the landlord class.[12]

[10] For a discussion of the *T'ai-p'ing ching*, see Chapter 6.

[11] For two recent Western studies of these revolts, see Paul Michaud, "The Revolt of the Yellow Turbans," *Monumenta Serica*, 1958, pp. 47–127; and R. Stein, "Remarques sur les mouvements du Taoisme politiques-religieux au IIe siècle ap. J.-C.," *T'oung Pao*, vol. 50, 1963, pp. 1–78.

[12] E.g., Fan Wen-lan, *Chung-kuo T'ung-shih Chien-pien* (1961 ed.), vol. 2, p. 201; Ch'i Hsia *et al.*, *Ch'in Han Nung-min Chan-cheng Shih*, pp. 158 ff. However, Li Kuang-pi ("The Taiping Tao of Han Times and the Yellow Turban Uprising," *LKP*, pp. 59 ff.) is representative of the communist author who allows a more positive function for the role of religion in the Yellow Turban revolt.

REVOLTS OF THE
SIX-DYNASTIES PERIOD

The revolts of the six-dynasties period are associated in varying degrees with the tensions produced by the northern invasions and subsequent migrations. Because of the complex racial and social questions of the time and the paucity of research, these revolts receive relatively less attention in mainland historiography. There has been some discussion, however, of the revolts of the "vagrants" (*liu-min pao-tung*) in the first decade of the fourth century, of the revolts led by Sun En and Lu Hsun, A.D. 398–417, and by T'ang Yü-chih, A.D. 485, and of the early sixth-century revolts in north China culminating in the movement led by Ko Jung, A.D. 525–28.

The first of these disruptions occurred when people of all classes, many of whom had fled the invasions of east and north China, became involved in disputes in the upper Yangtze region. These disputes were products of frictions between new and old settlers[13] and between the different races, as well as of the usual social and political factors. Where there is discussion of these revolts at all on the mainland, references usually concern the revolt of certain minority tribes and vagrants under the leadership of Chang Ch'ang in Hupeh,[14] and especially the revolt led by Li T'e and Li Hsiung, which succeeded in taking Chengtu and organizing a government which endured from 302 to 347. The latter revolt proposed certain slogans of a supposedly progressive nature.[15]

The confused social nature of the period is revealed by the revolt in the lower Yangtze area led by Sun En and Lu Hsun

[13] According to Shih ("Some Chinese Rebel Ideologies," p. 170, citing the work of Wu Hsien-ch'ing) this was the primary cause of these revolts.

[14] E.g., Chien Po-tsan, "The Vagrants of the Late Western Chin and Their Revolts," in his *Chung-kuo Shih Lun-chi*, vol. 1, pp. 95–105.

[15] E.g., Chao Li-sheng and Kao Chao-yi, *Chung-kuo Nung-min Chan-cheng Shih Lun-wen Chi*, p. 41. For the "progressive" slogans proposed by Li T'e, see Chapter 6.

after 398. Both men were members of once prominent families, and the Sun family apparently sought to better its fortune by use of Taoist secret societies which were very popular in the Chekiang-Kiangsu area. When Sun En's uncle was killed by the eastern Ch'in government for his part in these activities, Sun En decided to revolt openly against the government. He enjoyed considerable success both on land and sea in the lower Yangtze delta area from 399 to 401 but was defeated and committed suicide in 402. Much of his army, supposedly numbering 200,000, melted away, but his son-in-law, Lu Hsun, led some survivors and new followers south by sea to Kwangtung. There he held out for several years before returning north, where he was defeated in battles in Anhui and Kiangsi shortly after 409. Remnants of the rebellion, which has been called "the first great pirate war in Chinese history," [16] survived until 417.

Mainland historians are ambivalent toward this rebellion because of the evident upper-class origins and motivations of its leaders, but most argue that what started as a manifestation of "internal governing-class contradictions" came to embrace basic social antagonisms of the peasantry against the landlords.[17] Similarly, another revolt in Chekiang in 485, in-

[16] Werner Eichhorn, "Description of the Rebellion of Sun En and earlier Taoist Rebellions," *Mittelungen des Institutes für Orientforschung*, no. 2, 1954, p. 352.

[17] Hsieh T'ien-tso, "Tentative Discussion of the Nature of the Uprising of Sun En and Lu Hsun," *HCS*, no. 2, 1962, according to summary in *Referentsii Sbornik, Sovremennaya Kitaiskaya Literatura po Obshestvennym Naukam* (Collected References, Contemporary Chinese Literature in the Social Sciences, hereafter *RS*) (Moscow: Akademiya Nauk), no. 49; and Chang Yi-tun, "Discussing the Peasant Uprising Led by Sun En and Lu Hsun," *LKP*, pp. 71 ff. According to Ts'ao Yung-nien ("A Tentative Discussion of the Transformation and Changes in the Late Ch'in Peasant Uprising," *LSYC*, no. 2, 1965, pp. 43–58) there are five views of the nature of this rebellion: (1) that it was a pure peasant uprising; (2) that Sun En's rebellion was a peasant rebellion but not the later revolt led by Lu Hsun after 402; (3) that after 400 it transformed from a peasant rebellion to a "five pecks of rice" (Taoist) rebellion; (4) that the whole affair was a result of contradictions within the governing class and hence was not a peasant rebellion against the landlord class; and (5) that it contained elements of a peasant rebellion but never developed into a true one. The author favors the third interpretation, advanced by Fan Wen-lan and others.

volving some 30,000 men under T'ang Yü-chih, is interpreted as reflecting the antagonisms of the peasantry against government oppression, especially against the corvée.[18]

In north China the relations between the Han Chinese, the Hsiung-nu, the Hsien-pi, and other minorities complicated the social composition of numerous revolts against the northern Wei in the early decades of the sixth century. The most important of these in communist historiography is the revolt led by Ko Jung in Hupeh, 525–28, which mainland authors insist infused class content into revolts of the minorities, such as that of the "six garrisons" along the Great Wall, 524–30.[19]

THE ANTI-SUI REVOLTS, A.D. 610–24

Of the more than 100 separate rebel forces which brought about the fall of the Sui in 618 and then contended for power, mainland historians describe several as peasant "righteous armies." The first of these major "peasant revolts" was led by Wang Po, an unwilling recruit for the first expedition sent by Sui Yang Ti against Korea. Wang rallied large numbers of other deserters in Hopeh and Shantung to his force before its defeat, 611–12. Another group, supposedly numbering several hundred thousand men, held out in the same area until well after the overthrow of the Sui, first under Tou Chien-te and then under Liu Hei-ta. The strongest peasant army, known as the Wa Kang Chün, was begun by a commoner, Chai Jang, but developed under an aristocrat, Li Mi, who had earlier participated in a revolt led by the Sui Minister

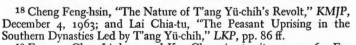

---

[18] Cheng Feng-hsin, "The Nature of T'ang Yü-chih's Revolt," *KMJP*, December 4, 1963; and Lai Chia-tu, "The Peasant Uprising in the Southern Dynasties Led by T'ang Yü-chih," *LKP*, pp. 86 ff.

[19] E.g., see Chao Li-sheng and Kao Chao-yi, *op. cit.*, pp. 44–67. For a Western commentary on these revolts, see E. Balazs, "La Révolte des six garrisons et la sécession des Wei, 524–534," Appendix no. 1 to *Le Traité économique du Souei chou* (Leiden: E. J. Brill, 1953), pp. 241–250. This work is also carried in *T'oung pao*, no. 42, 1954.

of Rites. Mainland historians consider this revolt the center
of the "people's war" prior to the overthrow of the Sui, a
distinction which then passed to Tou Chien-te's group. In
the Huai River area, a strong rebel force led by Tu Fu-wei
represented the southern flank of the "peasant armies." After
the defeat of the Sui, according to mainland historians, the
military aristocrats Li Yuan and Li Shih-min were able to use
and divert the force of the peasant wars to found the T'ang.
Several of the peasant rebellions, however, notably that led
by Tou Chien-te and his successor Liu Hei-ta, held out until
624.[20] Because of the upper-class origins of Li Mi and other
Sui rebel leaders and because of the complexities of the Marxist approach to disruptions which occur at the beginning of
renewed historical development, as was the case after the
founding of the T'ang, there has been considerable discussion
of these two problems in mainland interpretations of the Sui
peasant revolts.[21]

[20] The fullest Western treatment of the fall of the Sui and founding
of the T'ang is contained in Woodbridge Bingham, *The Founding of
the T'ang Dynasty: The Fall of Sui and Rise of T'ang, a Preliminary
Survey* (Baltimore: The Waverly Press, 1941). For the fullest com-
munist account of the Sui revolts see Ch'i Hsia, *Sui-mou Nung-min
Ch'i-yi* (Late Sui Peasant Uprisings) (Shanghai: Hua-tung Jen-min
Ch'u-pan She, 1954); and Ch'i Hsia, "On Several Problems in the Late
Sui Peasant Uprisings," *LKP*, pp. 97–118.

[21] For the discussions of the role played by Li Mi, see articles listed
in *SSP* bibliography, p. 533; Chao Li-sheng and Kao Chao-yi, *op. cit.*,
pp. 68 ff.; Sun Tso-min, *Chung-kuo Nung-min Chan-cheng Wen-t'i
T'an-su*, pp. 93–95; and Fang Jo-sheng, "On the Historical Function of
Li Mi," in *Chung-kuo Li-shih Jen-wu Lun-ts'ung* (Discussions on Chinese Historical Figures), Li Kuang-pi and Ch'ien Chün-hua (eds.)
(Peking: San-lien Shu-tien, 1957), pp. 82 ff. For a discussion of distinctions between the upper-class anti-Sui "Ch'i-ping" and the anti-Sui
"peasant uprisings" see Ch'en Kuo-tsan, "The Class Contradictions of
Sui Society and Their Relations with the Characteristics of the Late
Sui Peasant Uprisings," *KMJP*, July 9, 1959; and Kao Min, "On
Several Problems About the Late Sui Landlord Revolts," *KMJP*, August
6, 1959.

THE LATE T'ANG REVOLTS

The great rebellion led by Wang Hsien-chih and Huang Ch'ao (874–84) was preceded by the revolts of Ch'iu Fu, who led an estimated 30,000 vagrants and farmers against government tax policies in eastern Chekiang in 859 and 860,[22] and by that of P'ang Hsun, whose soldiers' mutiny allegedly transformed into a "peasant revolt" involving 100,000 people in the Hsüchow area in 869.[23] Although Wang Hsien-chih and Huang Ch'ao were fairly wealthy salt smugglers and Huang Ch'ao had several times attempted to pass the government examinations, Wang and Huang were, according to communist accounts, well suited to the leadership of a "people's war" against the decadent and oppressive Late T'ang. This was because their illegal activities and organization provided a nucleus for the disaffected peasants in the Shantung-Honan-Hopeh border area, who had been hard hit by government policies, drought, and floods.

The two leaders joined forces in revolt in 875, but then split the following year. According to the communists, Wang's wish to accept a government offer alienated the more class-conscious Huang Ch'ao, but, in fact, their dissension was due to Huang's own ambitions and feelings of neglect. Roaming their separate ways over much of the north China plain, Wang was killed in 878, and Huang Ch'ao moved south across the Yangtze, first to Fuchow and then to Canton in 879. There he attempted to bargain with the government for a post, and when that failed, he reportedly perpetrated a great slaughter of Arabic, Jewish, and Chinese merchants.

Returning to the north with plans to overthrow the corrupt T'ang and with an army said to have increased after earlier setbacks to 600,000 men, Huang Ch'ao took Loyang

[22] See Teng Kuang-ming, "A Tentative Discussion of the Late T'ang Peasant Uprisings," *LKP*, pp. 124–25.

[23] See *ibid.*, pp. 125–27; and Fu Chu-yü, "P'ang Hsun's Uprising in the Late T'ang," *SHYK*, no. 8, 1959.

and the capital, Ch'ang-an, in 881. The T'ang court, helped by Turkish mercenaries and because of rebel mistakes and desertions, was able to drive Huang Ch'ao out of the capital, briefly in 881 and for good in 883.[24]

However, the T'ang never really recovered from the rebellion. Some two decades after the defeat and death of Huang Ch'ao in 884, one of his former lieutenants, Chu Wen, was able to finish off the T'ang, to which he had earlier defected, and to found the first of the ephemeral "five dynasties." [25]

The rebellion of Huang Ch'ao understandably receives much attention both in the West [26] and in the communist world.[27] In Chinese communist historiography, its position as an example of a traditionally scorned but obviously important and allegedly "just" rebellion and its place in the transitional period between early and late feudalism make it especially important.

[24] Debates over the actions and popularity of the rebels in Ch'ang-an are especially numerous in communist historiography. See Chapter 6.

[25] The evaluation of Chu Wen is disputed because of his earlier contributions to the rebellion but ultimate betrayal of Huang Ch'ao; see Yang Chih-chiu, "The Great Uprising of Huang Ch'ao," in *LKP*, p. 151; and Hu Ju-lei, "On the Question of the Evaluation of Chu Wen," *KMJP*, September 17, 1959.

[26] See Howard Levy, *Biography of Huang Ch'ao* (Berkeley: University of California Press, 1961); Wolfram Eberhard, *Conquerors and Rulers: Social Forces in Medieval China* (Leiden: E. J. Brill, 1952), pp. 54 ff.; and Wang Gung-wu, *The Structure of Power in North China During the Five Dynasties* (Kuala Lumpur: University of Malaya Press, 1963), pp. 13 ff.

[27] For a leading Soviet account, see V. Rubin, "The Campaigns of Huang Ch'ao," in L. V. Simonovskaya (ed.), *Sbornik Statei po Istorii Stran Dalnego Vostoka* (Collected Articles on the History of Countries of the Far East) (Moscow: Moscow University, 1952). For a recent mainland account, see Lin Hua-ch'ing, *Huang Ch'ao* (Shanghai: Jen-min Ch'u-pan She, 1962). See also Howard Levy's criticisms of several earlier accounts in *JAS*, vol. 16, 1957, pp. 612–17.

REVOLTS OF THE SUNG PERIOD

The revolts of the Sung period are important in communist historiography more for the alleged advances in their ideology than for their size or impact on Sung political history. Mainland historians argue that the egalitarian slogans proposed by some of the Sung rebels revealed and reflected economic and social developments accompanying the transition to later Chinese feudalism.[28] The most important Sung revolts—according to one article there were over sixty,[29] and according to a looser reckoning, over 200 in the Southern Sung alone[30]—were those led by Wang Hsiao-po and Li Hsun in Szechwan, 993–95,[31] by Fang La in Fukien and Chekiang, 1120–22,[32] and by Chung Hsiang and Yang Yao in the area

[28] See Chapters 6, 7, and 8. A useful compendium of source materials for the three Sung revolts elaborated on here has recently appeared on the mainland. See Su Chin-yuan and Li Ch'un-p'u (eds.), *Sung-tai San-tzu Nung-min Ch'i-yi Shih-liao Hui-pien* (Collection of Sources on the Three Sung Peasant Uprisings) (Peking: Chung-hua Shu-chü, 1963).

[29] Kuan Lu-ch'üan, "On the Peasant Wars of the Two Sung," *LSYC*, no. 2, 1962.

[30] Hua Shan, "The Great Peasant Revolt in Kiangsi, Fukien, and Kwangtung in the Shao-ting, Tuan-p'ing Period (1228–1236) of the Southern Sung," *Wen Shih Che* (hereafter *WSC*), no. 3, 1956.

[31] A well-known scholar of the Republican period discussed this uprising. See Chang Yin-lin, "The Revolt of Wang Hsiao-po and Li Hsun in Szechwan, 993–5: An Unsuccessful Communist Movement," *Ch'ing-hua Hsueh-pao*, vol. 12, no. 2, 1937, pp. 315–35. This interpretation, which is quite close to current mainland interpretations, is disputed, paradoxically, by a scholar from communist East Germany who maintains that Wang Hsiao-po led a Szechwan independence movement against the Sung rather than a class struggle of the peasants against the landlords. See Werner Eichhorn, "Toward a History of the Uprising of Wang Hsiao-po and Li Hsun in Szechwan, 993–995," *Zeitschrift für Deutschen Morgenlandischen Gesellschaft*, vol. 105, 1955, pp. 192–209. Wu Han stressed both the social and separatist political factors in a brief essay published in 1946. See Wu Han, "Two Egalitarian Movements During the Sung," in *Li-shih te Ching-tzu* (The Mirror of History) (Shanghai: Sheng-huo Shu-tien, 1946), pp. 69–73. For a current mainland account see Yang Wei-min and Jen Shu-ming, "The Uprising of Wang Hsiao-po and Li Hsun in Early Northern Sung," *LKP*, pp. 154–66. See also *LSYC* 1958, no. 5.

[32] There has been a recent noncommunist study of this rebellion. See

around Tung T'ing lake in Hunan and Hupeh, 1130–35.[33]

In all of these revolts the leaders were men of some wealth[34] who utilized secret or religious societies and proposed popular programs calling for greater social justice. The usual social and political tensions were exacerbated in the case of the first by friction between the inhabitants of Szechwan and the Sung administrators, and in the case of the last two by the incursions of the Jurchen and by Sung policies toward the northern nomads. Accordingly, the uprisings of Fang La and of Chung Hsiang as well as some other Sung revolts[35] allegedly demonstrate the patriotic feelings as well as the resistance to oppression of the Chinese peasantry. Fang La's revolt is also noted for its connections with Buddhism and Manicheism and for the great loss of life caused by its disruptions and pacification.[36] The skirmishes (c. 1120) involving the "bandits" of Liang Shan Po, Shantung, the subject of the famous novel *Shui-hu Chuan*, are considered more in terms of later legends than for their intrinsic importance. Among other controversies concerning them is the question of their submission to the Sung and their subsequent part in the bloody suppression of Fang La's rebellion.[37]

Kao Yü-kung, "A Study of the Fang La Rebellion," unpublished Harvard University dissertation, 1962; and Kao Yü-kung, "The Fang La Rebellion," *HJAS*, vol. 24, 1962–63. See also Vincent Shih, "Some Chinese Rebel Ideologies," pp. 173–85. For a communist account see Ch'ien Chün-hua and Ch'i Hsia, "Fang La's Uprising," *LKP*, pp. 186–205; and Hsing Yueh, "The 'Ming Chiao' and Peasant Uprisings of the Sung Dynasty," (*LSCH*), no. 6, 1959, pp. 39–42.

[33] There are no Western studies of this revolt. For a Soviet account, see G. Ya. Smolin, *Krestyanskoye Vostaniye v Provintsiakh Hunan i Hupeh v 1130–1135* (The Peasant Uprising in the Provinces of Hunan and Hupeh in 1130–1135) (Moscow: Izdatelstvo vostochnoi literatury, 1961); and G. Ya. Smolin, "Peasant Uprising Under the Leadership of Chung Hsiang and Yang Yao," *Problemy Vostokovedeniye*, no. 1, 1960. For a mainland account see Teng-Kuang-ming, "Discussing the Uprising of Chung Hsiang and Yang Yao, *LKP*, pp. 205–15.

[34] See Muramatsu, *op. cit.*, p. 259.

[35] E.g., that of Li Ch'üan and Li T'an, who fought both the Sung and Jurchen in a rebellion in Shantung, 1205–62.

[36] Some traditional sources spoke of three million dead in the wake of Fang La's rebellion. See Kao Yü-kung, *HJAS*, vol. 24, 1963, p. 81.

[37] See Chang Cheng-liang, "An Investigation into Sung Chiang," *LKP*, pp. 167–85.

THE ANTI-MONGOL REVOLTS

In the fourteenth century the incidence of popular unrest reached a new high in China,[38] and it is generally recognized that the Mongol Yuan dynasty was overthrown by the force of the mass revolts which engulfed the country after about 1350. Communists historians seek to distinguish these revolts according to their social and racial content. They consider the early (1351–c. 1358) White Lotus revolts led by P'eng Ying-yü and then by Liu Fu-t'ung and Ni Wen-chun of the eastern and western wings of the movement, respectively, to have been class wars of the peasantry directed against social and economic exploitation by both native and Mongol landlords. Some later White Lotus leaders[39] as well as Fang Kuo-chen, Chang Shih-ch'eng, Kuo Tzu-hsing, and the Ming founder Chu Yuan-chang are considered to have been or to have become representatives of the landlord class in a national struggle against the Mongols. In other words, according to the communists, the latter group, and Chu in particular, were leaders of a "just" patriotic war but not of a still more progressive struggle for social justice, as were the earlier uprisings. After about 1358–60, class struggle against the landlords transformed into a national and racial struggle against the Mongols.[40]

[38] According to Chien Po-tsan (*Li-shih Wen-t'i Lun-ts'ung* [Collected Discussions of Problems in History] [Peking: Jen-min Ch'u-pan She, 1962], p. 113) there were more than 400 revolts in the 100 years of the Yuan dynasty, while another source speaks of up to 300 revolts in Shantung province alone. See L. V. Simonovskaya (ed.), *Ocherki Istorii Kitaya* (Outline History of China) (Moscow: Gosizdat, 1956), pp. 88–89. See also Wu Han, "The Uprising of the Red Army in the late Yuan," *HCS*, no. 11, 1954. See F. W. Mote, *The Poet Kao Ch'i* (Princeton: Princeton University Press, 1962), pp. 8 ff.; and Shih, "Some Chinese Rebel Ideologies," pp. 188–201, for leading Western accounts of some of these revolts.

[39] After 1360 Ming Yü-chen was perhaps the most "progressive" rebel leader. See Shih, *op. cit.*, pp. 200–201.

[40] For examples of this prevailing communist interpretation, see Tu Lieh-yuan, "On the Nature, Development and Two Stages of the Late Yuan Revolutionary Struggles," *Hsi-pei Ta-hsueh Hsueh-pao* (Journal

Because of the alleged peasant background but subsequent landlord affiliations of the Ming founder,[41] there has been considerable discussion of the proper evaluation of Chu Yuan-chang in mainland historiography. The earlier interpretation that Chu had "sold out" the peasant class[42] gave way to a more favorable evaluation in the mid-1950s,[43] but recently the emphasis has returned to the negative aspects of Chu's actions.[44] Other questions of great concern in the Chinese communist historiography of the Yuan revolts are their relations with the White Lotus and Maitreya sects of Buddhism.[45]

---

of Northwest University), no. 3, 1957, pp. 107–27; Lai Chia-tu, "A Tentative Discussion of the Great Uprising Led by Liu Fu-t'ung Against the Yuan," *LKP*, pp. 216–26; Yeh Fen, "Tentative Discussion of Ch'en Yü-liang," *KMJP*, August 14, 1963, p. 4; and L. A. Borovkova, "The Uprising of the Red Troops and the Rise of Chu Yuan-chang," *NAA*, no. 2, 1961, pp. 89–103. Some independent scholars before 1949 also distinguished an earlier social stage in the anti-Mongol revolts. See Meng Ssu-ming, "The Yuan Dynasty Social Class System," *Yen-ching Hsueh-pao* (Journal of Yenching University), no. 16, 1938; and Wang Ch'ung-wu, "On Ming T'ai-tsu's Revolt and the Changes in his Policies," *Chung-yang Yen-chiu Yuan* (Academia Sinica), no. 10, 1948.

[41] However, a recent Western study shows that Chu Yuan-chang's closest associates remained old peasant rebel comrades. See Romeyn Taylor, "Social and Political Origins of the Ming Dynasty," unpublished University of Chicago dissertation, 1960, pp. 60 ff.

[42] For instance, Wu Han, "How My Political Studies and Thought Progressed," *Tsai-Ch'ien-chin te Tao-lu-shang* (On the Road Ahead) (Peking: Ch'ing-nien Ch'u-pan She, 1950), p. 86; and *Chu Yuan-chang Chuan* (Biography of Chu Yuan-chang) (Peking: San-lien Shu-tien, 1949), pp. 136 and 140, compared Chu to Chiang Kai-shek in their "selling out" the revolution. See also Wang Tan-ts'en, *Chung-kuo Nung-min Ke-ming Shih-hua* (Talks on the History of the Chinese Peasant Revolution) (Shanghai: Kuo-chi Wen-hua Fu-wu She, 1952), pp. 247–91.

[43] E.g., Wang Ch'ung-wu "The Development and Transformation of the Late Yuan Peasant Revolt and Its Historical Significance," *LSYC*, no. 4, 1954, pp. 105–7.

[44] See Hsueh-shu Tung-t'ai column, "The Question of the Evaluation of Chu Yuan-chang," *KMJP*, March 20, 1959. Nor do Western students agree on the evaluation of Chu-Yuan-chang. See F. W. Mote, "The Growth of Chinese Despotism," *Oriens Extremus*, August 1961, especially pp. 20 ff. and p. 31; and also Mote, *The Poet Kao Ch'i*, pp. 166–167.

[45] E.g., see Chien Po-tsan, "The Anti-Tartar struggle of the Chinese People in the Yuan Dynasty," in *Chung-kuo Shih Lun-chi*, vol. 1, pp. 138–63.

THE REVOLTS OF THE
MIDDLE MING PERIOD

Some of the many revolts of the Ming receive special attention because of their alleged relation to the economic changes of "declining feudalism." Prior to the criticisms in the late 1950s of the stress on the existence of "roots of capitalism" in medieval China, leading historians described certain revolts of "miners" and "townsmen" during the fifteenth, sixteenth, and seventeenth centuries as "forerunners" of the modern Chinese workers' movement.[46] There was even speculation on the possibility of the later Ming peasant wars having led the transition to capitalism if the Manchus and then the "imperialists" had not intervened.[47] Because of the sensitivity of the periodization of modern history, however, in recent years these views have seldom been expressed, although historians continue to discuss various characteristics of an alleged seventy-seven revolts by miners and workers during the Ming.[48]

In addition there is discussion of the revolts led by T'ang Sai-erh (1420–21) in Shantung;[49] by Yeh Tsung-liu (1442–49) and Teng Mou-ch'i (1447–49) in Fukien, Chekiang, and Kiangsi;[50] by Huang Hsiao-yang in Kwangtung in the 1450s;[51]

[46] E.g., see Fan Wen-lan, *Chung-kuo T'ung-shih Chien-pien* (1961 edition), Preface, vol. 1, pp. 22–23. Hou Wai-lu and Shang Yüeh were among others sharing this view. See "On the Discussion of Problems of the Roots of Capitalism," *HCS*, 1956, no. 6, p. 64. See also Chapter 6.

[47] E.g., see Ch'i Hsia, "On the Question of the Nature of the Chinese Peasant Wars," *SSP*, p. 73; and Chao Li-sheng and Kao Chao-yi, *op. cit.*, p. 153.

[48] Li Lung-ch'ien, "A Tentative Discussion of the Resistance Struggles of the Ming Miners' Movements," *SHYK*, no. 3, 1959, p. 33. Liu Yen ("Early Urban Movements Following the Development of Urban Economy in Late Ming," *LSYC*, no. 6, 1955) discusses twenty-six revolts of the period 1596–1628.

[49] This revolt and many others of the Ming period are discussed in the last three chapters of Chao Li-sheng and Kao Chao-yi, *op. cit.*, pp. 128 ff. For a traditional account of some of these revolts, see Chao Yi, *Nien-erh Shih Cha-chi* (Notes on the Twenty-two Histories) (Taipei: Shih-chieh Shu-chü, 1958 reprint), chüan 36.

[50] Li Lung-ch'ien, "The Events and Characteristics of the Revolts of

by Liu T'ung (1464–65) and Li Yuan (1470–71) in Hupeh;[52] by Liu Liu and Liu Ch'i in north China from Hopeh to the Yangtze (1510–12);[53] and by some household slaves in the Wan Li period and at the end of the dynasty.[54]

THE REVOLTS OF THE LATE MING AND EARLY CH'ING (1627–45)

The great revolts affecting ten provinces of north China during the last seventeen years of the Ming also reflected the crisis of declining feudalism, according to mainland histori-

Yeh Tsung-liu and Teng Mou-ch'i in the Ming, Cheng-t'ung Period," *LKP*, pp. 227–51. Chao Li-sheng and Kao Chao-yi (*op. cit.*, p. 152) consider that these revolts marked the first social crisis of the Ming period, and the revolts of the early sixteenth the second. The Japanese scholar Miyazaki Ichisada ("Peasant Riots in Chinese History with Special Reference to the Affair of Teng Mou-ch'i," *Toyoshi Kenkyu*, vol. 10, no. 1, 1947) agrees that the revolt of Teng Mou-ch'i was a class-conscious revolt of peasants and workers against abuses of the time.

[51] P'eng Yi-lo, "The Social Background and Events of the Revolt of Huang Hsiao-yang in Canton in the Mid-Ming," *SHYK*, no. 10, 1957; and Hsu Hsu, "On Several Questions in the Revolt of Huang Hsiao-yang," *SHYK*, no. 11, 1958.

[52] Lai Chia-tu, *Ming-tai Yun-yang Nung-min Ch'i-yi* (Peasant Revolt at Yun-yang in the Ming Dynasty) (Wuhan: Hupeh Jen-min Ch'u-pan She, 1956); and Lai Chia-tu, "The Revolt of the Vagrants Led by Liu-T'ung and Li Yuan in Ching Hsiang Mountains in the Mid-Ming," *LKP*, pp. 252–66.

[53] Mu Hsuan, "Reminiscences of Liu Ch'i Amid Storm and Wave," *Hsin-hua Jih-pao* (Nanking), August 19, 1956; and Li Kuang-pi, "The Great Peasant Uprising of Liu Liu and Liu Ch'i in the Middle Ming," *LKP*, pp. 267–87, and Chao Li-sheng and Kao Chao-yi, *op. cit.*, pp. 134 ff.

[54] Hsieh Kuo-chen wrote an early article on the Ming slave revolts, terming them "class movements." See Hsieh Kuo-chen, "Investigations into the Ming Slave Revolts," in *Ming-ch'ing chih Chi Tang-she Yun-tung K'ao*. Among other senior historians, Wu Han has also written on the subject. See Wu Han, *Teng-hsia chi* (Collections Under Lamplight) (Peking: San-lien Shu-tien, 1960), pp. 76–83. For a recent mainland account see Chin Yi-tien, "Discussing the Ming Household Slaves from the Point of View of the Late Ming Slave Revolts in South China," *KMJP*, October 9, 1963. For a noncommunist account, see Saeki Yuichi, "On a Mass Movement at the End of the Ming," *Toyoshi Kenkyu*, vol. 16, no. 1, 1957, pp. 26–57.

ans. As with the earlier Ming revolts, however, this feature is not stressed lest it impinge on the prevailing theory of the intrusion of imperialism and the transition to a semi-colonial, semi-feudal society in the nineteenth century.[55]

The late Ming revolts originated in Shensi, Shansi, and Kansu as early as 1627 with as many as thirty-six separate and ten major "vagrant bandit gangs." Following a series of ups and downs, temporary surrenders, and renewed outbursts over much of north, central, and west China,[56] the rebels gradually coalesced into two groups under Chang Hsien-chung and Li Tzu-ch'eng.

Chang Hsien-chung, the son of a farmer and cloth dealer, was a rebellious youth who deserted the Ming army to become one of the leading commanders of the "disorganized raiding" of the 1630s and the leading rival of Li Tzu-ch'eng as well as of the Ming after 1643.[57] Following the ravaging of much of north and central China, Chang invaded Szechwan

[55] Liao-ning Ta-hsueh Li-shih hsi (Liaoning University History Department), "Criticize the Mistaken Viewpoint of Shang Yüeh on Rural Class Relations and Peasant Wars of the Ming-Ch'ing Period," *KMJP*, July 21, 1960; and Jung Sheng, "Tentative Discussion of Some Characteristics of the Peasant Class Struggles of the Ming and Ch'ing," *SSP*, pp. 1–24.

[56] The most complete account of these revolts in a noncommunist source is contained in James Parsons, "The Rebellion of Chang Hsien-chung as an Example of the Internal Disturbances in China During the Late Ming Dynasty," unpublished University of California doctoral dissertation, 1954; and Li Wen-chih, *Wan-ming Min-pien* (People's Revolts of the Late Ming) (Shanghai: Chung-hua Shu-chü, 1948). For leading communist sources see L. V. Simonovskaya, *Velikaya Krestyanskaya Voina v Kitai*, 1628–1645 (Great Peasant War in China) (Moscow: Uchpedgiz, 1958); and articles in *LKP* and in Li Kuang-pi (ed.), *Ming-Ch'ing Shih Lun-ts'ung*. Source materials for the Ming period are contained in Cheng T'ien-t'ing and Sun Yüeh (eds.), *Mingmou Nung-min Ch'i-yi Shih-liao* (Source Materials on the Late Ming Peasant Uprisings) (Shanghai: Chung-hua Shu-chü, 1954).

[57] James Parsons, "The Culmination of a Chinese Peasant Rebellion: Chang Hsien-chung in Szechwan, 1644–46," *JAS*, May 1957, together with Parsons' dissertation, cited above, provide most of the information given here on Chang Hsien-chung. For some communist accounts see Hsieh Kuo-chen, "Chang Hsien-chung and the Peasant Uprising," *LSCH*, February 1952, pp. 10 ff.; and Sun Tz'u-chou, "Investigation of the Record of Chang Hsien-chung, in Szechwan," *LSYC*, no. 1, 1957, pp. 47–57.

in 1644 with perhaps 100,000 men and established an infamous government in Chengtu. There his harsh policies prior to collapse and defeat by the Manchus—according to one tradition he killed 600 million people—constitute a dilemma for communist as well as noncommunist historians.[58] Some senior mainland historians condemned Chang unequivocally for his brutalities,[59] but recently there have been attacks on such "continuations of traditional slanders" of the righteous revolt of Chang Hsien-chung.[60] Several Jesuit observers noted the early popularity of Chang Hsien-chung, and a leading Western student of the revolt relates occasions when the rebels distributed some of their booty to the poor as well as other constructive acts. He concluded that Chang's army was "not just a disorganized rabble. Rather even from the limited amount of information available, it is apparent that they had definite organization, disciplinary regulations, and methods of operation." [61]

Li Tzu-ch'eng, the son of a prosperous farmer, was born in northeast Shensi not far from Yenan. He, too, joined the Ming army after a row with some local gentry, only to desert and join his maternal uncle in banditry in the northwest mountains. By 1635 he was one of the more prominent rebel leaders,[62] but by 1639 the fortunes of Li and the other rebels

[58] See Parsons, "The Culmination of a Chinese Peasant Rebellion," pp. 395–96.

[59] E.g., Lü Chen-yü, *Chien-ming Chung-kuo T'ung-shih* (A Simplified General History of China) (Peking: Jen-min Ch'u-pan She, 1961, 2 vols.), vol. 2, pp. 844–47.

[60] Chou Ku-cheng was so accused. See Chao Ch'eng-te and Ho Ch'un-liang, *op. cit.*, KMJP, November 10, 1958. For communist criticisms and refutations of traditional slanders of Chang Hsien-chung, see Sun Tz'u-chou, *op. cit.*, LSYC, no. 1, 1957; Ch'en Teng-yuan, "Chang Hsien-chung," *Shensi Jih-pao*, June 2, 1957 (this article was also carried in *Hsi-pei Ta-hsueh Hsueh-pao*, no. 3, 1957), and "The Birth of a Graduation Thesis," JMJP, August 26, 1962.

[61] Parsons, dissertation, p. 242. For the Jesuit account and reports of rebel generosity see *ibid.*, pp. 18, 122, 147, and 154. See also *ibid.*, p. 173, and Parsons, "Attitudes Toward the Late Ming Rebellions," *Oriens Extremus*, December 1959.

[62] Other leaders were Kao Ying-hsiang, then the senior commander, the Moslem Ma Shou-ying, and Lo Ju-ts'ai, who was killed by Li Tzu-ch'eng in 1643.

had sunk to a low ebb. Continuing natural disasters and Ming oppression, however, together with the recruitment of some literati and the formulation of an attractive program, enabled dramatic development of Li's forces after 1640. His support was concentrated in Honan and Hupeh, where he made his capital at Hsiangyang, returning periodically to the northwest. Li took Kaifeng in 1642, Sian in 1643, and moved on Peking in 1644 with an army said to number 400,000 men. The capital fell to the rebels in April 1644, ending two and a half centuries of Ming rule. Li's success was short-lived, and the rebels were driven from the capital by an alliance of Manchu and Chinese forces a month later. Li was defeated and killed in Hupeh in the spring of 1645.[63]

Problems of special consideration in the mainland historiography of the late Ming revolts include the egalitarian programs of the rebels and their behavior in Peking and elsewhere, the role of gentry advisers such as Li Yen,[64] and the way in which the rebellions demonstrated political strengths and weaknesses of the peasant class.[65] Finally, there is much discussion of the struggle against the Manchus for fifteen years after 1644, conducted by remnants of Chang Hsien-chung's forces under Li Ting-kuo, and of Li Tzu-ch'eng's army under Li Kuo. After 1644 the hostility between the Chinese people and the Manchus supposedly superseded temporarily the opposition between the peasants and the

[63] For a representative mainland account of Li Tzu-ch'eng see Li Wen-chih, "The Late Ming Peasant Revolutionary Leader, Li Tzu-ch'eng," in Li Kuang-pi and Ch'ien Chün-hua (eds.), *Chung-kuo Li-shih Jen-wu Lun-ts'ung*, pp. 99–129.

[64] E.g., Kuo Mo-jo, *Chia-shen-nien San-pai-nien-chi* (Commemoration of the 300th Anniversary of Chia Shen Year) (Peking: Jen-min Ch'u-pan She, 1954 reprint); and Ts'ao Kuei-lin, "On Li Yen," *LSYC*, no. 4, 1964.

[65] Sun Tso-min has stressed the negative side of the late Ming rebellions in articles in *KMJP*, August 1, 1957; *HCS*, no. 3, 1962; and *Che-hsueh Yen-chiu*, no. 4, 1964; as did Weng Heng-sheng, "Some Ideas on the Piece: 'The Entry of Li Tzu-ch'eng's Army into Peking,'" *KMJP*, October 13, 1960. The latter article was refuted by Chou Wei-min, "On Questions of Ch'uang Wang Entering Peking," *KMJP*, November 24, 1960; and Sun Tso-min has been criticized repeatedly for his slanders of the late Ming revolts.

landlords, although this interpretation is sometimes disputed.[66] In any case, according to mainland historians, the peasants were the "true patriots" and the vanguard of the struggle against the barbarian invader.

THE TAIPING REBELLION

The Taiping Rebellion was the greatest pre-modern mass movement in history, lasting for over fifteen years, devastating much of central and south China, and affecting the lives of many millions of people. At least ten million people are estimated to have lost their lives as a result of this holocaust. All modern Chinese nationalists and revolutionaries have placed great emphasis on the role of the Taipings, and, not unnaturally, the Chinese communists most of all.[67]

[66] E.g., see Liu Ta-nien, "On Emperor K'ang Hsi of the Ch'ing Dynasty," *URS*, vol. 24, no. 22, citing *LSYC*, no. 3, 1961; "Peking Municipal Society of History Holds Annual Meeting . . . ," *ECMM*, 308, citing *LSYC*, no. 1, 1962; and Yang Shu-sen, "On Discussion of the Nature of the Struggle after the Ch'ing Government Entered the Passes," *Min-tzu T'uan-chieh* (Minority Unity), January 6, 1962.

[67] For the most comprehensive non-communist bibliography of works on the Taiping, see Teng Ssu-yü, *Historiography of the T'ai-p'ing Rebellion* (Cambridge: Harvard University Press, 1962). For non-communist interpretations, see Vincent Shih, "Interpretations of the T'ai-p'ings by non-Communist Writers," *Far Eastern Quarterly*, May 1951, pp. 248–257. The leading English accounts of the Taipings, are Franz Michael, *The Taiping Rebellion* and Vincent Shih, *The Taiping Ideology*. For communist works, see Albert Feuerwerker and S. Cheng, *Chinese Communist Studies of Modern Chinese History*, pp. 78 ff. According to *SCMP* 2418, p. 14, citing *NCNA*, January 11, 1961, over sixty books and reference volumes in 6 million words and over 400 articles on the subject of the Taipings had been published on the mainland. For a partial collection and bibliography of these articles, see Ching Yen and Lin Yen-shu (eds.), *T'ai-p'ing T'ien-kuo Ke-ming Hsing-chih Wen-t'i T'ao-lun Chi* (Collected Articles on the Nature of the TPTK Revolution) (Peking: San-lien Shu-tien, 1961). See also Lo Erh-kang, "The Discovery, Editing, and Publication of Source Materials on the TPTK," *JMJP*, August 20, 1961. Chien Yu-wen, the leading noncommunist scholar of the Taipings has made a critique of Marxist interpretations of the revolt, "The Marxian Interpretation of the T'ai-p'ing T'ien-kuo," *Proceedings of the Second Biennial Conference of the International Association of Asian Historians* (Taipei, 1962).

Mainland historians consider the Taiping Rebellion to have marked the beginning of the "old democratic revolution" in China, although, as with other revolts in transitional periods, there are many inconsistencies and problems of periodization.[68] These center around the degree to which the Taipings were influenced by and influenced the development of capitalism in China and their relation to the intrusion of "imperialism." Despite the presence of these two new forces in mid-nineteeth-century China, most mainland historians consider internal class contradictions to have remained primary until the Boxer movement.[69]

The rebellion broke into the open at Chin-t'ien, Kwangsi, in January 1851, following several years of preparation and teaching based on Hung Hsiu-ch'üan's understanding of Christianity. The movement then swept northward until its army, traditionally said to have grown to well over a million men and women, took Nanking in 1853. From that time onward, however, the movement lost its momentum and soon degenerated with factional strife and corrupt practices. Able young generals extended Taiping power through much of the lower Yangtze valley, but a revitalized force of conservative Chinese and Manchus was able to take advantage of declining rebel morale and other weaknesses to crush the rebellion in 1864.[70]

[68] Supposedly, the "old democratic revolution" began with the Opium War, 1840, and the "new democratic revolution" lasted from 1919 to 1949.

[69] See Ching Yen and Lin Yen-shu (eds.), *T'ai-p'ing T'ien-kuo Ke-ming Hsing-chih Wen-t'i T'ao-lun Chi.* Following considerable discussion in the later 'fifties, the views of Kuo Yi-sheng (see *ibid.*, pp. 354 ff.) and others to the effect that the presence of significant numbers of urban workers and miners explained the high revolutionary consciousness of the Taipings have been rejected by most because of their implications for the periodization of modern Chinese history.

[70] The works of Lo Erh-kang have been particularly important on the mainland for the record of the Taiping movement. Fan Wen-lan's *Chung-kuo Chin-tai shih* (History of Modern China) (Peking: Jen-min Ch'u-pan She, 1961, first published in 1947) remains the most authoritative orthodox interpretation. Mou An-shih's *T'ai-p'ing T'ien-kuo* (Shanghai: Jen-min Ch'u-pan She, 1959) is one of the better recent accounts, while Shen Yuan, "Hung Hsiu-ch'uan and the TPTK Revolution," *LSYC*, no. 1, 1963, pp. 49–94, gives another recent interpretation.

The ideology and nature of the Taiping movement,[71] the role of key leaders, and relations with other secret society and minority revolts, as well as the problems associated with the periodization of Chinese history, are questions of particular concern in the mainland historiography of the Taiping Rebellion.

OTHER REVOLTS OF
THE CH'ING DYNASTY

Of an alleged 100 or more revolts other than the Taiping occurring in the Ch'ing period, those of the White Lotus, of the Miao and Moslem minorities, of the Nien, and of the Boxers are the most important. The White Lotus society of Buddhism was involved in many popular revolts from the Sung dynasty onward, especially in the Yuan and Ch'ing periods. From the 1770s White Lotus societies became extremely active in Honan, Shantung, and many provinces of north and west China. Their adherents joined a general revolt against oppressive social, religious, and political conditions in 1796, calling for the overthrow of the Ch'ing and restoration of the Ming dynasty. By 1799 perhaps 100,000 rebels were operating in scattered areas of five provinces of north and west China. Because of government corruption and inefficiency, they were not suppressed until five years later.[72]

See Chapter 5 for further discussion of Li Hsiu-Ch'eng and Taiping leaders.

[71] For documentation in English for the Taiping ideology see Michael, *op. cit.*, vols. 2 and 3; and J. C. Cheng, *Chinese Sources for the T'ai-p'ing Rebellion, 1850–1864* (Hong Kong: Hong Kong University Press, 1963). For leading noncommunist interpretations of Taiping ideology see Eugene P. Boardman, *Christian Influences upon the Ideology of the T'ai-p'ing Rebellion* (Madison: University of Wisconsin Press, 1952); Boardman, "Millenary Aspects of the T'ai-p'ing Rebellion," in Sylvia Thrupp (ed.), *Millennial Dreams in Action* (The Hague: Mouton, 1962); Vincent Shih, "The Ideology of the T'ai-p'ing T'ien-kuo," *Sinologica*, vol. 3, 1953; and Shih's *The Taiping Ideology.*

[72] For a comprehensive noncommunist study of the White Lotus

There were many revolts by the minority races of China during the Ch'ing, of which the most important were those of the Miao of Kweichow and Hunan in 1735–36, 1795–1806, and 1855–72,[73] of the Moslems in Kansu in the 1780s[74] and in both the southwest and northwest during the Taiping period.[75] The relation of the latter revolts to the Taiping movement receives particular attention in the mainland press. The Moslem rebellions in the northwest were also factors in the controversial revolt of Yakoob Beg and in the Nien movement.

Praise of the revolts of the minorities went to such extremes during the early 1950s that a leading historian felt compelled to warn that although "there was fighting by national minorities against the oppression of the dominant Han race, one cannot say that every time a national minority took up the sword to kill the Han, it meant [progressive] revolution." [76] Hence, some minority revolts, particularly if allegedly involved in "imperialist plots" such as that of Yakoob

---

uprising see Suzuki Chusei, *Shincho Chukishi Kenkyu* (A Study of Mid-Ch'ing History) (Toyohashi: Aichi University Research Institute, 1952). The author is indebted to the unpublished translation of this work by Harold Khan of the University of London. See also Columbia University doctoral dissertation (1967) by Richard Chu. For representative communist accounts, see Wang Chu-lou, "The Great White Lotus Uprising of 1796–1805," *LKP*, pp. 321–55; Yang K'uan, "Tentative Discussion of the Characteristics of the White Lotus Teaching," *KMJP*, March 15, 1961; Shao Hsun-cheng, "Secret Societies, Religion and the Peasant Wars," *SSP*, pp. 369–84; and E. B. Porshneva, "People's Uprising of 1796–1803," *Kratkiye Soobscheniye* (Brief Notices) (Moscow: Akademiya Nayk, 1962), no. 53.

[73] Ma Shao-ch'iao, *Ch'ing-tai Miao-min Ch'i-yi* (Miao Uprisings of the Ch'ing Dynasty) (Wuhan: Hupeh Jen-min Ch'u-pan She, 1956). For a discussion of the second of these uprisings, see Wang Chu-lou, "The Great Miao Uprising of 1795," in Li Kuang-pi (ed.), *Ming-Ch'ing Shih Lun-ts'ung*, pp. 247–63.

[74] Wang Chu-lou, "The Moslem People's Uprising of the 1780s," in *ibid.*, pp. 226–46.

[75] See Lin Kan (ed.), *Ch'ing-tai Hui-min Ch'i-yi* (Uprisings of the Moslems in the Ch'ing Dynasty) (Shanghai: Hsin-chih-shih Ch'u-pan She, 1957). For source materials on these uprisings see Pai Shou-yi, *Hui-min Ch'i-yi* (Shanghai: Shen-chou Kuo-kuang She, 1953). For a noncommunist reference, see Marshall Broomhall, *Islam in China: A Neglected Problem* (London: Morgan and Scott, 1910).

[76] Chien Po-tsan, in *HCS*, no. 3, 1959, as cited in *CNA* 326. Chien is himself of minority ancestry.

Beg in Turkestan in the 1870s, are now judged reactionary.[77]

Numerous revolts of secret societies in the nineteenth century are discussed in mainland historiography,[78] while the Nien and Boxer rebellions, which grew out of secret societies, are considered major "class wars." The Nien "bandits," or Nien army as it was later called, developed into a coordinated rebellion after 1851, following a half-century of isolated secret-society activities. At first centered in the Huai valley in northern Anhui, the Nien cavalry later roamed through much of north China, splitting into an eastern and a western wing in 1866 before being finally annihilated in 1868.

Both communist and noncommunist scholars consider the Nien to have been less politically conscious than the Taipings.[79] The communists attribute this relative "backwardness" to the wealth and secret-society status of early Nien

[77] See Ch'eng Su-lo, "The Reactionary Nature of the Uighur Rebel Movement and Yakoob Beg in Sinkiang in the Late Nineteenth Century," *LKP*, pp. 385–400. Some mainland historians praised Yakoob Beg for revolting against the Ch'ing until considerable attention to the role of the English in this rebellion forced the communists to term it a "reactionary movement." See Kuo Ying-te, "Correction of my Former Mistaken Approach to the Evaluation of Yakoob Beg," *KMJP*, June 21, 1956. A similar situation arose with some of the minority revolts of the southwest. E.g., see Hsueh-shu Tung-t'ai column, "Some Yunnan Historical Workers Propose a Different Evaluation of Tu Wen-hsiu," *JMJP*, October 14, 1961.

[78] Especially the uprising of the T'ien-li Chiao in north China, 1813 (see Hsiao Yu-min, "The Uprising of the T'ien-li Chiao in the Chia Ch'ing Reign of the Ch'ing," *LKP*, pp. 356–69) and the secret-society uprisings of the Taiping period in the cities of south and east China. See articles in *SHYK*, no. 2, 1958, and no. 9, 1959, for accounts of the Small Knife society revolts of 1853, and in *KMJP*, March 28, 1962, for consideration of the T'ien-ti hui leader Ch'en K'ai. See also Wang T'ien-chang, "The Secret Societies of the Latter Half of the Nineteenth Century," *LSYC*, no. 2, 1963. For documentation on these revolts see Feuerwerker and Cheng, *op. cit.*, pp. 97 ff.

[79] E.g., Teng Ssu-yü, *The Nien Army and Their Guerilla Warfare, 1851–1868* (Paris: Mouton and Co., 1961), pp. 113–14. Teng's book is the most recent and thorough study of the Nien. See also S. T. Chiang, *The Nien Rebellion* (Seattle: University of Washington Press, 1954). For a communist account, see Chiang Ti, *Nien-chün Shih Ch'u-T'an* (Preliminary Investigation of the History of the Nien Army) (Peking: San-lien Shu-tien, 1956). For documentation and other studies prepared on the Nien, see Feuerwerker and Cheng, *op. cit.*, pp. 97 ff.

leaders such as Chang Lo-hsing.[80] They also argue, however, that the Nien did have a more "progressive side," and that this was greatly increased after contact with the Taipings from 1853 onward and especially after absorption of many of the defeated Taipings, including Lai Wen-kuang, later the most prominent leader of the eastern wing of the Nien.[81] There is further discussion of the relations of the Nien with the Moslem revolt in the northwest[82] and with the revolt of Sung Ching-shih in Shantung.

The Boxer movement also had its roots in the White Lotus and other secret societies. From 1898 it rapidly gained strength in Shantung, Hopeh, and other areas of north China. Because of the reaction of the Ch'ing court to the threats of the Western powers on the one hand, and because the rebels were hard-pressed by the government forces on the other, an apparent understanding was reached in late 1899 and 1900 between the court and the formerly despised rebels.[83] In any case, by this date at the latest the rebellion was directed primarily into anti-Christian and anti-Western channels and led to the well-known occupation of Peking and

[80] E.g., Chiang Ti, *op. cit.*, pp. 14–15.

[81] There is much discussion of the periodization of the history of the Nien and of the relation of the Nien to the Taipings. Lo Erh-kang particularly stresses the closeness of the relationship between the later Nien struggles and the Taipings, although he does not deny an earlier history of the Nien independent of the Taipings as implied by Teng Ssu-yü (Preface to *The Nien Army and Their Guerrilla Warfare, 1851–1868, op. cit.*). See Lo Erh-kang, "The Real Name of the Nien Chün," *An-hui Shih-hsueh* (Anhui History Studies), no. 1, 1960; and Preface to *T'ai-p'ing T'ien-kuo Hsin-chün te Yun-tung chan* (The Mobile Warfare of the T'ai-p'ing New Army) (Shanghai: Shang-wu Yin-shu Kuan, 1955). This book was first published in 1939 as *Nien Chün te Yun-tung Chan* (The Mobile Warfare of the Nien Army). See also Chiang Ti, "On the Question of the Periodization of the History of the Nien Army," *KMJP*, July 5, 1956; and Chiang Ti, "The Relations of the Nien Uprising and the T'ai-p'ing T'ien-kuo," *LSYC*, no. 3, 1963.

[82] E.g., Lu Fang, "The United Anti-Ch'ing Struggle of the Western Nien Army and the Northwest Moslem Army," *SHYK*, no. 10, 1959, pp. 29–32.

[83] The latest noncommunist student of the Boxers supports this communist argument although of course with a different emphasis. See Victor Purcell, *The Boxer Uprising* (London: Cambridge University Press, 1963), pp. 173–222, especially pp. 183–84, 208 ff.

the allied relief expedition of 1900. According to the communists, the "anti-imperialist" content of the Boxer movement revealed the temporary ascendancy of the "contradiction against imperialism" over the "contradiction between the landlords and the peasants." Hence, mainland historians consider the Boxer rebellion the "last large-scale spontaneous peasant war in Chinese history" and also the "first large-scale people's resistance to imperialism." [84]

The struggle against the landlords and the Manchus continued, however, according to mainland historians, who point to the slogan "Wipe out the Ch'ing, destroy the foreigners" (*Sao-ch'ing Mieh-yang*), with which a 1902 uprising replaced the Boxer slogan "Uphold the Ch'ing, destroy the foreigner" (*Fu-ch'ing Mieh-yang*).[85] Actually, communist treatment of the Boxers has been marked by an unusual amount of diversity because of the obviously backward as well as anti-imperialist aspects of the movement. Communist leaders have moved from an early ambivalent criticism of the Boxers[86] to the present affirmation of both its "peasant class" and "anti-imperialist" content. Chou En-lai recently termed it "one of the cornerstones of the Chinese revolution." [87]

[84] Chien Po-tsan, "The Yi Ho-t'uan Movement," *LSCH*, no. 5, 1958, pp. 7–16.

[85] For a recent article on the significance of the 1902 slogan, see Ku Yi-chün, "On Several Problems Regarding Ching T'ing-pin's 'Wipe out the Ch'ing, Destroy the Foreigner' Revolt," *KMJP*, December 9, 1960.

[86] E.g., Ch'en Tu-hsiu's views, see Chapter 3.

[87] According to Shih Ssu-ch'ün, "On the Sixtieth Anniversary of the Yi Ho T'uan Anti-Imperialist Struggle," *LSYC*, no. 6, 1960, p. 13. For some representative communist treatments of the Boxers, see Chin Chia-jui, *Yi Ho T'uan Yun-tung* (The Boxer Movement) (Shanghai: Jen-min Ch'u-pan She, 1957); and Lin Shu-yü, "The Struggle of the Boxers in Chih-li," in *LKP*, pp. 401–15. For other communist sources and documentation, see Feuerwerker and Cheng, *op. cit.*, pp. 114 ff.

Abbreviations

CB	*Current Background*
CCP	Chinese Communist Party
CHYC	*Che-hsueh Yen-chiu*
CKCN(P)	*Chung-kuo Ch'ing-nien (Pao)*
CNA	*China News Analysis*
ECMM	*Extracts China Mainland Magazines*
FEQ	*Far Eastern Quarterly*
HCS	*Hsin Chien She*
HJAS	*Harvard Journal of Asiatic Studies*
JAS	*Journal of Asian Studies*
JMJP	*Jen-min Jih-pao*
JPRS	*Joint Publications Research Service*
KMJP	*Kuang-ming Jih-pao*
KMT	Kuomintang
LKP	Li Kuang-pi (ed.), *Chung-kuo Nung-min Ch'i-yi Lun-chi*
LSCH	*Li-shih Chiao-hsueh*
LSCHWT	*Li-shih Chiao-hsueh Wen-t'i*
LSYC	*Li-shih Yen-chiu*
MESW	Karl Marx and Frederick Engels, *Selected Works in Two Volumes*
NAA	*Narody Azii i Afriki*
PV	*Problemy Vostokovedeniye*
SCMM	*Selections China Mainland Magazines*
SCMP	*Survey China Mainland Press*
SHYK	*Shih-hsueh Yueh-k'an*
SSP	Shih Shao-pin (ed.), *Chung-kuo Feng-chien She-hui Nung-min Chan-cheng Wen-t'i T'ao-lun Chi*
SWMTT	*Selected Works of Mao Tse-tung*, New York edition, 1954, 4 vols.
SWMTT	(Peking Edition) *Selected Works of Mao Tse-tung*, Peking Edition, 1961, vol. 4.
TPTK	*T'ai-p'ing T'ien-kuo*

URS	Union Research Service
VI	Voprosy Istorii
WSC	Wen Shih Che

Bibliography

BIBLIOGRAPHIES AND REFERENCES

Bibliography of Asian Studies, published annually as a separate issue of *The Journal of Asian Studies*.

Ch'üan-kuo Chu-yao Pao-k'an Tzu-liao So-yin (Index to Important Periodicals of the Entire Country). Shanghai, 1955– .

Ch'üan-kuo Tsung Shu-mu (General Bibliography for the Entire Country). Peking: Hsin-hua Shu-tien, 1949– .

Chung-kuo Shih-hsueh Lun-wen So-yin (Index of Articles on Chinese Historical Studies). Peking: K'o-hsueh Ch'u-pan She, 1957.

Fairbank, John K., and Masataka Banno. *Japanese Studies of Modern China*. Rutland: C. E. Tuttle, 1955.

Feuerwerker, A., and S. Cheng. *Chinese Communist Studies of Modern Chinese History*. Cambridge: Harvard University Press, 1961.

Hua-tung Shih-fan, Ta-hsueh Li-shih Hsi, eds. *Chung-kuo Ku-tai chi Chung-shih-chi Shih Pao-k'an Lun-wen Tzu-liao So-yin* (Index to Periodical Literature for the Ancient and Medieval History of China). Shanghai, 1959.

Nunn, G. R. *Chinese Periodicals, International Holdings, 1949–1960*. Ann Arbor: Association for Asian Studies, 1961.

Referentsii Sbornik, Sovremennaya Kitaiskaya Literatura po Obshestvennym Naukam. Moscow: Fundamentalnaya Biblioteka Obshestvennyk Nauk, Akademiya Nauk. Mimeographed abstracts, issued quarterly 1953–55, and bimonthly thereafter.

Revue Bibliographique de Sinologie. Paris: Ecole Pratique des Hautes Etudes, University of Paris, 1955– .

Skachkov, P. E. *Bibliografia Kitaya*. Moscow: Izdatelstvo Vostochnoi Literatury, 1959. (See also the 1932 edition of this work.)

Sorich, Richard, ed. for United States Joint Publications Research

Service. *Contemporary China: A Bibliography.* New York: Joint Committee on Contemporary China, 1961.

Teng, Ssu-yü. *The Historiography of the Taiping Rebellion.* Cambridge: Harvard University Press, 1962.

——. *Japanese Studies on Japan and the Far East: A Short Biographical and Bibliographical Introduction.* Hong Kong: Hong Kong University Press, 1961.

Wang Chih-chiu and Sung Kuo-chu, eds. *Chung-hsueh Li-shih Chiao-shih Shou-ts'e* (Handbook for Middle School History Teachers). Shanghai: Shanghai Chiao-yü Ch'u-pan She, 1958.

BOOKS IN CHINESE AND JAPANESE

Ah Ying. *Li Ch'uang-wang* (The Dashing King Li [Tzu-ch'eng]). Shanghai: Hsin-hua Shu-tien, 1949.

Chang Ching-lu. *Chung-kuo Ch'u-pan Shih-liao Pu-pien* (Expanded Edition of Historical Materials on Chinese Publishing). Peking: Chung-hua Shu-chü, 1957.

Chang Hsiang-shan. *Jen-min Ch'ün-chung ho Ke-jen tsai Li-shih-shang te Tso-yung* (The Function of the Masses and the Individual in History). Peking: Ch'ing-nien Ch'u-pan She, 1954.

Chang Hsun-hui. *Chung-kuo Ku-tai Shih-chi Hsiao Tu-fa* (School Reader for Ancient Chinese Historical Sources). Peking: Chung-hua Shu-chü, 1962.

Chao Li-sheng and Kao Chao-yi. *Chung-kuo Nung-min Chan-cheng Shih Lun-wen Chi* (Collected Articles on Chinese Peasant Wars). Shanghai: Hsin Chih-shih Ch'u-pan She, 1955.

Chao Yi. *Nien-erh Shih Cha-chi* (Notes on the Twenty-two Histories). Taipei: Shih-chieh Shu-chü, 1958 (reprint).

Ch'en Hsü-lu. *Lun Li-shih Jen-wu P'ing-chia Wen-t'i* (A Discussion of the Problem of the Evaluation of Personages in History). Shanghai: Hsin Chih-shih Ch'u-pan She, 1956.

Ch'en Kung-po. *Chung-kuo Li-shih-shang te Ke-ming* (Revolutions in Chinese History). Shanghai: Fu-tan Shu-tien, 1928.

Ch'en Pai-ch'en. *Sung Ching-shih Li-shih Tiao-ch'a Chi* (Record of the Investigation into the History of Sung Ching-shih). Peking: Jen-min Ch'u-pan She, 1957.

Ch'en Shou. *San-kuo Chih* (Record of the Three Kingdoms). Peking: Chung-hua Shu-chü, 1959 (reprint).

Ch'en Ta. *Jen-k'ou Wen-t'i* (The Population Problem). Shanghai: Shang-wu Yin-shu Kuan, 1935.

Cheng T'ien-t'ing and Sun Yueh, eds. *Ming-mou Nung-min Ch'i-yi Shih-liao* (Source Materials on the Late Ming Peasant Uprisings). Shanghai: Chung-hua Shu-chü, 1954.

Ch'i Hsia. *Sui-mou Nung-min Ch'i-yi* (The Late Sui Peasant Uprisings). Shanghai: Hua-tung Jen-min Ch'u-pan She, 1954.

Ch'i Hsia *et al. Ch'in-Han Nung-min Chan-cheng Shih* (History of the Peasant Wars of the Ch'in and Han). Peking: San-lien Shu-tien, 1962.

Chiang Chung-cheng Ch'üan-chi (Collected Works of Chiang K'ai-shek), 2 vols. Shanghai: Min-tzu Ch'u-pan She, 1937.

Chiang K'ai-shek. *Lu-shan Hsün-lien Chi* (Collected Training Speeches at Lu Shan). N.p., vol. 1, 1933–34.

Chiang Meng-lin. *T'u-ti Wen-t'i yu Jen-k'ou* (The Land Problem and Population). Taipei, 1954.

Chiang Ti. *Nien-chün Shih Ch'u-t'an* (Preliminary Investigation into the History of the Nien Army). Peking: San-lien Shu-tien, 1956.

Chiao-yü Tzu-liao She, ed. *Hsueh-hsiao-chung te Ai-kuo Chu-yi Chiao-yü* (The Education of Patriotism in the Schools). Peking: Jen-min Ch'u-pan She, 1951.

Chien Po-tsan. *Chung-kuo Shih-kang* (Outline of Chinese History), 2 vols. Shanghai: Sheng-huo Shu-tien, 1946.

——. *Chung-kuo Shih Lun-chi* (Collected Essays on Chinese History), 2 vols. Shanghai: Kuo-chi Wen-hua Fu-wu She, 1947.

——. *Li-shih Wen-t'i Lun-ts'ung* (Collected Discussions of Problems in History). Peking: Jen-min Ch'u-pan She, 1962.

Chien Yu-wen. *T'ai-p'ing T'ien-kuo Ch'üan-shih* (Complete History of the TPTK), 2 vols. Hong Kong: Chien-shih Meng-chin Shu-shih, 1962.

Ch'ien Mu. *Kuo-shih Hsin-lun* (New Discussions of the National History). Kowloon: Ch'iu-ching Yin-wu, 1955.

——. *Kuo-shih Ta-kang* (Outline of National History). Shanghai: Shang-wu Yin-shu Kuan, 1944.

Ch'ih-fei Fan-tung Wen-chien Hui-pien (Collected Documents on the Reactionary Red Bandits). Nanking, 1935.

Chin Chia-jui. *Yi Ho T'uan Yun-tung* (The Boxer Movement). Shanghai: Jen-min Ch'u-pan She, 1957.

Chin Yü-fu. *Chung-kuo Shih-hsueh-shih* (History of Chinese Historiography). Peking: Chung-hua Shu-chu, 1962 (revised edition).

Ching Chih. *Chung-kuo Li-shih* (Chinese History). Shanghai: Tu-shu Sheng-kuo Ch'u-pan She, 1939.

Ching Yen and Lin Yen-shu, eds. *T'ai-p'ing T'ien-kuo Ke-ming Hsing-chih Wen-t'i T'ao-lun Chi* (Collected Articles on the

Nature of the TPTK Revolution). Peking: San-lien Shu-tien, 1961.

Ch'ing Ju-chi. *Mei-Kuo Ch'in-hua Shih* (History of American Aggression Against China). Peking: Jen-min Ch'pan She 1962– , several vols.

Chou Ku-ch'eng. *Chung-kuo T'ung-shih* (General History of China), 2 vols. Shanghai: K'ai-ming Shu-tien, 1936.

Chu Hsi. *T'ung-chien Kang-mu* (Outline and Digest for the General Mirror). N.p., n.d.

Chuang Wei. *Chung-kuo Nung-min Ch'i-yi te Ku-shih* (Stories of the Chinese Peasant Uprisings). Shanghai: Hua-tung Jen-min Ch'u-pan She, 1952.

Chung-hsueh Chiao-hsueh Tsan-K'ao Tzu-liao (Reference Materials for High School Education). Tientsin: T'ienchin Chiao-yü She, 1950.

Chung-hua Jen-min Kung-ho-kuo Kao-teng Chiao-yü-pu, eds. *K'ai-hsueh Chih-tao* (Guide for Beginning School). Peking, 1957.

Chung-kuo Ch'ing-nien Ch'u-pan She, eds. *Mei-ti-kuo Chu-yi Ch'in-hua Tsui-hsing Lu* (Record of the Heinous Activities of American Imperialist Aggression Against China). Peking, 1965.

Chung-kuo Jen-min Ta-hsueh, Chung-kuo Li-shih Chiao Yen Shih, eds. (Chinese History Teaching and Research Section of China's People's University). *Chung-kuo Tzu-pen Chu-i Meng-ya Wen-t'i T'ao Lun Chi* (Collected Essays on the Problems Relating to the Roots of Chinese Capitalism). Peking: K'o-hsueh Ch'u-pan She, 1959.

Fan Ti-jui. *Chung-kuo Ku-tai Nung-min Yun-tung* (Peasant Movements in Ancient China). Shanghai, 1938.

Fan Wen-lan. *Chung-kuo Chin-tai Shih* (History of Modern China), 2 vols. Peking: Jen-min Ch'u-pan She, 1961 (revised edition).

——. *Chung-kuo T'ung-shih Chien-pien* (A Simple General History of China), 2 vols. Shanghai: Hsin Chih-shih Shu-tien, 1947. See also: Peking: Jen-min Ch'u-pan She, 1961 (revised edition).

——. *TPTK Ke-ming Yun-tung.* Hong Kong: Hsin Min-chu Ch'u-pan She, 1948.

Feng Ting. *Kung-jen Chieh-chi te Li-shih Jen-wu* (Historical Tasks of the Working Class). Shanghai: Hua-tung Jen-min Ch'u-pan She, 1953.

Ho Kan-chih. *Chung-kuo Ch'i-meng Yun-tung Shih* (The History of China's Movement for Enlightenment). Shanghai: Sheng-huo Shu-tien, 1947.

Hou Wai-lu. *Su-lien Li-shih Hsueh-chieh Chu Lun-cheng*

Chieh-ta (Exposition of the Debates in Soviet Historical Circles). Shanghai: Chien-kuo Shu-tien, 1946.

—— (ed.). *Chung-kuo Li-tai Ta-t'ung Li-hsiang* (The Great Unity Ideal in Chinese History). Peking: K'o-hsueh Ch'u-pan She, 1959.

—— *et al.*, eds. *Chung-kuo Ssu-hsiang T'ung-shih* (A General History of Chinese Thought), 4 vols. Peking: Jen-min Ch'u-pan She, 1957–59.

Hsiao-hsueh Kao-nien-chi, Li-shih Chiao-hsueh Shou-ts'e (History-Teaching Handbook for Upper Elementary School). Shanghai: Shang-wu Yin-shu Kuan, 1951.

Hsiao Yi-shan. *Ch'ing-tai T'ung-shih* (General History of the Ch'ing Period), 5 vols. Taipei: Shang-wu Yin-shu Kuan, 1963.

Hsieh Kuo-chen, ed. *Ch'ing-ch'u Nung-min Ch'i-yi Tzu-liao Chi-lu* (Collected Materials on the Early Ch'ing Peasant Uprisings). Shanghai: Hsin Chih-shih Ch'u-pan She, 1956.

——. *Ming-Ch'ing chih Chi Tang-she Yun-tung K'ao* (Investigations of the Political Societies of the Ming-Ch'ing Period). Shanghai: Shang-wu Yin-shu Kuan, 1934.

Hsu T'e-li *et al.*, eds. *Lun Ai-kuo Chu-yi te Chiao-yü* (On the Education of Patriotism). Peking: Ch'un-ch'ung Shu-tien, 1951.

Hsueh Nung-shan. *Chung-kuo Nung-min Chan-cheng chih Shih te Yen-chiu* (Study of the History of Chinese Peasant Wars), vol. 1. Shanghai: Shen-chou Kuo-kuang She, 1933.

Hua Kang. *T'ai-p'ing T'ien-kuo Ke-ming Chan-cheng Shih* (History of the Taiping Revolutionary War). Shanghai: Hai-yen Shu-tien, 1949.

Jen Chieh. *Chung-kuo Nung-min Ke-ming Shih-hua* (Talks on the Chinese Peasant Revolutions). Peking: T'ung-su Tu-wu Ch'u-pan She, 1956.

Jung Meng-yuan. *Chung-kuo Chin-pai-nien Ke-ming Shih-lueh* (Brief History of the Chinese Revolution in the Last One Hundred Years). Peking: San-lien Shu-tien, 1954.

——. *Li-shih Jen-wu te P'ing-chia Wen-t'i* (The Problem of Evaluation of Historical Persons). Shanghai: Hua-tung Jen-min Ch'u-pan She, 1954.

Kao-chi Chung-hsueh K'o-pen Chung-kuo Li-shih (Upper-Level High School Text of Chinese History), 4 vols. Peking: Jen-min Ch'u-pan She, 1958.

K'o Tzu-chi (Kautsky). *Chieh-chi Cheng-tou* (Class Struggle), Yun Tai-ying, translator. Shanghai: Hsin Ch'ing Nien She, 1921.

Kung-tso T'ung-hsun ([Military] Work Bulletin), January–July 1961. Released by United States Department of State.

Kuo Chan-po. *Chin Wu-shih-nien Chung-kuo Ssu-hsiang Shih*
(History of the Last Fifty Years of Chinese Thought). Pe-
king: Jen-wen Shu-tien, 1936.
Kuo Mo-jo. *Chia-shen-nien San-pai-nien-chi* (Commemoration of
the Three-hundredth Anniversary of Chia-shen Year [1644]).
Peking: Jen-min Ch'u-pan She, 1954 (reprint).
———. *Chung-kuo Ku-tai She-hui Yen-chiu* (Research in Ancient
Chinese Society). Peking: K'o-hsueh Ch'u-pan She, 1960
(reprint).
———. *Kuo Mo-jo Hsuan-chi* (Selected Writings). Peking: K'ai-
ming Shu-tien, 1951.
Lai Chia-tu. *Ming-tai Yun-yang Nung-min Ch'i-yi* (Peasant Re-
volt at Yun-yang in the Ming Dynasty). Wuhan: Hupei
Jen-min Ch'u-pan She, 1956.
Lao Kan. *Ch'in Han Shih* (History of the Ch'in and Han). Tai-
pei: Chung-kuo Wen-hua Fu-wu She, 1952.
Li Chi, chief editor for Chung-kuo Li-shih Yen-chiu She. *Chung-
kuo Nei-luan Wai-huo Li-shih Ts'ung-shu* (Collected Books
on the History of China's Internal Disruptions and Foreign
Disasters), 36 vols. Shanghai: Shen-chou Kuo-kuang She,
1936–47.
Li Kuang-pi, ed. *Ming Ch'ing Shih Lun-ts'ung* (Collected Discussions on Ming-Ching History). Wuhan: Hupeh Jen-min
Ch'u-pan She, 1957.
Li Kuang-pi and Ch'ien Chün-hua, eds. *Chung-kuo Li-shih
Jen-wu Lun-ts'ung* (Compilation of Discussions on Chinese
Historical Figures). Peking: San-lien Shu-tien, 1957.
Li Kuang-pi, Ch'ien Chün-hua, and Lai Hsin-hsia, eds. *Chung-
kuo Nung-min Ch'i-yi Lun-chi* (Collected Discussions on
the Chinese Peasant Uprisings). Peking: San-lien Shu-tien,
1958 (reprint of a 1954 edition published by LSCH Yueh-
k'an She with the deletion and addition of several articles).
Li-shih Yen-chiu Pien-chi Pu (LSYC Editorial Department), eds.
Chung-kuo Ku-tai Fen-ch'i Wen-ti T'ao-lun Chi (Collected
Discussions on the Problem of Periodization of Ancient
China). Peking: San-lien Shu-tien, 1957.
———. *Chung-kuo Li-tai T'u-ti Chih-tu Wen-t'i T'ao-lun Chi*
(Collected Discussions on the Problem of China's Land
System Through the Ages). Peking: San-lien Shu-tien, 1957.
Li Shou-ch'ang (Li Ta-chao). *Shih-hsueh Yao-lun* (Discussion of
the Essentials of Historiography). Shanghai: Shang-wu Yin-
shu Kuan, 1924.
Li Ta. *Hsien-tai She-hui Hsueh* (Modern Sociology). Shanghai:
K'un-lun Shu-tien, 1929 (2d edition).
Li Ta-chao Hsuan-chi (Selected Works of Li Ta-chao). Peking:
Jen-min Ch'u-pan She, 1962.

Li Wen-chih. *Wan-ming Min-pien* (People's Revolts of the Late Ming). Shanghai: Chung-hua Shu-chu, 1948.

Lin Hua-ch'ing. *Huang Ch'ao*. Shanghai: Jen-min Ch'u-pan She, 1962.

Lin Kan. *Ch'ing-tai Hui-min Ch'i-yi* (Uprisings of the Moslems in the Ch'ing Dynasty). Shanghai: Hsin-chih-shih Ch'u-pan She, 1954.

Liu Chih-chi. *Shih T'ung* (Generalities on History). N.p., n.d.

Liu K'ai-yang. *Ch'in-mou Nung-min Chan-cheng Shih-lueh* (Brief History of the Late Ch'in Peasant War). Peking: Shang-wu Yin-shu Kuan, 1959.

Liu Ta-nien. *Mei-Kuo Ch'in-hua Shih* (History of American Aggression Against China). Peking: Jen-min Ch'u-pan She, 1951.

Lo Erh-kang. *Nien-chün te Yun-tung Chan* (The Mobile War of the Nien Army). Changsha: Shang-wu Yin-shu Kuan, 1939.

——. *T'ai-p'ing T'ien-kuo Hsin-chün te Yun-tung Chan* (The Mobile War of the TPTK New Army). Shanghai: Shang-wu Yin-shu Kuan, 1955.

——. *T'ai-p'ing T'ien-kuo Shih-kang* (Outline History of the TPTK). Shanghai: Shang-wu Yin-shu Kuan, 1937.

——. *T'ai-p'ing T'ien-kuo Shih-kao* (A Draft History of the TPTK). Peking: K'ai-ming Shu-tien, 1951.

——. *T'ai-p'ing T'ien-kuo Shih Shih-k'ao* (Investigation of Events in the History of the TPTK). Peking: San-lien Shu-tien, 1955.

Lü Chen-yü. *Chien-ming Chung-kuo T'ung-shih* (A Simplified General History of China). Peking: Jen-min Ch'u-pan She, 1961 (revised edition).

——. *Chung-kuo She-hui Shih Chu Wen-t'i* (Some Questions in the History of Chinese Society). Peking: San-lien Shu-tien, 1961 (First published, 1940).

——. *Shih Ch'ien-ch'i Chung-kuo She-hui Yen-chiu* (Researches into Chinese Society Before the Historical Period), 4 vols. Peiping: Jen-wen Shu-tien, 1934.

——. *Shih Lun-chi* (Discussions of History). Peking: San-lien Shu-tien, 1960.

Ma-k'o-ssu Chu-yi Ching-tien Tso-chia Lun Li-shih K'o-hsueh (Marxist Classic Writers on Historical Science). Peking: Jen-min Ch'u-pan She, 1962.

Ma-k'o-ssu En-ko-ssu Lun Chung-kuo (Marx and Engels on China). Peking: Jen-min Ch'u-pan She, 1957.

Ma Shao-ch'iao. *Ch'ing-tai Miao-min Ch'i-yi* (Mios Uprisings of the Ch'ing Dynasty). Wuhan: Hupeh Jen-min Ch'u-pan She, 1956.

Mao Tse-tung. *Hunan Nung-min Yun-tung K'ao-ch'ao Pao-kao*

(Report of an Investigation into the Peasant Movement in Hunan). Shanghai: Hsin-hua Shu-tien, 1949.

——. *Mao Tse-tung Hsuan-chi* (Selected Works of Mao Tse-tung). Mukden: Tung-pei Shu-tien, 1948.

Mou An-shih. *T'ai-p'ing T'ien-kuo* (The Heavenly Kingdom of Great Peace). Shanghai: Jen-min Ch'u-pan She, 1959.

Nan-k'ai Ta-hsueh, Li-shih Hsi, eds., *Chung-kuo Feng-chien She-hui T'u-ti So-yu Chih* (Landlolding Systems in Chinese Feudal Society). Peking: San-Lien Shu-tien, 1962.

Nieh Ch'ung-ch'i. *Erh-ch'ien-nien Lai Mi-hsin Chih T'uan* (Two Thousand Years of Secret Societies). N.p., n.d.

Pai Shou-yi. *Hui-min Ch'i-yi* (The Moslem Rebellions), 4 vols. Shanghai: Shen-chou Kuo-kuang She, 1953.

Pai T'ao. *Chung-kuo Nung-min Ch'i-yi te Ku-shih* (Stories of Chinese Peasant Revolts). Harbin: Kuang-hua Shu-tien, 1949.

Pan Ku. *Han Shu* (History of the Han).

Pei-ching Ta-hsueh Wen-hsueh Hsi (Peking University Literature Department), eds. *Chung-kuo Li-tai Nung-min Wen-t'i Wen-hsueh Tzu-liao* (Literary Materials on the Peasant Question in Chinese History). Peking: Chung-hua Shu-chü, 1959.

Shang Yueh. *Chung-kuo Li-shih Kang-yao* (Outline of Chinese History). Hong Kong: San-lien Shu-tien, 1957.

Shen Hui and P'an Hsia. *Ku-chin Liu-k'ou Ho-chuan* (Biographies of Ancient and Modern Bandits). Taipei: Shanghai Yin-shua-ch'ang, 1951.

Shen K'uo. *Meng-ch'i Pi-t'an* (Notes Taken at Meng Ch'i).

Shih-chieh T'ung-shih (General History of the World), 2 vols. E. M. Ju-ka-fu, ed., translated from the Russian edition published by Akademiia Nauk. Peking: San-lien Shu-tien, 1960.

Shih Shao-pin, ed. *Chung-kuo Feng-chien She-hui Nung-min Chan-cheng Wen-t'i T'ao-lun Chi* (Collected Articles on the Problem of Peasant Wars in Chinese Feudal Society). Peking: San-lien Shu-tien, 1962.

Ssu-ma Ch'ien. *Shih Chi* (Record of History). Peking: Ku-chi Ch'u-pan She, 1956 (reprint).

Ssu-ma Kuang. *Tzu-chih T'ung-chien* (Comprehensive Mirror for Self-Government), 10 vols. Peking: Ku-chi Ch'u-pan She, 1956 (reprint).

Su Chin-yuan and Li Ch'un-p'u, eds. *Sung-tai San-tzu Nung-min Ch'i-yi Shih-liao Hui-pien* (Collection of Sources on the Three Sung Peasant Uprisings). Peking: Chung-hua Shu-chü, 1963.

Sun Tso-min. *Chung-kuo Nung-min Chan-cheng Wen-t'i T'an-su*

(An Investigation into Problems of Chinese Peasant Wars).
Shanghai: Hsin Chih-shih Ch'u-pan She, 1956.

Sung Yang. *Chung-kuo Nung-min Ke-ming Yun-tung Shih-hua*
(Talks on the History of the Chinese Peasant Revolutionary
Movements). Tientsin: Tu-che Shu-tien, 1949.

Suzuki Chusei. *Shincho Chukishi Kenkyu* (A Study of Mid-
Ch'ing History). Toyohashi: Aichi University Research Institute,
1952.

Taiping T'ien-kuo Ke-ming Yun-tung Lun-wen Chi (Articles on
the Taiping Revolutionary Movement). Peking: San-lien
Shu-tien, 1950.

T'an Pi-t'ao. *Wai-kuo Shih K'o-pen* (Text of the History of Foreign Countries). Shanghai: K'ai-ming Shu-tien, 1950.

T'ao Hsi-sheng. *Chung-kuo She-hui chih Shih te Fen-hsi* (Analysis of History of Chinese Society). Shanghai: Hsin Sheng-
ming Shu-chü, 1929.

———. *Chung-kuo She-hui Hsien-hsiang Shih-ling* (Collected Miscellany on Chinese Social Phenomena). Shanghai: Hsin
Sheng-ming Shu-chü, 1931.

———. *Chung-kuo She-hui yü Chung-kuo Ke-ming* (Chinese Society and Revolution). Shanghai: Hsin Sheng-ming Shu-
chü, 1929.

Teng Yun-t'e (Teng T'o). *Chung-kuo Chiu-huang Shih* (History
of Chinese Disaster Relief). Shanghai: Shang-wu Yin-shu
Kuan, 1937.

*Ti-yi-tzu Kuo-nei Ke-ming Chan-cheng Shih-ch'i te Nung-min
Yun-tung* (The Peasant Movement During the Period of
the First Revolutionary Civil War). Peking: Jen-min Ch'u-
pan She, 1953.

Tsai Ch'ien-chin te Tao-lu-shang (On the Road Ahead). Peking:
Ch'ing-nien Ch'u-pan She, 1950.

Ts'ai Hsueh-ts'un. *Chung-kuo Li-shih-shang te Nung-min Chan-
cheng* (The Peasant Wars in Chinese History). Shanghai:
Ya-tung Shu-tien, 1933.

Tung Chia-tsun. *Chung-kuo Nu-li She-hui Shih* (History of Chinese Slave Society). Canton: She-hui Hsueh-she, 1955.

Wang Chih-chiu. *Kao-chi Chung-hsueh K'o-pen Shih-chieh Ku-
tai Shih* (Advanced High School Text of World History).
Peking: Jen-min Ch'u-pan She, 1954.

Wang Chung-ming, ed. *Chung-kuo Nung-min Wen-t'i yü Nung-
min Yun-tung* (The Chinese Peasant Question and the
Peasant Movement). Shanghai: P'ing-fan Shu-chu, 1929.

Wang Chung-ying. *Kuan-yü Chung-kuo Nu-li She-hui te Wa-
chieh chi Feng-chien Kuan-hsi te Hsing-ch'eng Wen-t'i* (On
the Problem of the Breakup of Chinese Slave Society and

the Formation of Feudal Relations). Wuhan: Hupeh Jen-min Ch'u-pan She, 1957.

Wang Tan-ts'en. *Chung-kuo Nung-min Ke-ming Shih-hua* (Talks on the History of the Chinese Peasant Revolutions). Shang-hai: Kuo-chi Wen-hua Fu-wu She, 1952.

Weng Ta-tsao. *Huang Ch'ao Lun* (On Huang Ch'ao). Shanghai: Shang-wu Yin-shu Kuan, 1950.

Wu Ch'uan-ch'i. *Kuo-tu Shih-ch'i te Chieh-chi yü Chieh-chi Tou-cheng* (Classes and Class Struggle in Past Times). Peking: Jen-min Ch'u-pan She, 1955.

Wu Han. *Chu Yuan-chang Chuan* (Biography of Chu Yuan-chang). Peking: San-lien Shu-tien, 1949 (Published earlier as *Ming T'ai-tsu*, Chungking: Shong-li Ch'u-pan She, 1944).

——, ed. *Chung-kuo Li-shih Hsiao Ts'ung-shu* (Little Chinese History Library). Peking: Chung-hua Shu-chü, 1958 *et seq.*

——. *Hai Jui Pa-kuan* (The Dismissal of Hai Jui). Peking: Pei-ching Ch'u-pan She, 1961.

——. *Li-shih te Ching-tzu* (The Mirror of History). Shanghai: Sheng-kuo Shu-tien, 1946.

——. *Teng-hsia Chi* (Collections Under Lamplight). Peking: San-lien Shu-tien, 1960.

—— *et al. Tsen-yang Kai-tsao* (How to Reform). Hong Kong: Ho-tso Shu-tien, 1950.

Wu Hsun yü Wu Hsun Chuan P'i-p'an (Criticism of Wu Hsun and of the Biography of Wu Hsun). Canton: Hua-nan Jen-min Ch'u-pan She, n.d. (c. 1952).

Wu Su-chih. *Lu-lin-chün Ch'i-yi te Ku-shih* (Stories of the Up-rising of the Green Forest Army). Wuhan: Ch'un-yi T'ang, 1956.

Wu Yü-chang. *Chung-kuo Li-shih Chiao Ch'eng-hsü Lun* (Dis-cussion of the Processes of Teaching Chinese History). Shanghai: Hsin-hua Shu-tien, 1950.

Yang Jung-kuo. *Chien-ming Chung-kuo Ssu-hsiang Shih* (Simpli-fied History of Chinese Thought). Peking: Chung-kuo Ch'ing-nien Ch'u-pan She, 1962.

Yeh Ch'ing. *Chieh-chi Tou-cheng Lun P'i-p'an* (Critique of the Theory of Class Struggle). Taipei: Po-mi-erh Shu-tien, 1952.

Yeh Huo-sheng. *Ming-mou Nung-min Ch'i-yi-chün Lien-ming K'ang-man Hsiao-shih* (A Small History of the Late Ming Peasant Rebel Army and Its Fight with the Ming Against the Ch'ing). Peking: Jen-min Ch'u-pan Shih, 1951.

Yuan Ting-chi. *Chang Hsien-chung*. Peking, 1963.

ARTICLES IN CHINESE

In order to keep an already bulky bibliography in hand, the titles of articles in Chinese are given in English translation only, the journal indicating the language consulted. Titles of books and journals are given in transliteration from the original with English translations.

An Ming. "Resolutely Hit the Sabotaging Activities of Reactionary Taoist Sects," *SCMP* 1092, citing *JMJP*, July 7, 1955.

"Anhui University History Department Holds Discussion of Chinese Peasant Wars," *KMJP*, April 3, 1961.

"The Anti-British Corps and the Sheng-p'ing Study Society," *CKCNP*, February 17, 1956.

"The Anti-Party, Anti-Socialism, Anti-Marxism Political Thought and Academic Viewpoint of Comrade Wu Han," *JMJP*, April 10, 1966.

Chang Cheng-liang. "An Investigation into Sung Chiang," *LKP*.

Chang Ch'i-chih. "Is It Historical Materialism or Subjective Idealism?" *CHYC*, no. 5, 1964.

Chang Heng-shou. "A Tentative Discussion of the Nature of Society in Han Times," *LSYC*, September 1957.

Chang Pao-kuang *et al.* "The Problem of Vagabondism in the History of the Chinese Peasant Wars," *SSP*.

Chang Pin. "Some Ideas on the Book *Chung-kuo Nung-min Chan-cheng Wen-t'i T'an-su*," *KMJP*, March 17, 1958.

Chang Shih-te and Wu T'ing-tung. "The Special Characteristics of Chung Hsiang and Yang Yao's Peasant Revolt," *LSCHWT*, 1958, no. 3 (March).

Chang Yi-tun. "Discussing the Peasant Uprising Led by Sun En and Lu Hsun," *LKP*.

Chang Yin-lin. "The Revolt of Wang Hsiao-po and Li Hsun in Szechwan, 993–95: An Unsuccessful Communist Movement," *Ch'ing-hua Hsueh-pao* (Tsinghua Journal), vol. 12, no. 2, 1937.

Chang Yu-lin. "The Method of Marxist Class Analysis and Historicism," *LSYC*, no. 3, 1963.

Chao Ch'eng-te. "Criticize Mr. Chou Ku-ch'eng's *General History*," *KMJP*, November 10, 1958.

Chao Hsi-yen *et al.* "Criticize Several Mistaken Views on the Historical Function of Chinese Peasant Wars in [Sun Tso-min's Book] . . . *T'an-su*," *SSP*.

Chao Li-shang. "Some Ideas on the Section of Chung-kuo Li-shih Kang-yao Devoted to the Peasant Wars," *WSC*, no. 3, 1955.

Ch'en Ch'ang-yuan. "Several Questions About Sun Tso-min's *Chung-kuo Nung-min Chan-cheng Wen-t'i T'an-su*," *WSC*, no. 11, 1958.

Ch'en Chia-cheng and Lung Te-yü. "On the Relation Between the Ancient Chinese Peasant Wars and the 'Four Authorities,' " *SSP*.

Ch'en Hsueh-wen. "Problems in the Historical Viewpoint and Methodology of the *TPTK Shih-kao*," *KMJP*, February 19, 1959.

Ch'en Kuo-tsan. "The Class Contradictions of Sui Society and Their Relations with the Characteristics of the Late Sui Peasant Uprisings," *KMJP*, July 9, 1959.

Ch'en Pai-chen. "Peasant Revolutionary Hero Sung Ching-shih and His Black Flag Army," *JMJP*, July 24, 1952.

Ch'en Teng-yuan. "Chang Hsien-chung," *Shensi Jih-pao*, June 2, 1957. (This article was also carried in *Hsi-pei Ta-hsueh Hsueh-pao*, no. 3, 1957.)

Ch'en Tu-hsiu. "Basic Differences in the Ideas of Oriental and Occidental Peoples," *Hsing Ch'ing Nien*, vol. 1, no. 4, 1915.

———. "Our Two Mistaken Views of the Yi Ho T'uan," *Hsiang-tao Chou-pao*, no. 81, September 3, 1924.

Cheng Feng-hsin. "The Nature of T'ang Yu-chih's Revolt," *KMJP*, December 4, 1963.

Cheng T'ien-t'ing. "Professors' Views in Respect of 'Contention of Diverse Schools of Thought,' " *URS*, vol. 7, no. 20, citing *JMJP*, April 21 and 22, 1957.

Ch'eng Su-lo. "The Reactionary Nature of the Uighur Rebel Movement and Yakoob Beg in Sinkiang in the Late Nineteenth Century," *LKP*.

Chi Cheng-te. "The Collection and Editing of Traditional Stories of the Nien," *JMJP*, September 15, 1960.

Chi Chien. "The Relation of the Late Sui Peasant Uprisings with T'ang T'ai-tsung's 'chen kuan' Government," *KMJP*, May 30, 1953.

Chi Tun-yü. "Is the Theory of Two Types of Revolution Economic Determinism?" *CHYC*, no. 5, 1964.

Chi Wen-fu. "Profoundly and Thoroughly Observe the Viewpoint of the Class Struggle in Historical Research," *SCMP* 2500, citing *KMJP*, April 28, 1961.

Ch'i Hsia. "On the Question of the Nature of the Chinese Peasant Wars," *SSP*.

———. "On Several Problems in the Late Sui Peasant Uprisings," *LKP*.

——. "Regarding Research on the History of Our Country's Peasant Wars," *JMJP*, December 4, 1956.

Ch'i Li-huang. "On the Double Nature of 'Peasant Government' in Chinese Feudal Society and Its Necessary Transformation into a Feudal Government," *LSYC*, no. 3, 1962.

Ch'i Lung-wei. "Discussing Current Prejudices in Research on the History of the T'ai-p'ing T'ien-kuo," *KMJP*, May 23, 1957.

——. "From the Inscription on [a Taiping Relic] Discussing the Prejudice in the Present Research Work on the TPTK," *KMJP*, May 23, 1957.

——. "The Spirit of Anti-Imperialism and Patriotism of the TPTK," *KMJP*, January 5, 1961.

Ch'i Pen-yü *et al.* "Comrade Chien Po-tsan's Historical Views Must Be Criticized," *JMJP*, March 25, 1966.

——. "Criticize Li Hsiu-ch'eng's Autobiography," *LSYC*, no. 4, 1963.

——. "How Shall We Treat Li Hsiu-ch'eng's Treacherous Surrender?" *LSYC*, no. 4, 1964.

——. "Study History for the Sake of Revolution," *SCMM* 506, citing *Hung Ch'i*, no. 13, December 1965.

Ch'i Ssu-ho. "A Criticism of Modern Chinese Historiography," *Ta Chung*, vol. 1, 1946.

Chiang Ti. "On the Question of the Periodization of the History of the Nien Army," *KMJP*, July 5, 1956.

——. "The Relations of the Nien Uprising and the T'ai-p'ing T'ien-kuo," *LSYC*, no. 3, 1963.

Chiang Yi-jen. "Regarding Several Questions in the Sung Peasant Revolt Led by Wang Hsiao-po, Li Hsun, and Chang Yu," *LSYC*, no. 5, 1958.

Chien Po-tsan. "Discussion of China's Ancient Peasant Wars," in Chien Po-tsan, *Li-shih Wen-t'i Lun-ts'ung.*

——. "On the Question of Overthrowing the Dynastic System of History," *KMJP*, March 28, 1959.

——. "Oppose the Restoration of Capitalist Class Social Science," *JMJP*, July 15, 1958.

——. "Regarding the Problem of Public and Private Slaves During the Two Han," *LSYC*, 1954, no. 4.

——. "Some Problems in Contemporary Historical Studies," *Hung Ch'i*, 1959, no. 10.

——. "Tentative Views on the Handling of Several Historical Problems," *KMJP*, December 22, 1961.

——. "The Yi Ho T'uan Movement," *LSCH*, no. 5, 1958.

Ch'ien Chün-hua and Ch'i Hsia. "Fang La's Uprising," *LKP.*

Chin Yi-tien. "Discussing the Ming Household Slaves from the

Point of View of the Late Ming Slave Revolts in South China," *KMJP*, October 9, 1963.

Chin Ying-hsi. "How Chou Ku-ch'eng Defends Ch'in Kuei, Favors Capitulation, and Calumniates Advocates of War," *SCMM* 439, citing *Hung Ch'i*, nos. 17–18, September 1964.

"Chinese Historians Meet in Peking in Commemoration of the 110th Anniversary of the Taiping," *SCMP* 2514, citing *JMJP*, May 31, 1961.

Ching Wu. "The Alliance of the Imperialist and Feudal Forces Which Ravaged China in the T'ai-p'ing Period," *KMJP*, May 12, 1955.

Chou Pao-chu. "Discussion of a Problem in the History of the Late T'ang Peasant War," *SHYK*, no. 6, 1959.

Chou Tzu-ch'iang. "The Class Struggle in the Transition Period Between Slavery and Feudalism in China," *LSYC*, nos. 5 and 6, 1964.

Chou Wei-min. "On Questions of Ch'uang Wang Entering Peking," *KMJP*, November 24, 1960.

Chou Yü-t'ung. "China's New Historiography of the Last Fifty Years," *Hsueh lin*, vol. 1, 1941.

Chu Ta-chün *et al.* "Criticism of the History of the Ch'in-Han Peasant Wars," *LSYC*, no. 4, 1963.

Chu Tso-yun. "Rightist Chao Li-sheng and the Struggle Between Two Roads over the Direction of Our Higher Education Policy," *WSC*, no. 6, 1958.

"Comrade Chien Po-tsan's Anti-Marxist Historical Viewpoint," *JMJP*, April 23, 1966.

"Departments of Szechwan Normal Institute and Chungshan University Eagerly Discuss the Question of the Center of World History," *SCMP* 2531, citing *KMJP*, May 7, 1961.

"The Differences and Connections Between Peasant Revolts and Wars," *Wen Hui Pao* (Shanghai) July 9, 1961.

"Discussion of Problems in the Peasant Wars in Our Country's Feudal Society," *KMJP*, June 20, 1962.

Fan Wen-lan. "Remember the One Hundred and Fifth Anniversary of the Revolt of the TPTK," *JMJP*, January 11, 1956.

Fang Chih-kuang *et al.* "Discussion of Several Problems in the History of the Peasant Wars in China's Feudal Society," *SSP*.

Feng Chih. "Did Fang La's Revolt Promulgate Slogans of Equality?" *KMJP*, September 29, 1960.

"The Form of Land Ownership Under Feudal Society in China," *SCMP* 2479, citing *KMJP*, March 11, 1961.

Fu Chu-yü. "P'ang Hsun's Uprising in the Late T'ang," *SHYK*, no. 8, 1959.

HCS, eds. "On the Questions of the Nature, Function and Distinguishing Characteristics of the Peasant Wars in Chinese History," *SSP*.

Ho Ch'ang-ch'ün. "On the Slogans of the Yellow Turban Peasant Uprising," *LSYC*, no. 6, 1959.

Ho Jo-chun. "Extirpate the Reactionary Capitalist Class Views of the Upper Level Modern Chinese History Text Edited by Sung Yun-piao," *SHYK*, no. 5, 1958.

Ho Kan-chih. "Problem of the Laws of Development of Feudal Society," *Shih-ti She-hui Lun-wen Chai-yao Yueh K'an* (Abstract Monthly), October 1936.

Ho Lin-t'ien. "How to Look on the Two Mistaken Traditions Concerning Huang Ch'ao and the Boxers," *Hsiao-hsueh Chiao-shih* (Elementary School Teacher), September 1954.

Ho Tzu-ch'uan. "Ch'in Shih-huang," *HCS*, no. 4, 1959.

Hou Wai-lu. "The Development of the Peasant Wars and Their Programs and Slogans in Early and Late Periods of China's Feudal Society," *SSP*.

———. "Historical Characteristics of the Peasant Wars of the T'ang and Sung," *HCS*, March 1964.

Hsiang Yang. "On Two Problems in the Chinese Revolutionary Wars," *KMJP*, no. 4, 1962.

Hsiao Shu. "The Peasant Question in the Socialist Revolution," *Peking Review*, no. 21, May 26, 1961.

Hsiao Yu-min. "The Uprising of the T'ien-li Chiao in the Chia Ch'ing Reign of the Ch'ing," *LKP*.

Hsieh Kuo-chen. "Chang Hsien-chung and the Peasant Uprising," *LSCH*, February 1952.

———. "Notes of Materials on the Function of the Late Ming and Early Ch'ing Peasant Revolts," *LSYC*, no. 3, 1962.

Hsieh T'ien-tso. "Tentative Discussion of the Nature of the Uprising of Sun En and Lu Hsun," *HCS*, no. 2, 1962.

Hsin Shih-hsueh, no. 8. "The Leading Opportunist and Traitor, Li Hsiu-ch'eng," *KMJP*, June 13, 1967.

Hsing Yueh. "The 'Ming Chiao' and Peasant Uprisings of the Sung Dynasty," *LSCH*, no. 6, 1959.

Hsiung Te-chi. "The Relationship of the Thought and Author of the Taiping Ching with the Yellow Turbans and the T'ienshih Tao," *LSYC*, no. 4, 1962.

Hsu Hsu. "On Several Questions in the Revolt of Huang Hsiaoyang," *SHYK*, no. 11, 1958.

Hsueh-shu Tung-t'ai column. "Chien Po-tsan Discusses the Problems of the Chinese Peasant Wars," *JMJP*, November 18, 1961.

———. "Discussion of Several Problems in the History of the Chinese Peasant Wars," *JMJP*, May 18, 1962.

——. "Historical Circles Discuss the Nature of the T'ai-p'ing Tao and the Yellow Turban Uprising," *JMJP*, December 15, 1960.

——. "Some Yunnan Historical Workers Propose a Different Evaluation of Tu Wen-hsiu," *JMJP*, October 14, 1961.

Hu Cheng-ssu. "The Changes in Class Relations and Major Contradictions at the Time of the Opium War," *LSCHWT*, no. 8, 1958.

Hu Ju-lei. "The Historical Function of the Late T'ang Peasant Wars," *LSYC*, no. 1, 1963.

——. "On the Question of the Evaluation of Chu Wen," *KMJP*, September 17, 1959.

Hua Shan. "The Great Peasant Revolt in Kiangsi, Fukien, and Kwangtung in the Shao-ting, Tuan-p'ing Period (1228–36) of the Southern Sung," *WSC*, no. 3, 1956.

Huang Yuan-ch'i. "The Spread and Development of Chinese Historical Science Under the Glorious Reflection of the October Socialist Revolution," *SHYK*, 1957, no. 11.

Hung Ch'i-hsiang. "America's First Aggressive Action Against the Chinese Revolution," *Ta Kung Pao* (Hong Kong), May 3, 1951.

Jen Chi-yü. "The Function of the Peasant Revolutionary Struggles for the History of Chinese Philosophy," *SSP*.

Jung Sheng. "Ideas on the Most Fundamental Difference Between Slaves and Serfs," *WSC*, no. 2, 1958.

——. Lung Sheng-yun and Ho Ling-hsiu. "Tentative Views on the Relation Between Peasant Wars and Religion in China," *SCMP* 2370 citing *JMJP*, October 17, 1960.

——. "Tentative Discussion of Some Special Characteristics of the Ming and Ch'ing Peasant Class Struggles," *SSP*.

Kao Min. "On Several Problems About the Late Sui Landlord Revolts," *KMJP*, August 6, 1959.

——. "A Tentative Discussion of the Question of the Stages of Development of the Peasant Uprisings and Wars in Our Country's Feudal Society," *SSP*.

Ku Ch'en. "The Role of Mass Power in History," *Hsin Sheng Ming* (New Life), vol. 3, no. 1, 1930.

Ku Feng. "Kuan Lu-ch'uan Discusses the Special Features of the Chinese Peasant Wars," *Nan-fang Jih-pao*, Canton, May 8, 1962.

Ku Yi-chun. "On Several Problems Regarding Ching T'ing-pin's 'Wipe Out the Ch'ing, Destroy the Foreigners' Revolt,'" *KMJP*, December 9, 1960.

Kuan Lu-ch'üan. "On the Peasant Wars of the Two Sung," *LSYC*, no. 2, 1962.

Kung P'eng-chiu. "Investigation into the Mobile Tactics of the Late Ming Peasant Army," *LSCH*, no. 3, 1959.

Kuo Jen-min. "Tentative Discussion of Several Problems in the Great Late Ch'in Peasant Revolt," *SHYK*, no. 7, 1958.

Kuo Mo-jo. "Genius and Hard Work," *SCMM* 323, citing *CKCN*, June 29, 1962.

——. Historical Studies in War-time China," VI, vols. 5–6, 1945.

——. "On Several Problems of Contemporary Historical Research," *HCS*, no. 4, 1959, and *KMJP*, April 8, 1959.

——. "The Processes of Historical Development of the Chinese Peasant Revolts," *SSP*.

Kuo Ying-te. "Correction of My Former Mistaken Approach to the Evaluation of Yakoob Beg," *KMJP*, June 21, 1956.

Lai Chia-tu. "The Peasant Uprising in the Southern Dynasties Led by T'ang Yü-chih," *LKP*.

——. "The Revolt of the Vagrants Led by Liu T'ung and Li Yuan in the Ching-hsiang Mountains in the Mid-Ming," *LKP*.

——. "A Tentative Discussion of the Great Uprising Led by Liu Fu-t'ung Against the Yuan," *LKP*.

Lai Hsin-hsia. "On the Peasant Revolt Led by Pai Lang in the Early Republic," *LKP*.

——. "A Tentative Discussion of the Great Peasant Revolt of the Late Kuang-hsu Reign in Kwangsi," *LKP*.

Li Chih-ch'in. "Expose and Criticize the Capitalist Class Reactionary Historical Viewpoint of Ch'en Teng-yuan in the Teaching of Ancient History," *Hsi-pei Ta-hsueh Hsueh-pao*, (Jen-wen K'o-hsueh), no. 1, 1958.

Li Kuang-pi. "The Great Peasant Uprising of Liu Liu and Liu Ch'i in the Middle Ming," *LKP*.

——. "The Taiping Tao of Han Times and the Yellow Turban Uprising," *LKP*.

Li Lung-ch'ien. "The Events and Characteristics of the Revolts of Yeh Tsung-liu and Teng Mou-ch'i in the Ming, Cheng-t'ung Period," *LKP*.

——. "A Tentative Discussion of the Resistance Struggles of the Ming Miners' Movements," *SHYK*, no. 3, 1959.

Li Shao-chung. "[The Slogan] 'Support the Ch'ing, Destroy the Foreigners' of the Yi-ho T'uan," *KMJP*, February 16, 1956.

Li Shih-yueh. "Anti-Christian Movements in the Thirty Years Before Chia-niu Year," *LSYC*, no. 6, 1958.

——. "Features of the Anti-Christian Struggle After the Boxer Movement," *KMJP*, July 9, 1959.

——. "On the Nature of the Yi-ho T'uan Movement and Its

Slogan 'Support the Ch'ing, Destroy the Foreigners,' "
KMJP, October 27, 1960.

——. "The Struggle Against 'Carving the Melon' of the People of Northeast China Before and After the Boxers," *SHYK*, no. 5, 1959.

Li Shu. "Comrade Mao Tse-tung's 'Reform Our Studies' and China's Science of History," *SCMP* 2546, citing *JMJP*, July 8, 1961.

Li Ta-chao. "Youth and the Village" (1919), in *Li Ta-chao Hsuan-chi* (Peking: Jen-min Ch'u-pan She, 1962).

Li T'ien-tso. "The Problem of the Special Characteristics of the Chinese Peasant Wars," *SSP*.

Li Ting-fang. "The Revolts of the Red Eyebrows and Green Forest [Army]," *LKP*.

Li Wei-han. "The Struggle for Proletarian Leadership in the New Democratic Revolution in China," *Peking Review*, February 23, 1962.

Li Wen-chih. "The Function of the Revolution of the TPTK in the Transformation of the Feudal Productive Relations," *KMJP*, January 16, 1961.

——. "The Late Ming Peasant Revolutionary Leader, Li Tzu-ch'eng," in Li Kuang-pi and Ch'ien Chün-hua, eds., *Chung-kuo Li-shih Jen-wu Lun-ts'ung*.

Li Yin-nung. "On How to Understand Chairman Mao Regarding the Function of the Peasant Revolts," *SSP*.

——. "On the Question of the Awareness of Feudal Governors of the Force of Peasant Revolutions," *Yang-ch'eng Wan-pao*, September 7, 1961.

Liang Jen-kan. "Religious Reform Was the Ideological Form of the Ancient and Medieval Class Struggles," *KMJP*, December 22, 1960.

Liang Tso-kan. "A Brief Discussion of the 'Dark and Chaotic Periods' in History," *KMJP*, August 16, 1956.

——. "Oppose Vulgar Interpretations of the Principle 'Class Struggle Is the Motive Force of Social Development,' "
KMJP, May 24, 1956.

Liang Yuan-tung. "The Forms of Struggle in Chinese History," *Shih Ti Shih* (Historical and Geographical Knowledge), vol. 5, no. 15, 1936.

Liao-ning Ta-hsueh Li-shih hsi (Liaoning University History Department). "Criticize the Mistaken Viewpoint of Shang Yueh on Rural Class Relations and Peasant Wars of the Ming-Ch'ing Period," *KMJP*, July 21, 1960.

——. "The Nature and Characteristics of the Chinese Peasant Wars," *SSP*.

Lin Piao. "Long Live the Victory of People's War," *Peking Review*, September 3, 1965.

Lin Shu-yü. "The Struggle of the Boxers in Chih-li," *LKP*.

Lin Yen-shu *et al.* "Regarding the Discussion of the Evaluation of Ts'ao Ts'ao," *SHYK*, no. 9, 1959.

Lin Yi-chou. "The Peasant Question in the Democratic Revolution," *Peking Review*, March 31, 1961, no. 13.

Liu Chih-chien. "A Brief Discussion of Selection and Use of Historical Materials," *KMJP*, August 6, 1959.

Liu Ch'üan. "A Tentative Discussion of the Question of the Goals of the Chinese Peasant Uprisings," *KMJP*, September 17, 1959.

Liu Chung-jih. "Doubts on the Doubts of the Late Ming Equal Field System," *LSYC*, no. 5, 1962.

Liu Shao-ch'i. "The Victory of Marxism-Leninism in China," *Peking Review*, October 1, 1959.

Liu Ta-nien. "On Emperor K'ang Hsi of the Ch'ing Dynasty," *URS*, vol. 24, no. 22, citing *LSYC*, no. 3, 1961.

———. "Historical Science in the New China," *LSYC*, 1962, no. 2.

———. "Present State of China's Historical Science," *KMJP*, July 22, 1953.

———. "What Did the Yi-ho T'uan Movement Show?" *SCMP* 2341, citing *JMJP*, August 30, 1960.

Liu Yao-t'ing *et al.* "The Development of Historical Science in the Light of Ten Years of Struggle on the Intellectual Front," *SHYK*, nos. 10 & 11, 1959.

Liu Yen. "Early Urban Movements Following the Development of Urban Economy in Late Ming," *LSYC*, no. 6, 1955.

Liu Yi-nan. "Criticize *Nan-Ming Shih-lueh*," *LSYC*, no. 9, 1958.

Lo Erh-kang. "Criticism of the Harms and Deceits of the Rightist Line in Science as Considered from the Point of View of Historical Studies," *KMJP*, August 28, 1957.

———. "The Discovery, Editing, and Publication of Source Materials on the TPTK," *JMJP*, August 20, 1961.

———. "Materials on the TPTK," *Wen-hui-pao* (Hong Kong) March 22, 1956.

———. "My Investigations in Writings on the History of the TPTK," *KMJP*, March 3, 1955.

———. "The Problem of Population Pressure Before the Revolution of the Taiping Heavenly Kingdom," *Chung-kuo She-hui Ching-chi Shih Chi-k'an* (Chinese Social and Economic History Review), vol. 8, no. 1, 1949.

———. "The Real Name of the Nien Chün," *An-hui Shih-hsueh*, no. 1, 1960.

Lu Fang. "The United Anti-Ch'ing Struggle of the Western

Nien Army and the Northwest Moslem Army," *SHYK*, no. 10, 1959.

Lü Chen-yü. "Historical Science Must Be Developed on the Basis of Comrade Mao Tse-tung's Thought," *LSYC*, no. 5, 1960.

———. "How to Study History," *CKCN*, October 6, 1961.

Lung Sheng-yun. "On the Land Policy of the TPTK," *LSYC*, no. 6, 1963.

———. "On the Question of Prejudice in Research Work on the History of the TPTK," *KMJP*, March 3, 1958.

Ma Chang-shou. "Eliminate the Influence of Capitalist Class Historiography on Our Historical Circles," *Hsi-pei Ta-hsueh Hsueh-pao* (Jen-wen K'o-hsueh) (Journal of Northwest University in the Humanities), no. 1, 1958.

Ma K'ai-liang. "An Example of a Capitalist Class Idealist Historical Outlook," *Jen-wen K'o-hsueh Tsa-chih* (Magazine of Human Sciences), no. 5, 1958.

(Mao) Jun-chih (Mao Tse-tung). "The Bitter Sufferings of the Peasants in Kiangsu and Chekiang," *Hsiang Tao Chou-pao*, no. 179, October 25, 1926.

Mao Tse-tung. "Introducing a Cooperative," *SCMP* 1784, citing *Hung Ch'i*, 1958, no. 1.

Meng Ssu-ming. "The Yuan Dynasty Social Class System," *Yenching Hsueh-pao* (Journal of Yenching University), no. 16, 1938.

Meng Ssu-yuan. "The Social and Class System of the Yuan," *Yen-ching Hsueh-pao* (Journal of Yenching University), no. 16, 1938.

Mu Hsuan. "Reminiscences of Liu Ch'i amid Storm and Wave," *Hsin-hua Jih-pao* (Nanking), August 19, 1956.

"Never Forget the Past," *SCMP* 3072, citing *Kung-jen Jih-pao*, September 8, 1963.

"New Conflict in Academic Ideology," *URS*, vol. 32, no. 25, September 24, 1963.

Ning K'o. "The Question of Monarchism in the History of the Chinese Peasant Wars," *SSP*.

———. "The Question of Spontaneity and Consciousness of the Chinese Peasant Wars," *SCMM* 311, citing *Hung Ch'i*, no. 7, April 1, 1962.

———. "Some Ideas on 'Correctly Evaluate the Function of Peasant Uprisings in Chinese History,' " *KMJP*, June 7, 1956.

"On the Discussion of Problems of the Roots of Capitalism," *HCS*, no. 6, 1956.

"The One Hundred and Tenth Anniversary of the TPTK in the Shanghai Press," *SCMP* 2420, citing NCNA (Shanghai) January 13, 1961.

"Opening of Discussion of Problems of Peasant Wars in Chinese

Feudal Society by Historical Circles," *KMJP*, September 20, 1960.

Pa Chin. "Writers' Courage and Sense of Responsibility," *SCMM* 323, citing *Shanghai Wen-hsueh*, no. 5, 1962.

Pai Shou-yi. "Aspects of Spring in the Historical Fields," *KMJP*, October 15, 1959.

——. "The Characteristics of the Peasant Wars in Chinese History," *HCS*, nos. 8 and 9, 1960.

——. "On the Nature of the Peasant Wars in Chinese Feudal Society," *SSP*.

——. "Special Characteristics of the Peasant Wars in Chinese History," *SSP*.

P'an Te-shen. "On the Function, Characteristics, and Nature of the Peasant Revolts and Wars in the Later Period of Chinese Feudal Society," *SSP*.

"Peking Municipal Society of History Holds Annual Meeting . . . ," *ECMM* 308, citing *LSYC*, no. 1, 1962.

P'eng Yi-lo. "The Social Background and Events of the Revolt of Huang Hsiao-yang in Canton in the Mid-Ming," *SHYK*, no. 10, 1957.

"Put Down the Rebellion in Tibet Thoroughly," *JMJP*, March 31, 1959.

"The Question of the Evaluation of Chu Yuan-chang," *KMJP*, March 20, 1959.

"Remember the Hundredth Anniversary of the Revolution of the TPTK," *JMJP*, January 11, 1951.

"Report of Investigation of Wu Hsun and His Contemporary Peasant Rebel Leader Sung Ching-shih," *JMJP*, July 24, 1951.

"Report on Kuangtung Historical Conference," *SCMP* 2514, citing *KMJP*, May 19, 1961.

"Shantung Historical Circles Discuss Problems of the Chinese Peasant Wars," *KMJP*, October 11, 1960.

Shao Hsun-cheng. "Secret Societies, Religion and the Peasant Wars," *SSP*.

Shih Hung-ping (Shih Shao-pin). "Use the Invincible Thought of Mao Tse-tung to Occupy the Battleground in Historic Studies," *KMJP*, May 30, 1967.

Shih Shao-pin. "On the Discussion of Problems in the Peasant Revolutionary Wars in Chinese Feudal Society," *SSP*.

——. "Resolutely Support the Direction of the Revolution in Historical Science," *JMJP*, March 27, 1966.

——. "Why Protect Wu Han," *JMJP*, June 3, 1966.

Shih Ssu-ch'ün. "On the Sixtieth Anniversary of the Yi Ho T'uan Anti-Imperialist Struggle," *LSYC*, no. 6, 1960 (Translated in *Political Information on Communist China*, no. 14, *JPRS* 8312).

Shih Tse. "On the Government of the TPTK Revolution," *KMJP*, June 17, 1964.

"Some Academic Problems Discussed at the Annual Meeting of the Kuang-t'ung History Society," *SCMP* 2446, citing *KMJP*, January 6, 1961.

"Some Problems in the History of the Peasant Wars," *KMJP*, November 7, 1961.

Su Hsing. "Ch'en Sheng, the First Leader of a Chinese Peasant Revolt," *CKCN*, no. 72, August 1951.

Sun Tso-min. "The Battle of Ch'u-Han," *KMJP*, May 10, 1956.

——. "Is It Supporting Class Analysis or Destroying Class Analysis?" *CHYC*, no. 4, 1964.

——. "The Question of the Blows of the Chinese Peasant Wars Against the Feudal System," *SSP*.

——. "Regarding the Book *Chung-kuo Nung-min Chan-cheng Wen-t'i T'an-su*," *KMJP*, May 26, 1958.

——. "A Tentative Discussion of the Nature of Li Tzu-ch'eng's Ta Hsun Government," *HCS*, no. 3, 1962.

——. "The Use of Historicism and Class Viewpoint in the Research on the History of Our Country's Peasant Wars," *JMJP*, February 27, 1964.

Sun Tso-min and Fan Hsueh-yi. "Correctly Evaluate the Function of Peasant Uprisings in Chinese History," *KMJP*, April 12, 1956.

Sun Tz'u-chou. "Investigation of the Record of Chang Hsien-chung in Szechwan," *LSYC*, no. 1, 1957.

Sung Hsi-min and Wang Hsin-yeh. "A Criticism of One of the False Views of Chao Li-sheng on the Question of the Peasant Wars," *WSC*, no. 12, 1958.

Ta Jen. "Huang Ch'ao's Revolt Also Raised the Land Problem," *KMJP*, April 12, 1961.

Tai Yi. "On the Causes of the Outbreak of the Revolution of the TPTK," *KMJP*, January 11, 1961.

"Talk Freely About and Evaluate Personalities," *SCMP* 2457, citing *KMJP*, January 15, 1961.

T'ang Hsing. "Criticize Wu Feng's *Sui-t'ang Wu-tai Shih*," *LSYC*, no. 9, 1958.

T'ang Yu-yuan. "Regarding Some Questions on the Class Contradictions in China's Feudal Society," *LSYC*, nos. 5 and 6, 1964.

T'ao Hsi-sheng. "Various Revolts in Sung Times," *Chung-shan Wen-hua Chiao-yü Kuan Chi-k'an*, vol. 1, no. 2, 1934.

Teng Kuang-ming. "Discussing the Uprising of Chung Hsiang and Yang Yao," *LKP*.

————. "A Tentative Discussion of the Late T'ang Peasant Uprisings," *LKP*.

Teng T'o. "The Thought of Mao Tse-tung Opens the Way for the Development of China's Science of History," *ECMM* 264, citing *LSYC*, no. 1, 1961.

"Three Thoughts on the Historical Drama," *JPRS*, May 8, 1962, citing *Hung Ch'i*, March 16, 1962.

T'ien Chang-wu. "Is It Historical Materialism or Is It Economic Determinism?" *KMJP*, May 14, 1964.

T'ien-chin Shih-fan Ta-hsueh Li-shih hsi, "Regarding the Heated Controversy over the Problem of the Laws of Development of the Chinese Peasant Wars," *SSP*.

T'ien Han. "Problems of Choosing a Theme," *URS*, vol. 25, citing *Wen-yi-hsueh*, no. 7, 1961.

T'ien Ju-kang. "The Resistance Movement of the Foochow People Against the English Aggressors and the Chinese Traitors in 1852," *KMJP*, July 4, 1957.

"Tientsin Historians Discuss Some Questions in the History of the Chinese Peasant Wars," *SCMM* 308, citing *LSYC*, no. 1, 1962.

Ting Yi. "American Aid to the Manchu-Ch'ing in Destroying the Revolutionary Movement," *Ta Kung Pao* (Hong Kong), December 14, 1950.

Ts'ai Mei-piao. "Discussion of Several Questions in the Debate on the History of the Chinese Peasant Wars," *LSYC*, no. 4, 1961.

————. "*Kuo-shih Chin-wen* [a book by Ch'en Teng-yuan] Should Be Criticized," *LSYC*, no. 11, 1958.

————. "More on Several Problems in the History of the Chinese Peasant Wars," *HCS*, no. 11, 1962.

Ts'ao Kuei-lin. "On Li Yen," *LSYC*, no. 4, 1964.

Ts'ao Kuo-she. "Discussion of the Land and Tax Policy of the T'ai-p'ing T'ien-kuo," *Chung-shan Ta-hsueh Hsueh-pao* (Journal of Sun Yat-sen University), no. 9, 1959.

Ts'ao Yung-nien. "On the Slogans of Ch'en Sheng and Wu Kuang," *KMJP*, August 14, 1963.

————. "A Tentative Discussion of the Transformation and Changes in the Late Ch'in Peasant Uprising," *LSYC*, no. 2, 1965.

Ts'en Ch'ung-mien. "How to Regard the Laws of Development of Our Country's Peasant Wars," *SSP*.

Tu Lieh-yuan. "On the Nature, Development, and Two Stages of the Late Yuan Revolutionary Struggles," *Hsi-pei Ta-hsueh Hsueh-pao* (Journal of Northwest University), no. 3, 1957.

Tuan Wen-yuan. "Discussion of the Problem of Li Mi," *KMJP*, no. 9, 1953.

Tung Chia-tsun. "On the Question of Monarchism," *SSP.*

"Various Provinces of China Compile Revolutionary History," *SCMP* 2525, citing *NCNA* (Peking), January 19, 1961.

Wang Chu-lou. "The Great White Lotus Uprising of 1796–1805," *LKP.*

Wang Ch'ung-wu. "On Ming T'ai-tsu's Revolt and the Changes in his Policies," *Chung-yang Yen-chiu Yuan,* (Li Shih Yü-yen So), vol. 10, 1948.

——. "On the Development and Transformation of the Late Yuan Peasant Revolt and Its Historical Significance," *LSYC,* no. 4, 1954.

Wang Hsin-yeh and Sung Hsi-min. "Criticize One of Chao Li-sheng's Absurd Theories . . . His Distortion and Slanders of the Peasants and Peasant Uprisings," *WSC,* no. 12, 1958.

Wang Hsing-ya. "Purge the Reactionary Hero-Centered Viewpoint from the Research and Teaching of History," *SHYK,* no. 10, 1958.

——. "The Reactionary Nature of Capitalist Class Rightist Chao Li-sheng's Research on the History of the Chinese Peasant Wars," *WSC,* no. 12, 1958.

Wang Li-ching. "Analysis of the Peasant Wars in Chinese History and the Road for the Solution of the Peasant Problem," *Chung-kuo Ching-chi* (Chinese Economy), vol. 1, no. 1, April 1933.

Wang P'ing-sheng. "Regarding the Article 'A Tentative Discussion of Peasant Uprisings of the Mid-Northern Sung,'" *SHYK,* no. 9, 1959.

Wang Shou-yi. "Doubts About the Equal Land Slogan of the Late Ming Peasant Army," *LSYC,* no. 2, 1962.

Wang Ssu-chih. "On the Question of the Nature of the Peasant Wars," *SSP.*

—— *et al.* "Discussion of the Nature of Han Society," *LSYC,* no. 1, 1955.

Wang Tan-ts'en. "Regarding [My Book] Chung-kuo Nung-min Ke-ming Shih-hua," *KMJP,* August 22, 1953.

Wang T'ien-chang. "The Secret Societies of the Latter Half of the Nineteenth Century," *LSYC,* no. 2, 1963.

Wang T'ien-chiang. "The Class Composition of the Local Officials of the TPTK," *LSYC,* no. 3, 1958.

Wang Yi. "On Several Problems in the Evaluation of the Peasant Wars," *KMJP,* July 19, 1956.

Wei Fu-ch'ang. "Discussion of Problems in Professor Chang Shun-hui's Chung-kuo Li-shih Yao-chi Chieh-shao," *SHYK,* no. 6, 1960.

Wei Kan-chih. "Extirpate Capitalist Class Academic Views in

the Teaching of Ancient Chinese History," *SHYK*, no. 9, 1958.

Wei Li. "Introduction of the Classical Works of Marxism-Leninism to China . . . ," *SCMP* 2021, citing *JMJP*, May 5, 1959.

Weng Heng-sheng. "Some Ideas on the Piece 'The Entry of Li Tzu-ch'eng's Army into Peking,' " *KMJP*, October 13, 1960.

"What Was the Function of the Peasant Wars in History?" *Wen Hui-pao* (Shanghai) June 9, 1959.

Wu Ch'uan-ch'i. "We Cannot Say the Peasant Wars Are a Continuation of Feudal Landlord Policies," *KMJP*, April 3, 1964.

Wu Feng. "On the Class Struggle and Internal Governing Class Struggles in the Early T'ang," *HCS*, no. 1, 1962.

Wu Han. "On Appraisal of Figures of History," *SCMP* 2721, citing *JMJP*, March 23, 1962.

——. "On the True Nature of History," *KMJP*, December 3, 1960.

——. "The Uprising of the Red Army in the late Yuan," *HCS*, no. 11, 1954.

Wu Shih-mo. "Did the Peasant Class Strike the Feudal System and Demand the Establishment of a New Social System or Not?" *SSP*.

Wu T'ien-ying. "Two Points at Issue Arising from Discussions on the Questions of the Peasant Wars," *SCMM* 552, citing *HCS*, February 20, 1966.

Wu T'ing-ch'iu. "Establish a New System of World History," *SCMP* 2503, citing *KMJP*, April 9–10, 1961.

Wu Yen-nan. "On the Historical Function of the Chinese Peasant Revolts and Wars," *SSP*.

——. "On the Question of Goals and Peasant Governments in the Peasant Revolts and Wars," *SHYK*, no. 6, 1960.

——. "A Tentative Discussion of the Characteristics of the Peasant Revolts of the End of the Sui and T'ang," *SHYK*, no. 11, 1959.

Yang Chih-chiu. "The Great Uprising of Huang Ch'ao," in *LKP*.

——. "On the Function of Revolutionary Ideology of the Chinese Peasant Wars and Its Relation with Religion," *SSP*.

Yang K'uan. "Another Discussion of the Functions of Revolutionary Thought in the Chinese Peasant Wars and Their Relations with Religion," *SSP*.

——. "On the Historical Function of the Class Struggle in Ch'un-ch'iu Chan-kuo Times," *WSC*, no. 8, 1954.

——. "On the *T'ai-p'ing Ching*," *Hsueh-shu Yueh-k'an*, no. 9, 1959.

——. "A Tentative Discussion of the Characteristics of the White Lotus Teaching," *KMJP*, March 15, 1961.

Yang Shu-sen. "On Discussion of the Nature of the Struggle After the Ch'ing Government Entered the Passes," *Min-tzu T'uan-chieh* (Minority Unity), January 6, 1962.

Yang Wei-min and Jen Shu-ming. "The Uprising of Wang Hsiao-po and Li Hsun in the Early Northern Sung," *LKP*.

Yao Wen-yuan. "Criticize Mr. Chou Ku-ch'eng's Contradictory Outlook," *KMJP*, May 10, 1964.

——. "A Review of the New Historical Play 'Hai Jui Dismissed from Office' " (Shanghai), *WHP*, November 10, 1965.

Yeh Fen. "Tentative Discussion of Ch'en Yü-liang," *KMJP*, August 14, 1963.

Yen Hsun. "Regarding Some Views on the Yi-ho T'uan," *KMJP*, January 20, 1955.

Yin Ch'i-min, Fan Wen-lan, *et al.* "Lectures on Chinese History," serialized in *Ch'ün Chung* (Masses), Chungking, May 30, 1944.

Yin Hsiang-hao. "One Cannot Confuse the Question of Dark Periods of History and the Function of Peasant Revolts," *KMJP*, June 21, 1956.

Yu Yen-kuang. "The Kuangtung Peasant Movement in the First Internal Revolutionary War Period," *LSYC*, 1958, no. 9.

Yuan T'ing-chung. "Remember the Sixtieth Anniversary of the Yi-ho T'uan Movement, Its Anti-Imperialist Struggle, and Historical Significance," *KMJP*, September 29, 1960.

BOOKS IN WESTERN LANGUAGES

Alley, Rewi, trans. *Poems of Revolt*. Peking: New World Press, 1962.

Arendt, Hannah. *On Revolution*. New York: The Viking Press, 1963.

Balazs, Etienne. *Chinese Civilization and Bureaucracy*. New Haven: Yale University Press, 1964.

——. *Le Traité économique du Souei-chou*. Leiden: E. J. Brill, 1953.

Barber, Bernard. *Social Stratification*. New York: Harcourt, Brace and Company, Inc., 1957.

Barghorn, F. C. *Soviet Russian Nationalism*. New York: Oxford University Press, 1956.

Beasley, W. G., and E. G. Pulleyblank, eds. *Historians of China and Japan*. London: Oxford University Press, 1961.

Bendix, R., and S. M. Lipset, eds. *Class, Status and Power.* Glencoe: Free Press, 1953.

Bensing, Manfred, and Siegfried Hoyer. *Der Deutsche Bauernkrieg, 1524–26.* Berlin: Deutscher Militärverlag, 1965.

Beqiraj, Mehmet: *Peasantry in Revolution.* Ithaca: Center for International Studies, Cornell University, 1966.

Bielenstein, Hans. *The Restoration of the Han Dynasty,* 2 vols. Göteborg: Elanders Boktryckeri AB, 1953 and 1959.

Bingham, Woodbridge. *The Founding of the T'ang Dynasty: The Fall of Sui and Rise of T'ang: A Preliminary Survey.* Baltimore: The Waverly Press, 1941.

Black, C. E., ed. *Rewriting Russian History.* New York: Vintage Books, 1962.

———. *The Transformation of Russian Society.* Cambridge: Harvard University Press, 1960.

Bloch, Marc. *Feudal Society.* Chicago: University of Chicago Press, 1961.

Boardman, Eugene. *Christian Influences upon the Ideology of the T'ai-p'ing Rebellion.* Madison: University of Wisconsin Press, 1952.

Bober, M. M. *Karl Marx's Interpretation of History.* Cambridge: Harvard University Press, 1950.

Boissonade, P. *Life and Work in Medieval Europe.* New York: Alfred A. Knopf, 1927.

Borton, Hugh. *Peasant Uprisings in Japan of the Tokugawa Period.* Tokyo: Transactions of the Asiatic Society of Japan, 2d series, vol. 16, 1938.

Brière, O. *Fifty Years of Chinese Philosophy.* London: George Allen & Unwin, 1956.

Brinton, Crane. *Anatomy of Revolution.* Englewood Cliffs, N.J.: Prentice-Hall, 1952.

Broomhall, Marshall. *Islam in China: A Neglected Problem.* London: Morgan & Scott, 1910.

Buck, Pearl, trans. *All Men Are Brothers,* 2 vols. New York: Grove Press, n.d. (reprint).

Chavannes, E. *Les Mémoires historiques de Se-ma Ts'ien.* Paris: E. Leroux, 1895–1905.

Ch'en, Jerome. *Mao and the Chinese Revolution.* London: Oxford University Press, 1965.

Ch'en Po-ta. *Notes on Mao Tse-tung's "Report of an Investigation into the Peasant Movement in Hunan."* Peking: Foreign Languages Press, 1954.

Ch'en, Theodore H. E. *Teacher Training in Communist China.* Washington: U. S. Department of Health, Education and Welfare, 1960.

———. *Thought Reform of the Chinese Intellectual.* Hong Kong: Hong Kong University Press, 1960.

Cheng, J. C. *Chinese Sources for the T'ai-p'ing Rebellion, 1850–1864.* Hong Kong: Hong Kong University Press, 1963.

Chesneaux, Jean. *Les Sociétés Secrètes en Chine.* Paris: Julliard, 1965.

Chi Ch'ao-ting. *Key Economic Areas of Chinese History.* London: George Allen & Unwin, 1936.

Chiang Kai-shek. *China's Destiny.* New York: Macmillan Co., 1947.

———. *Soviet Russia in China.* New York: Farrar, Straus and Cudahy, 1957.

Chiang, S. T. *The Nien Rebellion.* Seattle: University of Washington Press, 1954.

Chou Tse-tsung. *The May Fourth Movement.* Cambridge: Harvard University Press, 1960.

Chou Yung-te. *Social Mobility in China.* New York: Atherton Press, 1966.

Ch'u T'ung-tsu. *Law and Society in Traditional China.* Paris: Mouton, 1961.

Clubb, O. Edmund. *Twentieth Century China.* New York: Columbia University Press, 1964.

Cohn, Norman. *The Pursuit of the Millennium.* Harper Torchbook, 1961.

Cole, G. D. H. *History of Socialist Thought.* London: Macmillan & Co., 1955.

Contradictions: Rectification in China. China Viewpoints (Hong Kong), 1958.

Cozer, Lewis. *The Functions of Social Conflict.* New York: Free Press, 1956.

Crook, David and Isabel. *Revolution in a Chinese Village, Ten Mile Inn.* London: Routledge, 1959.

Dahrendorf, Ralf. *Class and Class Conflict in Industrial Society.* Stanford: Stanford University Press, 1959.

de Bary, W. T., *et al.*, eds. *Sources of the Chinese Tradition.* New York: Columbia University Press, 1960.

Deutsch, Karl. *Nationalism and Social Communication.* Cambridge: M.I.T. Press, 1966.

Doolin, Dennis J., ed. *Communist China: The Politics of Student Opposition.* Stanford: Stanford University Press, 1964.

Dubs, H. H., trans. *Pan Ku's History of the Former Han Dynasty.* Baltimore: Waverly Press, 1955.

Eberhard, Wolfram. *Conquerors and Rulers: Social Forces in Medieval China.* Leiden: E. J. Brill, 1952.

Eckstein, Harry, ed. *Internal War.* New York: The Free Press of Glencoe, 1964.

Engels, F. *Anti-Duhring*. New York: International Publishers
Co., 1939.
——. *The Peasant War in Germany*. Moscow: Foreign Languages Publishing House, 1956.
Fainsod, Merle. *How Russia is Ruled*. Cambridge: Harvard University Press, 1959.
Favre, B. *Les Sociétés secrètes en Chine*. Paris: Maisonneuve, 1933.
Fei Hsiao-t'ung. *China's Gentry: Essays in Rural-Urban Relations*. Chicago: University of Chicago Press, 1953.
Feuerwerker, Albert, ed. *Chinese Communist Historiography*. Cambridge: M.I.T. Press, 1966.
Feuerwerker, Albert, and S. Cheng. *Chinese Communist Studies of Modern Chinese History*. Cambridge: Harvard University, East Asian Research Center, 1961.
Florinsky, M. T. *Russia: A History and an Interpretation*. New York: The Macmillan Company, 1953.
Fokkema, D. D. W. *Literary Doctrine in China and Soviet Influence*. Paris: Mouton, 1965.
Franke, Wolfgang. *Das Jahrhundert der Chinesischen Revolution, 1861–1949*. Munich: R. Oldenbourg, 1958.
Frazer, Stuart, ed. *Chinese Communist Education*. Nashville: Vanderbilt University Press, 1965.
Fried, Morton. *The Fabric of Chinese Society*. New York: Praeger, 1953.
Friedrich, Carl J., ed. *Revolution*. New York: Atherton Press, 1967.
Gardner, C. S. *Chinese Traditional Historiography*. Cambridge: Harvard University Press, 1961, 2d printing.
Goldman, Merle. *Literary Dissent in Communist China*. Cambridge: Harvard University Press, 1967.
Goodrich, L. Carrington. *Literary Inquisition of Ch'ien Lung*. Baltimore: Waverly Press, 1935.
Gottschalk, L., ed. *Generalization in the Writing of History*. Chicago: University of Chicago Press, 1963.
Han Yu-shan. *Elements of Chinese Historiography*. Hollywood: W. M. Hawley, 1955.
The Historical Experience of the Dictatorship of the Proletariat. Peking: Foreign Languages Press, 1959.
Ho Ping-ti. *The Ladder of Success in Imperial China*. New York: Columbia University Press, 1962.
——. *Studies on the Population of China, 1368–1953*. Cambridge: Harvard University Press, 1959.
Hobsbawm, E. J. *Primitive Rebels*. Manchester: Manchester University Press, 1959.
Hsiao Kung-ch'uan. *Rural China: Imperial Control in the Nine-*

teenth Century. Seattle: University of Washington Press, 1960.

Hsiao Tso-liang. *Power Relations Within the Chinese Communist Movement, 1930–1934.* Seattle: University of Washington Press, 1962.

Hsu, Francis. *Under the Ancestors' Shadow.* New York: Columbia University Press, 1948.

Hu Sheng. *Imperialism and Chinese Politics.* Peking: Foreign Languages Press, 1955.

Huang Sung-k'ang. *Li Ta-chao and the Impact of Marxism on Modern Chinese Thinking.* Paris: Mouton, 1966.

Hummel, A. W., ed. *Eminent Chinese of the Ch'ing Period,* 2 vols. Washington: Government Printing Office, 1943.

Hunt, R. N. Carew. *Marxism, Past and Present.* London: Geoffrey Bles, 1954.

Hunter, W. W. *The Annals of Rural Bengal,* 3 vols. London, 1868.

Israel, John. *Student Nationalism in China, 1927–1937.* Stanford: Stanford University Press, 1966.

Johnson, Chalmers. *Communist Policies Toward the Intellectual Class.* Kowloon: Union Research Institute, 1959.

——. *Peasant Nationalism and Communist Power.* Stanford: Stanford University Press, 1962.

——. *Revolution and the Social System.* Stanford: The Hoover Institution, 1964.

Joussain, André. *La Loi des révolutions.* Paris: Flammarion, 1950.

Kautsky, John H. *Political Change in Underdeveloped Countries.* New York: John Wiley & Sons, 1962.

Kautsky, Karl. *The Class Struggle.* Chicago: Charles H. Kerr & Co., 1910.

——. *Communism in Central Europe in the Time of the Reformation.* New York: Russell & Russell, 1959.

Keep, John, ed. *Contemporary History in the Soviet Mirror.* New York: Praeger, 1964.

Kirby, E. S. *Introduction to the Economic History of China.* London: George Allen & Unwin, 1954.

——, ed. *Contemporary China, 1958–1959.* Hong Kong: Hong Kong University Press, 1964.

Kracke, E. A. *Civil Service in Early Sung China, 960–1067.* Cambridge: Harvard University Press, 1953.

Kwok, D. W. Y. *Scientism in Chinese Thought, 1900–1950.* New Haven: Yale University Press, 1965.

Lanternari, Vittorio. *The Religions of the Oppressed.* New York: Alfred A. Knopf, 1963.

Lattimore, Owen. *Inner Asian Frontiers of China.* New York: Capitol Publishing Co., 1951.

Legge, James, trans. *The Four Books.* Shanghai: The Chinese Book Co., n.d.

Lenin, V. I. *Alliance of the Working Class and the Peasantry.* Moscow: Foreign Languages Publishing House, 1959.

———. *Collected Works.* Moscow: Foreign Languages Publishing House, 1959–1965.

———. *Collected Works of V. I. Lenin.* New York: International Publishers Co., 1942.

———. *Marx, Engels, Marxism.* Moscow: Cooperative Publishing Society, 1934.

———. *Selected Works in Twelve Volumes.* New York: International Publishers Co., n.d.

———. *Selected Works in Two Volumes.* Moscow: Foreign Languages Publishing House, 1950.

———. *Sochineniye* (Works), vol. 29. Moscow, 1950.

Levenson, Joseph R. *Confucian China and Its Modern Fate,* 3 vols. Berkeley: University of California Press, 1958–65.

———. *Liang Ch'i-ch'ao and the Mind of Modern China.* Cambridge: Harvard University Press, 1953.

Levy, Howard. *The Biography of Huang Ch'ao.* Berkeley: University of California Press, 1961.

Lewis, John. *Leadership in Communist China.* Ithaca: Cornell University Press, 1963.

Liao, W. K., trans. *The Han Fei-tzu.* London: Arthur Probsthain, 1959.

Lichtheim, George. *Marxism: An Historical and Critical Study.* New York: Praeger, 1961.

Lin Mou-sheng. *Men and Ideas.* New York: The John Day Company, 1942.

Linton, Ralph. *The Study of Man.* New York: D. Appleton-Century Company, 1936.

Liu, James J. Y. *Chinese Knight Errant.* Chicago: University of Chicago Press, 1966.

Liu Shao-ch'i. *How to Be a Good Communist.* Peking: Foreign Languages Press, 1951.

———. *On the Party.* Peking: Foreign Languages Press, 1951.

Lowe, D. M. *The Function of China in Marx, Lenin, and Mao.* Berkeley: University of California Press, 1966.

Lukacs, Georg. *Histoire et conscience de class,* trans. from the German edition of 1923 by Kostas Axelos and Jacqueline Bois. Paris: Les Editions de Minuit, 1960.

Mao Tse-tung. "In Commemoration of Sun Yat-sen," in *Dr. Sun Yat-sen: Commemorative Articles and Speeches.* Peking: Foreign Languages Press, 1957.

———. *On Guerrilla Warfare,* trans. by S. B. Griffith. New York: Praeger, 1961.

——. *On the Correct Handling of Contradictions Among the People*. Peking: Foreign Languages Press, 1960.

——. *Selected Works of Mao Tse-tung*, 4 vols. New York: International Publishers, 1954; and vol. 4, Peking: Foreign Languages Press, 1961.

Mannheim, Karl. *Ideology and Utopia*. New York: Harvest Book, n.d. (reprint).

Marsh, Robert. *The Mandarins*. New York: Free Press, 1961.

Marx, Karl. *Capital*, 3 vols. Moscow: Foreign Languages Publishing House, 1957.

——. *Marx on China: Articles in New York Daily Tribune, 1853–1860*. London: Lawrence & Wiswart, 1951.

——. *The Poverty of Philosophy*. Moscow: Foreign Languages Publishing House, n.d., 3d impression.

Marx, Karl, and Friedrich Engels. *The German Ideology*. New York: New World paperback edition, 1963.

——. *K. Marx and F. Engels on Religion*. Moscow: Foreign Languages Publishing House, 1957.

——. *Selected Works in Two Volumes*. Moscow: Foreign Languages Publishing House, 1958.

Mazour, Anatole G. *Modern Russian Historiography*. Princeton: D. Van Nostrand Company, 1958, 2d edition.

Meadows, Thomas Taylor. *The Chinese and Their Rebellions*. Stanford: Academic Reprints, n.d.

Mehnert, Klaus. *Stalin Versus Marx: The Stalinist Historical Doctrine*. London: George Allen & Unwin, 1952.

Meisner, Maurice. *Li Ta-chao and the Origins of Chinese Marxism*. Cambridge: Harvard University Press, 1967.

Michael, Franz. *The Taiping Rebellion*, 3 vols. Seattle: University of Washington Press, 1966.

Mills, C. Wright, ed. *Images of Man*. New York: George Braziller, 1961.

Mitrany, David. *Marx Against the Peasant*. Chapel Hill: University of North Carolina Press, 1951.

Moore, Barrington. *Social Origins of Dictatorship and Democracy*. Boston: Beacon Press, 1966.

Morgan, W. P. *Triad Societies in Hong Kong*. Hong Kong: Government Printing Office, 1960.

Mote, F. W. *The Poet Kao Ch'i*. Princeton: Princeton University Press, 1962.

Namier, L. B. *Avenues of History*. London: Hamilton, 1952.

Nechkina, M. V., ed. *Istoriya i Istoriki* (History and Historians). Moscow: Nauka, 1965.

Nivison, David. *The Life and Thought of Chang Hsueh-ch'eng*. Stanford: Stanford University Press, 1966.

Nomad, Max. *Aspects of Revolt.* New York: Brookman Associates, 1959.

Norman, E. H. *Soldier and Peasant in Japan: The Origins of Conscription.* New York: Institute of Pacific Relations, 1943.

Ossowski, Stanislaw. *Class Structure in the Social Consciousness.* New York: Free Press, 1963.

Outline History of the USSR. Moscow: Foreign Languages Publishing House, 1960.

Payne, Robert. *Portrait of a Revolutionary.* New York: Abelard-Schuman, 1961.

Peake, Cyrus H. *Nationalism and Education in Modern China.* New York: Columbia University Press, 1932.

Plamenatz, John. *German Marxism and Russian Communism.* London: Longmans, Green & Co., 1954.

Plekhanov, G. V. *The Development of the Monist View of History.* Moscow: Foreign Languages Publishing House, 1956.

———. *The Role of the Individual in History.* New York: International Publishers Co., 1940.

Popper, Karl. *The Open Society and Its Enemies,* 2 vols. Princeton: Princeton University Press, 1963.

———. *The Poverty of Historicism.* New York: Harper Torchbook, 1962.

Proceedings of the Eighth National Congress of the Chinese People's Congress. Peking: Foreign Languages Press, 1956.

Pulleyblank, E. C. *The Background of the Rebellion of An Lu-shan.* London: Oxford University Press, 1955.

Purcell, Victor. *The Boxer Uprising.* London: Cambridge University Press, 1963.

Redfield, Robert. *Peasant Society and Culture.* Chicago: University of Chicago Press, 1958.

Reischauer, Edwin O., and John K. Fairbank. *East Asia: The Great Tradition.* Boston: Houghton Mifflin Company, 1960.

Rignano, Eugenie. *Le Materialisme historique.* Bologna: Nicola Zanichelli, n.d.

Rudé, George. *The Crowd in History, 1730–1848.* New York: John Wiley and Sons, 1964.

Rue, John E. *Mao Tse-tung in Opposition, 1927–35.* Stanford: Stanford University Press, 1966.

Safarov, G. *Klassy i Klassovaya Borba v Kitaiskii Istorii* (Classes and Class Struggle in Chinese History). Moscow: Gos. Izdat., 1928.

Sansom, Sir George B. *A History of Japan, 1334–1615.* Stanford: Stanford University Press, 1961.

Sarkisyanz, E. *Buddhist Backgrounds of the Burmese Revolution.* The Hague: Martinus Nykoff, 1965.

Scalapino, Robert A., and George T. Yu. *The Chinese Anarchist Movement.* Berkeley: University of California, Center For Chinese Studies, 1961.

Schram, Stuart. *The Political Thought of Mao Tse-tung.* New York: Praeger, 1963.

———. *Mao Tse-tung.* New York: Simon & Shuster, 1967.

Schwartz, Benjamin. *Chinese Communism and the Rise of Mao.* Cambridge: Harvard University Press, 1958, 3d edition.

———. *In Search of Wealth and Power: Yen Fu and the West.* Cambridge: Harvard University Press, 1964.

Schurmann, H. Franz. *Ideology and Organization in Communist China.* Berkeley: University of California Press, 1966.

Shih Ch'eng-chih. *People's Resistance in Mainland China.* Hong Kong: Union Research Institute Press, 1956.

Shih, Vincent Y. C. *The Taiping Ideology.* Seattle: University of Washington Press, 1967.

Shteppa, K. F. *Russian Historians and the Soviet State.* New Brunswick: Rutgers University Press, 1962.

Simonovskaya, L. V. *Antifeodalnaya Voina v Kitai v 17 b* (Antifeudal War in China in the Seventeenth Century). Moscow, 1966.

———, ed. *Ocherki Istorii Kitaya* (Outline History of China). Moscow: Gosizdat, 1956.

———, ed. *Sbornik Statei po Istorii Stran Dalnego Vostoka* (Collected Articles on the History of Countries of the Far East). Moscow: Moscow University, 1952.

———. *Velikaya Krestyanskaya Voina v Kitai, 1628–1645* (Great Peasant War in China, 1628–1645). Moscow: Uchpedgiz, 1958.

Smedley, Agnes. *The Great Road.* New York: Monthly Review Press, 1956.

Smirin, M. M. *Narodnaya Reformatsiya Thomasa Muntzer i Velikaya Krestyanskaya Voina* (The People's Reformation of Thomas Muntzer and the Great Peasant War). Moscow: Akademiya Nauk, 2d edition, 1955.

Smolin, G. Ya. *Krestyanskoye Vostaniye v Provintsiakh Hunan i Hupei v 1130–1135* (Peasant Uprising in the Provinces of Hunan and Hupeh from 1130–1135). Moscow: Izdatelstvo Vostochnoi Literatury, 1961.

Snow, Edgar. *Red Star over China.* New York: Random House, 1938.

Sorokin, Pitirim. *The Sociology of Revolution.* Philadelphia: J. B. Lippincott Company, 1925.

Sorokin, Pitirim, and Carle C. Zimmerman. *Principles of Rural-Urban Sociology.* New York: Henry Holt, 1929.

Stalin, J. *Dialectical and Historical Materialism.* New York: International Publishers Co., 1942.
——. *Foundations of Leninism.* Moscow, 1934.
——. *History of the Communist Party of the Soviet Union, Short Course.* Moscow: Foreign Languages Publishing House, 1957.
——. *Selected Writings.* New York: International Publishers Co., 1942
——. *Works.* Moscow: Foreign Languages Publishing House, 1955.
Stern, Fritz, ed. *The Varieties of History.* New York: Meridian Books, 1957.
Struve, V. V., ed. *Drevny Vostok* (Ancient East). Moscow: Uchpedgiz, 1958.
Sumner, B. H. *A Short History of Russia.* New York: Harcourt, Brace & World, 1949.
Sun Yat-sen. *San-min Chu-yi* (The Three Principles of the People), trans. by Frank W. Price. Chungking: Ministry of Information of the Republic of China, 1943.
Swarup, Shanti. *A Study of the Chinese Communist Movement, 1927–1934.* London: Oxford University Press, 1966.
Talmon, J. *Political Messianism.* New York: Praeger, 1960.
Tan, Chester. *The Boxer Catastrophe.* New York: Columbia University Press, 1955.
Teng, Ssu-yü. *Historiography of the Taiping Rebellion.* Cambridge: Harvard University Press, 1962.
——. *New Light on the History of the Taiping Rebellion.* Cambridge: Harvard University Press, 1950.
——. *The Nien Army and Their Guerilla Warfare, 1851–1868.* Paris: Mouton and Co., 1961.
Teng, Ssu-yü, and John K. Fairbank, eds. *China's Response to the West.* Cambridge: Harvard University Press, 1954.
Treadgold, D. *Lenin and His Rivals: The Struggle for Russia's Future.* New York: Praeger, 1955.
Trotsky, Leon. *The Chinese Revolution* (Bulletin of Marxist Studies, no. 1). New York: Pioneer Publishers, n.d.
Tucker, Robert C. *The Soviet Political Mind.* New York: Praeger, 1963.
Wang Gung-wu. *The Structure of Power in North China During the Five Dynasties.* Kuala Lumpur: University of Malaya Press, 1963.
Wang, Y. C. *Chinese Intellectuals and the West.* Chapel Hill: University of North Carolina Press, 1966.
Watson, Burton. *Records of the Grand Historian of China,* 2 vols. New York: Columbia University Press, 1961.

——. *Ssu-ma Ch'ien, Grand Historian of China*. New York: Columbia University Press, 1961.

Wiegand, H. J. *A Close-Up of the German Peasant War*. New Haven: Yale University Press, 1942.

Wilbur, C. Martin. *Slavery in China During the Former Han Dynasty*. Chicago: Field Museum of Natural History, 1943 (Anthropological Series, vol. 34).

Wittfogel, Karl A. *Oriental Despotism*. New Haven: Yale University Press, 1963.

Wright, Arthur F., ed. *The Confucian Persuasion*. Stanford: Stanford University Press, 1960.

——, ed. *Studies in Chinese Thought*. Chicago: University of Chicago Press, 1953.

Yang, C. K. *Religion in Chinese Society*. Berkeley: University of California Press, 1961.

Yang Lien-sheng. *Studies in Chinese Institutional History*. Cambridge: Harvard University Press, 1961.

ARTICLES AND UNPUBLISHED MATERIALS
IN LANGUAGES OTHER THAN CHINESE

Balazs, E. "The Social Crisis and Political Philosophy at the End of the Han" (in French), *T'oung Pao*, 39, lvr. 1–3.

Baranovsky, M. I. "Anglo-American Capitalist Suppressors of the Taiping Uprising" (in Russian), VI, no. 1, 1952.

Belyelubsky, F. B. "On the Social Character of the Taiping Leadership" (in Russian), NAA, no. 1, 1963.

Boardman, Eugene. "Millenary Aspects of the T'ai-p'ing Rebellion," in Sylvia Thrupp, ed., *Millennial Dreams in Action*. The Hague: Mouton, 1962.

Bodde, Derk. "Harmony and Conflict in Chinese Philosophy," in Arthur F. Wright, ed., *Studies in Chinese Thought*. Chicago: University of Chicago Press, 1953.

Borovkova, L. A. "The Uprising of the Red Troops and the Rise of Chu Yuan-chang" (in Russian), NAA, no. 2, 1961.

Bowman, Herbert E. "Soviet Literary and Historical Scholarship," in C. E. Black, ed., *The Transformation of Russian Society*. Cambridge: Harvard University Press, 1960.

Butterfield, Fox. "The Legend of Sung Ching-shih: An Episode in Communist Historiography," *Harvard Papers on China*, no. 18, 1964.

Chien Yu-wen. "The Marxian Interpretation of the T'ai-p'ing T'ien-kuo," *Proceedings of the Second Biennial Conference of the International Association of Asian Historians*, held at Taipei, October 1962.

Chou Tse-tung. "Yen Fu," in Howard Boorman, ed., *Men and Politics in Modern China: Preliminary Fifty Biographies.* New York: Columbia University Press, 1960.

Chu, Richard Y. D. "An Introductory Study of the White Lotus in Chinese History," unpublished Columbia University doctoral dissertation, 1967.

Crawford, Robert B. "The Social and Political Philosophy of the *Shih Chi*," *JAS*, vol. 22, no. 4, August 1963.

de Bary, W. T. "Huang Tsung-hsi, a Plan for the Prince," unpublished Columbia University doctoral dissertation, 1953.

Delyusin, L. P. "Review of Research on the TPTK" (in Russian), *NAA*, no. 5, 1962.

Demieville, P. "Chang Hsueh-ch'eng and His Historiography," in W. G. Beasley and E. G. Pulleyblank, eds., *Historians of China and Japan*. London: Oxford University Press, 1961.

Eberhard, W. "The Formation of a New Dynasty," in *Sonderdruck aus Beiträge zur Gesellungs und Volkwissenschaft: Festschrift zum Achtzigsten Geburtstag von Prof. R. Thurnwald*. Berlin: Verlag Gebr. Mann, 1950.

Eckstein, Harry. "On the Etiology of Internal Wars," *History and Theory*, vol. 4, no. 2, 1965.

Eichhorn, Werner. "Description of the Rebellion of Sun En and Earlier Taoist Rebellions" (in English), *Mittelungen des Institutes für Orientforshung*, no. 2, 1954.

———. "Towards a History of the Uprising of Wang Hsiao-po and Li Hsun in Szechwan" (in German), *Zeitschrift für Deutschen Morgenlandischen Gesellschaft*, vol. 105, 1955.

Fei Hsiao-t'ung. "Peasantry and Gentry: An Interpretation of Chinese Social Structure and Its Changes," *American Journal of Sociology*, 1946.

Feuerwerker, Albert. "China's History in Marxian Dress," *American Historical Review*, no. 1, 1961.

———. "Rewriting Chinese History: Interpreting the Past in People's China," *University of Toronto Quarterly*, Supplement, The Far East, 1961.

Gayn, Mark. "Peking Has a Yenan Complex," *New York Times Magazine*, January 30, 1966.

Gillin, Donald G. "China's First Five-Year Plan: Industrialization Under the Warlords as Reflected in the Policies of Yen Hsi-shan in Shansi Province, 1930–1937," *JAS*, February 1965.

Glantz, Oscar. "Class Consciousness and Political Solidarity," *American Sociological Review*, vol. 23, August 1958.

Harrison, James P. "Communist Interpretations of Chinese Peasant Wars," *China Quarterly*, October–December 1965.

——. "The Ideological Training of Intellectuals in Communist China," *Asian Survey*, October 1965.

——. "The Li Li-san Line and the CCP in 1930," *China Quarterly*, nos. 14 and 15, 1963.

——. "Peking's Remembrance of Things Past," *Problems of Communism*, June 1966.

Ho Ping-ti. "Aspects of Social Mobility in China," *Comparative Studies in Society and History*, June 1959.

——. "Records of China's Grand Historian: Some Problems of Translation," *Pacific Affairs*, Summer 1963.

Houn, F. W. "The Eighth Central Committee of the CCP," *American Political Science Review*, June 1957.

How, Julie. "The Development of Ch'en Tu-hsiu's Thought, 1915–1938," unpublished Columbia University master's essay, 1949.

Hsia, C. T. "Comparative Approaches to Water Margin," *Yearbook of Comparative and General Literature*, no. 11, 1962.

Hulsewé, A. F. P. "Notes on the Historiography of the Han Period," in W. G. Beasley and E. G. Pulleyblank, eds., *Historians of China and Japan*. London: Oxford University Press, 1961.

Ikeda, Makoto. "Rebellion in the Szechuan District in the Early Sung Period" (in Japanese), *Rekishigaku Kenkyu* 152, July 1951.

Ilyushechkin, V. P. "Agrarian Policies of the Taipings" (in Russian), *NAA*, no. 4, 1962.

Johnson, Chalmers. "Social Science in China Scholarship," *World Politics*, January 1965.

Kao Yü-kung. "The Fang La Rebellion," *HJAS*, vol. 24, 1962–1963.

——. "A Study of the Fang La Rebellion," unpublished Harvard University doctoral dissertation, 1962.

Kuhn, Philip. "The T'uan-Lien Local Defense System," *HJAS*, 1967.

Kuo Mo-jo. "Historical Studies in Wartime China" (in Russian), *VI*, vols. 5–6 (1945).

Kuo T'ing-yi. "The Totalitarian Rule of the T'ai-p'ing Heavenly Kingdom," *Annals of Academia Sinica*, no. 11, part 1, 1955.

Lee, J. S. "The Periodic Recurrence of Internecine Wars in China," *Journal of Science and Arts*, 1931.

Lee, Robert H. G. "The Study of History, Some Contemporary Views," in John E. Lane, ed., *Researches in the Social Sciences on China*. New York: East Asian Institute of Columbia University (private distribution), 1957.

Lei Hai-tsung. "The Periodization of Chinese History and of World History," *Chinese Social and Political Science Review*, 1936–37.

Levenson, Joseph R. "History Under Chairman Mao," *Soviet Survey*, Spring 1958.

Levine, Steven. "Trotsky on China," *Harvard Papers on China*, no. 18, 1964.

Levy, Howard. "The Bifurcation of the Yellow Turbans in Later Han," *Oriens*, nos. 13–14, 1960–61.

——. "Review of Books on Huang Ch'ao," *JAS*, August 1957.

——. "Yellow Turban Religion and Rebellion at the End of the Han," *Journal of the American Oriental Society*, no. 76, 1956.

Lewis, John W. "China's Secret Military Papers," *China Quarterly*, April–June 1964.

Lichtheim, George. "The Transmutations of a Doctrine," *Problems of Communism*, July–August 1966.

Linko, G. M., *et al.* "On a Teaching Theme: Peasant War in China for the Eighth Grade" (in Russian), *Prepodavaniye v Shkole*, no. 1, 1953.

Maspero, Henri. "Les Régimes fonciers en Chine des origines aux temps modernes," in *Mélanges posthumes sur les religions et l'histoire de la Chine*, vol. 3. Paris: Études Historiques, Civilisations du Sud, 1950.

Masubichi Tatsuo. "The Yu Hsia and the Social Order in the Han Period," *Annals of the Hitotsubashi Academy*, October 1952.

Matsui Shuichi. "Study of the Rebellions in Huai and Yangtze Areas in the Ninth Century" (in Japanese), *Shigaku Zasshi*, vol. 66, no. 2.

Mavrodin, V. V., *et al.* "On the Characteristics of the Peasant Wars in Russia" (in Russian), VI, no. 2, 1956.

Meisner, Maurice. "Li Ta-chao and the Chinese Communist Treatment of the Materialist Conception of History," *China Quarterly*, no. 24, October–December 1965.

Michaud, Paul. "The Revolt of the Yellow Turbans," *Monumenta Serica*, 1958.

Miyazaki Ichisada. "Peasant Riots in Chinese History with Special Reference to the Affair of Teng Mou-ch'i" (in Japanese), *Toyoshi Kenkyu*, vol. 10, no. 1, 1947.

Moore, Barrington. "A Comparative Analysis of the Class Struggle," *American Sociological Review*, no. 10, 1945.

Mote, F. W. "The Growth of Chinese Despotism," *Oriens Extremus*, August 1961.

Muramatsu, Yuji. "Some Themes in Chinese Rebel Ideologies,"

in Arthur F. Wright, ed., *The Confucian Persuasion*. Stanford: Stanford University Press, 1960.

Nechkina, M. "The Uprising of Razin and Pugachov in the Conception of M. N. Pokrovsky" (in Russian), in *Protiv Istoricheskii Kontseptsii M. N. Pokrovskogo*. Moscow, 1939.

Nikiforov, V. N. "Some Problems of Chinese History at the XXV International Congress of Orientalists," *JPRS* 8619 (non-series), citing *Problemy Vostokovedeniye*, no. 1, 1961.

Ohanjanian, A. "Taiping Agrarian Policy: Some Chinese and Soviet Views," *Pacific Affairs*, vol. 29 (1966).

Oliver, Adam. "Rectification of Mainland China Intellectuals, 1964–65," *Asian Survey*, October 1965.

Parsons, James. "Attitudes Toward the Late Ming Rebellions," *Oriens Extremus*, December 1959.

——. "The Culmination of a Chinese Peasant Rebellion: Chang Hsien-chung in Szechwan, 1644–45," *JAS*, May 1957.

——. "The Rebellion of Chang Hsien-chung as an Example of Internal Disturbances in China During the Late Ming Dynasty," unpublished University of California doctoral dissertation, 1954.

Perelomov, L. S. "On the Character of the Driving Forces of the War of 209–202 B.C. in China" (in Russian), *NAA*, no. 1, 1962.

Pokora, Timoteus. "On the Origins of the Notions T'ai-p'ing and Ta-t'ung in Chinese Philosophy," *Archiv-Orientalni*, vol. 29, no. 3, 1961.

Porshneva, E. B. "People's Uprising of 1796–1803" (in Russian), *Kratkiye Soobscheniye* (Brief Notices), no. 53. Moscow: Akademiya Nauk, 1962.

Powell, Ralph. "Politico-Military Relationships in Communist China." Washington: U.S. Department of State, 1963.

Pozdnyeva, L. "Revolts of the Slaves and Poor" (in Russian), in V. V. Struve, ed. *Drevny Vostok* (Ancient East). Moscow: Uchpedgiz, 1958.

Pulleyblank, E. G. "Chinese Historical Criticism: Liu Chih-chi and Ssu-ma Kuang," in W. G. Beasley and E. G. Pulleyblank, eds., *Historians of China and Japan*. London: Oxford University Press, 1961.

——. "The Origins of Chattel Slavery in China," *Journal of the Economic and Social History of the Orient*, no. 1, 1957–58.

Rawlinson, Frank. "A Study of the Rebellions of China," *Chinese Recorder*, no. 36, March 1905.

Rubin, V. "The Campaigns of Huang Ch'ao" (in Russian), in L. V. Simonovskaya, ed., *Sbornik Statei po Istorii Stran Dalneyo Vostoka* (Collected Articles on the History of Countries of the Far East). Moscow: Moscow University, 1952.

Saeki Yuichi. "On a Mass Movement at the End of the Ming" (in Japanese), *Toyoshi Kenkyu*, vol. 16, no. 1, 1957.

Scalapino, Robert A., and H. Shiffren. "Early Socialist Currents in the Chinese Revolutionary Movement," *JAS*, May 1959.

Schram, Stuart. "Chinese and Leninist Components in the Thought of Mao Tse-tung," *Asian Survey*, June 1963.

Schurmann, H. Franz. "On Social Themes in Sung Tales," *HJAS*, June 1957.

Schwartz, Benjamin I. "Ch'en Tu-hsiu and the Acceptance of the Modern West," *Journal of the History of Ideas*, January 1951.

——. "The Intelligentsia in Communist China, a Tentative Comparison," *Daedalus*, Summer 1960.

——. "The Legend of the 'Legend of Maoism,'" *China Quarterly*, no. 2, Spring 1960.

——. "A Marxist Controversy on China," *FEQ*, February 1954.

Shih, Vincent. "The Ideology of the T'ai-p'ing T'ien-kuo," *Sinologica*, vol. 3, 1953.

——. "Interpretations of the T'ai-p'ings by Non-Communist Writers," *FEQ*, May 1951.

——. "Some Chinese Rebel Ideologies," *T'oung Pao*, no. 44, 1956. (This article is included also in Shih, *The Taiping Ideology*.)

Skazkin, S. D. "Peasant Wars Against the Exploiters in the Middle Ages" (in Russian), *Prepodavaniye v Schkole* (Teaching in the Schools), no. 3, 1952.

Smolin, G. Ya. "The Discussion by Chinese Historians on the Question of the Peasant Revolts in the Period of Feudalism" (in Russian), *NAA*, no. 2, 1962.

——. "Peasant Uprising Under the Leadership of Chung Hsiang and Yang Yao" (in Russian), *PV*, no. 1, 1960.

Stein, R. "Rémarques sur les Mouvements du Taoisme Politiques-Religieux au 11ᵉ Siècle ap. J.C.," *T'oung Pao*, vol. 50, 1963.

Taylor, Romeyn. "Social and Political Origins of the Ming Dynasty," unpublished University of Chicago doctoral dissertation, 1960.

Teng, Ssu-yü. "Chinese Historiography in the Last Fifty Years," *FEQ*, February 1949.

——. "A Political Interpretation of Chinese Rebellions," *Tsing Hua Journal of Chinese Studies*, September 1958.

Timofeyev, T. "Scientific Socialism and Petty Bourgeois Ideology," *Current Digest of the Soviet Press*, November 16, 1961, citing *Pravda*, October 24, 1966.

Travert, André. "The Attitudes of the Communist Party Towards

China's Cultural Legacy," in *Golden Jubilee Conference* (University of Hong Kong, 1961).

Uhalley, Stephen. "The Controversy over Li Hsiu-ch'eng," *JAS*, February 1966.

Van der Loon, P. "The Ancient Chinese Chronicles and the Growth of Historical Ideals," in W. G. Beasley and E. G. Pulleyblank, eds., *Historians of China and Japan*. London: Oxford University Press, 1961.

Van Slyke, Lyman P. "Liang Sou-min and the Rural Reconstruction Movement," *JAS*, August 1959.

Viatkin, R. V., and S. L. Tikvinsky. "On Questions in Chinese Historical Sciences" (in Russian), VI, no. 10, 1963.

Wang, Chang-ling. "Mainland Historians and the 'Great Cultural Revolution,'" *Issues and Studies*, vol. III, no. 7 (April 1967).

Wang, Yü-ch'uan. "The Development of Modern Social Science in China," *Pacific Affairs*, vol. 2, no. 3, 1938.

——. "The Rise of Land Tax and the Fall of Dynasties in Chinese History," *Pacific Affairs*, vol. 9, 1936.

Watson, Burton. "Memoirs of the Yu Hsia," unpublished Columbia University master's essay, 1951.

Wittfogel, Karl A. "Class Structure and Total Power in Oriental Despotism," in E. S. Kirby, ed., *Contemporary China*, no. 3. Hong Kong: Hong Kong University Press, 1960.

——. "The Foundations and Stages of Chinese Economic History" (in English), *Zeitschrift für Sozialforschung*, no. 4, 1935.

——. "The Legend of Maoism," *The China Quarterly*, nos. 1 and 2, 1960.

——. "The Marxist View of China," *The China Quarterly*, nos. 11 and 12, 1962.

——. "Marxist Views of Russian Society and Revolution," *World Politics*, vol. 12, July 1960.

——. "The Peasants," in F. M. Bochensky and G. Niemeyer, eds. *Handbook on Communism*. New York: Praeger, 1962.

Wright, Arthur F. "Harmony Versus Struggle," in L. Bryson, ed., *Thirteenth Symposium of Conference on Science, Philosophy, and Religion*. New York: Harper & Row, 1954.

Wright, Mary C. "From Revolution to Restoration: The Transformation of the KMT Ideology," *FEQ*, August 1955.

Wu Ta-k'un. "An Interpretation of Chinese Economic History," *Past and Present*, 1952.

Yao Shan-yü. "The Chronological Distribution of Floods and Droughts in Chinese History, 206 B.C. to 1911," *HJAS*, vol. 6, 1941–42.

Yaresh, Leo. "The 'Peasant Wars' In Soviet Historiography,"

American Slavic and East European Review, vol. 16, no. 3, October 1957.

——. "The Role of the Individual in History," in C. E. Black, ed., *Rewriting Russian History*.

Index

James P. Harrison

James P. Harrison is a member of the faculty of Hunter College of the City University of New York. He received his Ph.D. from Columbia in 1965 and presently lives in New York City with his wife and two daughters.